EUROPEAN STAGE

Gunilla Anderman

EUROPE ON STAGE

TRANSLATION AND THEATRE

OBERON BOOKS

LONDON

First published in 2005 by Oberon Books Ltd
521 Caledonian Road, London N7 9RH
Tel: 020 7607 3637 / Fax: 020 7607 3629
e-mail: oberon.books@btconnect.com
www.oberonbooks.com

A catalogue record for this book is available from the British Library.

ISBN: 1 84002 220 5

Printed in Great Britain by Antony Rowe Ltd, Chippenham

The cover photograph by Leonora Chan shows the curtains and proscenium arch decorations of Her Majesty's Theatre, London, designed for the original production of The Phantom of the Opera *(Maria Bjornson, Production Designer). With thanks to Really Useful Theatres.*

CONTENTS

Introduction, 7

Chapter 1
Europe on the English Stage, 13

Chapter 2
French Drama: the Forerunner, 33

Chapter 3
Henrik Ibsen, 75

Chapter 4
Anton Chekhov, 120

Chapter 5
August Strindberg, 158

Chapter 6
Gerhart Hauptmann, Arthur Schnitzler and Bertolt Brecht, 201

Chapter 7
Luigi Pirandello, Eduardo de Filippo and Dario Fo & Franca Rame, 238

Chapter 8
Federico García Lorca and Ramón del Valle-Inclán, 281

Chapter 9
Lost and Gained in Translation, 317

Bibliography, 341

Index, 357

INTRODUCTION

FOR ANYONE WITH AN INTEREST in the theatre travelling in Europe in 1892–3, the stage provided rich offerings. In Paris, Maurice Maeterlinck's *Pelléas et Mélisande* and Oscar Wilde's *Salomé* were premiering, while London saw the first opening of Bernard Shaw's *Widowers' Houses*. It was also the year that witnessed the first performances of Gerhart Hauptmann's *The Weavers*, *The Master Builder* by Henrik Ibsen and Arthur Schnitzler's *Anatol*.

Such an accumulation of dramatic talent is not frequently found, nor does it come about coincidentally: in the case of the 1892–3 European theatre season it represented the culmination of developments in the theatre as late nineteenth-century dramatists turned to naturalism, becoming detached observers recording the processes of society, as had scientists before them in their investigation of nature.

In a letter dated 25 May 1883, written from Rome to the actress Lucie Wolf, Ibsen announced that he had abandoned writing in verse and for several years had been practising 'the far more difficult art of writing in straightforward, truthful and naturalistic language'. At this time, everyday language on stage was not the norm. But for the world outside the theatre to be portrayed naturalistically, the language spoken on stage needed to be brought in line with the issues presented for debate.

In its discussion of the translation of European plays for the English stage, this book takes as its starting point the breakthrough of modern drama. In many respects, the social concerns of the dramatists who shaped modern drama are still with us today and the issues raised for debate are now all aired in the 'naturalistic language' which Ibsen, well over a century ago, declared to be his new written mode in preference to verse.

The present work is also primarily concerned with the translation of European playwrights for the English *stage* rather than the *page*. While a translation which faithfully reflects the original in every detail may be of great interest to a reader, it is often less helpful to a theatre audience. Unlike a theatre-goer, a reader is in a position to consult footnotes and encyclopaedias providing information about unfamiliar social and cultural concepts. With the exception of information in the performance programme, members of a theatre audience are left to fend for themselves when, during the course of a performance, they are confronted with unfamiliar and often bewildering information.

In order to explore and highlight translation issues that are of particular relevance to performance on stage, this book looks at some of the major European playwrights and the linguistic and cultural aspects of their work in the original language at risk of being lost or misread in translation, such as humour, imagery, allusions, dialects and socially determined use of language (Chapters 2–8). It also looks at the processes used to compensate for loss in translation, and the means used, often by British playwrights, to reintroduce lost humour and imagery and to relocate or update the European canon for the English stage. However, in discussing the amendments made to allow an English theatre audience better to understand and enjoy a European play in translation, my intention has been not to assess a translation as such; rather the aim has been to account for the changes sometimes necessary for a play originating in another language to make the transition onto the English stage.

In fact, throughout this work on European drama in translation I have been concerned not to label a particular translation as 'good' or 'bad', or to single out translations as 'correct', since such an evaluation would vary depending on the function of the translation. Different translations serve different purposes, and the vagaries of evaluation are perhaps most clearly demonstrated by theatre directors who consider 'absolutely awful' translations to be 'very useful' for their own artistic work (see Chapter 9).

Closely linked to the subject of adjusting the work of European playwrights for the English stage is the varying degree of difficulty which these dramatists have experienced in the process of gradually acquiring an authentic English voice. While, for instance, Ibsen and Chekhov may be viewed as 'honorary British dramatists', Strindberg continues to wait his turn, while Lorca still remains behind, bringing up the rear.

The nineteenth century saw the practice of two diametrically different approaches to translation for the stage, still more or less prevalent today. While the French comedies, popular on the London stage, were often adapted to the point of complete Anglicisation (see Chapter 2), William Archer's Ibsen translations remained faithfully close to the original Norwegian (see Chapter 3). The distinction between the two approaches to translation, the pros and cons of which have been the subject of debate since time immemorial (see Chapter 1), can be summed up as: either the translator brings the playwright to the audience, that is, the text is Anglicised; or alternatively, all foreign aspects of the play are left intact and the English audience is asked to travel abroad. As will be seen, this book looks at approaches to translation which range through the full spectrum between these two extremes.

❖

My own personal observations of a London audience's reaction to European drama in translation date back to the late 1970s when I was first commissioned to translate *Seven Girls* by Swedish playwright Carl-Johan Seth, which was staged at Charles Marowitz's Open Space Theatre in Tottenham Court Road. The critical reception of the play, which dealt with juvenile delinquency, and was closely linked to the debate taking place in Sweden at the time about penal reform and the open prison system, caught me by surprise. Why, asked one reviewer, were the wardens in an institution for girls not exclusively female? The question, unrelated to the subject of the play, would not have been asked by anyone in the play's country of origin, where for many years mixed education had been the norm. Issues that the playwright had never intended to raise threatened to overshadow those that he did wish to open up for debate. The play, I discovered, had been written on the basis of a set of shared cultural assumptions, many of which were sufficiently unfamiliar to members of an English audience to appear strange and bewildering.

Two years later *The Night of the Tribades*, a play that I translated by Swedish novelist and playwright Per Olov Enquist about August Strindberg, was staged at the Hampstead Theatre under the shortened title *The Tribades*, directed by Michael Rudman with Peter Woodthorpe as Strindberg and Susan Hampshire as his first wife Siri von Essen. Although a complimentary remark about my translation was flattering, it aroused my curiosity. Given the status of Swedish as a less well-known European language, the chances were slim that the reviewer would have known it. How then could the quality of a translation, normally understood to involve more than just one language, be evaluated without recourse to the original? I now learnt that *translation* seemed to mean different things to different people (see Chapter 1).

Next, in the early 1980s, I translated another play. Written by Swedish actor and playwright Stig-Ossian Ericsson, the play was a comedy, providing me with the opportunity to learn that being funny on stage was by no means a laughing matter. Under the title *Haven't We Met Before?*, the play was staged at The Mill at Sonning, starring John Alderton as an out-of-work actor, who successfully takes on the real-life role of a consultant in a hospital. What I learnt from this experience about the vagaries of translating humour was further reinforced in 1987 when I was commissioned to translate *Munich-Athens* by Swedish playwright Lars Norén for the then Soho Poly, a play about a modern couple left to confront each other during a forty-eight hour train journey, their aggression frequently aired through the use of punchy one-liners.

As a mediator of European plays onto the English stage I came to realise that the problems facing the translator of drama are as much culture-bound as they are linguistic. The reception of a play in translation is often unpredictably influenced by the extent that the 'foreign import' is felt to be too unfamiliar. The 'foreign feel' may be related to the loss of humour (see Chapter 9); the disappearance of the distinctive voice of the characters as expressed in the use of dialects and other language-specific characteristics which make audience identification difficult (see Chapters 1 and 9); and to allusions and culture-specific imagery that fail to travel between languages, the result of geographical and social differences between the speakers of the original language and the language into which a play is translated (see Chapter 9 as well as individual language chapters). Acknowledging that when translating a play, close attention needs to be paid to culture-linked as well as linguistic problems, each European language and country represented in this volume has been discussed from both angles.

In the discussion of the translation of French drama for the English stage, attention has also been given to the period preceding the introduction of modern drama on European stages. At the time, the work of Parisian playwrights, in different forms of adaptation, dominated the English stage in a manner similar to the present Anglo-American hegemony in Europe. Moreover, owing to the historical links and geographical proximity between France and the UK, translation between French and English may be seen as different in kind to translation from other European languages. As the first foreign language studied in the UK, widespread knowledge of French makes possible the use of French phrases and expressions in translation, while familiarity with the culture and society of France facilitates comprehension of allusions and cultural references. As a result, the chapter on French drama not only starts at an earlier point in time, it also looks at a wider range of playwrights in translation, including the recent success of French playwright Yasmina Reza.

For a book discussing the work in translation of dramatists writing in other European languages, which takes as its starting point the breakthrough of modern drama, certain names and languages choose themselves. Henrik Ibsen and August Strindberg, although quite different in their writing, often present similar translation problems due to the close linguistic relationship between Norwegian and Swedish. The special position held by Anton Chekhov on English-speaking stages made the choice of the Russian playwright obvious. As a German representative of modern drama, Gerhart Hauptmann, whose naturalist dialect work for long proved resistant to translation, also seemed an obvious candidate for inclusion, as did Austria's Arthur Schnitzler, disillusioned chronicler of Vienna at the turn of the century. In order to illustrate the problems in translation from Italian, the choice of Luigi Pirandello seemed unanswerable, as did Federico García Lorca in the case of Spanish drama.

This initial selection of European dramatists was later complemented by the inclusion of other, twentieth-century playwrights staged in English translation. In *The National Theatre and its Work 1963–1997*, Simon Callow chronicles three decades of National Theatre productions, concluding with a complete list of the close to five hundred productions mounted by the National Theatre since 1963. Excluding playwrights writing prior to the breakthrough of modern drama, a closer study of the productions of European plays in translation during this period by the National Theatre, custodian of the European dramatic canon on the English stage, unearthed some interesting information. Vying for the leading position with Chekhov and Ibsen in frequency of performance was Bertolt Brecht, which made me realise that any discussion about European theatre in English translation would not be complete without the performance history of this playwright's work. It similarly became obvious that discussion of some further European playwrights in translation also needed to be included. In 1973, Franco Zeffirelli directed *Saturday, Sunday, Monday* by the Italian playwright Eduardo de Filippo at the National Theatre, and over the decades other plays by the Neapolitan playwright were performed at the National, as well as at other West End theatres. Another twentieth-century Italian dramatist appearing at times on English-speaking stages, and periodically at the National Theatre, was the 1997 recipient of the Nobel Prize for Literature, Dario Fo, along with his wife Franca Rame. In the case of Spanish drama of more modern times at the National, there appeared to be little more than Lorca. However, interesting discussions of the staging of plays by Ramón Valle-Inclán in English translation had found their way into the available literature, complementing the discussion of the problems of transferring modern Spanish drama onto English-speaking stages (see Chapter 8). As a result, each individual language chapter, with the exception of Ibsen and Strindberg, discusses the performance history and translation problems of more than one national playwright. In the case of Russian theatre, while the work of Chekhov in English translation dominates the chapter, it also briefly acknowledges the interest shown more recently by English theatres in the staging of other Russian playwrights. Throughout, transliterations of titles have been provided. However, for ease of recognition, the commonly used names of playwrights and directors have been retained.

A further, general point concerns the dates for plays appearing in brackets. As far as possible, these refer to the date of publication.

In many respects, the issues linked to the translation of nineteenth-century drama remain relevant to the translation of European drama for the English stage today. At the time, the stream of translated plays flowed predominantly in one direction; English as well as other European stages imported French theatrical fare for performance in varying forms of adaptation (see Chapter 2). At the beginning of the twenty-first century, the stream remains uni-directional, although the focus is now on plays written in English. While Anglo-American drama is rapidly translated into the languages of Europe, plays written in other languages have, until recently, made only sporadic appearances on English-speaking stages. It is the purpose of this book to attempt to explore the nature of the linguistic and cultural obstacles that continue to confront European drama in its transfer onto the English stage.

I owe a great debt of gratitude to a large number of people, too many for all to be mentioned here. In particular, I benefited greatly from the help of the language specialists who commented on earlier drafts of individual chapters; Michael Holman, Michael Colenso, Nelly Chachibaia, Anne Ife, Rochelle Sibley, Gunnar Magnusson and Lois Greenaway. Toby Radford of the National Theatre Bookshop gave me invaluable help in providing me with access to performance programmes from past National Theatre productions. Thanks are also due to Anna Lass, Kay Windust, Sylvia Leone and Gillian James who helped with the preparation of the manuscript. Any mistakes are of course of my own making. I am also grateful to Peter Newmark for his encouragement and stimulating discussions over lunch. But, above all, to Benjamin Anderman and Steven Anderman who made it all possible.

Gunilla Anderman
Guildford, April 2005

Chapter 1

EUROPE ON THE ENGLISH STAGE

IN THE MIDDLE OF THE NINETEENTH CENTURY, the supremacy of French culture and language was such that when Victor Hugo was asked, during a visit to England, whether he didn't find it inconvenient not to speak any English, he replied, 'When England wishes to converse with me, it will learn to speak French.'[1]

Victor Hugo wrote at the height of a several-century-long period of French cultural domination, which placed French literature in a firmly-established central position in Europe. For translation, this meant that a norm was created against which foreign literature was compared and, not surprisingly, often found wanting. In the case of drama, plays in translation into French were accepted only on French terms and if they were adapted to French theatrical norms. For the first French stage production of *Hamlet* in 1769, in order to meet French audience expectations, the translator Jean-François Ducis felt the need to 'domesticate' Shakespeare's play for the Comédie Française. To fit the literary requirements of neo-classicism prevailing at the time and its demands for the unity of time, place and action, Hamlet never leaves Elsinore, where the action takes place during a 24-hour unbroken period of time, with sub-plots such as the death of Ophelia and the gravediggers' scene all removed. As a result, in translation into French, Shakespeare's play emerges in its adjusted form as having been written by a contemporary of Racine.[2] The position of cultural domination held by France for several centuries had left its mark on the approach taken to translation.

This illustrates how, when translating into a language of the status of, for example, eighteenth-century French, a high degree of adjustment is normally required in order to conform to the poetic norms prevailing in the target culture. For translation in the opposite direction, on the other hand, less adaptation is usually required, as familiarity with the culture and literary tradition of a language in a leading position can usually be assumed among the speakers of the languages of smaller nations.[3]

The supremacy of France brought about a French-speaking elite throughout Europe, able to converse with each other in French irrespective of their own native language. But the status of French was also such that speakers of the same language might use French to indicate their social status. As a result, the use of French became a powerful tool for dramatists wishing to illustrate dominance on stage. The device was used for example by Chekhov in *Three Sisters*, in order to show the social pretensions of the poorly-educated Natasha, who stoops to conquer only, in the end, to rule the household and, symbolically, the whole country. It is also one of the linguistic means used by Strindberg to lay bare Jean's social pretensions in *Miss Julie*, and, similarly, by Ibsen when in *Ghosts* Regine distances herself from provincial Norway by peppering her speech with *rendez-vous, pardon* and *merci*.

During the latter part of the twentieth century, however, the cultural dominance of French was challenged by the phenomenal spread of English, starting in earnest after World War II. During the last 25 years, English, reinforced by the now worldwide use of e-mail, has acquired a supranational momentum which has proved unstoppable. In no small measure, this new world domination of the English language has been helped by the United States. As the British Empire, which had helped to spread English all over the world, declined, the rise of American power and culture has ensured that the English language now holds the position once held by French. The joint Anglo-American literary tradition has also established its undisputed leadership. Not long after their publication in English, books by English and American writers appear in translation into the languages of Europe; television programmes, as well as full-length screen films, rapidly find their way into European homes and cinemas, dubbed or subtitled into the languages of individual nations. And in the case of English and American drama, classical as well as contemporary plays in translation are the standard fare at national and studio theatres in smaller European countries. Judging from the lesser frequency with which foreign plays in translation reach the English stage, there has been, until more recently, limited reciprocity, particularly in the case of plays written by contemporary European playwrights.

In many respects, the present-day Anglo-American literary situation resembles the French one, in particular in the heyday of its literary and linguistic European hegemony. While best-selling English and American writers of all genres travel with ease into other European languages, European works in English translation are rarely met with the same degree of enthusiasm. The deciding factor behind this one-way traffic is clearly not the size of population: with a population of well over eighty million, Germany is as open to the import of Anglo-American literature in translation as are the inhabitants of the smaller European nations. In a study undertaken on behalf of the European Commission in the early 1990s, the UK, with the second largest publishing industry in the world, had the lowest rate of translation of the then eleven member states. Figures showing the percentage of translated books out of a total publishing output of the member states at the time are exemplified in this table:

Country	Books published	Translated
Greece	4,693	36%
Portugal	6,430	44%
Germany	67,890	14%
Spain	43,896	24%
France	39,535	18%
UK	67,628	3%

The figures do not appear to have changed significantly during the decade following the publication of the Commission's study. On 20 February 1998, *The Bookseller* put the total number of books published in the UK at around 100,000 with a translation rate of 2–3 per cent, out of which a maximum of 380 titles (approximately 19 per cent) are likely to be in the literary domain. The number of books published in translation in Ireland closely reflects those in the UK, confirming the position held by translated literature in yet another English-speaking country.[4]

The same asymmetry holds true for Anglo-American theatre: while classical and contemporary playwrights writing in English figure prominently in translation on European stages, the same cannot be said about European playwrights in the UK and the USA. Again, this is hardly surprising. Most European youths are now learning English as their first foreign language and, through English-speaking films and television and American mass culture, audiences are not likely to be left dumbfounded by either British or American social and cultural references on stage. As a result, the translation of contemporary drama originating in the English-speaking world can usually remain faithful to the playwright's work with limited need for adaptations, versions or rewrites, an approach that also characterises the method of staging the work of other European playwrights in translation. In smaller European nations the learning of foreign languages plays an important role, as knowledge of other languages constitutes a lifeline to the outside world, and familiarity with the work of classic and contemporary European playwrights usually minimises the need for adaptation. As a result of this asymmetrical literary exchange, it is no coincidence that the candidate selected for the Nobel Prize in Literature frequently takes the English-speaking world by surprise. Chosen by a committee reflecting a long-established acceptance of literature, including drama, in translation, the criteria for selection are those of the speakers of Swedish, not always acting in accordance with the postulates of prevailing Anglo-American literary traditions. Conversely, European writers whose work departs markedly from that of the playwrights of the Anglo-American tradition are almost inevitably to be found wanting when their work appears in English translation. This gulf between literary traditions remains largely unacknowledged by European playwrights as well as English audiences.

The introduction of modern European drama onto the English stage has not been helped by the inclination of early translators into English to espouse a respectfully faithful approach to the task as they felt befitted the subject matter. While the light French theatrical fare appearing on the London stage during the early part of the nineteenth century lent itself to adaptation, Ibsen's modern drama did not. However, this difference in approach between the translation of French light comedies on the one hand, and the reverent treatment given to Ibsen by his translator William Archer on the other, reflects a continuing debate about translation that can be traced back to the days of the Romans, two thousand years ago. Should the translation stay as close as possible to the original or should it be adjusted to better meet the expectations of the target actors and speakers?

Having conquered Greece, the Romans set about adopting and imitating Greek civilisation. Wishing to emulate the defeated Greeks not only socially and politically but also in the arts, including poetry, it became necessary for well-to-do, educated Romans to learn Greek. Cicero and Horace, translators of the ancient Greek classics into Latin, were the first to draw the distinction between the word-for-word and the sense-for-sense approach to translation. The difference in approach is made clear in Cicero's *De optimo genere oratorum* v. 14, around 46 BC. Here Cicero rejects the word-for-word approach and explains that he has rendered the speeches by Aeschines and Demosthenes into Latin not only as a translator ('*ut interpres*'), but in addition, as a speaker ('*ut orator*'). In Odes iv.II, Horace discusses in detail the problems encountered when translating the Greek poet Pindar, stressing that what was involved was not a work being imitated but the art of emulation which entailed 'bending the techniques of another author to one's own subject and language'.[5]

Cicero's concept of a translation as having an independent value as a creative achievement was matched by the approach of St Jerome whose translation of the Bible, commissioned by Pope Damasus in 384 AD, marked a turning point in Bible translation. Jerome stated that he had rendered the text sense-for-sense and not word-for-word, following the principles as laid down by Cicero. Adhering to this approach was, however, not always free from dangerous consequences. Often referred to as the master of modern English, William Tyndale (1494–1536), paid with his life for rendering the Bible into accessible English, defying the Church which demanded exclusive access to the divine word of God in Latin.

In the seventeenth century, the importance of making the foreign 'import' as acceptable to an English readership as possible was acknowledged by Abraham Cowley (1618–67), who even went as far as declaring, in the 'Preface' to his *Pindarique Odes* (1656), that in his translations he had 'taken, left out and added what I please'. Cowley's somewhat cavalier approach also serves to exemplify one of the three basic principles of translation formulated by the poet John Dryden (1631–1700) towards the end of the century. Dryden called the type of translation favoured by Cowley 'imitation', an approach that allowed the translator to abandon the text if necessary in an attempt to recreate the 'spirit' of the original, not dissimilar to the type of rewrite often applied to European drama in English translation. For the word-for-word type of translation Dryden coined the term 'metaphrase' while he referred to Cicero's sense-for-sense, more balanced approach to translation as 'paraphrase'.

Owing to the deposition of James II, Dryden lost his long-held posts as Poet Laureate and Royal Historiographer, which had previously allowed him to devote his poetry to public issues. Instead he now turned to translation in order to voice his views, choosing foreign texts that lent themselves to this form of indirect social and political commentary. Receiving attractive contractual terms from his publisher, Dryden benefited handsomely from the subscriptions to his translations: his complete version of Virgil pocketed him more than £1000.[6] Dryden's approach also exercised considerable influence on Alexander Pope (1688–1744), whose translations of Homer's *Iliad* and *Odyssey* kept readers enthralled. In his *Life of Pope* (1779), Samuel Johnson comments that here was a translation of Homer made 'for his own age and his own nation'.[7] It was also at this time that the work of the translator was recognised as an artistic creation in its own right. The judicial pronouncements in *Burnett v Chetwood* (1720) established that a translation was not an infringe-ment of the original but an independent piece of work, as acknowledged in the current practice of displaying prominently the name of British playwrights as adapters of the work of European dramatists.

In Germany, during the early part of the nineteenth century, the role of translation became essential for the realisation of Goethe's concept of *Weltliteratur*, or world literature. The importance of keeping the original intact in translation was stressed in particular by Friedrich Schleiermacher (1768–1834). An ardent advocate of a return to the source text, Schleiermacher went as far as wanting the original to 'shine through' the translation, leaving readers in no doubt that what they were reading had its roots in another, different culture. The result was the concept of a 'hybrid' language used only for the purposes of translation. A later commentator, the translator and theorist Walter Benjamin (1892–1940), further reinforced these ideas:

> It is the task of the translator to release in his own language that pure language which is under the spell of another, to liberate the language imprisoned in a work in his re-creation of that work.[8]

Expressed in different terms, the translator should ensure that the text itself holds priority over its readers, whatever difficulties this may present. This approach resulted, in turn, in translated literature becoming the exclusive prerogative of a cultured and educated elite, in stark contrast to the earlier, more 'populist' approach of Dryden and Pope. Summed up, the two approaches have been described as 'Either the translator leaves the author in peace as much as possible and moves the reader towards him; or he leaves the reader in peace as much as possible, and moves the author towards him.'[9]

In England, during the post-romantic period, a time when English society underwent enormous changes, resulting in widespread personal and moral conflict, there were also opposing approaches to translation. For William Morris (1834–96), lover of native and artistic perfection, the legacy of the Romantic tradition provided an escape from the Victorian world and the everyday reality of increasing industrialisation. His translations of French medieval tales and Icelandic sagas show the deliberate use of an archaic style of language whereby the 'exotic' foreignness of the original is introduced to the reader; through this style of translation Morris revealed his own yearning for a simpler life of times past. Matthew Arnold (1822–88), on the other hand, chose to expound an approach to translation diametrically opposed to that of William Morris, and strongly rejected the archaising principle in translation. However, in both William Morris and Matthew Arnold, poets in their own right, translator and poet were found in one and the same person. This combination of language knowledge and subject matter expertise was also found at the time in the English playwrights who translated and adapted French plays for the London stage.

In the case of the early translators of modern drama on the other hand, the language of the original play was no longer French, narrowly restricting the pool of potential translators. When plays by modern European dramatists were first staged in English translation, toward the end of the nineteenth and beginning of the twentieth century, the combination of playwriting skill and knowledge of the foreign language was rarely if ever evident in one and the same translator. As a literary critic with experience of stage work and of having worked closely with the actress Elizabeth Robins on Ibsen productions, William Archer probably came closest to embracing the dual role of theatre practitioner and linguist. In the case of Strindberg, many of the early translations into English were done via other languages, in particular German. A devoted disciple, Strindberg's committed translator Emil Schering was firmly schooled in the tradition of word-for-word translation, and his over-dutiful renderings of the Swedish playwright's work resulted, not infrequently, in mistranslations as well as stylistic distortions. Although Chekhov fared better in terms of accuracy, still, in the early translations by Constance Burnett there is little evidence of the humour which is now known to be there in the original in some of Chekhov's major plays.

The frequently incurred loss of humour in translation constitutes one of the most difficult problems for a play when travelling from a European to an English stage. For English actors, often accustomed to measuring the success of their performance against the yardstick of the number of laughs they obtain from the audience, the absence of humour in the texts of translated plays is one reason why the offer of a part in a play in translation is not always met with enthusiasm.

In many other European countries, the classical distinction between comedy and tragedy remains more clear-cut, and the laughter amid tears characteristic of English stage work is less well established. This may sometimes result in English plays that are not sufficiently subtly interpreted in translation being targeted for criticism because of their 'superficiality', while drama travelling in the opposite direction often strikes English actors as 'solemn' and 'heavy'.

Sadly, many jokes do not travel well in translation: it is no coincidence that English humour, popular in other European countries, on film as well as television, is often enjoyed in the original and not in translation. For example, for the humour of Oscar Wilde's *The Importance of Being Earnest* to be captured in translation into another language, the name in the title of the play would need a man's name in that language to be identical in sound to an adjective meaning 'sincere'. Unless this hypothetical language is closely related to English, the chances for such a match are not very good. Still, if against the odds, this were to be the case, a translation covering all nuances of the English title of the play would still remain elusive, as in Victorian times the word 'earnest' also appears to have been used in the sense that 'gay' is now, as a term to denote homosexuality. Given the high rate of loss of humour in translation, the presence of puns and word-play in plays staged in translation into English is more likely to be the result of added, compensatory efforts, as for instance in Tom Stoppard's adaptation of Johann Nestroy's Viennese comedy *On the Razzle* (see Chapter 9).

Often relevant to characterisation or aspects of interpersonal communication on stage, allusions are also likely to cause problems in translation into English, in particular if originating in languages spoken in countries which normally receive limited reporting in the English-speaking press. When, for instance, in the run-up to the presidential election in 1992, a newspaper report on an appearance by Republican vice-presidential candidate Dan Quayle described him as having given 'one long Checkers speech' with the concluding question, 'Will he soon produce a dog?', worldwide American news transmission had ensured that the reference to President Nixon's defensive television appearance with his dog Checkers was understood by many Europeans.[10] It is, however, highly unlikely that a European politician would attract the same worldwide attention in the English-speaking media if accompanied by a dog for a televised interview. Instead, allusions to political and social events of a similar nature by European playwrights are likely to cause nothing but consternation in translation into English. In some cases this may also happen to certain types of allusions appearing in the work by British playwrights if the subject area is sufficiently deeply rooted in English culture. Although recognition of culturally derived allusions might be an easier task for a translator working out of English who can assume a fair degree of familiarity with English/American life, mistranslations still occur. As reported by Martin Esslin, a reference to cricket terminology in Harold Pinter's *The Birthday Party* appeared in German, in a translation that has now entered theatre history. When, in the play, Stanley is being brainwashed by the two terrorists, Goldberg and McCann, who keep hurling accusations at him, one of their questions is 'Who watered the wicket at Melbourne?' Consulting a dictionary, the German translator appears to have been led from 'wicket' to 'wicket gate', from which must have been inferred that the reference was to 'the gate of the city of Melbourne'. In combination with a less frequently found interpretation of the verb 'water', this resulted in the German *'Wer hat an das Stadttor von Melbourne gepinkelt?'* which, back-translated into English, yields, 'Who peed against the city gate of Melbourne?'[11]

A study of the translation of Pinter's use of allusions in translation into Swedish points to a similar lack of awareness on the part of translators of a number of English life- and culture-related allusions.[12] Nevertheless, baffled theatre audiences throughout Europe are still willing to suspend disbelief and accept what they do not understand as 'Pinteresque'. It is interesting to speculate what would have happened if Pinter had not been born in England but, say, in Finland. Would the cultural and linguistic allusions made by this hypothetical North European Pinter, referring perhaps to national sports such as skiing and skating, Nordic folk songs, trolls and related mythology, have been described in reverent terms and referred to as 'Pinteresque', or would reviewers have been inclined to reach for other less flattering adjectives?

Mistranslation of Pinter, which in some European countries has helped to nudge his plays closer to the realm of 'surrealism' than might have been the English playwright's own intention, stems from the fallacy that the meaning of a word in one language can simply be determined through the consultation of a dictionary. This approach to translation, which prevailed in Europe from the late eighteenth century until the 1960s, developed from the method used in the teaching of Greek and Latin. In the study of the classical languages, translation traditionally was the key; and in the nineteenth century, the most popular teaching exercises focused on translation into and out of English. The role of translation as practised in the classroom was that of examining students' acquisition of new vocabulary, learnt from memorising new words in the foreign language together with their English equivalents as set out in word lists and dictionaries.

When, in the mid-nineteenth century, the study of modern languages was first introduced as a serious pursuit, it was felt that in order to justify its newly-elevated place on the school curriculum, the teaching pattern of the classical languages should be replicated. In the UK, what became known as the grammar-translation method received a boost in 1858 when a system of public examinations was established, monitored by the universities of Oxford and Cambridge.[13] Like the classical languages, the emphasis was on written language and grammar with the spoken language receiving limited attention. As a result, in an educational context, the process of translation became inextricably associated with using word lists or dictionaries to establish one-to-one correspondences between a word in the learner's language and its 'equivalent' in the foreign language.

As part of the exercise, it was not uncommon for books designed for self-practice to contain an 'answer key' which presented the 'correct' translation, with alternative 'word solutions' listed in declining order of 'correctness'. Even today, at the beginning of the twenty-first century, studies involving large corpora comparing literary works in translation with originally written texts, show that the influence of the grammar-translation method is still felt. Translators tend to use words in translation that they would be less inclined to use when writing spontaneously in their own language, having learnt in childhood the so-called 'correct' meaning of foreign words.[14]

Commenting on early translations of *The Seagull* by Anton Chekhov, playwright Tom Stoppard has drawn attention to the fact that while these translations may differ on virtually every line, they nevertheless share a common approach, almost 'a philosophy' towards translation:

> They are as scrupulous as ledgers: everything on the Russian side of the line is accounted for on the English side, sentence by sentence, and the sentences themselves – allowing for the occasional flourish – faithfully carry over nouns, verbs and qualifiers.[15]

Not only does 'the ledger principle' often result in stylistic awkwardness, a further disadvantage related to this approach to translation is the ease with which the translator might fall into the trap of incorrectly translating 'false friends'. In closely-related European languages, the polysemy of Latin words has given rise to differences in meaning, which easily invites mistranslation. For example, the meaning of the English word 'sympathetic' has remained closer to the original than the German *sympatisch*, *sympathique* in French, *sympatisk* in Norwegian, *simpatico* in Italian or *simpático* in Spanish, where it has moved to the more generic sense of 'pleasant'. The French loan words that have infiltrated the English vocabulary, also at times result in incorrect translations (see Chapter 2 for discussion of *prétendre* and *luxure* transferred into English as their *faux amis*, 'pretend' and 'luxury').

As a corollary to the belief that the meaning of a word can be found solely through the consultation of a bilingual dictionary, nuances necessarily left unaccounted for in English translation because of lack of exact equivalents were dutifully explained through information contained in footnotes. In, for instance, the English translation of the work of Knut Hamsun, the Norwegian recipient of the 1920 Nobel Prize for Literature, readers encounter the unknown concept of 'Kvæns' as in: '...and he roared: "I have seen the Kvæns fight; just come back and I'll show you!"' In a note provided by T S Scott, the translator, the following information is then proffered: 'Kvæns = the name given by Norwegians to the Finns, in distinction to the Lapps, whom they call Finns'.[16] This piece of information, of doubtful value to the reader, is of even less use to a theatre audience with no access to the written text of a play. It is, however, the method whereby William Archer, in accordance with the practice of his age, provides information about discrepancies between Ibsen's Norwegian text and his own English translation (see Chapter 3).

With spoken varieties of classical Greek and Latin no longer in existence, modern language teaching methodology of the past also showed limited interest in the use of the spoken language. Early translators would replace the written word in the foreign language with the equivalent written word in English with little apparent concern that people rarely speak the way they write. Before naturalism reached the stage, the lack of knowledge about the spoken mode of language was, however, not of crucial importance in the theatre, as the way ordinary people spoke was not considered to be appropriate language for use on stage. When, in 1914, Shaw's *Pygmalion* first opened at *His Majesty's Theatre* in London with Herbert Beerbohm Tree as Professor Higgins and Mrs Patrick Campbell as Eliza Doolittle, the *Daily Express* took a Charing Cross flower girl, Eliza Keefe, along to the *Haymarket*, loftily reporting her reactions to the amusement of its readers: 'Well, I've never 'ad such a night in all me natural...'. What offended the papers was not the social inequity but the use of bad language on stage, especially 'not bloody likely', spoken in Act 3. Indignantly the *Daily Sketch* headline pronounced: 'Mrs Patrick Campbell swears on stage and cultured London roars with laughter'. In contrast, when the play opened in the New World, other anxieties found their expression in the recorded reactions to the play. Americans did not mind 'not bloody likely' as much as reports that Mrs Patrick Campbell was spotted smoking in the tea-room of the Plaza Hotel.[17]

As Bernard Shaw's passion with reforming English society grew, so did his interest in reforming language. In the early 1880s he had met Henry Sweet (1845–1912) whose interest in spoken language resulted in the publication of *A Handbook of Phonetics* in 1877. Adapted in 1890 as *A Primer of Spoken English*, it became the first scientifically-based description of educated London speech or Received Pronunciation (RP). In the preface to *Pygmalion*, which in the character of Professor Higgins contains obvious touches of Sweet, Shaw refers to Sweet's 'satanic contempt for all academic dignitaries and persons in general who thought more of Greek than phonetics'. Acknowledging the way in which dialect and sociolect interact in English to make language a unique indicator of class and education, Shaw famously remarks that 'it is impossible for an Englishman to open his mouth without making some other Englishman despise him'.[18]

The many social and geographical distinctions that are conveyed when speakers engage in conversation were, however, rarely captured by early English translators of modern drama. While plays originally written in French presented fewer problems in English translation, given the position of French as the first foreign language in the UK, other European plays did. Not surprisingly, the combination of a knowledge of a particular foreign language with an awareness of the intricacies of spoken language and the demands of the stage were, at the time, not easily found in one and the same person. However, as Europe started to open up again after the ravages of two world wars, and other countries gradually became more easily accessible through increased use of air travel, so did information about differences in language and culture. Around the mid-twentieth century, translators started to emerge who combined a knowledge of European languages with an interest in theatre, such as Eric Bentley (Brecht and Pirandello), John Willett (Brecht), Michael Meyer (Strindberg and Ibsen) and Frederick May (Pirandello). (See individual language chapters.) The transfer of a play from its original language and culture to another, has been likened to the action of an hourglass,[19] with the flow of the grains regulated through a number of filters imposed by the culture receiving the 'foreign import'. This filtration was now being monitored by the linguist and dramatic adapter in one and the same person. Slowly but surely, a number of different strategies emerged which, when applied to a foreign play in translation, would help to ensure a smoother transfer from source to target language.

The cultural and linguistic obstacles encountered in the transfer of a play from one language to another are sometimes most easily overcome by transporting it, either in time by placing it in a different historical period, or geographically through finding a different location. This process is not limited to inter-lingual relocation but may also be *intra*-lingual. In a heatedly debated article, Susan Bassnett has argued that the Bard himself would benefit from being 'translated' into modern English if his plays are to continue to attract the interest of the younger generation of today's school children.[20] In the case of moving a play between languages, its most far-reaching form might arguably be Eugene O'Neill's *The Iceman Cometh* as the consummate 'rewrite' of Ibsen's *The Wild Duck*, as has been suggested by Robert Brustein,[21] or *The Song of Roland* as the perfect translation of the *Poem of the Cid*, a proposal put forward by the poet Carlos Alvarez.[22] It has even been argued that many of the canonical plays such as those by Ibsen, Strindberg and Lorca are in fact various forms of 'translation' of the tragic plots from antiquity, sharing as they do an Athenian preoccupation with the negotiations between the claims of the family and of the world beyond, and 'the Athenian diagnosis of our ambivalence towards this demand'.[23]

Examples of transposition through geographical and/or historical re-location of modern European drama are numerous: Strindberg's *Miss Julie* has been set in England on the eve of the 1945 Labour victory election, as in Patrick Marber's *After Miss Julie* staged at the Donmar Warehouse theatre in 2003 (see Chapter 5), and *The Cherry Orchard* by Anton Chekhov (see Chapter 4) has been transported to the American South with an ex-slave rather than an ex-serf, and Trofimo crying, 'All America is our garden'. More recently, in her production at the Orange Tree in London, Janet Suzman relocated the play to South Africa. In 1996 the National Theatre production of Victor Hugo's *Le Roi s'amuse*, entitled *The Prince's Play* in a new verse translation by Tony Harrison, was set in an English music hall, and provides an example of a French play transposed to an English setting. A similar example of complete 'acculturation' of an Italian play would be British playwright Mike Stott's relocation of Eduardo de Filippo's *Natale in casa Cupiello* (*Christmas at the Cupiello's*) to Yorkshire under the title *Ducking Out* (see Chapter 7). An example from Spanish theatre is provided by the 1993 production of *Bohemian Lights* where David Johnston replaced the 1920 Madrid of Valle-Inclán by Dublin in 1915, the year before the Easter Rising (see Chapter 8). The permutations are many and varied: in *The Blue Room* David Hare transported Schnitzler's *fin de siècle* Vienna, in *Reigen* or *La Ronde*, to the end of the twentieth century and changed its original location into an unspecified, global metropolis (see Chapter 6). In contrast, by transplanting the same play to present-day Belfast, Carlo Gebler's *10 Rounds*, at the Tricycle theatre in the autumn of 2002, succeeded in replicating the sense in the original of an entire society being eroded, a feature arguably missing in the Hare/Mendes version at the Donmar, with its anonymous urban location.

In addition to naturalisation of a foreign play, there are other options available to make its 'foreignness' in translation less of an obstacle for English theatre audiences. In virtually all drama translation there is some degree of acculturation applied to the final product.[24] This process may not be total but simply take the form of neutralisation through toning down what is deemed to be too 'foreign', a practice extending as far back in history as the Romans. Translated from Greek into Latin, the Roman comedies retained their Greek setting and it was made perfectly clear early on in the play that the characters clad in the Greek mantle lived in a Greek city. The action was usually set in Athens, the city Roman audiences appear to have considered to be more Greek than any other location. According to Plautus, successful Roman adapter of Greek comedies into Latin: 'Now writers of comedy have this habit: they always allege that the scene of action is Athens, their object being to give the play a more Grecian air'.[25] Moving between closely related European cultures, similar steps are often taken simply through the replacement of a specific with a more generic reference.[26] For example, although flowers are often invested with a symbolic function, exactly what they symbolise may vary from culture to culture. In Strindberg's *The Ghost Sonata* hyacinths represent death and funerals, while in Lorca and Hispanic culture, this association appears to be more closely linked to dahlias (see Chapters 5, 8 and 9). By replacing Lorca's reference to 'dahlias of the sleeping moon' with the less specific 'frozen flowers', in David Johnston's translation 'frozen flowers of the sleeping moon' retains the symbol of death and sterility, a generic term subsuming the function of a more language and culture-specific reference.[27]

The decision as to the degree of acculturation required in English versions of European plays has more recently been left in the hands of British playwrights. In some cases, such as Christopher Hampton's translations of Yasmina Reza from French and Ödön von Horváth from German, the English playwright also knows the language in which the play was originally written. In other cases, on the other hand, the playwrights openly acknowledge that they do not know the source language. In an increasing number of instances, the name of the linguist who transferred the text into English is mentioned in the performance programme, usually referred to as having provided a 'literal' translation. On other occasions, however, failure to mention the manner in which a text written in another language has found its way into English inevitably results in one of two conclusions: the English playwright must have known the original language, or the work involved in helping the play to travel between languages was not considered to be of sufficient importance to warrant a mention.

Given the growing number of European plays now appearing on the English stage, the terminology related to English versions of the work by foreign playwrights constitutes a diffuse and poorly defined area where terms might profitably be more clearly defined. For most linguists the term 'translation' inevitably means that a text has changed languages; this is not, however, always the understanding of British playwrights or theatre managements. In the case of Arthur Schnitzler's *Undiscovered Country* staged at the National Theatre in 1979, Tom Stoppard, the British playwright who adapted the play, acknowledged the services of John Harrison, the German linguist provided by the National Theatre, in the Introduction to the 1986 published version of the play. However, any reference to the linguist as 'translator' or having acted as a 'human dictionary' failed to find its way into the performance programme. As in some cases 'versions' appear to be contractually more favourably remunerated,[28] it would seem to be in the interest of all parties involved to adopt uniformly the term 'version' or 'adaptation' for exclusively monolingual work; 'translated by' or 'translated and adapted by' might then be an appropriate description in cases where the source language is in fact known by the English playwright.

In the case of the 1992 Almeida production of Pirandello's *Rules of the Game*, the cover of the published English text described it as 'translated and adapted by David Hare' while on the inside it was referred to as 'a new version by David Hare', evidence that all three terms appear to be in common usage without being viewed as different activities or skills. When questioned on the subject, David Hare revealed that he had voiced a protest to the terms linked to his name on the grounds that he did not speak Italian but that in spite of his protestations 'they stuck them on'. When Hare suggested that the translator be credited, the argument offered was that Hare's name 'was better known'.[29] It is difficult to avoid the suspicion that the reason why the translator's name often does not appear or, if it does, it appears in very small letters in a less than prominent place in the performance programme, may be linked to something akin to fear among theatre managements that 'translated' works are not commercial. Theatre managements might have learnt from past reactions to translated plays that the public do not like an overly source-oriented approach to translation which, through its cultural and linguistic unfamiliarity, is accessible only to the initiated and converted, lacking in mass appeal. However, with the growing interest in European drama during the last decade and its often favourable critical reception, the use of appropriate terminology now seems to be due for renewed consideration.

The concept of 'literal' translation frequently used in performance programmes, arguably to indicate the degree of involvement of the linguist consulted, seems a particularly apt candidate for reconsideration. Even conjunctions such as 'and' and 'but' cannot always be replaced simply by their 'opposite numbers' in another language. In addition, virtually no word of substance can be translated without consideration of the associations with which it is customarily linked. Although a word such as 'die' describes the process of departing from this earth, it is not arbitrary, as many less than clearly laid-out dictionaries may lead us to believe, whether this act is referred to as for instance 'pass away' or 'kick the bucket'. While a statement such as 'my Aunt Emma has passed away' shows respect for a lost relative, describing her demise as having 'kicked the bucket' does not. And if, when alive, Aunt Emma had told us that her canary had 'passed away' rather than having died, we would have known that the old lady was sufficiently attached to her canary to have elevated its status to that of a human.

As translation always involves choosing one of a number of options, there is no such thing as a 'literal' translation, a concept that seems to suggest that this form of translation only involves replacing one word with another, from a store of knowledge readily accessible from a bilingual dictionary. In the case of English playwright Simon Gray, such a 'literal' rendering of the English text even resulted in a completely inaccurate translation of the original. Attending a rehearsal of one of his plays in translation into German, Simon Gray was taken aback by the appearance on stage of a character all covered in plaster. Enquiring as to the reasons for the emergence of this strange apparition, Simon Gray was shown his own script with his stage directions specifying that the character is to enter 'completely plastered'.[30]

In addition to such inherent dangers of 'literal' translation, questions need to be raised about the exact nature of this type of translation, what exactly is to be understood by 'literal'. In the *Concise Oxford Dictionary*, the following are the first three entries for 'literal':

1. Of, in, expressed by, letter(s) of alphabet.
2. Following the letter, text, or exact or original words (*translation, transcript,* etc).
3. Taking words in their usual or primary sense and applying the ordinary rules of grammar, without mysticism or allegory of metaphor.

Whereas following 1 and 2 may lead to 'plastered' in the sense of 'inebriated' being translated into German as 'covered in plaster', the approach as expressed in 3 may lead to a similar result. In translating the English 'it's raining cats and dogs', to take an example, a literal translation would be equivalent to a downpour of four-legged animals. In French, a more appropriate choice of metaphor would perhaps be 'it's raining like a cow urinating', while in Greek it would be 'it's raining legs of chairs'. In monolingual translation there are equally a number of ways in which to describe a heavy rainfall including in declining order of stylistic elevation, 'it's raining hard', 'it's coming down in buckets' and 'it's pissing outside', all equally appropriate given the right context and situation.

The individual and distinctive voices of the different characters in a play derive from a knowledge of their social and cultural background, as well as a host of other facts. This information in turn determines the linguistic options chosen to enable each character to speak in a voice of their own. To retain these voices in translation, however, matching options need to be found in the new language, something that can only happen if the text has been interpreted in accordance with the intentions of the original playwright. To some translators, deciding on which options to choose may even constitute the attraction of translation, an opinion voiced by Christopher Hampton when asked his reasons, as a playwright in his own right, for remaining interested in translation. What he liked about translation, Christopher Hampton pointed out, was the process, which he likened to 'a gigantic crossword involving a huge number of tiny decisions.' [31]

'The ideal' in translation is, according to Joseph Farrell, translator of Italian plays into English, a combination of 'fidelity and flair'. The fidelity of the translated text having previously been assured through the help of the linguist, the adapter or playwright (who may be the same person) contributes by making the necessary adjustments and adding the finishing touches to the text. As Farrell points out, in the case of Dario Fo, the writer Fo is regularly adapted on stage by Fo, the actor. Something equivalent needs to take place in translation in order to prevent an overly faithful reproduction of the original from appearing flat and uninteresting in its unadapted English form. [32]

In an article in the *Independent* of 18 May 1990, Miles Kington noted that:

> we [the English] are so used to ourselves that we hardly notice it any more, but foreigners arriving in Britain often complain that it is almost impossible to make out what the natives really mean; when we say, 'It wasn't half bad', we mean that it was wonderful, when we say almost anything, we usually mean something quite different, so no wonder foreigners find it 'hard going'.

During the decade that has passed, awareness seems to have increased that drama translation into English also needs to take account of the importance of pitching the verbal and emotional social intercourse at a more character-istically understated level, and to make adjustments in translation accordingly. For example, past translations of Italian drama have often been characterised by emotional outbursts which may have done little more than reinforce national stereotypes. However, this has gradually given way to an understanding that the universal element of emotions means that in translation they can be expressed in a more 'English' way – that is, in a form that will help to make an English audience recognise and experience them. In a translation of Luigi

Pirandello's *Naked* by William Murray dated 1962, Ersilia's distress is expressed in English using highly emotional language. However, in Nicholas Wright's 1998 version for the Almeida, it is left to the actress to express the same sentiments but within a more understated range of emotions:

Murray's translation:

GROTTI: (*He goes to her and attempts to embrace her.*) Ersilia. Ersilia.
ERSILIA: (*Violently, proudly, fending him off.*) No, damn you, leave me alone!
GROTTI: (*After her, reaching for her, wildly.*) No, no. Listen, listen.
ERSILIA: (*Defending herself.*) Leave me alone, I said!
GROTTI: (*Continuing.*) Oh God, let's cling together in our despair! [33]

Wright's version:

(*He moves quickly to her. Tries to embrace her.*)
ERSILIA: Leave me alone.
GROTTI: Listen.
ERSILIA: Don't touch me.
(*He stays beside her. Perhaps touches her. Gentler now than we've ever seen him.*)
GROTTI: I sometimes think that sharing grief is the same as love.[34]

Similarly, in the production of Eduardo de Filippo's *Filumena*, the same year, at the Piccadilly Theatre in the West End, the presumed hot-blooded passions of the Latin original were pitched at a lower, more easily recognisable Anglo-Saxon emotional temperature. Lauded for her performance in the part of Filumena, Judi Dench was accoladed for her 'sensuality' in a part engrained with a grim English introversion.

In the Europe of the twenty-first century, the contrasts may not be as stark as Schleiermacher's: no longer the choice between the translator leaving the European playwright in peace as much as possible and moving the English audience towards him, or leaving English audiences in peace as much as possible, and moving the European playwright towards them. Increasingly, it is beginning to look as if the two are now beginning to meet halfway. This was not the case, however, in the latter part of the nineteenth century, at the time of the breakthrough of modern drama.

Notes

1   G Robb, *Victor Hugo* (London, Picador, 1997), p. 324

2   R Heylen, *Translation, Poetics and the Stage: Six French Hamlets* (London, Routledge, 1993), pp. 26–44

3   Working within the framework of polysystem theory, the Tel Aviv translation theorist Even-Zohar has concluded that, 'Since peripheral literatures in the Western hemisphere tend more often than not to be identical to the literatures of smaller nations, as non-palatable as this idea may seem to us, we have no choice but to admit that within a group of relatable national literatures, such as the literatures of Europe, hierarchical relations are soon established, with the result that [...] some literatures take more peripheral positions.' I Even-Zohar, 'The position of translated literature within the literary polysystem', in L Venuti, (ed.), *The Translation Studies Reader* (London, Routledge, 2000), p. 194

4   T Hale, 'The imaginary quay from Waterloo Bridge to London Bridge: Translation, adaptation and genre', in M Salama-Carr (ed.), *On Translating French Literature and Film II* (Amsterdam, Rodopi, 2000), pp. 219–20, 236

5   L G Kelly, *The True Interpreter: A History of Translation Theory and Practice in the West* (Oxford, Blackwell, 1979), p. 44

6   L. Venuti, 'Neoclassicism and Enlightenment', in P France (ed.), *The Oxford Guide to Literature in English Translation* (Oxford, Oxford University Press, 2000), pp. 55–64

7   Discussed in L Venuti (ed.), *The Translation Studies Reader* (London, Routledge, 2000), p. 57

8   Quoted in L Venuti, *ibid.*, p. 22

9   Andre Lefevere (ed. and trans.), *Translating Literature: The German Tradition from Luther to Rosenzweig* (Amsterdam and Assen, van Gorcum, 1977), p. 74

10 R Leppihalme, *Culture Bumps. An Empirical Approach to the Translation of Allusions* (Cleveland, Multilingual Matters, 1997), p. 41

11 M Esslin, 'Pinter translated. On international non-communication', *Encounter* (1968), p. 45

12 See P Bergfeldt, *Insiderisms in Pinter; Problems in the Translation of Pinter's Formulaic Expressions into Swedish*, unpublished PhD dissertation (University of Surrey, 2003)

13 Discussed in K Malmkjær (ed.), 'Introduction: Translation and language teaching' in *Translation and Language Teaching. Language Teaching and Translation* (Manchester, St Jerome, 1998), p. 3

14 On this evidence, the case is strengthened for not introducing young students to traditional word lists and dictionaries until such a time that early behaviouristic patterns run less of a risk of affecting their language use in later life: see G Anderman, 'Finding the Right Word', in K. Malmkjær (ed.), *ibid.* pp. 39–48

15 Anton Chekhov, *The Seagull, A New Version*, Tom Stoppard (London, Faber & Faber, 1997)

16 J S Scott, *Children of the Age* (New York, Alfred A Knopf, 1924), p. 207. This example of the early nineteenth-century practice of providing information about 'untranslatable' concepts was brought to my attention by Per Qvale

17 R Butler, *My Fair Lady* performance programme (National Theatre, 2001)

18 Discussed in R Butler, *ibid.*

19 P Pavis, *Theatre at the Crossroads of Culture*, trans. Loren Kruger (London, Routledge, 1992)

20 *Independent*, 15 November 2001

21 Henrik Ibsen, *The Wild Duck,* adapt. Robert Brustein (Chicago, Ivan R. Dee, 1997)

22 Discussed in D Johnston (ed.), 'Introduction', *Stages of Translation* (Bath, Absolute Classics, 1996), p. 12

23 F Rosslyn, *Tragic Plots. A New Reading from Aeschylus to Lorca* (Aldershot, Ashgate, 2000), p. 6

24 S Aaltonen, *Acculturation of the Other. Irish Milieux in Finnish Drama Translation* (Joensuu, Joensuu University Press Oy, 1996)

25 Quoted in D Gilula, 'Greek drama in Rome: Some aspects of cultural transposition', in H Scolnicov and P Holland (eds.), *The Play Out Of Context: Transferring Plays from Culture to Culture* (Cambridge, Cambridge University Press, 1989), p. 102

26 S. Aaltonen, *op. cit.* pp. 74–5

27 'Theatre pragmatics', in D Johnston, *op. cit.* p. 65

28 See discussions in D Johnston, *ibid.*

29 'David Hare: Interview. Pirandello and Brecht', in D Johnston, *ibid.* p. 143

30 Discussed in *Platform Papers I: Translation* (London, National Theatre, 1992)

31 Discussed in G Anderman, *op. cit.* p. 39

32 J Farrell, 'Servant of many masters', in D Johnston, *op. cit.* p. 53

33 Luigi Pirandello, *To Clothe the Naked and Two Other Plays*, trans. W Murray (New York, E P Dutton & Co., Inc., 1962), pp. 57–8

34 Luigi Pirandello, *Naked*, adapt. N Wright, from a literal translation by G McFarlane (London, Nick Hern Books, 1998), p. 47

Chapter 2

FRENCH DRAMA: THE FORERUNNER

ALTHOUGH NOT THE MAIN FORCE behind the development of modern European drama, France was the country that laid the groundwork for the major changes to come in the art of playwriting as well as the working conditions for playwrights. It was in France that writing for the stage was turned into a profession, that provided playwrights with a living and in some cases a very comfortable lifestyle.

In the 1820s, the Parisian playwright in vogue was Eugène Scribe (1791–1861), the most popular playwright of the nineteenth century. Victorien Sardou, Scribe's most prominent follower and successor, was later to advise all young aspirants to 'Read Scribe! You'll learn theatre from him'. Scribe's gift included the ability to charm audiences, making them laugh at themselves without anger. Social and moral issues were however, not absent from his plays, and if audiences so chose, lessons could be learned. Without Scribe, whose total output may never be known – almost 400 plays have been documented, but his frequent use of pseudonyms has prevented an accurate accounting – the French theatre might have taken a very different turn; with him, it dominated European drama. It is Scribe who must be credited with restructuring French drama, and with moving it away from the sterility of neo-classic theory toward a concept of living theatre still practised today.[1] Scribe's plays, performed throughout Europe, figured prominently in Norwegian translation during Ibsen's stint as Artistic Director of the National Theatre in Christiania and his plays, in particular his early work, show clear signs of the influence of Scribe. If Ibsen is to be considered the father of Modern Drama, 'Scribe most undoubtedly is to be regarded as its grandfather'[2], and in years to come, aspiring playwrights were to be encouraged to read Ibsen, just as they had once been advised to study Scribe. Confiding his ambitions as a playwright to his agent, the legendary Peggy Ramsay, Willy Russell, author of *Educating Rita* as well as other West End successes, was reputedly told, 'Read Ibsen, darling, read Ibsen'.

By nature a generous man, Scribe did not stint when sharing the financial gains from his work with his collaborators, with whom he frequently co-operated, as was the custom at the time. Realising that he was part of a system in which managers could easily take advantage of young and inexperienced playwrights, Scribe took steps to strengthen the position of

French dramatists. Having studied law before he switched to writing plays, Scribe had a lawyer's awareness of the steps that needed to be taken and, in 1827, he moved to do something about the injustice of the prevailing system. With a number of other active authors, the *Société des Auteurs et Compositeurs Dramatiques* was established. The new association had four stated aims: to prevent managers from uniting against an author and 'freezing' him out; to establish fair rights for authors in Parisian as well as provincial theatres; to establish a common fund for needy authors and their heirs; and to provide a shared pool for operating and other expenses.[3]

As the result of Scribe's efforts, playwrights were helped to live by their pen. By the late 1820s, Scribe himself was a millionaire with an income of 60,000 francs a year, a mansion on the fashionable Rue Olivier-Saint-Georges, and a country house at Montelais, where a sign on the gate of 'Séricourt' greeted visitors with a frank:

> The theatre paid for this lovely place too;
> Thanks, passer-by – perhaps I owe you.[4]

A constant refrain in connection with Scribe is *'la pièce bien faite'*, the concept of 'the well-made play'. Not aspiring to immortality in the library, Scribe was a practitioner, intimately concerned with the demands of the stage, and his stagecraft was unparalleled. A master of the art of intrigue, he excelled in devising ingenious plots, providing his plays with a firm internal structure. Scribe's secret lay in the situations he built for his characters: keeping the audience focused in one direction he prepared a surprising yet perfectly logical dénouement. Time after time, the impossible is turned into the possible, disaster into hilarious comedy, while the complicated knot gets untangled in a completely unforeseen manner.

A collaborative effort with Délestre-Poirson, *Une Nuit de la Garde Nationale* (*A Night of the National Guard*), which opened to thunderous applause at the Vaudeville on 4 November 1815, brought Scribe his first real success. This *comédie-vaudeville* was an innovation, both in Scribe's own work and on the boulevard stage. His well-developed technique applied to a contemporary subject – the National Guard was greatly respected by Parisians for its services during a period when the city had twice been occupied by foreign troops – in combination with his use of colloquial language, proved to be a formula for success. Following the tumultuous reception of *Une Nuit...*, during the next five years, until 1820, Scribe was responsible for the production of at least 65 plays. Most were one-act *comédies-vaudevilles*, but the list also includes longer plays, comic operas and some three-act melodramas.

Although Scribe never lost his fundamentally comic view of life, *La Calomnie*

(*Calumny*, 1839) and *Une Chaîne* (*A Chain*, 1841) are examples of more thoughtful work: the first shows the devastating effect of malicious gossip on a small town, the second the problems in trying to escape from illicit romantic entanglements. In between *La Calomnie* and *Une Chaîne*, Scribe wrote *Le Verre d'eau* (*The Glass of Water*, 1840), a historical comedy in which he exemplified his favourite theme that far-reaching world events are often the result of a trivial set of circumstances. A glass of water which the Duchess of Marlborough spills over Queen Anne's dress sets in motion a chain of events: it causes her own disgrace, the fall of the Whig government and Bolingbroke's ascent to power which in turn result in a change in English foreign policy.

While the art of manipulation, the lynchpin in Scribe's work, had old French traditions – fully developed in eighteenth-century dramatists such as Marivaux and Beaumarchais – what was new in Scribe's work was the intentional sharpening of the intrigue. Through a complex middle structure of successive crises, tension mounts until a climax is reached in what the well-known French critic Francisque Sarcey (1827–99) labelled the *'scène à faire'*. This confrontation begins with the apparent downfall of the leading character, and ends in his triumph, with the audience knowing that the last act is normally reserved for the happy resolution of all the problems, while the preceding complications have been sufficiently intricate for everyone to have been left in the dark as to how it is all likely to end. What happened on stage had little to do with real life, and Sarcey is reported to have become most displeased with the well-known actress Madame Bartet for portraying, too convincingly, her grief at the unhappy fate of her beloved in the hands of the gendarmes. True emotions, he admonished her, belonged in real life and had no place on stage.[5]

In many respects, *Une Chaîne* may be viewed as the play which most clearly signals the type of influence that Scribe was to have on subsequent French playwrights such as Dumas *fils* (1824–95). The play treats the problems arising from a young man's earlier liaison, now that he is in love with a young girl, and it figures many of the characters and situations that were to become standard fare: the *grande dame* who has fallen for a young genius, the cuckolded husband, the threat of pistol duels, the young and innocent entering into marriage with no knowledge of the amorous liaisons of the future spouse, and the well-to-do and honourable out-of-town father-in-law. In this play, Scribe's strength and weaknesses are both apparent: the conflict and characters both anticipate the realistic drama which only a decade later was to become fully developed, but once the intriguing starts, the characters become mere puppets manipulated by the playwright, resulting in a theatrical chess game. Once attending a performance of one of his early plays, the plot of which he had forgotten, Scribe reportedly turned to the person sitting next to him, admitting his curiosity to find out 'how I managed to get out of this one'.[6]

For Scribe's plots to work, his characters often had to be created to fit the intrigue and the complexities of the plot as well as the dialogue. As a result, the way they speak is far removed from the kind of conversation in which ordinary people are likely to engage: it is theatre dialogue in which the clever excel in witticisms while the less gifted reveal their inferior abilities. Hardly surprising, then, that after thirty years of predictability of plot and dialogue, a new generation of French playwrights emerged, rejecting the set formula which, for many years, had earned Scribe consistent popularity. His ideas were now viewed as hopelessly outdated and out of touch with reality. After Scribe's death, on 20 February 1861, 'the young Turks had their day':[7] the *comédies-vaudevilles*, so popular during the early part of the century, started to disappear, and the boulevard theatres became filled with a different theatrical fare.

The French drama of the Second Empire, which came to exercise such an influence on modern European drama, called itself realistic, being influenced by the realistic French novel, whose interest in social problems and concerns it shared. In the hands of Dumas *fils* and Émile Augier (1820–89), the theatre became a platform for the airing of social issues, real people struggling with real problems. And, although the generation to come was later to try to free itself from what it saw as the Dumas-Augier school of clichés and their plot technique inherited from Scribe, the work of both playwrights helped to prepare the way for the arrival of naturalistic drama.

Having started his literary career as a poet, in 1848 Dumas *fils* wrote a novel, a romanticised account of his affair with Alphonsine Plessis, a well known Parisian courtesan better known as Marie Duplessis. Startlingly beautiful, she turned out to be only too happy to spend his money for Dumas *fils* to be able to continue the relationship. Only a few years after the break-up, Alphonsine, who suffered from consumption, died, aged only 23. At the suggestion of a friend, Dumas *fils* turned *La Dame aux camélias*, his novel of this true-to-life story, into a play which had its premiere in early 1852, and was subsequently staged in translation throughout Europe and the world.

Dumas *fils*' masterpiece, however, is generally considered to be *Le Demi-monde* (*The Half-World*, 1855). In this play, Dumas *fils*' 'half-world' is inhabited by marquis and marchionettes, counts and countesses, who to the outside world appear elegant and stylish, but this is only a veneer concealing fundamental cracks that reach to its core.

While the strength of his earlier work was the capturing of the feeling of atmosphere and milieu, in *Le Fils naturel* (*The Illegitimate Son*, 1858) Dumas *fils* turned his attention to the subject of illegitimacy. Born the illegitimate son of Alexandre Dumas, the author of *The Three Musketeers* who only acknowledged parenthood after he first reaped success in 1831, and never married Dumas *fils'* eight-years-older mother, he suffered from his illegitimacy particularly during his school years. Retaining his compassion for children born out of wedlock throughout his life, in *Le Fils naturel* Dumas *fils* dealt with the subject of illegitimate children and, through his efforts, succeeded in improving their situation. He continued increasingly to use the stage to raise problematic social issues, thus anticipating Ibsen's realistic social plays although, as he regretfully acknowledged before he died, he failed to achieve Ibsen's success in turning the stage into a forum for discussion of topical issues.

During the Second Empire French theatre had another representative of the realistic drama – Émile Augier. Augier did not share the startling success of Dumas *fils* but his portrayal of the encounters between the aristocracy of birth and that of money came to exert a considerable influence on the work of European playwrights at the time. But while the world of Dumas *fils* remains romantic and inhabited by aristocrats even when concerned with social equality, Augier's work is anti-romantic and moves solely among the middle classes. His first comedies were written in verse but when, following the example of Dumas *fils*, he turned to the realistic prose play, in 1854, he created his masterpiece, *Le Gendre de M. Poirier* (*Monsieur Poirier's Son-in-law*). In this play, the wealthy garment merchant Poirier has given his daughter's hand in marriage to Marquis Gaston de Presles. The conflict between father and son-in-law, and between the French aristocracy, having squandered their inheritance, and the emerging, moneyed middle classes, is finally resolved by Poirier's daughter who, through her understanding of both points of view, manages to reconcile her father and her husband.

With *Le Gendre de M. Poirier*, Augier rapidly gained European fame, scourging the world of courtesans while pointing a finger at parliamentary and political corruption. Often linking his plots to a love story, in his approach to political conflict Augier was a moralist: his influence can be seen more specifically in Bjørnson and Ibsen's social and political plays.

For material, Augier also drew on topical events outside France. At the time the building of the Suez Canal attracted attention and, in his play *La Contagion* (1866), the subject figures prominently. Here the protagonist is a young engineer named Lagarde who has the epoch-making idea of constructing a canal through the Algeciras peninsular in order to prevent Gibraltar from controlling the only access to the Mediterranean. Young, innocent, and unaccustomed to Parisian society, Lagarde is on his way to enter the world of financial intrigue when his eyes are opened. In the last act, he picks up the cudgels, taking a firm stand against corruption, and setting an example that was to be followed by Ibsen's Dr Stockmann in *An Enemy of the People*.

Aware of their virtues while scourging their hypocrisy, Augier's work, in many respects, represents the best values of the bourgeoisie: in *Les Fourchambault* (1878), for example, he discusses the social position of illegitimate children, making a son born out of wedlock the saviour of his family. Skilled in character portrayal and dialogue, Augier's plays, soon after they were written, were quickly translated into other languages and incorporated into the standard repertoires of European theatres. In fact, it does not seem unlikely that the amount of decadence and corruption that Bjørnson and Ibsen succeeded in unearthing amongst the inhabitants of the small Norwegian coastal towns may have been more characteristic of France during the Second Empire than the fishing population of Norway, still living under relatively primitive conditions. It was to take some time before both Norwegian playwrights were able to shake off the French influence and for more genuinely local issues to find their way into their work.

Also aiming his satirical wit at the French middle classes at this time was Victorien Sardou (1831–1908). With Sardou, the genre initiated by Scribe reached the peak of international popularity. No other nineteenth-century playwright has been staged so enthusiastically on both sides of the Atlantic and has had so many of his plays translated into so many languages; not even Scribe reigned as supreme in the world of theatre. Like Scribe, the greater the success of his plays on stage, the more rapid the descent of Sardou's reputation. But Scribe possessed an originality that Sardou lacked: he was the inventor of a theatre that, passed on, Sardou continued to use. In a historical perspective, however, his role is significant for the development of the modern drama if only viewed as an explanation for the intensity of the reaction of the naturalist movement towards the prevailing mode of theatre at the time. One of Sardou's most resounding European successes was *La Famille Benoîton* (1865) about a French middle-class family whose exorbitant wealth rests on the fortunes made from the sale of spring mattresses. Tumultuous events, however, force the different members of the family, accustomed to a life in luxury, to mend their ways and, before the curtain goes down, the Benoîton daughters appear on stage in simple muslin dresses, having bid farewell to their former, privileged existence.

The popularity throughout Europe of this moral tale was such that it created a new fashion for women in muslin dresses. When the play was staged in Sweden, Strindberg reminisced, in an article in the popular press in 1886, that the result of the attempt to scourge the French bourgeoisie for their pecuniary excesses was that the Swedish middle classes appeared in Benoîton dresses, Benoîton collars and Benoîton chains, and that the moral of Sardou's tale was to make anything labelled Benoîton an immediate sell-out.[8]

Sardou's historical plays were equally popular, and were performed in translation on all European stages. Unable, to an even greater extent than Scribe, to portray the complexity of human nature, during the last few decades of his life Sardou turned to writing bravura parts for actors, often in the form of expensively flamboyant tableaux from different periods of time, whose grandeur would cover up for their lack of psychological depth. In *Patrie* (1869) the period was the Renaissance, and in *Thermidor* (1891) it was the time of the revolution, also the case in *Robespierre* (1899), where the main role was played in London by Henry Irving. Sardou wrote a number of star vehicles for the leading British actor, which were translated from French into English before publication and then premiered in London.

The first master of the French light comedy was Eugène-Marin Labiche (1815–88) whose *Le Chapeau de paille d'Italie* (*The Italian Straw Hat*), written in collaboration with Marc-Michel, was first produced at the Théâtre du Palais-Royal in Paris in August 1851. In the eighty years following its creation, the play received more than a hundred productions in France alone, and in 1938 it was taken into the repertoire of the Comédie-Française where it has remained ever since. In England, it was staged in the 1880s and, throughout the years, British comedians and actors, from Jack Benny and Laurence Olivier to Tom Conti, have played the role of Fadinard, the hapless protagonist, who, on the morning of his wedding day, finds himself in desperate search of a replacement straw hat, which has been devoured by his horse, resulting in a delirious chase with its concomitant consequences. The hat, according to translator Kenneth McLeish, may well represent married stability and Fadinard, a confirmed bachelor and philanderer, is as much in a panic about finding it as not finding it. The play has also had its influence on other British media such as the sitcoms of John Cleese and Connie Booth, whose scripts for *Fawlty Towers* with their escalating lunacy were the fruit of much reading of Labiche and his successor Feydeau.[9]

With dramatists such as Scribe establishing the technique, Dumas *fils* and

Augier bringing social issues onto the stage, Sardou perfecting the Scribean genre, Labiche mastering the well-made farce and others such as collaborators Henri Meilhac (1831–97) and Ludovic Halévy (1834–1908) successfully turning the *comédie-vaudeville* into the operetta, the impact of French theatre during the Second Empire made itself known throughout Europe. In Britain, the French influence on cultural life peaked during the period 1850–70, to the extent that a number of newspapers systematically misinterpreted the title of a play, *Ours*, written in 1866 by T W Robertson (1829–71), the author of gently satirical social comedies, as *L'Ours*.[10] Since for anyone with a modicum of social pretensions, a knowledge of French was obligatory, 'translators' and 'adapters' were not difficult to find, with many of the resulting 'adaptations' hurriedly completed, and clearly undertaken with a view to financial gain. Given the modest remuneration to writers of original stage plays, the popularity at the time of 'adaptations' is hardly surprising. For a one-act farce the ordinary payment was ten shillings a night while comic dramas and pieces of the kind, in two or three acts, were paid at the rate of ten shillings an act per night. This, however, applied only to the London theatre: provincial rights were kept at a lower rate and there was nothing to be gained from American or Australian rights.[11] As a result, for writers lacking in material or with limited faith in their own powers of imagination, turning a Parisian success into an English-speaking London version must have seemed an attractive proposition. In the process, morals as well as situation were adapted in order to ensure protection of the English audiences' sensibilities. When in an old melodrama by Adolphe Phillipe Dennery (1811–99), a youth and a maiden are surprised by an avalanche ensconcing them together in a Swiss chalet for six months, the French play has them avow their love to one another. In the English adaptation, however, adjustments were made to conform to the Victorian moral code: the lovers maintain a cold reserve towards one another which lasts from the end of autumn till the beginning of summer, while the heroine instructs the hero in the French language.[12]

It was also common for an original French work to spawn more than one English version. In the case of for instance *Les Pauvres de Paris*, a play by Edouard Brisebarre and Eugène Nus, there is evidence of at least four English versions having been generated by the French original. One version, called *Poverty and Pride* (1857), originated from the pen of Charles Reade (1814–84), future author of *The Cloister and the Hearth*, who had purchased the English rights from the French playwrights. In addition, there were three other versions: *The Pride of Poverty* or *The Real Poor of London* by Ben Barnett and J B Johnstone, *Fraud and its Victims* by J Stirling Coyne and Dion

Boucicault's *The Streets of London* (1864) which was staged both in London and New York.[13] The French influence upon English theatre life appears to have been such that customary distinctions between original authorship, adaptation and translation became blurred. While in present-day theatre terminology a 'new play' from the pen of a contemporary British playwright would refer to an original new work, writing in 1871, Tom Taylor (1817–80), Charles Reade's friend and occasional collaborator, refers to the practice of using the term 'new play' to indicate that the material used had been re-worked, that is 'adapted'. The use of just 'play' on the other hand meant that the work was a translation, while a 'new and original play' would refer to a piece of work bearing only a very slight resemblance to another work.[14]

It was not uncommon for the oeuvre of English playwrights to consist almost exclusively of adaptations of French plays, as was the case with many of the plays by Charles Reade.[15] Charles Reade was, however, virtually unique among English playwrights, in acknowledging original authorship through payment. In return for the English rights to *Le Château de Grantier*, Reade paid £20 to the French writer Auguste Maquet (1813–86), half of which was to be paid back if Reade's adaptation was not performed within two years.

The route to the London stage for Maquet's play was not, however, to be a straight one. Having failed to interest theatre managers in his English version of the play, Charles Reade then proceeded to remove the stage directions and to transform the play into a novel, which was given the title *White Lies*. This narrative version in turn served as the basis for a stage adaptation entitled *The Double Marriage*, which finally reached the stage on 24 October 1867 as the opening piece at the new Queen's Theatre in Long Acre. By now familiar with the dénouement from the published novel the audience was not, however, amused and the play failed utterly.[16]

With a large number of English writers resorting to adaptations of French plays in preference to writing their own, the traffic of translations became almost exclusively unidirectional. In stark contrast to present-day practice, nearly every piece produced on the London stage did not originate in English, while there is little evidence of English plays appearing in translation in other languages. For some time, according to Sutherland Edwards, *Twice Killed* by John Oxenford (1812–77) was generally viewed as being an original work. Thus when a one-act opera by Grisar, on the same theme, was produced in Paris under the title *Bon Soir, Monsieur Pantalon!*, it was believed that at last a modern English play had been adapted into French. It turned out, however, that the story was an adaptation from the German, but it is noteworthy that neither in connection with the English nor the French version of the piece did the name of the original author appear.

The somewhat lawless borrowing of French plays for adaptation on the English stage came to an end in 1886 when, following the Berne Convention, legislative steps were taken to protect the property of playwrights for a period of fifty years following their death (see Chapter 9 for further discussion of copyright). Writing in 1900, Sutherland Edwards commented that:

> [A]t present, international rights have to be observed, and the right of translating a very successful French piece has to be largely paid for. French pieces have become more Parisian and less dependent upon plot; while owing partly to these causes but chiefly to the immense increase in the rates for dramatic work, a school at last has sprung up in England of original dramatists. At present too, every novelist desires, as in France, to present his work on the stage.[17]

Nevertheless, the influence of French theatre during the Victorian period was to be lasting and of subsequent importance to the extent 'that some understanding of it is a prerequisite to an analysis of the development of nineteenth-century English drama'.[18]

Due to the large number of *pièces bien faites* transferred from French into English during the Victorian period, English playwrights became acquainted with the craft of what was originally Scribean plot construction. Through the process of translating and adapting 'well-made' plays they acquired the French technique, learning to put down on the page what was likely to work on the stage. It has even been suggested that the assimilation of French literature during the nineteenth century helped to set English literature on its subsequent course.[19]

However, after decades of witty dialogue, cleverly woven plots and aristocratic settings, French interest in the traditional model started to wane. The conflicts were beginning to seem contrived, and the characters, however spontaneous and impulsive their behaviour, seemed to be experiencing their emotions in accordance with a set formula. Forgotten were the more irrational and illogical aspects of human nature, with the result that the people inhabiting the world on stage, like those of the earlier period of neo-classicism, often turned into mere abstractions. Voices of protest were raised and *une pièce bien faite*, the highest praise that could previously have been bestowed upon a playwright's work, no longer ranked as a compliment.

The most outspoken, dissenting voice came from Émile Zola (1840–1902).

In 1873, Zola dramatised his novel *Thérèse Raquin* (1867), often viewed as the starting point for the development of naturalist drama. Later, in a comprehensive statement in *Le Naturalisme au théâtre*, Zola set out his criticism of the theatre of his time. First appearing in Russian in *The Messenger of Europe*, a St Petersburg newspaper to which Turgenev had secured entry for him, it was later included in the volume *Le Roman experimental* (*The Experimental Novel*, 1880). Here Zola dismisses the theatre of Victorien Sardou, his contemporary and representative of the comedy of intrigue, as superficial, likening the well-made play to an amusing toy which has provided diversion for all of Europe. He also rejects Monsieur Dumas *fils* as a man of the theatre having succeeded, through his wit, in wringing the neck of reality. And in the case of Émile Augier, more human than Dumas *fils*, his inability to shake off social conventions, clichés and stereotypical characters has prevented him from introducing naturalism to the stage. Now, Zola continues, it is time for dramatists to give up theatre as clockwork and to place on stage men and women of flesh and blood. Recognising the time lag in development between the naturalistic novel and the still more conventional drama, Zola lambasts the Parisian stage for its mechanical plots, superficially drawn characters, stilted dialogue and overall remoteness from the real world. Embracing fully the new scientific faith sweeping the Western world, now Zola asks that what is shown on the stage should mirror what is happening in the world outside the theatre. Like the novel, the play should be uncompromisingly realistic and objective, aiming for an untarnished reflection of life without frills.

When naturalism crossed the Channel, it met Victorianism at the height of its power and self-assurance, and the reception accorded it was far from cordial. In the application of science to social and aesthetic theory, France was ahead of England and England looked upon France with mixed feelings of antagonism and admiration. Still, that continental realism and naturalism reached a wide audience in England is obvious from the large number of translations of the works of Balzac, Flaubert, the brothers de Goncourt, Daudet, Maupassant, Zola and Huysmans. First translated as early as 1834 with *Scenes from Parisian Life*, the next translation of a Balzac novel, *Mother and Daughter*, did not appear until 1842, but from then on until the end of the century, Balzac's fiction appeared regularly either in monthly or annual magazines or in book form. Initially hostile to these translations, as the century advanced English critics became increasingly persuaded of Balzac's genius, and the evolution of Balzac's literary reputation in England constitutes a revealing commentary on changing literary fashions. With each appearance of new French writing, the perceived threat shifted, leaving previous writers accepted as lesser evils. When Baudelaire threatened Victorian values, Balzac's reputation became less tarnished; Baudelaire in turn increased in acceptability as Zola and naturalism emerged in the literary arena.

English hostility to naturalism came from two separate groups: one included writers such as Oscar Wilde who were in disagreement, wholly or partially, on aesthetic or philosophic grounds; the other, represented by the clergy, the censor and members of the general public, whose views were reflected in the newspapers and the periodicals, objected on purely moral grounds. The controversy peaked in 1888 with an attack on the translations of the writings of Zola, leading to the trial of the publisher Henry Vizetelly (1820–94).

In 1842, Henry Vizetelly had founded the *Illustrated London News* and, the following year, the *Pictorial Times*; fame as a book publisher followed later. Vizetelly had become interested in contemporary literature during a lengthy sojourn in France, prompting his decision upon his return to England to publish a series of modestly-priced translations of novels of high repute in France. While the Victorians were indifferent to these translations, their reaction was to change drastically with Vizetelly's publication of Zola's work in English.

In France, Zola's literary breakthrough had come with *L'Assommoir* (*Drink*, 1877), a strong, socially-committed description of hardship and alcoholism in a Parisian working-class *arrondissement*. A year later, when Zola's novel had reached its forty-eighth edition in France but had not as yet been translated into English, H Schütz Wilson, in the *Gentleman's Magazine*, excused Zola's naturalism as possibly useful for social reform but drew attention to the important difference between English and French writers:

> English writers will not leave a celestial bed to prey on garbage. French writers sometimes do not shun even ordure. French literature knows but little reticence in the mention of such things. English writers avoid, with the reticence of fine shame, all allusion to the ignobler needs and functions of the body.[20]

In 1879, Zola put his working-class characters on stage, and on Whit-Monday the same year, *Drink*, a dramatisation by Charles Reade, was produced at the Princess's Theatre in London.[21] Making no effort to Anglicise the scenes and characters as had Boucicault in the case of *Les Pauvres de Paris*, Reade focused on conveying Zola's racking atmosphere of reality. When, during rehearsals, this resulted in the lessee of the Princess's starting to get cold feet, intimidated by contemporary criticism's violent antipathy to Zola, Reade agreed to take on a considerable share of the financial risk, receiving in return a corresponding division of the profits. This proved to be sound judgement by

Reade, who, instead of the usual royalties, received a fortune amounting to £20,000 from the successful production.[22]

Zola's novels were also popular, but controversial. In 1888 the controversy reached a climax. Pouncing upon *La Terre* (*Earth*), which Zola had completed the previous year, as well as including other naturalistic novels in the charges, the vice squad of the National Vigilance Association secured an indictment against the Vizetellys for trafficking in pornographic literature. Henry Vizetelly was convicted, fined £100 and placed on a year's probation. Elated by the victory, the Vigilance Association renewed their efforts. The following year, they hauled Vizetelly into court again, this time for publishing Flaubert, Bourget and Maupassant, resulting in a sentence of three months' imprisonment, which, owing to his age and physical condition, undoubtedly hastened his death in 1894. Nevertheless, during a visit made by Zola to London that year, the year before the Dreyfus trial, the *Spectator* registered the ironic fact that the country that in 1889 had sent Zola's publisher to prison, and a press that generally condemned his work, had now united to give him a welcome worthy of some master who had been taken to the heart of the English nation.[23]

Although less inclined to impose censorship on moral grounds than the Victorians, Parisian theatre managers did not unreservedly welcome the arrival of naturalist drama. Increasingly, it was becoming necessary to create private clubs or societies where the new drama could be staged free of censorship, for a select audience of like-minded adherents of these revolutionary ideas. Having assembled a number of progressive one-act plays which he had failed to find interest in staging, André Antoine (1858–1943), an employee of the Paris Gasworks and enthusiastic amateur actor, decided to produce them at his own expense. One of the plays in the programme was an adaptation of a novella by Zola, *Jacques Damour*. On 30 March 1887 the production opened in a little theatre holding only 400 spectators in the Passage des Élysées des-beaux-arts in Montmartre with Antoine himself giving a memorable performance as the haggard Jacques Damour returning home after ten years in exile to find that his wife has remarried. The realism of the scene and the natural acting style had an immense impact on the audience: the Théâtre Libre had been born. Subsequent success enabled Antoine to move to a better theatre; productions were extended to three performances, a subscription system was introduced and, gradually, full-length plays were offered: Tolstoy's *The Power of Darkness* in February 1888, Ibsen's *Ghosts* in May 1890 and *The Wild Duck* in April 1891, Strindberg's *Miss Julie* in 1893 and *The Father* in 1894.

By delving into dreams and states of mind, naturalism also carried within it the seeds of further developments, opening the way to symbolism which went on to explore deeper aspects of the human condition. Chekhov's work gives meticulously accurate pictures of reality: a real object like a cherry orchard in turn becomes a symbol of more complex social and psychological aspects of life. The same applies to the other great masters of modern drama: first viewed as social and realist criticisms, Ibsen's plays become increasingly rich in symbols as do Strindberg's later plays when he attempts to depict the state of his own internal mind rather than objective, external reality. The embodiment of this new approach was Maurice Maeterlinck (1862–1949), a Belgian poet. The year 1891 saw seminal performances of two of Maeterlinck's short atmospheric symbolist plays, *L'Intruse* (*The Intruder*) and *Les Aveugles* (*The Blind*). The cast list of *The Blind* included the actor Aurélien Lugné-Poe (1869–1940), soon to emerge as the leader of the symbolist movement in the theatre. In 1892, a production of Ibsen's *The Lady from the Sea* established Lugné-Poe as a leading director, and following the success of Maeterlinck's *Pelléas et Mélisande* at the Bouffes-du-Nord in Paris on 17 May 1893, he was able to launch his own company, the Théâtre de l'Œuvre which opened on 5 October 1893 with a production of Ibsen's *Rosmersholm*.

One of the performances of note at the Théâtre de l'Œuvre was Alfred Jarry's *Ubu Roi* (1896). In this satire on the French bourgeois' greed and craving for power, Ubu and his wife seize power and make themselves rulers of Poland, killing anyone standing in their way. The very first word uttered on stage is '*merdre*', probably the first time this taboo word had ever been heard on the French stage. In Kenneth McLeish's English translation (1997) it is delicately rendered as 'shikt'.[24] This word, the favourite coarse word of the play, exemplifies the language used by Jarry's characters in the Ubu cycle – *King Ubu*, and the sequels *Cuckold Ubu* and *Slave Ubu* – who for the most time speak in the language of playground slang, larded with secret words, puns and, in McLeish's terms, 'cocky, never-quite-gutter vocabulary'. The skits from which King Ubu originated were set in Poland and this location was retained in the play in order to convey a feudal, knightly resonance, which Jarry then sent up in the battle and court scenes. However, in a lecture given before the 1896 performance, Jarry let it be known that his 'Poland' was in fact a surreal, invented place, that is nowhere at all. In French, *pologne* also happens to be a particularly phallic kind of sausage, rather like the salamis and 'German' sausages which feature in pantomime and Punch and Judy shows.

In his translation, McLeish renamed Poland 'Baloney' and strove to match as far as possible the puns and slangy distortions of the original French with English schoolboy verve.

The anti-naturalistic strivings of the symbolists combined successfully with solid melodramatic effects brought Edmond Rostand (1868–1918) fame when only 29. *Cyrano de Bergerac* (1897), his best known work, was first given an English language performance in 1918 when it played to packed audiences, although the spectacular nature of the event turned it into a financial disaster. In 1970, the National Theatre presented a condensed English version of the play by Patrick Garland, simply called *Cyrano*. It was firmly built around the central figure with a great deal of the sub-plot and countless minor characters removed, acknowledging the likelihood that the original version, which was five hours long, would no longer appeal to present-day English theatre audiences. Rostand's five acts were reshaped into two, and turned into a prose version, with no attempt made to transfer into English the original French rhyming couplets.

Twenty-five years later, the National Theatre was home to another, very different *Cyrano*. Presented by the Tara Company, Rostand's play was now set in 1930s India, adapted by Jatinda Verma and rendered into verse by Ranjit Bolt, in a production which opened at the Cottesloe Theatre on 25 October 1995. The transposition of the original text to 1930s Raj India also brought about a reconfiguration of the character of Cyrano, from a lowly musketeer with a gift for poetry, into a prompt in a theatre in north India. In the company's quest to pursue the question of whether Cyrano is a sentimental hero and whether sentiment has a place in the modern world, the adaptation also served as a vehicle for re-examining the relationship between English and Indian theatre.[25]

Coinciding roughly in life span with Rostand, at a time when the future seemed to lie with symbolist fantasy or naturalist social comment, Georges Feydeau (1863–1921) resurrected the conventions of vaudeville and the well-made play. The first, after Labiche, to introduce reality into the fixed form of the vaudeville, he outlined his approach in an article published on 15 March 1908:

> I noticed that vaudevilles were invariably based on worn-out themes, and false, banal, ridiculous characters: mere puppets. It struck me that each of us, in life, gets mixed up in farcical situations without necessarily losing our individuality in the process... At once I set about looking for my

characters in living reality, determined to preserve their personalities intact. After a comic exposition, I would hurl them into burlesque situations.[26]

The son of an eminent Second Empire novelist, Feydeau, by his own account, wrote his first play around the age of six or seven, following a visit to the theatre. The epitome of the sophisticated boulevardier, his official career in the theatre began in 1880, with *Par la fenêtre* (*Through the Window*), followed in 1883 by *Amour et piano* (*Love and a Piano*). Altogether he wrote thirty-nine plays, including *Un Fil à la patte* (*A Cat among the Pigeons*, 1894), *Le Dindon* (*The Turkey*, 1896), *L'Hôtel du Libre-Échange* (*Hotel Free-Exchange*, 1896), *La Dame de chez Maxim* (*The Lady from Maxim's*, 1899), *Occupe-toi d'Amélie* (*Look After Amelia*, 1908) and *La Puce à l'oreille* (*The Flea in the Ear*, 1907). London productions of Feydeau's play include *L'Hôtel du Libre-Échange* as *Hotel Paradiso* (1958), *Cat Among the Pigeons* (1969), and *On Purge Bébé* as *The Purging*, adapted by Peter Barnes and presented at the Old Vic in 1976. In 1966, the National Theatre staged *La Puce à l'oreille* as *A Flea in Her Ear* at the Old Vic, translated by John Mortimer. This farce, with its mistaken identity plot, is perhaps the best-known Feydeau play to English audiences. *The Lady from Maxim's*, staged at the NT in 1977, also translated by John Mortimer, only had one previous London performance in English, at the Criterion Theatre in 1902. Then, in 1984, *L'Hôtel du Libre-Échange* reappeared on the programme of the National Theatre, this time with the title *A Little Hotel on the Side*. The translation was again by John Mortimer, admirably reproducing in English his version of the language of Feydeau's characters, which has been described as:

> [N]ot the good French of Labiche's heroes. It is chopped up, chaotic, slangy, elliptical, stuffed with a jumble of mad preposterous ideas, like the coat of a conjuror whose sleeves are full of fish, flowers, omelettes, bars of soap and cannon balls.[27]

Feydeau's comedy grows naturally out of the tradition of the 'well-made play' with its world of carefully motivated actions in rapid sequence inhabited by bourgeois urbanites with their wives and mistresses in the opulent mansions of the Second Empire, or in the Parisian underworld of seedy hotels and cafés. After the characters have jumped through an endless number of emotional and physical hoops, the happy ending is reached and all mysteries are explained. According to Feydeau, writing a play is like taking the role of a chemist, mixing 'elements together' in such a way as to be able to 'predict almost exactly the effect they will produce'. Taken at face value, in Feydeau's plays, relationships are reduced to the simple formula of 'two principal characters: the one who delivers the kicks to the backside and the one who receives them.'[28] Acquiring fresh meaning from existentialism and the theatre of the absurd, perhaps even post-modernism, Feydeau's work, which came to an end midway through World War I, seems to have reached maturity with the twentieth century.

About this time, a year before the outbreak of World War I, Sergei Diaghilev (1872–1929), the manager of the Ballets Russes which had burst upon the Parisian scene in 1909, decided to sever his links with the Russian state theatres, making Paris the permanent home of his company. Here he created a series of dazzling productions, including *Parade* (1917) with design by Picasso, music by Satie and a libretto by the twenty-eight year old Jean Cocteau (1889–1963). A famous example of an artist working in a number of media, Cocteau was also a dramatist, in love with the theatre, 'that red-and-gold sickness' as he called it.[29] In his theatre work Cocteau experimented with form, as in his surreal, dreamlike version of the myth of Orpheus, *Orphée*, which premiered in 1926, and the four, very different acts of his own version of the Oedipus story, *La Machine infernale* (*The Infernal Machine*), which opened in 1934. The year 1937 saw the premiere of *Chevaliers de la table ronde* (*Knights of the Round Table*) and, on 14 November the following year, *Les Parents terribles* opened at the Théâtre des Ambassadeurs. A lucrative run followed, terminated by the Municipal Council of Paris, after the owner of the theatre denounced the play as immoral. The following year, it reopened at the Théâtre des Bouffes-Parisiens where it ran to capacity audiences for another six months.

On 21 April 1994, fifty-six years after its Parisian premiere, *Les Parents terribles* opened at the Lyttelton Theatre in a new translation by Jeremy Sams. 'In Sams' witty translation,' wrote the *Guardian* critic Michael Billington, 'the play comes across as a piece of self-sustaining irony that owes as much to Feydeau as to classical tragedy': the production was described as not unlike 'a camp version of *Oedipus Rex*'.[30]

The theme of Cocteau's play is incestuous relations: the heroine, Yvonne, is a possessive, bedridden diabetic who does not take kindly to the news that her son Michael has fallen for Madeleine, a young bookbinder. Michael's announcement also meets with an unfavourable reaction from her husband George – once the passionate love object of Yvonne's spinster sister Léo – who, when he has not been devoting his time to trying to invent an underwater submachine gun, has been conducting a sexual relationship with Madeleine.

As an example of a recent, successful production of a twentieth-century

French play in English translation, the changes made by Sams for the National Theatre warrant a closer study. On the whole faithful to the original, a primary aim of Sams' approach to Cocteau's French text appears to have been his concern to condense and shorten the dialogue. Since the first half of the twentieth century, theatre traditions have changed from longer full-length evenings at the theatre to a practice of shorter, not infrequently one-act plays. In Sams' English version, dialogue is, for instance, omitted when action makes verbal comment superfluous. In one such instance, Léo asks about Yvonne:

> LÉO: *Où est-elle?*

> LEO: Where is she?

and receives the answer from Georges:

> GEORGES: *Là... Dans le cabinet de toilette.*

> GEORGES: There...in the toilet.[31]

Yvonne's appearance at the bathroom door makes this exchange superfluous and, in Sams' version, it is omitted.

Omissions also occur when the subject of the dialogue appears to be out of date, as in the conversation between Léo and Yvonne about Michel's military service in Act 1, Scene 2:

> LÉO: *A cause de ses bronches et du ministre, ma chère Yvonne. Ce service libérait Michel. Il ne fallait à aucun prix qu'il s'élogne. Il a vingt-deux ans.*

> LEO: Because of his 'weak chest' and the Minister, my dear Yvonne. This National Service would liberate Michael. He mustn't get out of it at any price. After all, he's 22.[32]

Similar reasons may underlie Sams' decision to cut discussions about the undesirable habits of the bourgeoisie, a favourite theme of Cocteau's. For example, in Act 1, Scene 2, Sams leaves out the following lines:

> LÉO: *Je n'accuse personne. Puisque je ne profite pas des avantages de la bourgeoisie, je me refuse aux mensonges qui viennent d'une vieille habitude sinistre de chuchoter et de fermer les portes dès qu'on parle de naissance, de fortune, d'amour, de mariage ou de mort.*

> LEO: I'm not accusing anybody. Since I don't benefit from middle-class advantages, I refuse to tell lies which come from an old, sinister habit of whispering and closing doors as soon as the subject of birth, wealth, love, marriage or death is mentioned.[33]

When rendering idioms, phrases and metaphors into English, Sams does not appear to depart from the original unless absolutely necessary. One such case concerns Léo's response to Michael's question:

> MICHEL: / – – – / *Où est papa?*
> LÉO: *Il ne supporte pas les scènes. Il a dû filer à l'anglaise.*[34]

In Sams' translation, Léo answers Michael:

> MICHAEL: / – – – / Where's Papa got to?
> LEO: He hates scenes – he's slipped off home.[35]

Here the literal translation of '*Il a dû filer à l'anglaise*', 'he must have run off the English way', means, according to a mono-lingual dictionary '*s'en aller sans permission en tachant de ne pas éveiller attention*', that is, getting away while trying not to attract attention. Not surprisingly, this has been translated as 'slipped off', an ordinary motion verb in place of the more colourful original.

In addition to adjustments necessitated by linguistic differences between French and English, Sams' changes often seem to be dictated by social and cultural factors. In Act 1, Scene 1, Yvonne refers to the family's unorthodox style of living as '*une famille qui habite une roulotte*' – they live in a 'horse-drawn gypsy caravan'.[36] More than half a century after Cocteau wrote the play, as we know, although gypsies have remained nomadic, their means of transport have changed from horse-drawn caravans; the metaphor of Cocteau's eccentric and disorganised family remains but, in Sams' version, has become re-located to a gypsy encampment.[37]

As a result of the cuts and inevitable adjustments dictated by changing times and habits, in Sams' English version Cocteau's play remains a family drama, but less encumbered by information which might divert attention from Cocteau's own, floridly theatrical portrayal of what today is commonly known as a dysfunctional family.

In translation between French and English, the translator is in the enviable position of being able to draw on a large number of French loan words, the use of which may help to reinforce the feel of authenticity of the original. Thus, when in *Les Parents terribles* Yvonne describes Léo in admiring terms:

> YVONNE: *[T]u as toujours été belle, ondulée, tirée à quatre épingles, élégante, brilliante...*[38]

Sams skilfully replaces the second adjective '*ondulée*' and the expression, '*tiré à quatre pingles*' (stretched out with four pins – that is, well-groomed) with '*soignée*', retaining the French flavour while shortening and sharpening the line:

> YVONNE: / – – – / You've always been so beautiful, so *soignée*, elegant, brilliant...[39]

The presence of French words in English has also been exploited in retaining the French title of the play, which is likely to be easily understood by an English audience due to the French origin of both the noun 'parents' and the adjective 'terribles'. The decision to leave a French play firmly anchored in French life and culture is clearly signalled by the title: to a theatre audience it indicates from the start that, although on a subject of mutual interest, this is safely a play not about 'us' but about 'them'. 'Significantly and appropriately,' Paul Taylor wrote in his review of Sean Mathias' production on 7 May 1994 in the *Independent*, 'the title has been left un-[A]nglicised.' Commenting on the translation he further stated:

> Given that the wranglings and rum goings-on in the convalescent murk of the mother's sleazily luxurious boudoir represent Gallic rather than Anglo-Saxon attitudes, it's a tribute to Jeremy Sams' translation that the first time you're made conscious of any cultural discrepancy is when the aunt makes a Yeatsian allusion to 'the rag and bone shop of the heart'.

When in 1995 the National Theatre's critically successful production of *Les Parents Terribles* moved to New York, it was acknowledged that the long-established links between France and the British might not cross the Atlantic intact. Fearing that the title might leave audiences in doubt as to what to expect (or possibly offend the sanctity of the family), Broadway producers opted for a new title. *Indiscretions*, the title finally chosen, called forth the indignant response from the *Daily News* theatre critic of 28 April 1995 that '[o]bviously the title was too difficult for us to understand'. The use of a more English sounding title might arguably also have invited expectations of a more naturalistic interpretation of Cocteau's fever dream – he reportedly knocked out the first draft of the play in eight opium-soaked days – than intended. The *Daily News* review of the New York staging went on to express reservations about the production, scourging the plot, the 'crude acting style' and the directorial touches 'deeply contemptuous of women'. Ironically, a less explicit title might in fact have helped towards greater understanding of the nature of Cocteau's play. Insufficient distancing from the text, a mistake frequently made in productions of European drama, may also have contributed to the American critics and general public perceiving the text as naturalistic.

Like Cocteau's *Les Parents terribles*, which in its wit and dark humour appears to have struck a familiar chord with British theatre audiences, lightheartedness and *ésprit* also seem to have been the necessary ingredients in the work of other French playwrights selected for performance on the English stage. In the case of the plays by novelist, *belle-lettriste* and diplomat Jean Giraudoux (1882–1944), *La Guerre de Troie n'aura pas lieu* (*The Trojan War Will Not Take Place*, 1935), a prophetic prophecy of the catastrophe which engulfed Europe four years after its staging, was produced in London in 1955. In an English version by Christopher Fry entitled *Tiger at the Gate* it became a resounding success, in no small measure due to the presence of the actor Michael Redgrave.[40] More literally translated by Fry as *The Trojan War Will Not Take Place*, the play was also staged at the Lyttelton Theatre in 1983, directed by Harold Pinter.

In June 1971, London theatregoers could also see *Amphitryon 38* (1929), Giraudoux's first original play for the stage. An early work, it is 'full of the frivolous jokes that [...] are so characteristic of the man. The title is one. Giraudoux pretended that the story of Jupiter and Amphitryon's unassailably virtuous wife was so hackneyed that novel treatment was impossible'.[41] Produced by Laurence Olivier and the National Theatre, the cast included Christopher Plummer, Geraldine McEwan and Constance Cummings in a version taken from the adaptations by S N Behrman and Roger Gellert. However, less buoyant works by Giraudoux have not been staged in London, perhaps because they do not fit the French playwright's English reputation as charming and lightweight, writing in accordance with the conventions of boulevard theatre between the wars.[42]

A similar fate to that of Giraudoux appears to have befallen Jean Anouilh (1910–87), whose plays in English translation emerge with an emphasis on laughter and comedy, often leaving the dark underside of this playwright's work insufficiently explored. Anouilh made his theatrical debut with *L'Hermine* (*The Ermine*), which was accepted for performance by Lugné-Poe at the Théâtre de L'Œuvre in February 1932. What was later to become one of his most successful plays, *Le Bal des voleurs* (*The Thieves' Carnival*), was written as early as 1932, but only staged in 1938 when Anouilh met the director André Barsacq. The co-operation with Barsacq, which continued until 1948, resulted in the production of what are generally considered to be Anouilh's best plays: *Eurydice* (1941), *Antigone* (1942) and *L'Invitation au château* (*Invitation to the Castle*, 1947), all produced at the Théâtre de L'Atelier. While before 1948 Anouilh was still considered as something of an avant-garde playwright, in the 1950s he became more of an establishment writer. *L'Alouette* (*The Lark*, 1953), about Joan of Arc, and *Becket* (1959), were highly successful and appeared to have been 'written with an almost visible desire to please the orchestra stalls'.[43]

It is clear by the titles Anouilh gave to the collections of his plays that he himself arranged them into categories. While early, naturalistic plays, pessimistic in their atmosphere, are termed '*pièces noires*', some of his more optimistic plays such as *The Thieves' Carnival* are labelled '*pièces roses*'. The 1940s and 1950s saw the emergence of '*pièces brillantes*', including *L'Invitation au château* and *La Répétition* (*The Rehearsal*, 1950), as well as his '*pièces grinçantes*' which set the audience's teeth on edge in plays such as *La Valse des toréadors* (*The Waltz of the Toreadors*, 1951) and *Pauvre Bitos* (*Poor Bitos*, 1956). *The Lark* and *Becket* on the other hand are classified by Anouilh as '*pièces costumés*'.

During the late 1960s and 1970s, Anouilh's more successful work includes *Cher Antoine* (*Dear Antoine*, 1969). In 1982, his last play, *Nombril* (*Navel*), was an immense success in Paris, but two years later it failed in the West End in a translation by Michael Frayn entitled *Number One*.

In all, Anouilh wrote more than forty plays, of which the early plays of the 1930s and the historically-based plays have received most critical and public acclaim. While translations into English of his later plays followed on closely from the originals, the early plays did not reach English audiences until after World War II, making Anouilh a popular and frequently performed playwright in English translation in the post-war West End. In 1949 Olivier directed Vivien Leigh in *Antigone*; a year later, Peter Brook directed Paul Scofield, Claire Bloom and Margaret Rutherford in *L'Invitation au château*, retitled *Ring Round the Moon*, and in 1955, Dorothy Tutin and Donald Pleasance in *The Lark*.

Early English translations of Anouilh's first real success, *Le Voyageur sans bagage* (*Traveller without Luggage*, 1936), about an amnesiac's return to what may be his long-lost family, bear the hallmarks of the birth pains of early modern drama translation. Little attention is paid to the difference between spoken and written language, nor to the socially-determined speech patterns of characters from opposing class backgrounds. In John Whiting's original translation for the *Collected Plays* (1966), replaced by that of Lucienne Hill, the main translator of Anouilh's plays, the colloquial language of the servants does not differ markedly from the caustic snobbery of the Duchess. Whiting's 'The working classes always come in large numbers, the better to defend themselves' does not compare favourably to Hill's high-handed Duchess who dismisses the lower classes as 'Safety in numbers – that's the peasant mentality all over.' [44]

Produced in 1944, during the German occupation of Paris, Anouilh's reworking of Sophocles' *Antigone* made him a controversial figure, many identifying Créon with the German occupiers and Antigone with the Resistance. Aware of the needs of a modern audience, Anouilh attempted to bridge the gap between past and present, substituting the somewhat awe-inspiring Greek characters for more ordinary men and women. Through skilful use of dialogue, variation in mood and pace is successfully conveyed: speeches of sustained emotional intensity from Antigone and Créon contrast with marked colloquialisms from the Nurse and the Guard. The contrast between the mythical and the modern is, however, delicately balanced and, at times, as in Lewis Galantière's 1946 American translation, upset through an over-emphasis on the modern; to have Antigone refer to her father as 'her dad' has been criticised as being excessively informal.[45] In contrast, Barbara Bray's more faithful translation for BBC Radio 3, published in 1987, scrupulously respects Anouilh's theatrical terminology used to underpin the life/theatre analogy.

After the defeat of the fascist powers in 1945, a London suffering from post-war austerity welcomed the poetic comedies of Christopher Fry (b. 1907), which offered verbal fireworks, frivolity and sentimental escapism – much the same theatrical fare as Anouilh's bitter-sweet romantic comedies, which had made his reputation before the war, and to which he now returned. As a result, Fry seemed ideally positioned to provide the definitive English translation of Anouilh's *L'Invitation au château* as *Ring Round the Moon*. Set in the winter garden of a château in the spring of 1912, at the centre of the plot is a patrician pair of twins, sweet and innocent Frédéric and sour and devious Horace. Like much of Anouilh's work, the play pits the forces of innocence, embodied by Isabelle, a girl of great purity, against those of an iniquitous and sophisticated society. However, unlike similarly-themed Anouilh works such as *Antigone* and *The Rehearsal*, in the end *Ring Round the Moon* allows love to triumph, defying the chilly currents of social oppression.

In order to ensure that greater prominence is awarded the 'feel good factor', *Ring Round the Moon* departs not insignificantly from the French text in its concern to emphasise the 'sweet' rather than the 'bitter' elements of the original. Starting with the title, it may be argued that *Invitation to the Castle*, Anouilh's original title in English translation, more closely reflects the way its focus on love, money and social class is closely related to the theme of man's fate, and while there is potentially an ominous note to be read into the original, any trace of danger has been lost in the more poetic title. A significant difference between the French and the English versions of the play is also illustrated by the different approaches taken by the productions in Paris and

London: for the London production the play was subtitled 'A charade with music'.

In its original French version, Anouilh's play also contains a number of less 'frothy' elements such as the insistence on the incompatibility between money and happiness. However, as a result of the omissions made in the adapted English version, this message is made considerably less clear. Thus Fry omits Hugo's (Horace's) cynical reflections on the charitable deeds of the rich at the beginning of Act 5 (Act 3, Scene 2 in Fry), while inserting, prior to Anouilh's Act 2, an amusing scene of his own (the beginning of his own Act 1, Scene 2), that turns Madame Desmermortes into a Lady Bracknell. This addition was, according to Fry, commissioned by Peter Brook in order to provide time for Claire Bloom in the part of Isabelle to change her dress where such a change was needed.[46] Fry also appears sensitive to pertinent differences between Gallic and Anglo-Saxon attitudes: while in the original, Romainville's protestations of sexual disinterest *'Je m'intéresse à cette jeune fille comme je m'intéresse à tous les arts'* ('I'm interested in this young girl as I'm interested in all the arts'), are those of the cultured Frenchman, Fry's counterpart 'I'm only interested in this girl as I'm interested in butterflies and old furniture', invokes English eccentricity.[47] Among omissions, the failure to include in the English version the full scene between Messerschmann, the millionaire made good, and his daughter, Diana, in Act 2, is particularly notable. In this scene, Diana recalls the time when they were poor and 'how we went from one frontier to another, crammed together in those railway trucks'. Fry admitted that the elimination of this passage as well as some other exchanges was 'a puzzle.' Thirty-five years were to pass before the shortening of the scene in English translation was discovered, prior to a planned production of the play at Manchester's Royal Exchange in 1985.[48]

The conscious or, as appears to be the case with Fry's translation, inadvertent omission of the more 'bitter' parts of Anouilh's 'bitter-sweet' observations on the human condition have resulted in gentler, watered-down English versions of the French playwright's work. Neither genuinely French nor properly English, but somehow caught in between, translations have yielded a playwright placed in no man's land, which has in turn coloured the reception of Anouilh's work on the English-speaking stage. For example, in 1999, an attempt at a revival of *Ring Round the Moon* in New York met with a typical critical response to both European theatre and Anouilh's plays in translation. Writing on 29 April 1999, Ben Brantley's review of the play in the *New York Times* began:

> Turning certain plays from French into English is like dragging vampires into the sunlight. They shriek, they curdle, they shrivel, while shedding

the elegant, arrogant authority they display in their natural element. There is in particular a French brand of theatrical whimsy, extensively practised around the middle of this century, that usually turns into dust in the mouths of American actors, however capable.

The review continues to describe *Ring Round the Moon* as 'an uneasy example of those Gallic fantasies, equal parts preciousness and cynicism, in which Anouilh specialised. It is the sort of work that makes you say, if you're feeling charitable, "Oh, those worldly, romantic French." ' What seems to have been forgotten by Brantley, however, is that 'those Gallic fantasies' are 'Gallic fantasies' mediated through English, not even in a translation originally aimed at an American audience. In addition, little consideration, if any, seems to have been given to the date of the translation; the New York production of the play in 1999 used Christopher Fry's translation first used on the London stage almost half a century earlier.

In the case of *Antigone*, another well-known, early play by Anouilh, a study of its translation history reveals other interesting facts; the play appears to exist in two English versions by the same translator, Lewis Galantière.[49] The first version was used for the production of the play in New York in 1946, while the London production with Laurence Olivier and Vivien Leigh at the Old Vic in February 1949 made use of the second. This version was published by Methuen in 1951 and included in *Volume 2* (1967) of *Jean Anouilh: The Collected Plays*.

In Galantière's 1946 version there are some significant departures from Anouilh's French text, which occur at the beginning of the play. Before the action begins on stage, the audience learns that Créon, the king, has ordered that Polynices, Antigone's brother, be left to rot unburied outside the city walls: we also know that Antigone, Créon's niece, will defy the edict. It is here, at the very outset of the play, when the Chorus talks about Antigone herself, emphasising her fatalism, her awareness that she must fulfil the role allotted to her, that some of the most drastic departures from the French original occur. The original reads:

> *Elle s'appelle Antigone et il va falloir qu'elle joue son rôle jusqu'au bout...*

In his 1949 version, Galantière translated this closely:

> When your name is Antigone, there is only one part you can play; and she will have to play hers through to the end.

In 1946, however, the translation was embellished:

> When you are on the side of the gods against the tyrant, of Man against the State, of purity against corruption – when, in short, your name is Antigone,

there is only one part you can play; and she will have to play hers through to the end.

In the 1946 version, Anouilh's portrayal of Créon was changed from that of a man who only reluctantly sets aside other interests to shoulder the burden of kingship, into that of a man with the character of a tyrant. In the 1949 version on the other hand, the translation retained Anouilh's own sympathetic portrayal of the king's character, and the prologue finishes on a more neutral note.

Arguably, an unadulterated English version of Anouilh's text might have served the interest of the playwright better in New York. Anouilh only achieved success on Broadway relatively late in his career, with *The Lark* in 1955, *The Waltz of the Toreadors* during the 1956–57 season, selected as best foreign play by the New York Drama Critics' Circle, and in 1960, *Becket. Antigone*, on the other hand, his most famous early play, ran for only 64 performances when staged in New York in 1946, with American reviewers expressing the same serious misconceptions about the true nature of the tragedy, which much later, were also expressed in New Zealand following a radio transmission of the play. On both occasions, the 'adapted' 1946 translation served as the basis for the performance text.

In the programme note for the New York production, reprinted as 'A Note by the Adapter', prefacing the Samuel French edition, the intentions of the translator in producing his 'adapted' version are clearly stated. Admitting to having introduced changes, Galantière declares that some aspects of Anouilh's text needed clarifying and highlighting in order for American audiences to be able 'to come away from M. Anouilh's play with the feeling that Antigone's case was stronger than Créon's'.[50] Bearing in mind that the play opened at the Cort Theatre in New York on 18 February, 1946, less than a year after World War II had come to an end, the translator's desire to draw a parallel with recent events and to warn against the carnage resulting from dictatorial rule is understandable if, in this case, seriously misguided. Instead of the subtleties at issue in the confrontation between the king and his niece in the French original, the theatre critic for *The Nation*, Joseph Wood Krutch, was led to see the New York production as centring on a conflict between the non-feeling arguments of 'a rationalising fascist dictator', and Antigone's impassioned 'conviction that necessity, the tyrant's plea, is never superior to the claim of fundamental human decency'.[51] Writing for the *New Republic*, Stark Young similarly perceived Antigone as motivated by 'respect for human instincts', standing against Créon's dictatorial 'malignity'.[52]

The reasons behind Galantière's decision to return to a more faithful rendering of the French text three years later for the London production belong to the realm of speculation. With a closer proximity to France and the knowledge of the French language that can generally be assumed among the educated middle-class British, objections to the 1946 translation might have been raised by the London production team which would have had easier access to the original French text. What we do know is that reviews of this production indicate that English theatre-goers were treated to a version of *Antigone* in translation that more closely reflected the author's intentions than the one that had been offered to New York audiences. Anouilh's *Antigone*, according to Worsley of the *New Statesman and Nation*, 'is placed in the position of having to make her individual protest in defiance not of tyranny and oppression, but of good sense, logic and reasonableness of things-as-they-are'. The characterisation of Créon is equally clearly conveyed: 'This Créon is not a cruel tyrant; he has been called in to restore order in a country devastated by the gang warfare between his two nephews, Antigone's brothers.'[53]

More recent revivals of Anouilh's plays in English translation have frequently borne the name of Jeremy Sams. In the autumn of 1991, Sams' version of *Becket* opened at the Theatre Royal Haymarket with Robert Lindsay and Derek Jacobi, the first major revival since the 1960 New York production with Laurence Olivier and the Aldwych staging in 1961, of a play that Kenneth Tynan described as a 'clever and witty chronicle of the relationship between Henry II and Thomas À Becket '. According to Paul Taylor in the *Independent* of 9 October 1991:

> [The production's] deliberately half-cod *Black Adder*-ish slant on history [was] nicely served by the adroit anachronisms in Jeremy Sams' witty translation, where Henry can accuse Becket of wanting to be a 'born-again Saxon' and where embezzlement can be blamed on 'a clever clerk, some creative accountant'.

The critical reaction to Sams' translation of Anouilh's *Colombe* for the Salisbury Playhouse's 1999 production was equally positive. The play follows the story of a virginal innocent whose straight-laced husband leaves her in the care of his actress mother while in the National Service, to find upon his return that she has discovered her true personality beyond her husband's shadow. Again Sams' translation is described as striking 'a near-perfect balance between period authenticity and modern comprehensibility'.[54]

English-speaking stages also intermittently mount productions of Jean-Paul Sartre (1905–80), a contemporary of Anouilh, although more outspoken in his social and political engagement. The first important play by Sartre, an existentialist treatment of the Orestes legend called *Les Mouches* (*The Flies*, 1943), was rendered into English by Stuart Gilbert in 1946, in a translation that has been quoted as remaining 'difficult to fault, in terms either of accuracy of meaning or of tone'.[55] Gilbert has also translated *Huis clos* (1944) (best known in English as *In Camera* (1946), or *No Exit* (1947)), Sartre's portrayal of the reciprocal purgatory created by three recently dead characters. This play, popular in English translation among student drama groups in the radical 1960s, was followed by Sartre's most important, and first, full-length play, *Les Mains sales* (*The Dirty Hands*, 1948, also known in English as *The Assassin* and *Red Gloves*). It was translated in 1949 as *Crime Passionel* by Kitty Black, who is also the translator of *Le Diable et le bon Dieu* (1951), in English best known as *Lucifer and the Lord* (1952) or *The Devil and the Good Lord* (1960). In these two plays, Sartre dramatises the struggle of the intellectual trying to break away from a concern with personal morality in order to achieve an impact upon the world of social and political reality. In the first play, Hugo, a young intellectual, fails to be an effective revolutionary because of his worries about his own worth and reality. In the second play, Goetz manages to break out of the vicious circle by abandoning such concerns in order to act. In the quest for authentic action, Hugo and Goetz stand for the two different sides of the coin: failure and success. About a decade later, Sartre chose another topical subject for airing on stage. In *Les Séquestrés d'Altona* (*The Condemned of Altona*, 1959), the theme *'qui perd gagne'*, loser wins, is dominant: the 1960 translation into English by Sylvia and George Leeson is even entitled *Loser Wins*,[56] although when published by Knopf, New York a year later, the title chosen was the more faithful translation of the original. The play reflects on Germany's extraordinary economic advances in the late 1950s, the result of its losing the war and suffering the destruction of its industry fifteen years earlier. This is represented in the character of Franz, son of successful shipbuilder Herr von Gerlach, whose sequestration is the consequence of his failure to come to terms with actions committed in the past.

In Kitty Black's translations, both *Crime Passionel* and *Lucifer and the Lord* display the frequently found weaknesses of earlier translation approaches paying too close attention to simple word equivalence. In the first of these two plays mistranslations occur and idioms go unrecognised: *'être fait comme un rat'* is rendered as 'to have the soul of a rat' instead of 'to be cornered';[57] the *faux amis 'prétendre'* and *'luxure'* are incorrectly translated into English as 'pretend' and 'luxury'.[58] Black appears to have been more successful in *Lucifer and the Lord* than in her translation of *Les Mains sales*.

When it first opened in France, *Les Mains sales* was a theatrical success, running from 2 April to 20 September 1949. At the centre of the play is the assassination of a professional politician, Hoederer, at the instigation of his supposed party allies in Illyria, a country which is on the verge of being annexed to the Eastern Bloc, in the closing stages of the World War II. Hugo, a young intellectual, whose troubled relationship with his wife Jessica, and ideological dispute with Hoederer form most of the substance of the play, carries out the murder. With time itself constituting an important part of the play, a weakness of Kitty Black's English translation is the failure to distinguish between tenses.[59] In view of the fact that Hugo is criticised for attaching too much importance to the past instead of planning for the future, the change of most of the past tenses in the first tableau into present tenses loses the irony of Hugo being preoccupied with the past, and, as a result, oblivious to the present danger he is in. The translation is also at times too literal, as when Louis, leader of the Communist Party opposed to Hoederer, discusses Hugo with Olga:

> *C'était un petit anarchiste indiscipliné, un intellectuel qui ne pensait qu'à prendre des attitudes...*[60]

> He's an undisciplined little anarchist, an intellectual who thought of nothing but taking up attitudes...[61]

At times, differences in social class reflected in speech also disappear in the English translation. In French, Slick and Georges, Hoederer's bodyguards, both speak in a colourful vernacular, their verbal antagonism towards Hugo being mainly a question of class. This is not always captured in Black's translation where at times the two express themselves in a manner not too dissimilar to well-bred, English gentlemen. When, for instance, Georges comments to Slick on seeing Hugo's wardrobe, '*Hé, Slick! Vise moi s'il est bien loque*',[62] ('Get a load of this – he's got nice rags'), this becomes from the lips of English George, 'Gee! What an outfit!'[63] There are also cuts, more numerous at the beginning of the play than in the middle, where politicians Le Prince, Karsky and Hoederer all juggle for power, and towards the end where Hoederer's life and later Hugo's are in question. Perhaps dictated by fear of endangering clarity in discussions of political and ideological matters, the lines chosen for omission are sometimes the ones conveying information about Sartre's characters, which when cut run the risk of making them more anonymous. Thus when Hugo who has just come out of prison says to Olga:

> *Il y a quelqu'un dans ta vie?*

> Is there someone in your life?

she answers:

De temps en temps – Pas en ce moment.

From time to time. Not at this moment.[64]

This tells us something about Olga and her attitude to men, information which is lost as the result of being cut in the translation.

In 2000, Richard Eyre produced *Les Mains sales* at the Almeida Theatre, as *The Novice*, in a translation of his own. In the performance programme, Eyre set out the reasons underlying his decision to stage the play. Familiar with Sartre's work after having appeared in two of his plays as a student actor, Eyre re-read *Les Mains sales* at a time when reports on peace negotiations in Northern Ireland and rancorous bickering between New and Old Labour filled newspaper front pages, and decided that Sartre's play might be a play for the times. In order to make obvious the parallel between past and present, Eyre shifted the play from its times. While creating plenty of 1940s *film noir* atmosphere, he removed all references to the Soviet Union which, in Sartre's original, are spelt out clearly: Illyria's contact with the USSR was interrupted by war and the local party elected to pursue its own line, whereas in the post-war world it has to kow-tow to Moscow orthodoxy. In Eyre's version, having committed the murder, Hugo is simply told by his minder, 'we've changed our policy'. However, although the opposing camps of communists and pragmatic compromisers do bring to mind the Blairite age, as the result of Eyre excising specific references, the Almeida production of the play left it somewhat floating in political limbo.

In the *Observer* of 14 May 2000, the Almeida production of *The Novice* was referred to as 'A fast-moving thriller of sex, politics and murder – from the pen of France's favourite thinker.' Under the heading of 'Yes but is it Sartre?' the reviewer raised the interesting question of the identity of the playwright in the original language and in translation. From the comments made about the production, it is clear that this reviewer liked her Sartre unadulterated, and his work to be viewed as philosophical and treated with reverence. But translation always entails making choices (see Chapter 1), and no writer in translation is likely to match in detail the impression formed by readers who know their work in the original. As a result, there are bound to be as many Sartres as there are languages into which he has been translated. In his *Guardian* review of 22 December 1992, of the English publication of *Witness to my Life: the Letters of Jean-Paul Sartre to Simone de Beauvoir, 1926–39*, entitled 'Too many translators…', Julian Evans observed that one of 'the first characteristics about this English Sartre is that he cannot write the clear, simple, sarcastic prose of his French counterpart'. While the longest letter of the collection, describing a visit to Naples, in French is a brilliantly-caught word-painting of one of Mussolini's cities, in English, Sartre's letter comes across as written by 'a knowledgeable American student writing for effect: arch, camp, pompous', as if he did not quite get things down 'in a literary enough way'. Not surprisingly, perhaps, it turns out that this translation was the result of the combined efforts of first an American translator whose translation was declined on the grounds that he did not understand French, then two editors recruited in order to patch up his work, followed by two more translators completing the job. Hopefully, other translations of Sartre are unlikely to entail such questionable collaboration, but it still raises doubts about the possibility of a definitive Sartre in English, as well as in other languages. In translation he will remain chameleon-like, while to a varying degree retaining some overlap with the French Sartre.

Also concerned with the events of the war and appalled by Nazi brutality and its devastation, Samuel Beckett (1906–89) used the collective spiritual despair of an age as the basis for *En attendant Godot* (1953), which catapulted him to fame. In the transformation of Beckett's French text into *Waiting for Godot* (1954), one aspect changed, leaving an impact throughout the literary world: in the original portrayal of Vladimir and Estragon in an absurd world, they are clowns invested with the function of filling in the intervals between those circus turns which are considered to be important. In Peter Hall's English production the two clowns are turned into tramps and the intervals occupy the whole show, symbolising Beckett's feeling that the only thing that ever happens is nothingness.

In turning his plays written in French into English and his English plays into French, Beckett provides interesting insights into the process of self-translation. Following the *succès de scandale* of *Godot* in January 1953 at the Théâtre Babylone in Paris, Beckett embarked upon nearly four decades of experimentation with the innate possibilities of two languages. A study of the changes he made when transferring his French text into English shows the steps he took to give the dialogue the lift needed to save it from the blandness often resulting from translation. In Act 2, a move from general to specific turns '*couvert de feuilles*' ('covered in leaves'), into 'the tree has three or four leaves.' Expressions are sharpened, as in turning '*Je me fais au goût*' ('I get used to the taste'), into the stronger 'I get used to the muck'; weight is added as when the meditation '*C'est long, mais ce sera bon*', ('It's long but it'll be good'), is turned into a quotation from the Book of Proverbs: 'Hope deferred maketh the heart sick' and Estragon's *'J'écoute'*, ('I'm listening'), is changed into 'I find this really most extraordinarily interesting'. Given the chance to create an alliteration in English, Beckett does not miss the opportunity: *'s'en prenant à la chaussure alors que c'est son pied le coupable'* ('blaming the shoe when it's his foot that's guilty'), becomes, sharpened, 'blaming on his boots the faults of his feet'. Later, when translating his play *Fin de partie* (1957) into *Endgame* (1958), Beckett was to describe the process of self-translation as 'heart breaking work', fearing that 'the loss incurred was even greater than with *Godot*'.[65]

Having lived his life in two different languages, Beckett had a heightened linguistic awareness, a sense which was shared by Eugène Ionesco (1909–94). Born in Romania to a French mother and a Romanian father, Ionesco spent his childhood partly in France and partly in Romania. After graduating in French literature from Bucharest University in 1933, he married in 1936 and three years later left for Paris, then residing in France for most of the rest of his life. With a highly-developed consciousness of the arbitrariness of attaching meanings to words – a likely consequence of his linguistic background – Ionesco's plays present in their often comical or grotesque form the paradoxes of verbal communication. In his early one-act plays, rational dialogue, a logical plot and consistent characters are discarded; people are reduced to empty objects and speech to empty clichés. The one-act sketch *La Cantatrice chauve* (*The Bald Prima Donna*, 1950) was followed, a year later, by *La Leçon* (*The Lesson*) and, two years later, by *Les Chaises* (*The Chairs*). Here chairs are set out for an invisible audience gathering to hear about 'the meaning of life', while the real audience is treated to the less than meaningful discussions of a very old couple passing their time with private games and half-remembered stories. Last seen in London in an original Theatre de Complicité and Royal Court production that received its London premiere on 19 November 1997, the play enjoyed a successful run. This was in no small measure due to English playwright Martin Crimp's translation, which effectively mixed recurring familiarity of address such as The Old Woman's use of 'poppet', 'my dear' and 'silly girl' with elevated nonsensical parlance such as The Old Man enquiring, 'Where are the snows of yesteryear?'

From 1950 and the appearance of *The Bald Prima Donna*, Ionesco exercised a powerful anti-realist influence on European drama, creating, together with the dramatist Arthur Adamov (1908–70), Samuel Beckett and Jean Genet (1910–86), the 'theatre of the absurd'. While in his famous antithesis of his most renowned plays, Beckett was influenced by the cadences of the Prayer Book familiar from his youth, Jean Genet was even more influenced by the Mass, regarding the elevation of the Host as a moment of drama never equalled in the theatre. All his plays – *Les Bonnes* (*The Maids*, 1947), *Les Nègres* (*The Blacks*, 1959), *Les Paravents* (*The Screens*, 1961) – are demonstrations of the power of ritual.[66]

In *Les Bonnes*, the maids want at the same time to kill and to become Madame, as the Priest turns Christ into a wafer that he eats and His blood into wine that he drinks. But they rarely talk of killing, they talk of ritual or ceremony:

> CLAIRE À SOLANGE: *Quand nous accomplissons la cérémonie, je protege mon cou. C'est moi que tu vises à travers Madame, c'est moi que suis en danger.*

> CLAIRE: (*To SOLANGE.*) When we finish the ceremony, I'll protect my neck. It's me that you're aiming at through Madame, it's me that's in danger.[67]

In *Le Balcon* (*The Balcony*, 1956), initially banned, theatre is identified with a brothel, both being a house of 'illusion'. The erotic fantasies played out by the actor's clients are transformed into symbolic reality when revolution wipes out all the state authorities. Image is all. *Le Balcon* had its world premiere at the Arts Theatre Club in London in April 1957. It was not performed in France until May 1960, when Peter Brook directed it at the Théâtre du Gymnase in Paris where it was an instant success. It was seen in New York in March 1960, and just over ten years later, in 1971, it was staged by the Royal Shakespeare Company in a translation by Barbara Wright and RSC director Terry Hands. More recently, on 15 June 1995, *Splendid's*, a two-act police thriller that Genet wrote in 1948 but which was never staged opened at The Lyric, Hammersmith. The action of this play takes place on the seventh floor of a luxury hotel, surrounded by police after it has been taken over by a group of criminals. Although originally praised by Jean-Paul Sartre and by Genet's American translator and sometime agent Bernard Frechtman, it was disliked by Genet, who was long assumed to have destroyed the only existing copy. It was considered lost until published in France in 1993, providing the French text used by director and translator Neil Bartlett for his English version at The Lyric. Introducing his translation of the play, Neil Bartlett avowed that '[t]his is not a version or adaptation of *Splendid's*; this is Genet's text, done in English. The only inventions are those mothered by necessity', signalling clearly that in this case the translator's strategy was one of 'foreignisation', that is, taking the English audience to the French text while refraining from any attempt at 'Anglicisation'. Forming part of this overall strategy is the approach taken to punctuation. According to a Publisher's Note accompanying Bartlett's 'Notes towards Performance of Jean Genet's *Splendid's*', 'Irregular punctuation has been retained to match that of the original'.[68] (See Chapters 4 and 5 for discussion of the translation of punctuation used by other European playwrights.)

Although through its foreignising approach spared some of the customary problems related to the process of English translation and adaptation, difficulties in the translation of *Splendid's*, described as a 'a camp rewrite of a *film noir*' still remain.[69] In particular, Neil Bartlett stresses the problem related to the translation of puns (see also Chapter 9). As he points out:

> Only in French can the word *rafale* be both a name and a burst of gunfire; can the words for submachine-gun, sequin and labour share an internally rhyming open vowel; can *châsse* suggest both a reliquary and an eyeball; can a *bergère* be both a shepherdess and an arm chair; can the actions of becoming a coward, letting off a gun, putting down a gun, lowering one's moral standards and holding one's fire be described by precisely the same verb.[70]

Unlike Neil Bartlett's translation strategy for Genet's *Splendid's*, Barbara Bray's approach to the translation of the work of Marguerite Duras (1914–96) is that of trying to interpret the writer's own 'music' rather than the individual word. Duras' unpossessive attitude towards the adaptation and translation of her text may be viewed in the light of her long experience of collaboration with others such as Alain Resnais and the making of *Hiroshima mon amour* (1960). The economy of Duras' dialogue 'arguably presents the translator with fewer problems than her narrative' and *Marguerite Duras: Four Plays* (1992) in translation by Barbara Bray is rendered 'in a largely faithful style'.[71] The volume includes *La Musica* (*La Musica Deuxième*, 1965), *Eden Cinema* (*L'Éden-cinéma*, 1977), *Savannah Bay* (1982) and *India Song* (1973).[72] However, the staging of *La Musica*, commissioned by the Hampstead Theatre in 1992, caused the *Guardian* theatre critic to comment that 'for all the excellence of Barbara Bray's translation, it is difficult to convey in English Duras' musicality and subtle shifts of tone from *tu* to *vous*'. (See Chapter 9 for further discussion of the problems of translating into English the pronouns of address in other European languages.)

While for some time London theatre audiences were offered little more than a sprinkling of contemporary drama from France, as the twentieth century was drawing to a close, French theatre *esprit* reclaimed its position on the London stage. With *Art* (1994), a play in which the argument over an all-white, abstract painting threatens to expose the hidden tensions among three long-time male friends, playwright and actress Yasmina Reza won an Olivier Award for best comedy in 1997 and, the same year, a Tony Award in New York for best play. After *Art* followed London productions of two of Reza's earlier plays. In 1997, *Conversations après un enterrement* (*Conversations after a Burial*), her first play written in 1987, was warmly received when staged at the Almeida Theatre. A year later, the Royal Shakespeare Company presented *L'Homme du hasard* (*The Unexpected Man*, 1995), Reza's play about a writer sharing a train compartment with a woman in the process of reading his latest book. The play then travelled to New York where it was a success at the Promenade Theatre off Broadway. With *Trois versions de la vie* (*Life x 3*, 2000), Yasmina Reza's position as France's best known living writer, beyond the borders of her own country, was established; her new comedy of manners opened almost simultaneously in translation in Vienna and Athens as well as in Paris and London.

Like many of the French playwrights of the nineteenth century whose light comedies found their way across the Channel, Yasmina Reza combines her writing skill with professional theatre experience as an actress. In fact, when during rehearsals of *Trois versions de la vie* one of the actors pulled out, Reza stepped in and took over the part.

In *Life x 3*, the same situation is presented three times, but each time with crucially different nuances. The givens are that Henrie and Sonia are settling in for an evening at home, intermittently interrupted by offstage whimpering of their six-year-old son, when Hubert and Ines arrive for dinner one day earlier than expected. From this situation, three contrasting variations are then created.

The translation of all the London productions of Yasmina Reza's plays bear the name of Christopher Hampton, playwright, screenwriter and director as well as translator. In his role as translator, Hampton, a trained linguist with French and German, combines his thorough knowledge of theatrical convention with his equally well-founded stagecraft. (See Chapter 3 for discussion of Hampton's adaptations of Ibsen.) Sensitive to the need for Anglo-Saxon 'warmth' not to be ousted by elegant but, at times, cool Gallic wit, Hampton's translation of *Art* nicely succeeds in bridging the cultural gap, subtly conveying hidden emotions while at the same time retaining the play's humour. Although equally masterfully rendered in English, in the case of the translation of *Life x 3*, the more mechanistic plot construction and its accompanying devices shine through the English translation. Back on the London stage, it would seem, is the tightly controlled comedy, shrouded in French elegance and *esprit*. While not lacking in psychological insight, what can go wrong in the bourgeois family goes wrong, to hilarious effect. From the safety of their seats, the audience can lean back and with grim satisfaction observe the misfortunes of others. By the third time that Hubert and Ines ring the front door bell of Henri and Sonia to the surprise of their hosts, Scribe himself, had he been in the audience, would have been wanting to ask: 'How is she going to get out of this one?'

As Yasmina Reza has become more true to form, that is, French form, appreciation of her work in France has soared. Writing in the daily *Libération*, René Solis observed that Ms Reza had turned a soap operatic story set in an educated bourgeois home into a 'brilliant exercise, full of suspense, false clues and unexpected plot changes'. And in *Le Figaro*, Philippe Tesson found *Trois versions de la vie* a 'very beautiful work', praising the talent of Ms Reza in presenting familiar situations, only to destabilise them unexpectedly.[73] In the autumn of 2003 another more recent Gallic import, even more true to French form, reached the Albery Theatre. In *See You Next Tuesday*, Ronald Harwood's adaptation of Francis Veber's film *Le Dîner de cons*, two friends compete to invite as a dinner guest the most boring person they are able to find. All the ingredients once required for popular success on the French stage seem to remain as important as ever for a French play to travel successfully into English. *Plus ça change...*

The translation of French drama into English is a journey of a different kind from that of translation of plays originating in other European languages. Close historical and geographical proximity between France and England has helped to create a unique situation, unparalleled in the relationship that English speakers enjoy with speakers of other European languages. During the late eighteenth century, the close link between French and English culture was temporarily interrupted by the revolution of 1789 and the Napoleonic wars. However, after the introduction of serialised novels in the *feuilleton* section in the new cheap press in France, writers such as Alexandre Dumas *père* (1802–70), Eugène Sue (1804–57) and George Sand (1804–76) were promptly translated into English. The English were also frequent visitors to France and French literature was read not only in translation into English but also in the original. As a result, French influence even made itself known in the work of English writers, in the use of French terms and expressions, which, it was assumed, were commonly understood by a middle-class readership.

To an extent this practice has continued in more recent times as reflected in the translation into English of French plays, originating in past as well as present times. In John Mortimer's and Kenneth McLeish's Feydeau translations, the characters invariably retain their French-sounding names and servants address their superiors as 'Monsieur' and 'Madame'. Place, street and hotel names in French similarly present the English reader with few problems.

As the first foreign language taught at English schools, French language and literature have for some time formed part of the educational programme in the UK, with the consequent creation of literary texts required for educational purposes. As a result, over the years the demand has intensified for translations of, in particular, short stories and plays suitable for examination syllabuses at the secondary level. Hence, it is possible for English playwrights/ translators to assume that a French text is written in a language familiar to a number of theatregoers. Discussing the problems in translating Genet's use of French puns, Neil Bartlett is in the fortunate position to suggest that '[a]ny reader who thinks my choice too bold should consult the French text in order to trace the originals of my puns'.[74]

While familiarity with French literary texts in translation may have been instrumental in developing an interest in the French dramatic canon, the role of translation for other educational purposes might at times have had a less positive effect. As in other parts of Europe, in the UK translation has often been used as a method for the teaching of foreign languages (see Chapter 1). Reinforced by the approach used in the instruction of classical Greek and Latin, languages which are no longer spoken and whose non-changing nature make it possible to find conclusively 'correct' equivalents, translation was long viewed simply as the process of matching one word with its 'correct' equivalent in the foreign language, an approach that often yields unexpected results. In his introduction to the translation of Feydeau's La Puce à l'oreille, Steven Mulrine informs us that:

> The original French title, La Puce à l'oreille (literally 'The Flea in the Ear') has nothing of our English connotation of 'I gave him a flea in his ear'. It is slang for a sudden notion or idée fixe: a good English translation might be A Bee in Her Bonnet.[75]

The literal translation of the name of the French farce, which in the light of Mulrine's comment can only be viewed as a mistranslation, has, however, now become so firmly established as a title of Feydeau's play that it is unlikely it will ever be corrected.

In addition to the close historical and cultural interaction between the two countries, the languages of France and England have long shared a unique linguistic relationship. Following the Norman invasion in 1066, for several centuries, the language of the upper classes, the Church and the judiciary was French. This imposed influence on English set its linguistic development on a different course from that of the other Germanic languages such as German, Dutch and the Scandinavian languages with respect to word order as well as to word formation. In the latter case, English often draws on borrowed words from French as well as Latinate cognates as designations for new concepts and processes. In translation between French and English, this situation may be to the translator's advantage as well as disadvantage. Among the advantages is the ease with which French words move into English. While the title *Les Liaisons Dangereuses*, Christopher Hampton's dramatised version of the Laclos novel of 1782 for the Royal Shakespeare Company and subsequent screen version, caused no problems for English theatre-goers as both words occur in related forms in English, productions of the play in some other countries required a translation of the French title.

In other cases, however, the preponderance of words of French origin in English may be less than helpful. For a translator working from non-standard French into English, French cognates might if anything have to be avoided. While Anglo-Saxon words and expressions tend to belong more closely to everyday usage, French and Latinate vocabulary in English is often associated with a more elevated style of discourse. This problem, inherent in the translation of French dialect varieties into English, has been encountered by Findlay and Bowman in the translation into English of the plays by the Quebec playwright Michel Tremblay. Tremblay writes in a regional dialect of Montreal known as '*joual*', named after the way the speakers of the area pronounce the French for *cheval*. Tremblay's *Messe solennelle pour une pleine lune d'été* (*Solemn Mass for a Full Moon in Summer*, 2000), which was performed at the Barbican by the Traverse Theatre Company in May 2000, translated into Scots English by Martin Bowman and Bill Findlay, is a play written in a secular, vernacular mass. In the original French, the play contains words such as *apathie, violence* and *insensibilité*, words that belong naturally to a French text written in the vernacular idiom. In English on the other hand, the cognates – apathy, violence and insensibility – fit less comfortably into a non-standard vernacular. Yet there is little alternative available, as attempts to retrieve less well known Anglo-Saxon words belonging to an appropriate English vernacular might run the risk of unnecessarily belabouring the text in English translation.[76]

Although this problem is difficult to solve, translation between French and English is on the whole assisted by a number of factors: the large number of English speakers with a thorough knowledge of the source language from which they translate; the likelihood that English playwrights may combine a knowledge of French with the skills gained from the writing of their own plays; and the familiarity with French language, history and culture that can be assumed on the part of English theatre audiences reducing the impact of the confrontation with 'the otherness' of French drama. When the work of playwrights from other less familiar European countries is performed in translation on the English stage, the confrontation can be a more startling experience and the problems in linguistic and cultural transfer of a completely different order.

Notes

1   H Koon and R Switzer, *Eugène Scribe* (Boston, Twayne Publishers, 1980), p. 34

2   *Ibid.* p. 29

3   *Ibid.* p. 23

4   *Ibid.* p. 20

5   M Lamm, *Det moderna dramat* (Stockholm, Albert Bonniers, 1948), p.23

6   *Ibid.* p. 26

7   H Koon and R Switzer, *op. cit.* p. 34

8   M Lamm, *op. cit.* p. 59

9   Eugène Labiche and Marc-Michel, *An Italian Straw Hat*, trans. and intro. K McLeish (London, Nick Hern Books, 1996), p. xi

10 T Hale, 'The imaginary quay from Waterloo Bridge to London Bridge: Translation, adaptation and genre', in M Salama-Carr (ed.), *On Translating French Literature and Film* II (Amsterdam, Rodopi, 2000) pp. 220–4

11 H Sutherland Edwards, *Personal Recollections* (London, Cassell & Co., 1900)

12 *Ibid.* p. 50

13 M Elwin, *Charles Reade* (London, Jonathan Cape, 1931), pp. 123–6, 195

14 W Tolles, *Tom Taylor and the Victorian Drama* (New York, AMS, 1966, first published 1940), p. 20

15 H Sutherland Edwards, *op. cit.* p. 45; also discussed in T Hale, *op. cit.* pp. 220–3

16 M Elwin, *op. cit.* pp. 130–1, 193

17 H Sutherland Edwards, *op. cit.* pp. 179–80

18 W Tolles, *op. cit.* p. 19

19 T Hale, *op. cit.* pp. 234–6

20 'L'Assommoir', in *Gentleman's Magazine*, December 1878, XX, p. 745

21 'The Comédie Française et M Zola', in *Gentleman's Magazine*, July 1879, XXIII, pp. 60–73

22 M Elwin, *op. cit.* p. 341

23 'A Delicious Celebrity', *Spectator*, 30 September 1893, LXXI, p. 427

24 Alfred Jarry, *The Ubu Plays*, trans. and intro. K McLeish (London, Nick Hern Books, 1997)

25 Discussed in 'Adapting Cyrano' in *Cyrano* performance programme (National Theatre, 1995)

26 *A Flea in Her Ear* performance programme (National Theatre, 1966)

27 C Berton, *A Flea in Her Ear* performance programme (National Theatre, 1966)

28 Georges Feydeau, *A Flea in Her Ear*, trans. K McLeish (London, Nick Hern Books, 2000), p. xiii

29 Simon Callow, quoting in introduction to *Les Parents Terribles* performance programme (National Theatre, 1994)

30 *Guardian*, 7 May 1994

31 J Cocteau, *Les Parents terribles*, (Paris, Gallimard, 1938), p. 17

32 *Ibid.* p. 25; author's translation

33 *Ibid.* p. 27; author's translation

34 *Ibid.* p. 125; author's translation

35 J Cocteau, *Les Parents Terribles* (*Indiscretions*), trans. J Sams, introduced by Simon Callow, National Theatre performance text (London, Nick Hern Books, 1994)

36 J Cocteau, *Les Parents terribles*, *op. cit.* p. 22

37 J Cocteau, trans. J Sams, *op. cit*, p. 4

38 J Cocteau, *Les Parents terribles*, *op. cit.* p. 28

39 J Cocteau, trans. J Sams, *op. cit*, p. 7 (emphasis added)

40 H Hobson, *French Theatre Since 1830* (London, John Calder, 1978)

41 R Bryden, *Amphitryon* performance programme (National Theatre, 1971)

42 *Ibid.*

43 P Thody, *Anouilh* (Edinburgh, Oliver and Boyd, 1968), p. 6

44 P Reed, 'Jean Anouilh', in O. Classe (ed.), *Encyclopedia of Literary Translation into English*, Vol. I (London, Fitzroy Dearborn, 2000), p. 57

45 *Ibid.* p. 57

46 'Ring Round the Moon', *Lincoln Center Theater Review*, 21, 1999, p. 18

47 P Reed, *op. cit.* p. 57

48 *Lincoln Centre Theatre Review*, *op. cit.* p. 18

49 I Reid, 'Hazards of adaptation: Anouilh's Antigone in English', in O Zuber (ed.), *Languages in the Theatre. Problems in the Translation and Transposition of Drama* (Oxford, Pergamon Press, 1980), pp. 82–91

50 *Ibid.* p. 91

51 *The Nation*, 162, 2 March 1946, p. 269. Discussed in I Reid, *op. cit.* p. 90

52 *New Republic*, 114, 4 March 1946, pp. 317–18. Discussed in I Reid, *op. cit.* p. 90

53 *The New Statesman and National*, 37, 19 February 1949, pp. 317–18. Discussed in I Reid, *op. cit.* p. 90

54 T O'Connor Morse, *Independent*, 8 April 1999

55 P Reed, 'Jean-Paul Sartre', in O Classe (ed.), *op. cit.* Vol. II, pp. 1234–5

56 Jean-Paul Sartre, *Loser Wins* (*Les Séquestrés d'Altona*), trans. S & G Leeson, (London, Hamish Hamilton, 1960)

57 P Reed, *op. cit.* p. 1237

58 *Ibid.*

59 *Ibid.*

60 W D Redfearn (ed.), *Jean-Paul Sartre. Les Mains sales*, Twentieth Century Texts (London, Routledge, 1985), p. 58

61 Jean-Paul Sartre, *Crime Passionnel*, trans. K Black (London, Methuen, 1949), p. 14

62 W D Redfearn, *op. cit.* p. 88; author's translation

63 Jean-Paul Sartre, trans. K Black, *op. cit.* p. 36

64 W D Redfearn, *op. cit.* p. 53; author's translation

65 H Guest, 'Samuel Beckett', in O Classe (ed.), *op. cit.* Vol. I, pp. 122–3

66 H Hobson, *op. cit.* p. 239

67 Discussed in C Puzin, *Les Bonnes. Le Balcon. Jean Genet*, Collection Balises (Paris, Nathan, 1998), p. 117; author's translation

68 Discussed in Jean Genet, *Splendid's*, trans. N Bartlett (London, Faber and Faber, 1995), p. xvi

69 E Wilson, introduction to Jean Genet, trans. N Bartlett, *ibid.* p. viii.

70 *Ibid.* p. xiv

71 J Philips, 'Marguerite Duras' in O Classe (ed.), *op. cit.* p. 387

72 Marguerite Duras, *Four Plays*, trans. B Bray (London, Oberon Books, 1992)

73 A Riding, *New York Times*, 31 December 2000

74 Jean Genet, trans. N Bartlett, *op. cit.* p. xiv

75 Georges Feydeau, trans. K McLeish, *op. cit.* p. xvi

76 M Bowman, 'Scottish horses and Montreal trains. The translation of vernacular to vernacular', in C-A Upton (ed.), *Moving Target. Theatre Translation and Cultural Relocation* (Manchester, St Jerome, 2000), p. 32

Chapter 3

HENRIK IBSEN

DURING THE FOUR HUNDRED YEARS that Norway was united with Denmark, little Norwegian literature was published, although some writing in Danish would at times reveal distinctly Norwegian characteristics in the use of language and the portrayal of nature. It was to take separation from Denmark in 1814 for a national literature to start to emerge. With the publication in the 1840s of Norwegian ballads and folk tales which had remained alive in remote parts of the country during the years of Danish dominion, the young independent Norwegian nation received a further injection of cultural self-confidence. In line with the overall national movement, there was also a need for a national theatre promoting the Norwegian language and employing exclusively Norwegian actors, and in 1850 the *Norske Theater* was founded in Bergen.

The following year, on 26 October 1851, Henrik Ibsen (1828–1906) arrived at the theatre to take up an appointment which included assisting the theatre as a 'dramatic author'.[1] He remained in this post until July 1857 when he left Bergen to take up a post at the recently established Norwegian Theatre in the capital of Christiania.

Henrik Ibsen's exposure to the theatre had, however, started long before he was attached to the theatres of Bergen and Christiania. Every now and then travelling theatre companies would visit Skien, the small shipping and sawmill town where he was born, and the young Henrik Ibsen would accompany his mother to performances of French and Danish vaudevilles and comedies.

While the Norwegian 'national renaissance' influenced the youthful work of Ibsen and his friend and sometimes rival Bjørnstjerne Bjørnson (1832–1910), the inspiration that led away from Scandinavian late-romanticism to Ibsen's naturalistic prose plays came from Copenhagen, where, in the autumn of 1871, the literary critic Georg Brandes (1842–1927) began a landmark lecture series on the main currents in nineteenth-century European literature which, soon afterwards, appeared in print.

The programme outlined by Brandes asked the writer to face the real world and to help bring about 'liberty of the spirit, liberty of thought and of the human condition'.[2] With Brandes as the likely catalyst, the ten years between *Peer Gynt* (1867), Ibsen's kaleidoscopically-structured verse play, and

Samfundets støtter (*Pillars of Society*, 1877), his prose drama about small-town corruption, saw a radical change in Ibsen's conception of the world. Mountains and sea gave way to the security of the middle-class drawing room as rhymed speech yielded to everyday conversation. Ibsen now set out on his course to strip bare the murkier, real world behind the seemingly perfect family façade. In his refusal to compromise with conventions of virtue rewarded and sentimental resolutions, Ibsen triumphantly realised Zola's vision of real life on stage. In so doing, however, he shared Zola's fate in attracting fierce opposition from Victorian England when his plays first reached the English stage.

As in the case of the French naturalist writers, acceptance of Ibsen's work in English translation developed only gradually. His plays airing social issues on stage initially met with strong resistance, and took some time before gaining full acceptance, and his more personal, symbolic dramas were met even more begrudgingly. However, although initial opposition was strong, in some ways Ibsen must be deemed to have been fortunate. At the time *Ghosts* arrived in London, the rigid conventions of Victorian society, which worked against him, might, paradoxically, also have worked in his favour. To attract the interest of its own writing talent, the English stage at the time had to shift its focus from amiable society plays to something new. By offering plays which challenged accepted social norms and conventions, Ibsen inspired a band of committed supporters who rallied around him and his work. The group included Edmund Gosse, William Archer, Bernard Shaw and Eleanor Marx, some of whom also acted as his translators.

The play with which Ibsen first secured his reputation as a European playwright dealt with the subject of women's rights. *Et dukkehjem* (*A Doll's House*, 1879) portrays the marital conflict unfolding between Nora and Torvald Helmer. Having secretly borrowed money from Krogstad, now one of her husband's employees, Nora has to face up to the threat of blackmail or confess to her husband. In the end, Krogstad, now in a more generous frame of mind since reunited with Mrs Linde, his first love, withdraws his early threats, but by now Nora's disillusionment with Torvald, owing to the lack of understanding he displays in his reaction to her confession, is complete. Acknowledging her own need to grow up and cease to be her husband's 'doll', Nora's only way out is to leave her husband and children in order to try to find herself.

When *A Doll's House* was first published in Copenhagen on 4 December 1879 it was a huge success: edition after edition poured from the press and

Scandinavian theatres opened their doors to Nora, recognising that they were being confronted with a contribution to the topical subject of women's rights. The play rapidly became a *cause célèbre*, with members of the audience leaving the theatre engaged in heated debate. In Copenhagen, posters were displayed prominently at social gatherings with the request 'Please do not discuss *A Doll's House*' and in Christiania, hostesses wanting to avoid discord at social gatherings attached a similar plea to their social invitations.[3]

One of the most outspoken critics of the play was the Swedish playwright August Strindberg, whose main concern reputedly was with the practical consequences of the planned arrangement. Matters of childcare, he felt, would have been greatly facilitated if Nora had simply set to work finding herself while remaining under the same roof as the rest of the family.

The first English version of *A Doll's House* appeared in Copenhagen in 1879 and was the work of a Danish schoolteacher, T Weber, a translation that has long served as an illustration of the necessity of adapting drama in translation (see Chapter 9). Next followed a translation by Henriette Francis Lord, a version used for a reading that took place in Great Russell Street, the home of Karl Marx's daughter, Eleanor, and her common-law husband Edward Aveling, on 15 January 1886. On this occasion, the first time that Bernard Shaw appears to have encountered *A Doll's House*, the Marx-Avelings played hosts 'to a few people worth reading Nora to'. While Shaw took the part of Krogstad, May Morris, William Morris's daughter, played Mrs Linde, with Eleanor Marx and Max Aveling in the roles of Nora and Torvald. The evening 'turned out to be an auspicious one for "Ibsenism", a meeting point for a plethora of "isms" – Marxism, Socialism and Fabianism, that hailed Ibsen as the spokesman of their cause'.[4]

The first professional performance in England of *A Doll's House* did not take place until three years later, on 7 June 1889, at the small Novelty Theatre in Great Queen Street, away from the regular theatre district. The principal force behind the project was the acting couple Janet Achurch and Charles Charrington. Finding Miss Lord's translation somewhat stilted and cumbersome, they appealed for a new version to William Archer, who not only supplied his own translation but also volunteered to help at rehearsals and to share his knowledge of Ibsen's stagecraft.

The play, with Janet Achurch as a memorable Nora, opened to less than full houses, but they included two or three dozen critics. A B Walkley of the *Star* was one of the critics sensing that something new was happening:

> What is being done at the Novelty by this little band of Ibsenites marks the beginning of a dramatic revolution. There is a future for the stage after all.[5]

Originally planned for a single evening performance, the run was extended to three weeks and twenty-four performances. Many critics, however, reacted adversely, greeting the production with an outpouring of repulsion and anger, reactions that were to become the hallmark of the reception of early Ibsen productions in London. In an anonymous editorial in the *Hawk* of 30 July 1889, entitled 'Archer's Frog', Archer was referred to as 'the Frankenstein who had created the monster Ibsen'. Critics were not alone in going on the rampage. In December 1889, Robert Buchanan, a popular playwright of the time, published a long essay in the *Contemporary Review*, titled 'The Modern Drama and Its Critics' expressing his disgust. Drama, he felt, was poisoning itself, 'by exchanging the atmosphere of romantic reality for the air of the dissecting room'. Ibsen was termed 'a belated and very dwarfish Goethe, whose theme is the development of the Individual, the apotheosis of the prig' and Zola and Ibsen were referred to as 'bastard descendants of Goethe's armour'.[6]

The 1889 production of *A Doll's House* marked the first significant outburst of Ibsen mania. The pros and cons of the master's work were aired in the *Academy* in a series of critical confrontations between Herford, a staunch defender of the dramatist, and Wedmore, an outspoken critic. Wedmore was abetted by Clement Scott, formerly owner of the *Theatre* and critic for the *Sunday Times*, the *Observer*, the *Illustrated London News*, *Truth* and the *Daily Telegraph*, which was at the time the paper with the largest circulation in the world. The temperature of the controversy may be gauged by just a sample from Scott:

> Having flung upon the stage a congregation of men and women without affection, an unlovable, unlovely and detestable crew – the admirers of Ibsen, failing to convince us of the excellence of such creatures, turn around and abuse the wholesome minds that cannot swallow such unpalatable doctrine.[7]

Still, a number of other critics leapt to Ibsen's defence pointing out that '[he] is already a power in the world of today, and it is hard to see that his influence has much more than dawned'.[8]

The critical reviews were not, however, a true indication of the overall reception of the 1889 London performance of *A Doll's House*. For example, Elizabeth Robins, the American actress, later turned playwright, who was to play a number of leading parts in Ibsen's plays during the years to come, was so impressed by her visit to the Novelty Theatre that she went a second time, as did Bernard Shaw.[9] Ibsen became the subject of dinner party conversation, and everyone was asking about this 'strange' new playwright. Word about his work also found its way across the Atlantic and in the United States newspapers carried notices of the English production of *A Doll's House*, the play everybody was talking about in London.

In the campaign to get Ibsen onto the English stage, the staging of *A Doll's House* indicated the first signs of a grudging acceptance of foreign drama, different in kind from the previous customary French imports in varying degrees of adaptation. One reason for this acceptance of *A Doll's House* might have been that it embodied something new in technique as well as in content, providing a good reason for putting a Norwegian play in translation on the English stage. And while novel, it was not 'too novel' but sufficiently in tune with the Zeitgeist for the play to be assimilated into English culture – women's right to self-fulfilment was just starting to become an issue, as was the need for changes in the theatre. From this moment in time, continuing until 1897 when *John Gabriel Borkman* was staged by the New Century Theatre, the production of Ibsen's plays in England was to constitute the single most important influence which 'leads us away from the amiable inanities of popular plays of 1888 to the Shavian theatre of the early twentieth century'.[10]

With the 1891 theatre season the battle was resumed: *Rosmersholm, Ghosts, Hedda Gabler* and *The Lady from the Sea* were all staged in London; it was also the year that Bernard Shaw published *The Quintessence of Ibsenism*. The first of the new crop of plays, *Rosmersholm* (1886), about the fall of the honourable but conservative House of Rosmer to prepare the way for new, more modern political and religious ideas, opened at the Vaudeville on 23 February, but failed to arouse much enthusiasm. This reception differed sharply from that which the play was awarded in Russia, where, when it was first staged during the early part of the twentieth century, its discussion of political and moral issues echoed the debate in the Russian press; there the climate of the receiving culture was such that the play attracted the attention of the critics and met with a lively response.[11]

The next Ibsen play on the London stage was *Gengangere* (*Ghosts*, 1881), in a production which met with a hostility that overshadowed all previous English-speaking productions of the Norwegian playwright's work. When on 12 December 1881 the play was first published, there had been initial resistance in Scandinavia and Germany, but by 1883, the Royal National Theatres in both Copenhagen and Stockholm had accepted the play for performance. Three years later, the German theatre embraced *Gespenster*. In England, on the other hand, it was to take until 1897, when Queen Victoria attended a performance of the play, for *Ghosts* to achieve full acceptance. It was to take more than three decades before the place of the play in the European canon was acknowledged, from the cries of 'filth and obscenity' in 1891, to 1928, when a young John Gielgud played Oswald to Mrs Patrick Campbell's Mrs Alving. For the play to compete with the musicals in the West End took the better part of a century; in early 2001, London saw a critically acclaimed production of *Ghosts* at the Comedy Theatre with Francesca Annis as Mrs Alving and Anthony Andrews as Pastor Manders.

In *Ghosts*, Ibsen examined virtually all the topics regularly debated in the Norwegian and Danish newspapers during the 1870s and 1880s which he read during his exile in Italy and Germany, such as free love, venereal disease, prostitution, heredity, Darwinism and euthanasia. Uncovering the web of lies shrouding the misdeeds of the now deceased Captain Alving, *Ghosts* treats the theme of the sins of the father visited upon the son.

Oswald Alving returns, in poor health, to Norway from student life in Paris. He has been sent away at an early age by his mother to be educated in order to prevent him from realising the truth about his father and the existence of a half-sister. Knowing only too well the origin of the fatal hereditary, at the time unmentionable, disease from which Oswald is suffering, Mrs Alving realises that it will fall upon her to administer the final help needed to alleviate her son's pain.

On Friday 13 March 1891, an English-speaking version of *Ghosts* reached the stage of the Royalty Theatre in Soho, produced by J T Grein, a naturalised Dutchman, and his Independent Theatre. When Grein first started to think of producing Ibsen's play, he knew that for a public performance to take place a licence would be required. Following a conversation with Edward Smyth Pigott, the Lord Chamberlain's Examiner of plays from 1874 to 1895, Grein soon realised the futility of even applying for a licence to perform the play on an English stage. Asking why a licence would not be granted, as French farces were readily allowed in London theatres, Pigott's reply sheds interesting light on the concept of 'the other' and the distinction between 'us' and 'them': 'My dear young man,' Pigott answered, 'when French plays come to London with French players, I consider that the theatre in which they act is for the time being French territory.'[12]

This practice may remind us of a similar one, which also appears to have been in operation in the world of film as well as theatre as late as the 1960s. John Trevelyan, an examiner and secretary of the British Board of Film Censors throughout the 1950s and 1960s, recalls in his autobiography *What the Censor Saw* that the board developed a policy of being less strict towards subtitled films than English language ones, and tended to be more lenient towards sex scenes in French films.

Unable to offer a public performance of *Ghosts*, Grein settled for a subscription matinée performance of the play. Little did he know, however, that as the result of this single performance he was to gain the title of 'the best-abused man in London'.[13] In his review for the *Daily Telegraph* of 14 March, Clement Scott referred to *Ghosts* as:

> The sensation play that deals with subjects that hitherto have been to most men horrible and to all pure women loathsome. It is a wretched, deplorable, loathsome history, all must admit. It might have been a tragedy had it been treated by a man of genius…a mass of vulgarity, egotism, coarseness and absurdity…it is all dull, undramatic, uninteresting verbosity – formless, objectless, pointless.

And Clement Scott's was not a lone voice. The reaction to the play was such that, with the intention of ridiculing the opposition, William Archer was able to bring together a wide-ranging sample of abusive statements about *Ghosts* from the press. On 8 April 1891, under the title 'Ghosts and Gibberings', these appeared in the *Pall Mall Gazette* to the delight of Henry James, Bernard Shaw, and other Ibsen supporters.

Below is a sample of the collection:

> 'Abominable piece… Scandalous… Naked loathsomeness… Most dammed and repulsive production' (*Daily News*); 'Morbid, unhealthy. Unwholesome and disgusting story… A piece to bring the stage into disrepute and dishonour with every right-thinking man and woman' (*Lloyds*); 'Maunderings of nookshotten Norwegians' (*Black and White*).[14]

The enraged outcries of the London critics were echoed on the other side of the Atlantic but protestations in the American press did not peak until later, at a time when Ibsen's work had already started to become assimilated in Europe.

The English response to *Ghosts* closely mirrored earlier negative public reactions to Zola. When, in the 1880s, the best-selling translations of his books appeared, Zola was fiercely denounced (see Chapter 2). Epithets appearing in English reviews describing his work ranged from 'dirty, loathsome and disgusting' in the *Saturday Review* to 'obscene to the point of bestiality' in the *Methodist Times*.[15] But Ibsen's notoriety in 1890s England exceeded even that of Zola. Arising from the characteristically Victorian fear of the theatre and its power of presence and physical seductiveness, the stage was viewed as more dangerous than 'telling' on the page.

The importance of the prevailing cultural attitudes of the receiving culture in determining the success or failure of a play in translation may be gauged by a comparison of the reception of Ibsen's work in other European countries. In

France, Ibsen's breakthrough, which took place during virtually the same period of time, was radically different. On 29 May 1890, in a historic production at Théâtre Libre by André Antoine who had been introduced to Ibsen's play by Zola, *Les Revenants* was presented to French theatre audiences. Less concerned with Victorian morals than the English reviewers, the critical response of the French press focused less on taboo subjects being aired on stage. Instead the translation of the text came under scrutiny, as did its alien feel of idiom and spirit. Reacting against the 'infatuation felt by France for foreign literature, against the idolatry of our young writers for the Scandinavian drama', Edmond de Goncourt decried that the French acted

> [a]s if they were the literary servants of Tolstoy and Ibsen...whose qualities cannot be acclimated to the degree of latitude in which we live...we ought to leave the Slavic mists to Russian and Norwegian minds and not try to introduce them by force into our own clear intellects.[16]

In other words, why bother importing foreign and, by implication, inferior products from other parts of Europe, as France already had her own Zola, more than adequately providing for the French need for social realism.

As in France, the Russian staging of *Ghosts* caused no moral outrage, nor did *A Doll's House*, the first of Ibsen's plays to be performed in Russia. Translated from the German, *A Doll's House* was staged on 8 February 1884 in St Petersburg, where it met with limited interest. Wife leaving husband or husband leaving wife does not appear to have been viewed as sufficiently shocking a subject to cause the debate it had triggered off in Scandinavia, Germany and Victorian England. If anything, the plot was viewed as somewhat trivial and the subject matter a topic that had already been exhausted by Russia's own writers.

The appearance of *Ghosts* on the Russian stage also seems to have been uneventful. Having set his heart on the part of Oswald, Pavel Orlenev, a Russian actor with a fondness for parts involving displays of pain and suffering, miraculously succeeded in getting *Ghosts* passed by the censors. The play opened in St Petersburg on 7 January 1904 to notices of praise for Orlenev's tortured bravura performance which included sobbing and spitting, overly naturalistic aspects of his acting which appear to have caused discomfort to rather than impressed members of the audience.[17]

The next major Ibsen event of the 1891 London theatre season was *Hedda Gabler* (1890). In this play about a woman who, unable to adjust to the constraints of middle-class life, through her frustration fatally wrecks the lives of others as well as her own, Ibsen was working within an idiom more easily recognisable to English theatre audiences. Hedda, the 'bad' brown-haired heroine, cutting a striking figure when out riding with her father, is not dissimilar to the familiar adventuress of Victorian melodrama, in particular when juxtaposed with the 'good' blonde, Thea Elvsted. For a wicked adventuring wife to look beyond her staid husband for amusement was also a subject well known through popular French theatrical fare of the time. The fact that Hedda was also a lady with some pretensions to fashion might now seem trivial but was nevertheless not lacking in importance to London theatre audiences of the period, accustomed to the commercial function of late Victorian actresses advertising new fashions on stage. In short, much of the feel of *Hedda Gabler* was familiar to orthodox London theatregoers of 1891. The first Hedda on the English stage was Elizabeth Robins. Having failed to interest theatre managers in a production of *Hedda Gabler*, Robins, together with Marion Lea, another young American actress, decided to produce the play themselves. The play opened successfully on 20 April 1891 with Thomas Hardy in the audience as well as George Meredith, ordinarily not enamoured with the London theatre. Elizabeth Robins' Hedda also succeeded in awakening Henry James's interest in Ibsen.[18]

Nevertheless, the arrival of *Hedda Gabler* was not unanimously praised. Ibsen's Nora could hardly have been described as a model of unselfishness and charity and other virtues customarily associated with a female lead at the time. Now followed Hedda, revealing further unattractive aspects of the female psyche. As always Clement Scott was quick to voice his disapproval, here in the *Illustrated London News*:

> What a horrible story! What a hideous play... Miss Elizabeth Robins has done no doubt what she fully intended to do (!) She has made vice attractive by her art. She has almost ennobled crime. She has glorified an unwomanly woman.[19]

Hard on the heels of *Hedda Gabler* followed *Fruen fra havet* (*The Lady from the Sea*, 1888), which opened on 11 May 1891 in a translation by Eleanor Marx and directed by Edward Aveling. Potential interest in the subject, that of freedom of choice within the confines of marriage, seems to have been outweighed by the unfamiliar feel of the play, and the production was not a success. Not surprisingly, the conflict facing Ellida, brought up on a desolate skerry at the mouth of the fjord, who has to choose between her husband, the hard-working doctor Wangel, and the 'merman', the tantalising seafarer, must have seemed somewhat remote to London theatre audiences. The very being of Ellida, alien and perplexing, must have appeared, as Bernard Shaw noted, 'a much more fantastic person to English readers than to Norwegian ones'.[20] For Ibsen, on the other hand, the need to be close to the scenic beauty of his native Norway and the unspoilt wilderness of northern Europe is likely to have grown in strength during the years he spent in exile abroad, and the setting of Act 1 of *The Lady from the Sea* tells of his feelings. The play opens according to his stage directions, 'on a warm, clear summer's day'. The Norwegian flag is about to be hoisted following the Scandinavian custom of observing name-days of members of the family. On stage right, a bower of lilac trees with a table and a set of chairs provides shady refuge for summer refreshments. Further away there lies a field, beyond which a tree-lined road skirts a fjord. In the distance can be seen the peaks of high mountains. A beautiful setting but inevitably alien to the city dwellers of Victorian London, and, combined with the complex personality of Ellida, it is not surprising that English theatre audiences at the time might have experienced problems identifying with many aspects of the play.

All of the Ibsen productions of the 1891 theatre season occasioned extended debate; there were at least twenty important essays, minor articles and newspaper comments. Much of the reaction was hostile. In his *Quintessence of Ibsenism*, Shaw summarised the Ibsen phobia as it raged up to June of that year, listing a number of adverse newspaper reactions to *Ghosts*. Now, however, the opposition, led by clergymen, newspapers and numerous managers and producers, was met by a formidable group of Ibsen supporters including William Archer, Bernard Shaw, Edmund Gosse, Henry James, Arthur Symons and George Moore.

In the 1890s, a new Ibsen play was a European event, and within a few months of its publication in Copenhagen in December 1892, *Bygmester Solness* (*The Master Builder*) had been published in three German translations and two in English, one of which was American. Within a year of its completion, the play been staged in Berlin, Trondheim, Leipzig, Turku, Christiania, Stockholm, London, Chicago and Rome, with Paris following shortly afterwards.[21]

Unlike *A Doll's House* and other Ibsen plays on the London stage, *The Master Builder* was not built on the skeleton of a conventionally well-made play, or a play that could be used to promote social and political issues. Fearing that he will be replaced by the younger generation, Solness the master builder meets his fate in the young Hilde Wangel. Infatuated with her youthful company, he agrees to climb the scaffolding of his house in order to satisfy the younger woman's romantic notion of 'the ideal'. He manages to reach the top but, tired and middle-aged, he loses his balance and falls to his death.

Originally scheduled to run at the Trafalgar Square Theatre from 20 to 24 February 1893, the run of *The Master Builder* was extended to 3 March as the result of the unanimous critical praise for Elizabeth Robins' portrayal of Hilde Wangel. The play then moved to the Vaudeville where it played from 6 to 25 March. George Moore came to see it three times and a 'delighted' Oscar Wilde attended the final performance.[22] By this time the London theatre climate was such that an Ibsen play could be viewed as an artistic success in its own right and not only as a vehicle for debate of social reform, although the absence of more clearly defined social and political issues in the play lost Ibsen the support of some of his customary advocates. On 9 April 1893, shortly after the play had closed, Edward Aveling, Karl Marx's son-in-law, appeared as the main speaker at a gathering at the Playgoers Club. According to Aveling, the 'lack of power' in *The Master Builder* was to be ascribed to Solness's capitalist leanings. 'Ibsen,' he declared, 'had himself not gained sufficient awareness and enlightenment to embrace socialism,' something he held accountable for the pessimism of the play's conclusion. Had Ibsen been a socialist there would instead have been optimism, 'for hope springs eternal in the human breast that looks for the demolition of the present social system and the building of a nobler structure on its ruins'.[23]

Hedda Gabler and Halvard Solness, the master builder, were preceded almost a decade earlier by another larger-than-life Ibsen character, Dr Tomas Stockmann, the protagonist of *En folkefiende* (*An Enemy of the People*, 1882). On 11 June 1893, Herbert Beerbohm Tree, the actor-cum-manager of the Haymarket Theatre, decided to interrupt the successful run of Oscar Wilde's *A Woman of No Importance* in order to stage a matinée performance of *An Enemy of the People*, with himself in the role of Dr Stockmann.

An Enemy of the People is the play that resulted from Ibsen's disappointment at the scandalised reaction in Norway to *Ghosts* which had caused sales of the published text to drop, depriving him of his income for a year. In Ibsen's time, plays were read with the same care and interest now devoted to novels and, bringing up topical issues for discussion, new Ibsen plays were normally seized upon by the Scandinavian reading public. As an expression of his anger and disappointment with his countrymen, Ibsen set about drawing a number of analogies: Dr Tomas Stockmann writes an article about the pollution of water in the local baths just as Dr Ibsen, an honorary title which he always used after it was bestowed upon him by the University of Uppsala in 1877, pointed to the danger of hereditary disease in his play. And just as the

Christiania Theatre turned down Ibsen's play, the local newspaper refuses to publish Dr Stockmann's article. Still, both doctors stand firm and, in spite of much abuse, will not give up the struggle to tell the truth.[24]

Following the production of the play in 1893, Herbert Beerbohm Tree revived it during the theatre season of 1894 and again in June 1895 when, after a successful guest performance in Chicago earlier in the year, it reappeared on the Haymarket Theatre programme. The play also enjoyed an extended run in 1905 when Tree appeared as Stockmann in weekly matinée performances extending from November into January 1906.

Tree, however, had a fondness for alterations in the original text and, commenting on the performance text in the first production of *An Enemy of the People*, William Archer referred to it as being 'monstrously mutilated'.[25] A notable facet of Tree's portrayal of Tomas Stockmann was his development of the character, a form of English appropriation and acculturation which did not fail to please the reviewers. In for instance *The Theatre* of 1 July 1893, Tree's interpretation of Tomas Stockmann was praised, to the point that it was now viewed as an improvement on that of Ibsen's original:

> It is not very often that an actor improves upon his author when the latter is a genius. But Mr Beerbohm Tree has done it… Broader, more humane, and more sympathetic, the new Stockmann drives home the truth of the play with immeasurably increased force…[26]

By 1909, the acculturation of the part also allowed the *Athenaeum* to see in Tree's portrayal of Stockmann more typically English virtues: 'Such a hero, the cheerful, indomitable fighter, always delights Englishmen of every class.'[27] A similar process of appropriation appears to have taken place in the case of Nora of *A Doll's House*. When the Italian actress Eleonora Duse appeared as Nora in London in 1893, following critical acclaim in America, most English reviewers were disappointed with her interpretation. For the *Athenaeum* critic, for instance, Duse was simply not Ibsen's Nora, raising the question of how a reviewer without knowing Norwegian could know the Nora of the original. An even stronger degree of ownership is voiced in the response of the *Pall Mall Gazette*, where further explanation is offered as to the reason why Signora Duse fails in the part of Nora Helmer. It concludes:

> Her performance last night was powerful, picturesque, tragic, but it did not for one moment convince us that we were face to face with the real Nora Helmer. The woman she gave us was an interesting, attractive woman, but she was essentially a southern woman.

Implicit in these critics assertions is that their access to Ibsen's *A Doll's*

House through English is in some way closer to the true nature of Ibsen's play than the Italian Duse's portrayal.[28]

However, this process of Anglicisation of Ibsen's larger than life characters helped to create greater interest in Ibsen's work and was instrumental in wresting him from the exclusive control of his specialised band of admirers, eventually leading to acceptance in the commercial theatre. Until more recently, this was a rare honour for a playwright staged in translation.

Also helpful in promoting interest was Ibsen's concept of the strong man standing alone squarely facing his opponents represented by Tomas Stockmann in *An Enemy of the People*. Placing Ibsen above the 'puerility of radical politics', Edmund Gosse considered his strongest political conviction to be 'the belief that the State is the natural enemy of the individual'.[29] Other interpretations have been triggered by different political views and circumstances. During the run of *An Enemy of the People*, starting in 1905, the political situation prevailing in the UK helped to promote interest in the play. At one November matinée performance, members of the audience included Asquith, John Burns and Keir Hardie as well as the young Winston Churchill.[30] In the light of the political circumstances at the time, Ibsen's play presented an amusingly apt commentary on the political situation at home, since Balfour's defeated Conservatives were soon to experience all too acutely the power of the 'liberal majority' stigmatised in Ibsen's drama. Public comment to this effect moved Tree to write a letter to *The Times* which appeared on 25 January 1906, explaining that the topical lines from Act 4 of the play – 'The majority is always in the wrong – the great liberal majority is always wrong' – were really Ibsen's own, and not introduced for their suitability in the days of the General Election.[31]

Political circumstances also worked in favour of the introduction of *An Enemy of the People* in Russia where it became one of the greatest Ibsen successes of the Moscow Arts Theatre. With Stanislavsky in the lead role, the eponymous hero of the play, now re-titled *Dr Stockmann*, was turned into a short-sighted absent-minded professor with a commitment to 'the truth'. As one critic pointed out, it was surprising that the radical youth wishing to work with the people would take to their heart a play with the concluding line that 'the strongest man is the man who stands alone'. Nevertheless, the need for a hero who would face up to the ruling powers and tell the truth, overrode the complex psychology of Ibsen's drama. The play was seen as a fight between truth and lies, between badly needed reforms and conservative bureaucracy. In St Petersburg, during a performance which started immediately following a student confrontation with mounted police in the square outside the theatre, the audience's response to the play was such that members of the audience interrupted the performance, rushing onto the stage to shake Stanislavsky's hand.[32]

Another shift in interpretation of the play is found in the version of *An Enemy of the People* by American playwright Arthur Miller. During the 1940s and 1950s, the time of McCarthyism in the United States, Ibsen's theme of man standing alone against the crowd might have been read as reflecting a lack of trust in democracy. This led Miller in his own version of *An Enemy of the People* to leave out some passages to ensure that the apparent elitism would not seem relevant to Fascism.[33]

The year following the introduction of *An Enemy of the People* to the London stage, was a meagre year for Ibsen productions with the exception of *Vildanden* (*The Wild Duck*, 1884). The wild duck, from which the play derives its name, lives in captivity in the attic room of the Ekdal family, and belongs to Hedvig, a young girl. Both are innocent spirits of goodness who fall victim to circumstances set in motion by the arrival of Gregers Werle, whose zest for 'the truth' triggers off a chain of events ultimately leading to Hedvig's death.

The play opened to lukewarm interest at the Royalty Theatre on 4 May 1894 with no reviews in the *Gentleman's Magazine* or the *Saturday Review*. *The Theatre* made the point that 'It is obviously symbolic. But of what?'[34] And then, of course, Clement Scott:

> To call such an eccentricity as this a masterpiece, to classify it at all as dramatic literature or to make a fuss about so feeble a production, is to insult dramatic literature and outrage common sense...[35]

In brief, *The Wild Duck* failed to stimulate critical controversy and to conquer the imagination of the ordinary critic and playgoer. Its English stage history was now suspended until 1905 when Harley Granville-Barker decided to resurrect it for production at the Court Theatre.

In contrast, *Lille Eyolf* (*Little Eyolf*, 1894), the next Ibsen play to be staged in London, might be viewed as a success. It reached the Avenue Theatre on 23 November 1896; all five performances were well attended and the run of the play was extended. The play, involving Alfred Allmers and his wife Rita, their crippled son Eyolf who follows the Rat-Wife out to sea and meets his fate by drowning, and Alfred's sister Asta, is a barely-disguised discussion of marital problems. In addition to Elizabeth Robins as Asta and Janet Achurch as Rita, the production boasted the presence of Mrs Patrick Campbell in the part of the Rat-Wife. In spite of moralists' objections to airing marital problems on stage, *Little Eyolf* was favourably received, partly due to the star quality of Mrs Campbell, partly due to its own artistic merit. Still, not long after its much-talked about London season, interest receded, perhaps as a result of attention now focusing on yet another Ibsen offering.

With the proceeds from the successful production of *Little Eyolf*, Elizabeth Robins had founded the New Century Theatre. The first production of the company was to be the new Ibsen play *John Gabriel Borkman* (1896). The eponymous protagonist of the play shares a house with his wife Gunhild but the two lead separate lives. Gunhild's sole concern is the future of Erhart, their only child, while Borkman is obsessively preoccupied with the past and the events that have prevented him from reaching the top of the financial world. As the play closes, Erhart has thwarted the plans laid for him by three bitter people – his parents and his aunt, Ella, his mother's twin sister and the real love of his father – leaving his father to die and his mother and aunt to become reconciled over his dead body.

The production opened on 3 May 1897, but, in spite of Bernard Shaw helping to herald the arrival of the play and Henry James expressing his enthusiasm, it was not received favourably. The lack of success was, according to Bernard Shaw, to be attributed to the capricious financial condition of the production. In words that could be used today, more than a century later, to describe the conditions often relating to the staging of contemporary European drama in English translation at underfunded venues, he concludes:

> For my part, I beg the *New Century Theatre*, when the next Ibsen play is ready for mounting, to apply to me for assistance. If I have a ten-pound note, they shall have it; if not, I can at least lend them a couple of decent chairs.[36]

While both *The Master Builder* and *John Gabriel Borkman* show the destructive face of genius, *Naar vi døde vaagner* (*When We Dead Awaken*, 1899), Ibsen's next play, which was also to be his last, focuses on the mission of the artist overriding all other considerations. Returning to Norway from abroad, the wealthy and fêted artist Arnold Rubek meets Irene, the muse and love of his life. Feeling that he has betrayed Irene's as well as his own youthful ideals, Rubek leaves Maja, his young wife, and, together with Irene, sets out to reach the top of a mountain, but they fail, stopped short by the force of a rapidly advancing avalanche.

In a letter to his brother Charles, written in December 1899, William Archer comments first on recent British reverses in the Boer War, then on Ibsen's new play. 'Well, here's a cheerful end to the century! And to cheer you up a little more, I send you a hurried line to say that at last the Old Man is an old man and the new play is a sad fiasco.' [37] Although clearly not enthusiastic about the play Archer duly translated it, and on 25 January *When We Dead Awaken* reached the Imperial Theatre where it ran for two days. Archer never revised his first unfavourable impression. He predicted accurately, however, that Bernard Shaw would laud it. On 21 February 1900, Archer received a postcard from Shaw, referring to the play as powerful and highly moral. The published version of the play also yielded a response from James Joyce, moving him to write an article called 'Ibsen's New Drama' for the *Fortnightly Review* in April 1900. In it he suggests that *When We Dead Awaken* may rank with the greatest of Ibsen's work.[38]

Thus, during his own lifetime, acceptance of Ibsen's work developed only gradually. However, although initial opposition was strong, in contrast to other playwrights writing in less well-known European languages whose work has never reached the English stage, in some ways Ibsen was lucky. Challenging the social as well as the political climate of the day, he was successful in attracting a band of committed supporters, some of whom were translators, including Edmund Gosse, William Archer and Eleanor Marx. It is certainly true that the factors firing Eleanor Marx's efforts as a translator were largely the social and political ideas of Ibsen's plays: she reportedly started to study Norwegian for the sole purpose of being able to translate Ibsen. Edmund Gosse, on the other hand, devoted considerable time to studying the Norwegian language as well as the literature and culture of the country, while, for William Archer, Norwegian was a natural second language which he learnt at a very young age during summers spent with relatives in Norway.

During the latter part of the nineteenth century Edmund Gosse (1849–1928) was the principal medium through which Scandinavia was introduced into English literature. Gosse not only introduced Ibsen to the English public but he was also the editor of Bjørnstjerne Bjørnson. Gosse's Ibsen campaign started well before Archer's and almost twenty years before the great Ibsen controversy of the early 1890s turned Ibsen into a household name in Britain.

Initially, Gosse appears to have developed an interest in the literature of Northern Europe for the purpose of advancing his career as a literary critic: as a young aspiring writer looking for openings he was advised by the literary editor of the *Spectator* to develop an expertise in a little-known field such as Scandinavian literature.[39] Gosse followed the advice given, first visiting Norway in 1871 at the age of twenty-two, the year which, on 3 May, saw the publication of Ibsen's selected *Poems*. The following year Gosse wrote a review of the book for the *Spectator*, the first critical discussion of Ibsen in England. This was followed by further articles in the *Spectator* as well as in the *Academy*, *Fortnightly Review* and *Frazer's Magazine* over the next couple of years. Gosse continued to act as a publicist for Ibsen, including a chapter on Ibsen in his *Studies in the Literature of Northern Europe* in 1879, reissued as *Northern Studies* in 1890. Above all, in 1907 Gosse published a separate volume, *Ibsen*, which remained the standard introduction to Ibsen for many years.

In the 1840s, many Norwegian writers began to attempt to 'Norwegianise' their language: the resulting Dano-Norwegian was a fusion of Danish and Norwegian following Denmark's rule over Norway for close to four centuries. It is difficult to know exactly how good Gosse's command of Dano-Norwegian actually was but, from all the evidence, his linguistic skills appear to have been considerable: his distinguished literary contacts in Scandinavia all wrote to him in their own language and translated quotations sprinkle his essays, the best being the short lyrical poems requiring delicate metrical and rhyming skills. He reportedly regularly received compliments on his mastery of the language in Denmark, although at times with the qualification that he spoke it like a Swede, that is 'not correctly but very prettily'.[40]

Given his interest in Scandinavian literature and the work of Ibsen it is not surprising that Gosse would also be approached to act as an Ibsen translator. Having discovered that he could obtain the theatrical rights to *Hedda Gabler* by publishing the text in English at the same time as it appeared in Copenhagen and Christiania, during the latter part of 1890 the publisher William Heinemann turned to Gosse and commissioned him to do a translation. This became the standard 'literary' version for some years, going into five editions from 1891 to 1906, until the joint Archer/Gosse version in 1907. Together with Archer, Gosse also translated *The Master Builder*. As a translator, Gosse appears to have striven for a respectfully close rather than an actable version of the original. According to the *Westminster Review*:

> *Hedda Gabler* is one of the poorest plays it has ever been our lot to read. The dialogue is trivial, dull and clumsily expressed, and in the English version it is further disfigured by the use of quasi-fashionable tricks of speech, such as 'It is too lovely of you' to do so and so. We did at least expect good English from Mr Gosse.[41]

By 1879, Gosse's knowledge of Scandinavian literature had secured him the position to which he had aspired and he was eager to throw his nets more widely. His interest in Ibsen, however, appears to have been more than merely a stepping stone in his own literary career. In the Epilogue to his auto-biographical *Father and Son* which appeared in 1907, the year which also saw the publication of his book on Ibsen, Gosse pointedly contrasted the dramatist with his own father, who was a representative of a spiritual Puritanism which he himself had come to reject.

A similar distancing from a puritanical background with Ibsen as a potentially new father figure replacing his own also characterised William Archer's campaign to bring the 'Master's' work onto the English stage. William Archer (1856–1924) grew up in a religious environment in Perth where much of the Sabbath was spent reading the Bible. Leaving this world behind him, in his search for an identity of his own, Archer was first attracted to the progressivism and 'the value of Liberty and Individuality' of John Stuart Mill, before discovering Ibsen and his plays, which revealed the real world behind the façade of the bourgeois drawing room.[42]

William Archer's link with Norway and Norwegian was a natural development of having spent the summers of his childhood in the village of Larvik where his grandfather had moved to raise his family, including Archer's father. As a result of his prolonged visits to Norway, Archer grew so familiar with the Norwegian language that, at the age of four, during an extended stay in Larvik, for a while he was unable to speak English. He would then, at intervals, lose his command of Norwegian which, in turn, he would regain on subsequent visits with the end result that Norwegian became a natural second language to him.

On one of his visits to Larvik, William Archer stumbled across *Kjærlighedens komedie* (*Love's Comedy*), an early Ibsen play which had been printed as an 1862 New Year Supplement to a Norwegian magazine. A copious reader, he quickly finished the play, then moved on to reading everything that Ibsen had written including his recently published play *Kejser og Galilæer* (*Emperor and Galilean*, 1873). Archer's first attempt at an Ibsen translation was his adaptation of *Pillars of Society*, which he retitled *Quicksands* and which, when staged in London in 1880, was not a success. Perhaps it was the shame and regret with which he viewed his early attempt at adapting Ibsen that later came to determine his approach as a translator: he would scrupulously ensure that every word Ibsen wrote was accurately transferred from Norwegian into English.

Today, over a century later, it is not uncommon to view Archer as 'a staid, even austere Scotsman who reduced Ibsen to a drawing room dramatist of well-made plays' or to complain, as does Eric Bentley in *The Playwright as Thinker*, that Archer 'shackled the master' with a Victorian style.[43] Archer translated for the time in which he lived. He was the first to point out that his translations failed to capture the full beauty and power of Ibsen's language.

Instead, he felt it was his task to provide accurate renderings of Ibsen's Norwegian texts in translations where nuances lost were explained in the form of footnotes. Help to turn Archer's translations into actable dialogue was also at hand from the actress Elizabeth Robins. In the case of *Hedda Gabler*, her work on the two then available translations, by Gosse and by Archer, was considerable, but she lay no claims on translation rights, graciously acknowledging that permission was given for the actors 'to collaborate on a somewhat more speakable version for stage use'.[44]

Rather more of an intractable problem than turning Archer's somewhat stilted English into the spoken vernacular is his word-for-word approach to the translation of idioms and metaphors. In *Little Eyolf*, to take one example, Ibsen uses an idiomatic Norwegian expression which translates literally into English as 'to promise someone gold and green forests', meaning to make grandiose but untenable promises. In Archer's word-for-word translation, the meaning of this commonly-used Norwegian idiomatic expression is less than clear. In his painstakingly faithful approach Archer often tackles similar idioms head on, with the result that his translations become overburdened with images more startling than those in the original, which in turn tend to detract from Ibsen's own verbal imagery so carefully interwoven into the texture of his plays. Devoted to Ibsen, the artist, Archer clung over-conscientiously to the letter, with the result that Ibsen's intentions are at times far from clear in English translation. Stumbling blocks to the reader and tongue twisters to the actor, they have helped to fuel the often-expressed belief that Ibsen is difficult and obscure.[45]

Less important aspects of Archer's translations such as stage directions and character descriptions also emerge in English as awkward, to the point of creating a less attractive English version of the original. Preparing for her part as Hilde Wangel in *The Master Builder*, Elizabeth Robins is floored by the description of the character she is about to play and predicts a similar reaction from her countryman Henry James:

> He'll faint when he hears! This is her portrait: Middle height, supple (graceful), delicately built, a little sunburnt, wears a 'tourist's dress' with a skirt fastened up (or pinned up). Sailor collar turned away from the throat and a little sailor hat on her head. Has a knapsack on her back; rug in a shawl-strap and alpenstock! How I hate her!!![46]

These directives read as if the Archer/Gosse translation team had opened a Norwegian-English dictionary and written down the first word on offer with little thought to its context of use. Had they ventured further amongst synonyms listed Elizabeth Robins might have been slightly less appalled at the prospect of taking on the role of Hilde Wangel:

> Average height, agile, slender, delicately built, light tan and dressed in hiking outfit with skirt hitched up, open-neck sailor collar with small, matching hat. On her back a knapsack with a blanket rolled up with a leather strap and an alpenstock.

The awkwardness of many of these early translations may, at least in part, have prompted Henry James' prophecy as expressed in his review of the first production of *Hedda Gabler* in 1891:

> His cause may be said to be lost; we shall never take [Ibsen] to our hearts because he is not pleasant enough, nor light enough, nor casual enough; he is too far from Piccadilly and our glorious standards.[47]

As other European playwrights have had to learn, it is indeed a long way to Piccadilly, even though in the case of Ibsen it proved not to be as long as Henry James predicted.

The years that have passed since Henry James made his pronouncement have seen Ibsen's work become increasingly more accessible in translation. Although it is a well-known fact that Ibsen was born a Norwegian, it is not infrequently forgotten that his plays were written in another language, that the words spoken on English-speaking stages are not his own. It is not always remembered that Ibsen's work is only known in English through the mediation of translation.

It is also easy to forget that in many cases it is the English and not the Norwegian Ibsen that serves as the basis for translation into other languages. Most, if not all, of the numerous versions of *A Doll's House* in China appear to have been translated from English and the same seems to hold true for Bangladesh. In other words, the Ibsen known in translation is far better known than the Ibsen of the original Norwegian.

Following its independence from Denmark in 1814, in the Norway of Ibsen's time there was a Norwegian National Theatre able to offer him a post at the age of 23. Previous generations of aspiring Norwegian playwrights, however, would have been more inclined to look to Copenhagen than to Bergen for furtherance of their artistic ambitions. As a matter of course, Ludvig Holberg (1684–1754) left his native Bergen to complete his education in Copenhagen, then the capital of Denmark-Norway. After the opening of its first public theatre in 1722, Holberg, often referred to as the father of Scandinavian drama and also known as 'the Danish Molière', wrote more than thirty comedies. Some of these plays on the theme of human folly have been translated into English; new translations by Michael Meyer of *Jeppe paa Bjerget* (*Jeppe of the Hill*, 1722) and *Den vægelsindede* (*Scatterbrain*, 1723) appeared in 1999.[48]

The language of Holberg's satirical vernacular comedies does not however, lend itself easily to translation. Nor does translation do full justice to the work of Bjørnstjerne Bjørnson (1832–1910). The 1903 recipient of the Nobel Prize for Literature, Bjørnson initiated the debate on women's rights in 1877 with his short story *Magnhild*, and in 1883, followed *A Doll's House* and *Ghosts* with his feminist play *En hanske* (*A Gauntlet*). Neither the work of Holberg nor of Bjørnson has managed to leave as lasting a mark in English translation as has that of Ibsen. The reason why these two playwrights have not attracted a wider and more lasting European interest has been ascribed to the difficulties of transferring their work in translation. It has been suggested that 'while Ibsen loses much in translation, Bjørnson loses more but Holberg loses everything – his greatest charm is his style which is bereft of all its aroma in another idiom.'[49]

Style is, however, not the only linguistic factor to be considered when a play changes language. Problems in translation may also occur at other levels: one such level is the phonological level when the sound system of one language is fundamentally different from that of another. In the case of Norwegian and English this can be illustrated by an example from *Little Eyolf*, when not long before the curtain goes down, Rita Allmers and her husband have the following exchange:

> ALLMERS: My first feeling for you was not love, Rita.
> RITA: What was it then?

Allmers gives a one-word reply:

> ALLMERS: Fear.[50]

Here 'fear' is the translation of the noun *skrekk* in Norwegian, a word that contains a combination of consonants which, when they occur in combination achieve a much harsher sound effect than does 'fear' in English. As Northam comments:

> There is no English word that I can think of capable of applying the whiplash
> of the Norwegian *skrekk*. Alfred's single word needs to be felt almost as a
> physical blow because the revelation is so vital for all its brevity...[51]

However, the linguistic level with which the translator is usually most concerned, is the lexical level, the domain of the word. At times, a word in one language lacks an equivalent in another, which may result in the foreign word being borrowed, as in the case of the Norwegian *fjord*. On other occasions, a corresponding word may exist but it does not fully cover the meaning of the original. An example of this is the Norwegian *gengangere*, the word which serves as the original title of Ibsen's play *Ghosts*. In English, 'ghosts' fails to convey the force of the word *gengangere*, which means 'something that walks again', conveying more exclusively the sense of something condemned to reappear over and over again.[52] This form of translation loss, involving the failure to convey part of the original meaning of a word in translation, is difficult to avoid in any attempt to transfer a text written in one language to another.

In spite of Norwegian and English being relatively closely related, both belonging to the Germanic language family, the English language has not always been kind to Ibsen. The language of English Ibsen, Arthur Miller opines, 'lyrical as it may sound in Scandinavia, does not sing in translation, although his ideas often do.'[53]

Although less frequently found in English, a linguistic feature characterising the Germanic language family is the frequent use of a device whereby two words are joined together in order to create a new word with a different meaning. While the process does exist in English, as in the case of 'rail' and 'way' combining to form 'railway', the formation of compounds has remained more productive in Norwegian and other Germanic languages. English, on the other hand, has developed in a different direction, drawing on imported loan words to enrich its vocabulary, a process triggered by the imposed influence of French for several centuries. This conveniently places the translator working into English in a position to draw on pairs such as 'begin' and 'commence', the former Anglo-Saxon and the latter of French origin, as stylistic variants, not available to the same extent in other Germanic languages. In these languages, which do not share the unique linguistic history and greatly enriched vocabulary of English, new words continue to be created through the process of putting two or more words together in order to form new concepts.

As the meaning of a new word that has been formed is usually 'transparent' from the two words put together to create it, translation is usually facilitated if the process is in use in target as well as source language. However, while the meaning of each of the two words put together may be relatively easy to comprehend in English, finding a one-word equivalent may be more difficult. The Norwegian word *liv* (life) may for instance combine with *kraft* (power) to form *livskraft* (life-power); with *glädje* (joy) to form *livsglädje* (life-joy), and with *mod* (courage) to form *livsmod* (life-courage). While *livskraft* might possibly be rendered as 'energy' or 'spirit', drawing on the English Greco-Latin word stock, *livsglädje* translated as 'joy of life' is not only three words instead of one, but also belongs to a different, more elevated style in English than it does in Norwegian: evidence that the meaning of the word is difficult to capture in English is the occasional resort to the French *joie de vivre*.

To convey the concept of *livsmod* (life-courage), the somewhat melodramatic ring to 'courage to face life' is unlikely to find favour with the actress on whose lot it falls to use the phrase on stage. In a conversation between Hedda and her husband at the beginning of Act 3 in *Hedda Gabler*, the word is used by Hedda to refer to her friend Eilert Løvborg. Relating the events of the previous evening at the social gathering at Judge Brack's house, Tesman tells Hedda that he had an opportunity to listen to Løvborg read from his new, recently completed book. 'It is one of the most remarkable books ever written', Tesman says to his wife. 'Such talent', he concludes, 'and yet the man is irredeemable.' To which Hedda answers:

> HEDDA: *Du mener vel, at han har mere **livsmod** end de andre?*

> HEDDA: You mean that he has more **life-courage** than the others? [54]

In the Dover Thrift Editions, the anonymous translator has decided simply to omit the first part of the compound, resulting in an incorrect interpretation of the meaning of the original:

> HEDDA: I suppose you mean that he has more **courage** than the rest.[55]

This is also the solution for which McFarlane opts:

> HEDDA: I suppose you mean he's got more **courage** than the rest.[56]

A solution frequently used when translating compounds into English is to treat the two parts as individual words, a method which has the disadvantage of making a line longer as well as losing part of its meaning. This is the approach favoured by John Osborne, who divides Ibsen's compound into 'pride' and 'life':

> HEDDA: You mean he has more **pride** – more **life** – than the others? [57]

In a more recent American version of *Hedda Gabler*, a similar, 'wordier' method is used:

> HEDDA: You mean – what – ? That he has an appetite for life? That he's more courageous than most people? [58]

One of the innovative aspects of Ibsen's use of the Norwegian language lies in his skill in finding two already existing words which he then combines to create a new, original image. Unfortunately, the resulting neologism, often startling in its novel use in Norwegian, frequently fails to make the transition into English. A well-known example is the word *lysrædd* which Ibsen uses in *Ghosts*, literally meaning 'light-frightened', an apt expression to describe the atmosphere prevailing in the Alving household with its elaborate web of lies carefully keeping in the dark everything that does not stand up to closer scrutiny.[59] Using this device, Ibsen consistently links words together creating new concepts, which then recur at intervals to form part of the thinking of his characters. Entering into the very architecture of his plays, they become key words or expressions and need ideally to be translated consistently as their repeated use reinforces what Ibsen is telling us about his characters.

In the introduction to his translation of *An Enemy of the People* for the 1997 National Theatre production, Christopher Hampton describes his working method as an Ibsen translator. Acknowledging that he is not a speaker of Norwegian but, as a trained linguist, accustomed to translating from French and German, Hampton has devised what he calls 'his own, slightly eccentric method of tackling Ibsen.'[60] Working from the original text, with a Norwegian dictionary, he is supported by a translation prepared by a Norwegian speaker as well as the original German translation. Already well acquainted with the difficulties posed by transferring compounds from German into English, it is a short step for Hampton to deal with the same problem in translation between Norwegian and English. German, in other words, assumes the role of a linguistic bridge between Norwegian and English.

The close similarity in the use made of compound formation in German and Norwegian was noted already in early Ibsen translation. As an example of a translation problem in *John Gabriel Borkman*, William Archer mentions having difficulties with the expression '*overskurkens moral*' where the first part of Ibsen's innovative compound means 'over', 'above' (German *über*) and the second part translates as 'scoundrel'. Archer astutely notes the similarity between Ibsen's word and Nietzsche's *Übermensch*.[61] What Ibsen seems to have done here is to create a new compound, using Nietzsche's concept as a springboard. But while the first part of the word travels with ease between German and Norwegian, translation into English with its preference for Latinate prefixes, is more problematic. Evidence of the untranslatability of neologisms containing *über* into English has been provided by its recent extensive use as a loan prefix in English. On 12 July 2002, the *Guardian* described Mike Ovitz of the powerful Hollywood agency CAA as an 'über-agent', followed just over two weeks later by a reference in the *Observer Magazine* of 28 July to 'über-hairdressers'. Ibsen's novel use of *über* in a new and different context would have caused amusement to theatregoers in Scandinavia but at the time, the humour is likely to have been lost in translation into English. It is doubtful that Archer's attempt at a translation, 'the morals of the higher rascality', would have had much resonance with an English audience, adding fuel to Clement Scott's complaint that 'Ibsen might be a mighty genius, but he has no sense of humour'.[62]

The lack of humour that so many critics have decried in Ibsen's work may at least in part be attributed to the difficulty of capturing in translation Ibsen's innovative compounds, used for comic effect in a manner similar to the way puns and word games are employed by British playwrights. In *The Wild Duck*, Relling tells Gregers Werle, the 'truth-teller', using yet another compound, that his is a complicated case, that he is suffering from a condition known as *'rettskaffenhetsfeber'* ('doing-the-honourable-thing-fever') as well as *'tillbedjansdille'* ('need-to-worship-someone-obsession'). What Relling means is that it is Gregers Werle's need to pay respect to upright and honourable idols, men who are not like his own father, that has resulted in wreaking immeasurable damage to the Ekdal household. Spoken by someone in the medical profession, the effect of Relling's lines in the original is highly amusing and the humorous effect is heightened as Relling further develops the medical image by referring to Werle's condition as acute. In English translation, Michael Meyer chooses 'this tiresome rash of righteousness' for the first 'illness' and 'live in a perpetual delirium of hero worship', for the second, in both cases 'wordy' lines with little of the humour retained:

> RELLING: Oh, yes. Yours is a complicated case. To begin with, you've this tiresome rash of righteousness; and what's worse, you live in a perpetual delirium of hero-worship.[63]

The male members of the Ekdal family also suffer from an acute condition: they are bent on living a 'life-lie'. So too are the regular customers at the bar of Harry Hope's saloon in O'Neill's American answer to *The Wild Duck*, *The Iceman Cometh*, but perhaps it is symptomatic of the difference in language and culture that the characters inhabiting O'Neill's world are viewed as cherishing their pipe dreams rather than suffering from the more Germanic condition of a 'life-lie-need'.

Lack of linguistic means to transfer Ibsen's innovative verbal constructions may also result in a somewhat banal and melodramatic English. When, just before the curtain goes down, John Gabriel Borkman's wife and twin sister are reunited over the dead body of the man they both loved, Ibsen puts two words together to form 'heart-cold', a new concept:

ELLA: (*With a painful smile.*) One dead man and two shadows...is what the cold has made of us.

MRS B answers, using Ibsen's new compound:

MRS B: *Ja,* **hjertekulden** *– Og så kan vel vi to rekke hinannen handen, da Ella.*

MRS B: Yes...the **cold heart**. (*Pause.*) Now we two can join hands, Ella.[64]

In the Norwegian text, '*hjertekulden*', literally the 'heart-cold', draws on the multiple references to cold which are scattered throughout the play, physically in the form of snow and ice and emotionally in the damage resulting from the denial of feelings. In English translation, however, the 'cold heart' conveys nothing innovative, if anything the phrase is somewhat banal, the line becoming 'a sitting target for those English critics who belabour Ibsen for the absence from his language of Shakespearean inventiveness and metaphorical volubility'.[65] At times, however, translation of Ibsen's compounds does succeed in yielding happy solutions. Archer's translation of Ibsen's '*luftslott*', literally 'air-castles', as 'castles in the air', has stayed in English in 'building castles in the air' as has the other lasting image in *The Master Builder*, that of 'the younger generation knocking at the door'. Nevertheless, these successful translations seem, on the whole, to be exceptions rather than the rule, and the fact remains that a major hurdle in the translation of Ibsen into English is the problem presented by his imaginative, lexical innovations.

If the translation of compounds ranks high on the translator's list of problem areas in transferring Ibsen's plays into English, a further difference between English and other Germanic languages presents yet another problem of near 'untranslatability'. While in English an adjective preceded by the definite article 'the' usually has to be followed by a noun, it is possible in Norwegian to use constructions involving adjectives unaccompanied by nouns. Thus Nora can use a phrase such as '*det vidunderlige*' ('the miraculous [thing]'), without indicating exactly what it is that is so miraculous. In *A Doll's House*, this is Nora's favourite rhetorical phrase which, as it becomes increasingly obvious that there is no place for this notion of hers in the real world, she is forced to give up.

Wisely, in this instance most translators avoid propping up the adjective by choosing the word 'thing', that is 'the miraculous thing', instead opting for the related noun 'miracle'. This means, however, that while the Norwegian adjectival construction, that is 'the miraculous', is open-ended, replacing the adjective with a noun tends to make it more specific and less open to audience interpretation and imagination. Then, at the very end of the play, at the time when Nora is about to leave her home to enter 'the real world', Ibsen raises the emotional temperature even further by putting the adjective *vidunderlig* in the superlative; now Nora uses the phrase *'det vidunderligste'*, ('the most miraculous [thing]') to refer to the possibility that Torvald, her husband, may not always remain a stranger to her. This escalation from 'miraculous' to 'most miraculous' is important in that it might now be possible to read into this new variation on the phrase a certain sense of hope, to interpret it as an attempt on Ibsen's part to temper the tragedy of a mother having to leave her three small children.[66]

Having settled for 'miracle' in the first instance, translators now have little choice but to continue on their chosen path, resulting in the English Nora speaking of 'miracle of miracles',[67] a translation which, although less economical and elegant than the original, nevertheless succeeds in capturing the intended escalation. Alternatively, the attempt to capture the intricate pattern of Ibsen's keywords interwoven into the text may just have to be abandoned, with the translator acknowledging what seems to be a genuine case of translation loss. This seems to be the approach taken by Frank McGuiness in his 1996 version of *A Doll's House* where, preceding her departure, Nora simply states that if her husband is not to remain a stranger 'then something glorious would have to happen'.[68]

Other linguistically linked problems may also create obstacles for the Ibsen translator. The type of language used by Ibsen's characters may for instance serve to illustrate some aspect of their personality. As pointed out by Inga-Stina Ewbank, unlike the characters inhabiting Chekhov's world who long to be other than they are, those of Ibsen's plays strive to be themselves.[69] The single-mindedness with which they pursue this aim, together with Ibsen's concern with personal commitment, makes for a combination of human characteristics with which English tradition continues to feel uneasy: total devotion to a calling tends to be viewed as simplistic, at times even suspicious. As an example, Ewbank points to *Brand* (1866), Ibsen's perhaps most explicit attack on 'the spirit of compromise'; the critical reception of the 1978 National Theatre production clearly showed this play of Ibsen's to be alien territory. A similar reaction to earlier stagings of *John Gabriel Borkman* could be sensed in Jack Tinker's review of the much-praised National Theatre production of the play in 1996. Instead of 'stifling giggles' Tinker admits to 'fighting back tears' as the result of Paul Scofield giving 'Borkman's monstrous self-absorption a very human face'.[70] Borkman's dilemma however may be viewed as stemming as much from the single-mindedness needed for anyone not born into money and social position to succeed in business, as from simple 'self-absorption'. Perhaps only a sufficiently nuanced performance such as that given by Scofield could succeed in giving English Borkman 'a very human face', in helping to remove entrenched reservations about the intrinsic 'otherness' in the human qualities of single-mindedness and total commitment.

Not surprisingly, those Ibsen characters showing more easily recognisable English features seem to have been some of the first to find favour with English audiences. A particular favourite seems to have been the world-weary cynic Dr Relling in *The Wild Duck*. 'I confess to a preference for the merry cynic, Dr Relling,' Edmund Gosse admitted, 'with his monstrous set of immoral paradoxes.'[71] These sentiments were echoed in an unsigned notice by Clement Scott in the *Daily Telegraph*, 5 May 1894:

> The hero of last night's experiment was without a doubt Mr Lawrence Irving who played the common-sense Dr Relling...he knew the man he was playing, he lived in the part, his enunciation and style were alike excellent...

The uncompromising structure of the Ibsen world which makes his single-minded characters more difficult for an English audience to accept than his world-weary cynics is carefully reflected in his language, in his use of contrasts such as *up* versus *down*. The Master Builder climbs up high and falls down, as do Rubek and Irene in *When We Dead Awaken* and, in *The Wild Duck*, the bird comes from 'the bottom of the sea' but is kept in captivity 'up in the attic', also used by old Ekdal for his make-believe bear-shooting expeditions. In addition to the up/down contrast, bipolarity also occurs in the form of *hot* versus *cold*. The closeness versus distance to the tiled stove as the centre of warmth in *Hedda Gabler* may be viewed as a barometer, registering Hedda's emotional stance and, at the same time, constituting the opposition between *light* and *dark*. When Hedda first appears on stage she asks that the curtains be drawn over the glass doors opening on to the veranda. A moment later she crosses the room to the side opposite to the glass doors and stands by the stove with its dark tiles.[72] In this way, Ibsen weaves together the language, the human characters and even the stage set which all interact to convey an overall, uncompromising emotional climate, at odds with the more favoured English style of indirectness and understatement.

In addition to the difficulties more immediately linked to language, there is in Ibsen, as in the work of any foreign playwright, the problem of transferring unfamiliar social and cultural references. On the whole, however, such references do not seem to occur in Ibsen's plays with the same frequency as they do in the work of fellow Scandinavian August Strindberg. For instance, Ibsen's first play to be translated into English, *Pillars of Society*, contains few references to Norwegian food and drink or forms of socially or culturally related rituals likely to defy translation into another language. Still, in both Ibsen and Strindberg a 'false friend' in the shape of the name of a drink recurs and may serve as an example of a social-cultural problem in translation, the existence of which seems to have escaped a number of translators.

The first act of *The Wild Duck*, a social gathering takes place at the Werle residence where Mrs Sørby, soon to marry Werle senior, a wealthy businessman, is acting as the hostess. After dinner, Mrs Sørby calls for the gentlemen to repair to the drawing-room and join her for drinks, tempting her guests with a glass of *'punsch'* as it is spelt in Norwegian, the drink *à la mode* in Scandinavia at the time of Ibsen. In use and content, this drink has little to do with the drink known as 'punch' in English; Scandinavian 'punch' is an arrack-based alcoholic liquor reminiscent of rum, made of sugar cane and rice with molasses and palm juice, which through the addition of sugar and water, has acquired a deep golden-yellow colour and a distinct arrack flavour. Right up to the middle of the nineteenth century, Scandinavians would mix their own 'punch', which would be drunk hot. For example, in Act 1 of *An Enemy of the People* Mrs Stockmann brings drinks and invites her guests to help themselves, in response to her husband's request for *toddyen* (the toddy). Here in the McFarlane & Arup translation:

> MRS STOCKMANN: Here we are – this is arrack, and here, this is rum
> and here is the cognac. Please help yourselves.[73]

In Christopher Hampton's 1997 version, Tomas Stockmann asks his wife not only for the toddy but for the *hot* toddy:

> TOMAS STOCKMANN: Katrine, let's have the *hot* toddy.

Mrs Stockmann brings a tray with a kettle, glasses, decanters and so on.

> MRS STOCKMANN: Now; this is arrack and this one is rum; and here
> is the brandy. Everyone help themselves.[74]

The presence of the kettle amongst the articles on the tray would seem to suggest that Stockmann's dinner guests might adhere to the older tradition of taking their 'punch' hot, mixing the arrack, water, sugar, lemon and tea themselves. Here Hampton's concession to an English audience is to insert the adjective 'hot' into his translation of Tomas Stockmann's line in order to help bring about the associations needed, making a possibly unfamiliar social event easier to understand in translation.

In *The Wild Duck*, on the other hand, which was written in 1884, two years later than *An Enemy of the People*, we do not know with certainty whether Mrs Sørby is offering a hot or a cold, bottled version of the drink, which had also become popular. What we do know, however, is that it she is not likely to be serving English punch, a completely different drink. Yet in most translations of *The Wild Duck* the 'false friend' effect has resulted in translations where this is the drink being offered:

> MRS SØRBY: (*To the guests in the other room.*) Gentlemen, please! If anyone wants a glass of punch, he must come in here.[75]

One solution to the problem would be to replace 'punch' with another drink likely to be offered on this type of occasion. As brandy was also common at the time, the absence of 'punch' as an after-dinner drink in English middle-class society could easily be remedied in translation by Mrs Sørby offering her guests another drink such as cognac.

Not surprisingly a number of translators have simply transferred the word from Norwegian into English, a mistake also repeatedly made by translators of Strindberg's plays from Swedish. It may seem a minor point, but still one that adds a foreign feel to the text: punch as currently understood in English is not the type of drink likely to be served after a formal meal to the participants in a gentlemen's dinner party during the latter part of the nineteenth century.

Its middle-class associations also makes Scandinavian 'punch' an obvious choice of drink offered in *Hedda Gabler*, given the eponymous heroine's social and cultural background and ambitions. It is mentioned on several occasions, the first time when Eilert Løvborg makes the fatal error of deciding to stay behind with Hedda and Thea Elvsted, declining the invitation from Judge Brack to join Jørgen Tesman and himself for a social gathering. Hedda, hardly unaware of Løvborg's fondness for drink, arranges for refreshments to be served. Later, her orders having been carried out, Hedda addresses the company pointing in the direction of the inner room. The close, literal Dover Thrift Edition of *Hedda Gabler* provides her with the following line:

> HEDDA: Will you not take a glass of cold punch, gentlemen?

Aware of his own weakness, Eilert Løvborg declines but is egged on by Judge Brack:

> BRACK: Why, bless me – cold punch is surely not poison.[76]

What is noticeable here is the repeated use of the adjective 'cold' together with the drink that Hedda is offering her guests. Served on a hot summer's day, the use of 'cold' as in a 'glass of cold white wine' might seem more attractive than simply 'a glass of white wine'. But this hardly seems applicable to the scene in Hedda's drawing-room, nor does it seem likely that the adjective 'cold' would recur accidentally in a text written by such a fastidious craftsman as Ibsen, rarely putting a 'word' wrong. Instead, the mention of the drink in its cold, now new and sophisticated bottled form might be viewed as an indication of the lifestyle to which Hedda is accustomed and still aspires. Serving the drink in the newly popular fashion provides further evidence of her efforts to raise the social status of the Tesman household.

Another social/cultural translation problem in *Hedda Gabler* is the reference made throughout the play to Eilert Løvborg having 'vine leaves in his hair'. This key phrase is first used at the end of Act 2 when Hedda offers Thea Elvsted a cup of tea while the two women wait for Eilert Løvborg to return. In order to illustrate the shortcomings of the popularly held view that a word-for-word translation most closely reveals the intentions of the playwright, the version quoted here is the Dover Thrift Editions translation of *Hedda Gabler*. This series of translations of classic plays does not give the name of the translator and specifically states that the translation 'may be used in its entirety, in adaptation or in any other way for theatrical productions, professional and amateur, in the United States, without fee, permission or acknowledgement'. It is difficult to avoid forming the impression that the series has been prepared to give director and actors a free hand to transform the translated text into what they feel might make a more 'acceptable' performance text. While this approach may undoubtedly solve some problems inherent in translation for the stage, it does not constitute a *deus ex machina*, and leaves a number of problems unresolved:

> HEDDA: And then – at ten o'clock – Eilert Løvborg will be here – with vine leaves in his hair. [77]

The phrase is repeated in Act 3 when Tesman tells Hedda about the previous evening's gathering at Judge Brack's home. When Hedda enquires about the outcome of the evening, Tesman is forced to acknowledge that it ended in a drinking bout. Hedda then turns to Tesman enquiring about Løvborg:

> HEDDA: Had he vine leaves in his hair?

Hedda's question, not surprisingly, appears somewhat bewildering to Tesman:

> TESMAN: Vine leaves? No, I saw nothing of the sort.[78]

Later, in Act 3, the 'vine leaves' reappear yet again. Having lost his manuscript, his and Thea's 'child', Løvborg now threatens to 'put an end to it all'. At this point Hedda steps closer pleading with him:

> HEDDA: (*A step nearer him.*) Eilert Løvborg – listen to me – Will you not try to – to do it beautifully? [79]

Literally, in Norwegian, Hedda seeks his assurance that it will happen 'in beauty'; to which Løvborg answers with a smile, repeating the phrase 'in beauty' in Norwegian, here translated as 'beautifully':

> LØVBORG: Beautifully? With vine leaves in my hair, as you used to dream in the old days...

Hedda then replies:

> HEDDA: No, no. I have lost my faith in the vine leaves. But beautifully nevertheless...

And, later as Løvborg is about to leave, sticking the pistol that Hedda has handed him in his pocket, she repeats:

> HEDDA: And beautifully, Eilert Løvborg – Promise me that!

There are two problems here which Ibsen translators have to contend with and for which they have attempted to find their own different solutions; how to interpret the phrase 'vine leaves in his hair' and how to translate Hedda's suggestion that Løvborg puts an end to his own life 'in beauty'. In both cases, the expressions occur more than once, indicating that Ibsen must have used them for a specific purpose which in turn means that they should not just be paraphrased and buried in the text. Ibsen would not have repeated them throughout the play if he had not been pointing explicitly to some aspect of Hedda that makes her use these expressions.

Looking first at the second key phrase, Hedda's plea that Eilert Løvborg does it 'in beauty' constitutes a translation problem that does not lend itself to an easy solution. At the time Ibsen wrote the play, Hedda's insistence that Løvborg takes his own life 'in beauty' would not have seemed as puzzling as it does today. In 1889, only a year before *Hedda Gabler* was published, Elvira Madigan, a circus performer, and Count Sixten Sparre of Sweden had chosen to seek death in idyllic surroundings in Denmark rather than face the social consequences of their liaison. At the time, their tragic fate became the focus of newspaper reports as well as the subject of a popular ballad, and in 1972, close to a century later, their tragedy was turned into a film directed by the Swedish director, Bo Wideberg. The couple's decision to face death rather than bow to social conventions in turn mirrored another incident that had taken place only six months earlier. In what is known as the Mayerling tragedy,

Archduke Rupert, the Crown Prince of Austria, killed Marie Vestera, the woman he loved and then himself, in defiance of the Emperor's order that he end the liaison.

The phrase do it 'in beauty' appears to have caused problems in translation right from the start, from the first performance of *Hedda Gabler* on the English stage. William Archer translated the phrase as 'beautifully' which, however, developed into a bone of contention with 'Hedda', the actress Elizabeth Robins, who wanted to substitute 'gracefully' for 'beautifully' but Archer, as always committed to a close reading of Ibsen's texts, was not to be moved, and in the end managed to persuade Robins to accept 'beautifully'. In fact, Hedda's apparent obsession with 'the beautiful' was to become one of the targets of the anti-Ibsen campaign conducted by *Punch* in the form of parodies of his plays; these started to appear in 1891 and were the work of Thomas Anstey Guthrie, writing under the pen name of F Anstey. Guthrie was quick to seize on Ibsen's use of adjectives, pointing to what he viewed as an absurdly joyful morbidity, which included Hedda's fondness for 'beautiful deaths'.[80]

Another translation alternative for 'in beauty' is offered by John Osborne whose decision to use 'perfection' is not far off the mark semantically, although it fails to do full justice to the poetic tone of the original. Osborne's translation does not however accurately reflect Ibsen's repeated use of the phrase. Instead he alternates between 'perfection', 'perfectly' and 'beautifully':

> HEDDA: (*A step nearer.*) Eilert Løvborg, listen to me. When you do it, think of perfection.

And just before the end of Act 3:

> HEDDA: Beautifully, Eilert Løvborg. Perfectly. Promise me![81]

The allusion to past events, now long forgotten, and the awkwardness with which Ibsen's phrase translates into English combine to make 'do it in beauty' a well known stumbling block in *Hedda* translations. Another recurring key phrase, Eilert Løvborg's 'vine leaves', might pose an even greater challenge for the translator. As in the previous case, Ibsen chooses his words with care in order to tell us something about Hedda. When she refers to Løvborg wearing vine leaves in his hair she indicates yet again her yearning for beauty in a world she sees filled only with middle-class trivia.

In the discussion of Løvborg and 'vine leaves in his hair', Ibsen lets Hedda draw on not easily accessible linguistic as well as cultural aspects of Norwegian life. When first performed on stage in Munich and Copenhagen, Hedda's announcement that 'At ten o'clock Løvborg will be back with vine leaves in his hair' was reportedly met with peals of derisive laughter.[82]

What then is Hedda likely to be referring to when she talks about Løvborg shrouded in vine leaves? Sprinchorn suggests that what she has in mind is an image of Løvborg as the god Dionysus as painted by Nietzsche. In 1889, the year preceding the publication of *Hedda Gabler, The Twilight of the Gods* had appeared in print. Here Nietzsche describes his Dionysian superman as a 'highly cultured human being who, keeping himself in check and having reverence for himself, dares to allow himself the whole compass and wealth of natural being – a man to whom nothing is forbidden, except weakness...' [83]

But this godlike image is not the only interpretation to give to Hedda's choice of expression. Within the field of arts and humanities in Scandinavia, the degree of doctorate is symbolised not by donning a hat, but by a wreath of laurel leaves. Thus the reference to leaves crowning Løvborg's hair may also, at one time, have been Hedda's prediction of a future, brilliant academic career for the man acknowledged even by her husband as his foremost rival for the university post to which he himself aspires. It is also difficult to believe that Ibsen's choice of the name 'Løvborg' is accidental, given the care with which he assigned names to his characters. The name 'Løvborg' is yet another compound, the first part of which means 'leaves' while *borg*, the second part, is the Norwegian for 'fortress'. Implicit in Hedda's own, intimate description of her 'young God' there might also have been the acknowledgement of his Bacchanalian leanings, that among the academic 'leaves' making up the 'fortress' there were also other 'leaves'. It would seem much less likely, however, that Hedda would have been referring exclusively to this aspect of Løvborg's character as this would fail to explain her later statement that she has now 'lost faith in the vine leaves', that all she wants is for him to do 'it beautifully'. A predominantly Bacchanalian reading found early favour by the critics when *Hedda Gabler* was first performed in English and is also the interpretation chosen by John Osborne who replaces 'vine leaves in his hair' with 'wine and roses'. This may result, however, in an interpretation of upper class Hedda as being content to idle the days away while striving to stave off boredom which is in fact the description Osborne gives of her:

> LØVBORG: Perfection? (*He smiles.*) All wine and roses, as you liked to
>   say...[84]

Hedda's dilemma, Osborne states in his introduction to his version of *Hedda Gabler*, is one of boredom. His interpretation offers an interesting illustration of an adapter choosing to emphasise an aspect of a character in the work of a foreign playwright which has been singled out for attention in his own work rather than that of the original author.

A further problem in the translation of *Hedda Gabler*, as well as in other Ibsen plays such as *A Doll's House, Ghosts, The Wild Duck, Rosmersholm* and *The Lady from the Sea*, is the difficulty in capturing the distinction in the use of the formal/informal pronouns of address in Norwegian, corresponding to the you/thou distinction no longer observed in English. This is also a problem when translating from many other European languages. In *Hedda Gabler*, the change in the use of pronominal address is linked in an interesting way to movement on stage. Just as Ibsen makes use of verbal and psychological bipolarity, he also exploits the different dimensions of the stage, the action shifting between up and down. Thus, in the set for *Hedda Gabler*, there is a downstage area represented by a drawing room and an upstage area, the inner room, where just before the curtain goes down Hedda will shoot herself. This is Hedda's domain, her refuge, this is where she goes when her husband pleads with her to please his aunt and address her with *du*, the informal pronoun of address in Norwegian.[85] Hedda however, not only refuses to use the more intimate *du* when addressing others to whom she does not wish to become close, she also refuses to let others use it to address her. Thus when Eilert Løvborg attempts to address her with *du*, she rebukes him:

> LØVBORG: May I say *du* when we are alone?
> HEDDA: No. You may think it; but you mustn't say it.
> LØVBORG: Ah, I understand. It is an offence against George Tesman, whom you* love.[86]

In the Dover Thrift Edition, the asterisk following the word *you* refers to an explanatory note at the bottom of the page providing the information that from this point on Løvborg will use *De*, the formal pronoun of address in Norwegian when addressing Hedda. The same method of annotation is used in Act 1 of the Archer/Gosse translation when Hedda declines to use *du* to Miss Tesman. Trying to persuade her to be more approachable, her husband pleads with her: 'if only you could prevail upon yourself to say *du* to her.' Here the Archer/Gosse version provides a footnote, containing the following information:

> 1. *Du* = thou, Tesman means 'If you could persuade yourself to *tutoyer* her.'[87]

In a number of more recent translations, such as that by John Osborne, the solution found involves Hedda rebuking Løvborg for using her maiden name and not the one given to her by marriage:

LØVBORG: (*Who has not taken his eyes off her, quietly and slowly.*)
    Hedda Gabler!
HEDDA: (*Quick glance.*) Sh!
LØVBORG: (*Again quietly.*) Hedda Gabler.
HEDDA: (*Looking at the album.*) Yes that used to be my name, when we
    knew each other first.[88]

The problem of translating the Norwegian pronouns of address increases in difficulty, when the characters themselves become involved in discussions of the way they address each other. This, for instance, is the case in one of the scenes in *A Doll's House*, the play where Ibsen first appears to have made use of the distinction between the formal and informal use of pronouns of address to dramatic effect. In Act 2 a discussion takes place where Nora and Helmer are talking about Krogstad, the employee at the bank who, unbeknown to Helmer, is attempting to use an incriminating note signed by Nora to his advantage. Helmer is wary of Krogstad as he feels he is constantly causing him embarrassment by addressing him in public with *du*, the familiar pronoun of address. Allowing other employees to hear him addressed in this fashion by someone in an inferior position makes Helmer fear that his social standing amongst his peers is being challenged:

HELMER: We call each other *du*... He believes that gives him the right
    to use a familiar tone to me: so he keeps blurting out: *du, du*
    Helmer.[89]

In order to solve this problem, the American translator Rolf Fjelde draws on the familiarity achieved through the use of first names as opposed to surnames:

HELMER: We're on a first-name basis...and so every other second he
    comes booming out with 'yes, Torvald' and 'Sure thing, Torvald'.[90]

This may be a workable solution although it may not fully capture the high degree of intimacy which Ibsen signals must have existed in the past between Hedda and Løvborg; for two people at the time to address each other as *du* warranted a higher degree of intimacy than the mere use of first names.

Another linguistic feature absent in English, also contributing towards the problems facing the Ibsen translator, is the frequent use made of so-called particles. Norwegian, again like a number of other European languages, makes regular use of a set of monosyllabic words we may refer to here as particles, which subtly reflect the attitude of the speaker or, at other times, serve to elicit a particular response from the person spoken to. In regular use in Norwegian, most notably in the spoken language, particles such as *ja, jo, ju, så, nok, vel*, to mention but a few, occur with great frequency in dialogue and lack one-word equivalents in English. Attempts to transfer the meaning of these particles into English often yield stylistically awkward translations or, alternatively, they are missed out in translation. Failing to capture the right meaning of these little words in English translation has been quoted as one of the reasons for inaccuracy in the interpretation of much drama translation. In the case of Ibsen, Ackerholt discusses a line from *A Doll's House*, which contains the particles *dog* and *vel*:

> *De har dog vel tid et oyeblikk?*

> You have *dog vel* time for a moment?

As a translation Akerholt suggests:

> You have perhaps time for a moment? [91]

She acknowledges, however, the failure of her translation to capture the feeling of uncertainty and appeal expressed in Norwegian through the use of the two words *dog* and *vel*.

Particles modifying the meaning of what different characters say occur on more or less every page of an Ibsen play and, at times, are virtually untranslatable. One such case is found in the reconciliation scene at the end of *John Gabriel Borkman*, where Ella and Mrs B meet over the body of the man they both loved. In the original Norwegian, Ella's line contains the particle *nok*:

> ELLA: *Det var **nok** snarere kulden some draebte ham.*

> ELLA: It was **nok** rather the cold that killed him.

Her work with Peter Hall on the production of *John Gabriel Borkman* at the Old Vic in 1975 and at the Lyttelton in 1976 provided Inga-Stina Ewbank with the opportunity to compare ways in which different translators have attempted to solve the problem presented by the presence of *nok* in this sentence. Here *nok*, according to Ewbank, implies an 'opinion held guardedly but firmly and, as the sentence is constructed in the third person, held grammatically away from the speaker'.[92] However, the ways in which Ella's line has been reconstructed differ considerably in English translation. For instance, in Michael Meyer's version ' I think it was the cold that killed him', Ewbank hears a false note of first person speculation. Arvid Paulson's method-acting influenced translation, on the other hand, she feels 'really goes to town on that subjective speculative note, expanding Ibsen's eight words to fifteen and losing the rhythm of the dialogue altogether: 'I would say it was the – coldness – the coldness he felt that took his life'.' (See Chapter 9 for a discussion of the translation of particles in other European languages.)

An accurate interpretation and rendering of particles in translation into English is perhaps nowhere of greater importance than in the lines spoken at crucial points in Ibsen's dramas, such as the last line before the curtain goes down. In the final line of *Hedda Gabler* a particle occurs in the original Norwegian. After hearing the pistol shot from the adjacent room, in the original, and in the Archer/Gosse translation, Judge Brack says:[93]

> BRACK: (*Halvt afmægtig i lænestolen.*) *Men, gud seg forbarme – sligt noe gjør man da ikke!*

> BRACK: (*Half fainting in the armchair.*) Good God! – People don't do such things.

Although the Dover Thrift Edition aims to be a word-for-word rendering of Ibsen's text in English, it still differs in one important respect from the original: it contains no indication of the presence of the particle '*da*' in the Norwegian. As the anonymous translator has been at such pains to indicate in the form of footnotes in other parts of the translated text the problems in transferring Ibsen's text into English, the only possible conclusion to be drawn is that particles are not considered to be important. This tendency to handle the problem of particle translation by simply ignoring its presence can at times yield a happy solution: stress and pronunciation often succeed in capturing their subtle nuance in meaning. At other times, however, the failure to transfer a particular attitude expressed by a particle may result in an English translation missing out on a nuance. For example, the anonymous translator of the Dover Thrift Editions gives a translation of the last line in *Hedda Gabler* identical to that of the Archer/Gosse version above.[94]

Thus both translations read as if there is no particle present in Judge Brack's concluding line in Norwegian, yet if Ibsen had intended for Brack merely to make a comment, there would have been little point in including the particle *da*. Examining more closely the meaning of this word in Norwegian, we find that one of its functions is to help reinforce an expression of astonishment and incredulity. The feelings eliciting this reaction in Judge Brack may however, most easily be understood if we return briefly to the social context of Hedda's drawing room.

Beyond the Norwegian middle-class world of the late 1890s lay the world of the proud descendants of the Vikings. Replaced by the bourgeoisie, they had left behind only a few relics like Hedda. This middle class was itself divided, between a Bohemian group formulating its own code of ethics and the tradesmen whose middle-class values they rejected. In Hedda's drawing room we witness the two groups meeting head on. 'I only wanted to show,' Ibsen said, 'what results from the contact between two social classes that do not understand each other.'[95] While the Tesman family represents the middle-class at its best, Judge Brack typifies the Philistines, to the extent that even his name is the Swedish word *bracka* meaning Philistine. By possessing Hedda, truly cultured and in possession of what he himself lacks, Brack sees a chance to rise in social status, an ambition thwarted as Hedda, triumphant even in death, has the last word.

One of the reasons underlying the use of particles in conversation is the speaker's wish to involve the addressee, implicitly asking for their agreement. In other words, Brack may, rather than commenting on the situation, in fact be addressing Hedda.

A further observation has been made by Svetlana Klimenko, who has drawn attention to the fact that *'sligt noe'*, the phrase also contained in Brack's concluding line, is an expression that recurs throughout *Hedda Gabler*. It is in fact the most frequently repeated phrase in the play, used by different characters no less than twelve times.[96] Thea Elvsted uses the phrase to refer to her more than just casual relationship with Eilert Løvborg:

> Å, **sligt noe** kan jo ikke lægges dølgsmål på allikevel.

> Oh, there's no hiding **that sort of thing**, anyway.

Hedda also uses the phrase when talking to Brack about her rudeness to Miss Tesman:

> Ja, ser De, – **sligt noe** kommer over mig ret som det er. Og så kan jeg ikke lade være.

> Yes, you see, **that sort of thing** suddenly comes over me. And then I can't help myself.

She also uses it in her discussion with Brack about motherhood:

> Jeg har ikke anlegg til **sligt noe**, herr assessor.

> I've no aptitude for **that sort of thing**, Judge.

In addition, there are nine more instances of this key phrase, all used as in the case of Hedda and Thea whenever someone touches on a taboo subject or a topic too close for comfort. Among these, two lines, both of Judge Brack's, are of particular interest in the way they relate to his concluding lines at the end of the play. As Klimenko points out, the last line of the play is in fact similar to an earlier line of Judge Brack's when, in response to his advances, Hedda tells him that she would rather die than succumb to him. Brack responds in Norwegian:

> **Sligt noe** siger man. Men man gjør det ikke.

One *says* **that sort of thing**. But one doesn't *do* it.

The similarity with the concluding line of the play does not seem to be a mere coincidence:

Men, gud seg forbarme, – **sligt noe** *gjør man da ikke*!

But, God almighty... One doesn't *do* **that sort of thing**.

Just as Hedda admonishes Løvborg when he attempts to be too intimate and address her informally that he 'may think it but not say it', one may also 'say it but not do it'. We do know, however, that Hedda did do it. But then Hedda was never going to play it by the rules, her birth and upbringing had placed her above the rules dictating middle-class behaviour, the target of Ibsen's scorn as he was writing in his expatriate exile. Thus we seem to be faced with a variation on yet another key phrase, the impact of which, repeated twice within a short time span, is obviously going to lose some of its force if translated differently into English each time it is used. However, as shown by Klimenko's table of five translations of Brack's two lines, in the transfer from Norwegian into English, much of the rhythm of repetition and patterning has disappeared. Gone also is the obvious allusion to Judge Brack's previous exchange with Hedda, with Hampton's translation most closely capturing the repeated use of the same words contained in the two lines.[97]

IBSEN (1880) *Sligt noe* siger *man. Men man* gjør *det ikke.*
Men, gud seg forbarme, – sligt noe gjør *man da ikke!*

MEYER (1962) People say that. They never do it.
But, good God, people don't do such things.

FABER (1966) People say that, but they never do![98]
GoodGod! But people don't do things like that!

McFARLANE / ARUP (1966) People say such things. But they don't do them.
But, God Almighty...people don't do things like that!

HAMPTON (1972) People say things like that. But they never do them.
What do you mean, my God, people don't do things like that!

OSBORNE (1978) That's what people say. It's not the same as doing it.
God have mercy! People don't – DO that kind of thing.

In the English translation of the last of Judge Brack's lines, yet another hurdle remains. The Norwegian word '*man*' as used in this sentence corresponds to *man* in German, to *on* in French and, at times, 'one' in English. At other times 'people' may also be an appropriate choice. On this occasion, it was the word chosen by all the five translators in Klimenko's table. If, however, 'people' is replaced by 'one' and the particle *da* is rendered in English as is commonly the case by an added 'tag' such as 'you know', Judge Brack's line, with some 'padding' in brackets to bring out the underlying meaning more clearly, may be read as follows:

> BRACK: (But Hedda dear,) one (really) doesn't do that sort of thing, you know.

Viewed as a comment on the class-based doctrine that there are 'certain things one just doesn't do', Brack's words are addressed to Hedda; he is telling her that resorting to the use of a pistol is 'simply not on'. Nevertheless, he knows that she has upstaged him and his carefully laid plans: she remains, even in death, the undisputed winner as confirmed by Ibsen's choice of adjective in his stage direction describing Brack in the armchair. In the original Norwegian the word '*afmæktig*' means not only 'fainted', the description chosen by most translators, but above all 'powerless' and 'weak.'

By not playing by the rules, Hedda has deprived Brack of his power. For the concluding line of his play, Ibsen was never going to make it easy for his audience. It is elusive enough in Norwegian: to mediate it through translation into English is likely to require an über-translator.

Notes

1   J McFarlane (ed.), *The Cambridge Companion to Ibsen* (Cambridge, Cambridge University Press, 1994), p. xiv

2   B Hemmer, 'Ibsen and the realistic problem drama', in J McFarlane (ed.), *ibid.* p. 69

3   G Ackerman, *Ibsen and the English Stage 1889–1903* (New York and London, Garland Publishing, 1987), p. 18

4   E Durbach, 'A century of Ibsen criticism', in J McFarlane (ed.), *op. cit.* p. 233

5   *The Star*, 9 June 1889

6   R Buchanan, 'The modern drama and its critics', *The Contemporary Review*, 56, Dec 1889, pp. 908–25

7   Discussed in C Decker, *The Victorian Conscience* (New York, Twayne Publishers, 1952), p. 121

8   *Ibid.* p. 122

9   G Ackerman, *op. cit.* p. 52

10 *Ibid.* p. 15

11 N Å Nilsson, *Ibsen in Russland* (Stockholm, Almqvist & Wiksell, 1958), pp. 106–7

12 Cutting file, Houghton Library Theatre Collection: untitled clippings dated 30 May 1914

13 G Ackerman, *op. cit.* p. 143

14 For further quotations from press reviews see T Postlewait (ed.), *William Archer on Ibsen: the Major Essays, 1889–1919* (Westport, Conn., Greenwood Press, 1984), pp. 23–7

15 G Becker, *Documents of Modern Realism* (Princetown University Press, 1963), pp. 350–83

16 Discussed in G Ackerman, *op. cit.* p. 136

17 N Å Nilsson, *op. cit.* p. 85, ff

18 'On the Occasion of Hedda Gabler', *New Review*, June 1981. Discussed in G Ackerman, *op. cit.* pp. 203–6

19 T Postlewait, *op. cit.* p. 41

20 George Bernard Shaw, *The Quintessence of Ibsenism* (New York, Dover Publications, 1904), p. 57

21 Discussed in M Robinson, 'England's Ibsen, or performing Ibsen's dramas of contemporary life today', *Scandinavica*, 39(2), 2000, pp. 172–3

22 G Ackerman, *op. cit.* p. 257

23 *Ibid.* pp. 259–60

24 R Ferguson, *Henrik Ibsen. A New Biography* (London, Richard Cohen Books, 1996), p. 250

25 W Archer, *The Theatrical World for 1893* (London, 1893), p. 166. Discussed in G Ackerman, *op. cit.* p. 304

26 Discussed in G Ackerman, *op. cit.* p. 307

27 *Athenaeum*, 6 May 1909

28 G Marshall, 'Duse and Ibsen in the 1890s', in I-S Ewbank, O Lausund and B Tysdahl (eds.) *Anglo-Scandinavian Cross-Currents* (Norwich, Norvik Press, 1999), pp. 207–8

29 E Bredsdorff, *Sir Edmond Gosse's Correspondence with Scandinavian Writers* (Copenhagen, 1960). Discussed in O Lausund, 'Edmund Gosse: Ibsen's first prophet to English readers', in I-S Ewbank, O Lausund, B Tysdahl (eds.) *op. cit.* p. 149

30 G Ackerman, *op. cit.* p. 319

31 *Ibid.*

32 N Å Nilsson, *op. cit.* pp. 53–62

33 A Miller, 'Ibsen and the drama of today', in J McFarlane, *op. cit.* p. 229

34 'The Wild Duck', *The Theatre*, 1 June 1894, p. 330

35 Discussed in G Ackerman, *op. cit.* p. 346

36 *Ibid.* p. 415

37 C Archer, *William Archer: Life, Work and Friendships* (Yale University Press, 1931), pp. 261–2

38 G Ackerman, *op. cit.* pp. 445–7

39 E Charteris, *The Life and Letters of Sir Edmund Gosse* (London, Collins, 1931), pp. 42–3.

40 A Thwaite, *Edmund Gosse: A Literary Landscape*, (Oxford, Granite Impex, 1984), p. 2

41 'Belles Lettres', *Westminster Review*, March 1891, pp. 347–8

42 T Postlewait, *Prophet of the New Drama. William Archer and the Ibsen Compaign* (Westport, Conn., 1986), p. 123

43 Discussed in T Postlewait, *ibid.* p. 6

44 E Robins, *Ibsen and the Actress* 2nd Series, XV (London, Hogarth Essays, 1928), pp. 15–16

45 E Le Gallienne, *Eight Plays by Henrik Ibsen* (New York, McGraw-Hill, 1992), Introduction, p. viii

46 Discussed in G Ackerman, *op. cit.* p. 239

47 'On the Occasion of Hedda Gabler', *New Review*, iv, June 1891

48 *Three Danish Comedies* (Heiberg, *No*; Holberg, *Jeppe of the Hill*, *The Scatterbrain*), trans. M Meyer, (London, Oberon Books, 1999)

49 T Postlewait, *op. cit.* p. 167

50 Henrik Ibsen, *Plays: Three* (*Rosmersholm*, *The Lady from the Sea*, *Little Eyolf*), trans. M Meyer, (London, Eyre Methuen, 1980), p. 267

51 J Northam, *Ibsen, A Critical Study* (Cambridge, Cambridge University Press, 1973), pp 201–2

52 R Ferguson, *op. cit.* p. 264

53 A Miller, 'Ibsen and the drama of today', in J McFarlane (ed.) *op. cit.* pp. 228–9

54 Henrik Ibsen, *Collected Works* (*Samlade værker* (*SV*) (Vol. V), 1907), p. 137. Translations are my own unless otherwise indicated.

55 Henrik Ibsen, *Hedda Gabler* (Dover Thrift Editions: New York, Dover Publications, 1990), p. 49

56 Henrik Ibsen, The Oxford IBSEN (Vol. VII): *The Lady from the Sea*, *Hedda Gabler*, *The Master Builder*, ed. J McFarlane , trans. J McFarlane and L Arup (London, New York, Toronto, Oxford University Press, 1966), p. 236

57 *Strindberg's The Father and Ibsen's Hedda Gabler*, adapt. J Osborne (London, Faber and Faber, 1989)

58 Henrik Ibsen, *Hedda Gabler*, adapt. J R Baitz, from a trans. by A-C Hanes Harvey (New York, Grove Press, 2000), p. 69

59 Ibsen SV, *op. cit.* p. 107

60 Henrik Ibsen, *An Enemy of the People*, trans. C Hampton, (London, Faber and Faber, 1997), pp. v-vi

61 T Postlewait, *op. cit.* p. 284

62 George Bernard Shaw, *Our Theatres in the Nineties*, III, (London, Constable, 1948), pp. 32–3

63 Henrik Ibsen, *Plays: One (Ghosts, The Wild Duck, The Master Builder)*, trans. M Meyer (London, Methuen Drama, 1980), pp. 201–2

64 I-S Ewbank, 'Ibsen on the English Stage: the proof of the pudding is in the eating', in E Durbach (ed.) *Ibsen in the Theatre* (London: Macmillan, 1980), pp. 41–3: translation by Ewbank.

65 *Ibid.* p. 42

66 B Hemmer, 'Ibsen and the realistic problem drama', in J McFarlane (ed.), *op. cit.* p. 83

67 Henrik Ibsen, *A Doll's House*, trans. M Meyer, with Commentary and Notes by Nan Worrall (London, Methuen, 1985)

68 Henrik Ibsen, *A Doll's House*, adapt. F McGuiness (New York, Dramatists Play Service, 1998), p. 67

69 I-S Ewbank, *op. cit.* p. 31 ff.

70 J Inverne, *Jack Tinker. A Life in Review* (London, Oberon Books, 1997), p. 119

71 M Egan, *Ibsen: The Critical Heritage* (London, Routledge, 1972), p. 189

72 E Sprinchorn, 'The unspoken text in Hedda Gabler', in F J Marker and C Innes (eds.) *Modernism in European Drama: Ibsen, Strindberg, Pirandello, Beckett* (Toronto and London, Toronto Press, 1998)

73 Ibsen trans. McFarlane and Arup, *op. cit.* p. 32

74 *An Enemy of the People*, trans. C Hampton, *op. cit.* p. 12

75 Ibsen, *Plays: One*, trans. M Meyer, *op. cit.* p. 124

76 *Hedda Gabler*, Dover Thrift Editions, *op. cit.* p. 35

77 *Ibid.* p. 45

78 *Ibid.* p. 49

79 *Ibid.* p. 59

80 T Rem, 'Cheerfully dark: Punchian parodies of Ibsen in the early 1890s', in I-S Ewbank, O Lausund, B Tysdahl (eds.) *op. cit.* pp. 215–18

81 *The Father* and *Hedda Gabler*, adapt. J Osborne, *op. cit.* pp. 125–6

82 W Brachvogel, *Hedda Gabler in München. Freie Bühne für Modernes Leben*, 21, (1891), pp. 117–18; E Davidsen, *Henrik Ibsen og Det Konglige Teater* (Copenhagen, 1980), p. 177. Discussed in E Sprinchorn, *op. cit.* pp. 54–5

83 Discussed in E Sprinchorn, *op. cit.* p. 50

84 *The Father* and *Hedda Gabler*, adapt. J Osborne, *op. cit.* p. 125

85 E Sprinchorn, *op. cit.* pp. 42–3

86 *Hedda Gabler*, Dover Thrift Editions, *op. cit.* pp. 37–8

87 Henrik Ibsen, *The Collected Works* (Vol. X): *Hedda Gabler, The Master Builder*, trans. E Gosse and W Archer (New York, Charles Scribners' Sons, 1907), p. 27

88 *The Father* and *Hedda Gabler*, adapt. J Osborne, *op. cit.* p. 101

89 Discussed in R Amundsen Le Maire, 'Ibsen's use of the pronouns of address in some of his prose plays', *Scandinavica* 20 (1), 1980, pp. 43–61

90 Henrik Ibsen, *Four Major Plays* (*A Doll's House, Ghosts, Hedda Gabler, The Master Builder*), trans. Rolf Fjelde (New York, Signet Classics, 1965), p. 78

91 M B Akerholt, 'Henrik Ibsen in English translation', in O Zuber (ed.) *The Languages of Theatre. Problems in the Translation and Transposition of Drama* (Oxford, Pergamon Press, 1980), p. 43

92 I-S Ewbank, 'Ibsen's language: literary text and theatrical context', in G K Hunter and C J Rawson (eds.) *The Yearbook of English Studies* (London, Modern Humanities Research Association, 1979), p. 107

93 *Hedda Gabler*, trans. Gosse and Archer, *op. cit.* p. 185

94 see *Hedda Gabler*, Dover Thrift Editions, *op. cit.* p. 172

95 E Sprinchorn, *op. cit.* p. 45

96 S Klimenko, 'Who killed Hedda Gabler? Playing the evidence of discourse against the alibi of the *mise en scène*', *Assaph. Studies in the Theatre*, 16, 2000, pp. 34–6; author's translation

97 *Ibid.*

98 Henrik Ibsen, *Hedda Gabler*, adapt. M Faber (London, Heinemann, 1966)

Chapter 4
ANTON CHEKHOV

DURING THE FIRST HALF of the nineteenth century, the Russian stage began to attract the attention of major writers such as Griboedov, Lermontov and Gogol. Alexander Griboedov (1795–1829) inaugurated a tradition of bitter comedy which, considering that he was writing in the age of Scribe, was characterised by a striking simplicity of plot. Griboedov died young, as did Mikhail Lermontov (1814–41), but Lermontov's early works such as *Lyudi i strasti* (*Men and Passions*, 1830) and *Strannyi chelovek* (*A Strange Man*, 1831) reveal that a Russian trend towards realism had emerged as early as the 1830s. A landmark play of this period was *Revizor* (1836) by Nikolai Gogol (1809–52), which had as its subject small town corruption as revealed by the arrival of a man mistakenly believed to be the Inspector General. Better known in English as *The Inspector General* or sometimes *The Government Inspector*, the play was only saved from the clutches of the censor by the Tsar's presence and enjoyment of the play at its opening at the Alexandrinsky Theatre: it was later to become firmly established in the Russian repertory.

The development of social comedy from Griboedov to Chekhov reached its zenith with Gogol. However, the half-century that separated Gogol from Chekhov was a period which also saw the work of Ivan Turgenev (1818–83), Alexander Ostrovsky (1823–86) and Leo Tolstoy (1828–1910). Turgenev's early theatrical experiments had a marked romantic flavour: in 1848 he completed *Nakhlebnik* (*The Parasite*) and a year later, *Kholastyak* (*The Bachelor*), both comedies showing the influence of Gogol. His only major play is *Mesyats v derevne* (*A Month in the Country*, 1850), a psychologically complex comedy about love. Owing to the censor and the play's departure from the traditionally burlesque style of comedy, it did not have its first successful production until 1879, when it baffled audiences as well as critics with the newness of its form. Turgenev, however, was primarily a novelist and his masterful novel, *Ottsy i deti* (*Fathers and Sons*, 1862), remains an outstanding example of nineteenth-century Russian realism.

The central figure in Russian theatre in the 1860s and 1870s was Alexander Ostrovsky: with the great majority of Ostrovsky's plays dealing with common people, the end was now in sight for aristocratic comedy. The process of democratisation of Russian theatre had begun, the concern for the 'lower orders' reflecting changes in society at large that had transformed the old way of life in Russia. Ostrovsky's first play, *Nesostoyatelnyi dolzhnik* (*The Bankrupt*, 1847), later reworked as *Svoi lyudi – sochtemsya* (*It's a Family Affair – We'll Settle It Ourselves*, 1850), was a vicious satire on the merchant class and was banned from production by the censor. After the emancipation of the serfs in 1861, Ostrovsky moved towards a style of drama that 'attempted a more subtle exposition of the conflict between the new industrial age and the stagnation of the old world', a theme reflected in *Groza* (*The Storm*, 1860).[1]

Another important writer at this time was Leo Tolstoy. In addition to the moralistic adaptations of his own stories for the stage in the 1880s and 1890s, Tolstoy also wrote *Vlast' t'my* (*The Power of Darkness*, 1886), a true drama remarkable for its 'illusion of life', the hallmark of his novels. Not surprisingly, his gloomy portrayal of Russian peasants as murderers and villains fell foul of the censor and the first performance of *The Power of Darkness* took place in translation into French in 1888 at Antoine's Théâtre Libre in Paris. The year that he wrote *The Power of Darkness* Tolstoy also began working on *Plody prosveshcheniya* (*The Fruits of Enlightenment*), a light comedy exposing the idle nobility as more superstitious than their supposedly ignorant servants. It was presented for a private performance at the Hunter's Club in Moscow in 1891 and was later included in the national repertory.

Towards the end of the century, the Imperial Theatres offered a repertory including, on the one hand, Griboedov, Gogol and Ostrovsky, and, on the other, classical European playwrights such as Shakespeare, Molière, Hugo and Schiller. The everyday theatrical fare, however, consisted partly of translations of Scribe, Dumas *fils* and Feydeau, and partly of plays written by a group of Russian writers often referred to by theatre administrators as 'our own playwrights'. Prominent among these playwrights were 'authors of spiritless concoctions made to please this or that actor and especially officials of the Imperial Theatrical Administration'.[2]

However, under the pressure of public opinion and progressive men in the theatre, including Ostrovsky, the monopoly of the Imperial Theatres was abolished. As from 1882, private theatrical enterprises were allowed throughout the Empire. Nevertheless, the effects of the abolition of the monopoly were not felt until the early 1890s, leaving the Imperial Theatres to continue their stranglehold upon the theatrical life of Russia. During the second half of the nineteenth century the most important among these theatres was the Maly Theatre, generally viewed as the citadel of realism. Principles of realism were not, however, always applied to the style of acting. In the performance of the foreign classics, in particular, the acting style was characterised by dated French techniques involving shouts and whispers, gesticulations and conventional postures. But change was on its way and towards the end of the 1890s accepted theatrical practice was to come under serious scrutiny.

The change came with the creation of the Moscow Art Theatre (MAT), which turned Moscow into the new centre of the naturalistic movement. In 1897, Nemirovich-Danchenko (1858–1943), playwright, director and teacher, and Konstantin Stanislavsky (1863–1938), actor and director, met in a restaurant at the Slavyansky Bazaar in Moscow. Following an eighteen-hour conversation they were ready to present a manifesto demanding a new kind of theatre that would dispense with the French and German farces, the actor star system and the old declamatory acting style.

These changes, which were embraced by the MAT, were to help ensure the success in 1898 of *Chaika* (*The Seagull*, 1896) by Anton Chekhov (1860–1904). While the staging of the play two years earlier at the Alexandrinsky Theatre in St Petersburg had thrown Chekhov into despair, the production of *The Seagull* at the MAT in 1898 inaugurated a new era in Russian theatre.

Although plays by Chekhov, the dramatist who changed the face of European theatre, have appeared more frequently in performance on the English stage than any other Russian playwright, the Russian dramatists foreshadowing Chekhov's work have not been strangers to the English stage during recent decades. In March 1979, the National Theatre at the Olivier staged Leo Tolstoy's *The Fruits of Enlightenment* and, in the late 1980s, when greed and conniving go-getters were lampooned on stage, around the time of Caryl Churchill's *Serious Money*, Ostrovsky enjoyed a vogue with the staging of Cheek by Jowl's *A Family Affair* and the Old Vic production of *Na vsyakogo mudretsa dovol'no prostoty* (*Too Clever by Half*, 1868).

The late 1990s saw renewed interest in Russian drama. In November 1998, the Almeida Theatre presented Ostrovsky's *The Storm*. Early the next year, the London theatre had the opportunity to enjoy a Russian week with Gorky's *Vassa* (*Vassa Zheleznova*, 1909) at the Albery Theatre and Ostrovsky's *Les* (*The Forest*, 1871) at the National Theatre, which opened at the Lyttelton on 28 January, adapted by the English playwright Alan Ayckbourn. In his article on Ostrovsky's play about two itinerant, free-spirited thespians who turn the country estate of tight-fisted widow Raisa Pavlovna upside down, Paul Taylor did not find it hard 'to hear faint pre-echoes of those axe blows at the end of

The Cherry Orchard (written 33 years later), or see Vosmibratov as a forerunner of Chekhov's Lopakhin'.[3]

Turgenev, on the other hand, has paradoxically been placed in the situation whereby the term Chekhovian is often applied to his comedy, *A Month in the Country*, although it was written 46 years before Chekhov wrote *The Seagull*. In Turgenev's play, Belyaev, a new tutor, causes turmoil when he arrives on the Islayev country estate, becoming the object of the affections not only of Natalya, an older woman, but also her seventeen-year-old ward, Vera. Recent productions of *A Month in the Country* include productions at the Albery Theatre in 1994 and a Royal Shakespeare Company production in 1998. Ironically, as was pointed out by Richard Freeborn, translator of the text used in the 1994 Albery Theatre production, which starred Helen Mirren as Natalya and John Hurt as Rakitin her faithful admirer, the play's belated success is due to the popularity of Chekhov's work and the ensemble playing of the MAT.[4]

Brian Friel expressed similar sentiments in his introduction to the Royal Shakespeare Company performance programme for his adaptation of *A Month in the Country*, which opened at the Swan Theatre on 25 November 1998:

> [Turgenev] fashioned a new kind of dramatic situation and a new kind of dramatic character where for the first time psychological and poetic elements create a theatre of moods and where the actor resides in informal emotion and secret turmoil and not in external events. We now have a name for that kind of drama: we call it Chekhovian.

Among Russian writers following after Chekhov, Maxim Gorky (1868–1936) displayed the most pronounced Chekhovian influence in his plays, clearly discernible in *Dachniki* (*Summer Folk*, 1904). This play, about the emergence of a new class of professionals in Russia and the conflict of values facing them, has had several successful London stagings during the last few decades, including a critically lauded National Theatre production at the Olivier in 1999, in an English version by British playwright Nick Dear.

In the case of Chekhov, it was his style as a dramatist that was revolutionary. Even though Ibsen was the first playwright to gain gradual acceptance for the theatre of naturalism, he found it difficult to throw off the shackles of some of the old theatrical conventions completely. His social drama required a stage environment of the greatest possible realism but Ibsen still tended to continue, structurally, to adhere to the principles of the well-made play. It was left to

Chekhov to take the decisive step beyond Ibsen, jettisoning the last remnants of closely-knit plot structure and renouncing the convention of characters attempting to explain themselves to the audience. A scientist and a physician, Chekhov rebelled against the artificiality of conventional dramatic structure. Rather, life should be as it is and people as they are. In real life, people engage in eating, drinking, and flirting while, at the same time, making their fortunes or ruining their own lives. Everything on stage should be just as simple or as complicated. Portraying life as it is, Chekhov's drama rejects moralising, just as it eschews the neat solutions required by the playwrights of traditional drama. With Chekhov, 'open form' entered the theatre. His renunciation of rhetorical explicitness also went much further than Ibsen's attempts at realistic dialogue. Seemingly casual conversations, silences and hesitations in his characters' speech resulted in a new kind of stage language, a new form of poetry. Capturing the lyrical nuances of the language of the moment is, however, far from easy. Nor, paradoxically, is it easy to reproduce on stage the ordinariness and triviality of everyday life. Combined with the absence of a defined plot and the emphasis on 'situation', these factors all contributed initially to Chekhov's plays meeting with grudging acceptance, not only in translation, but even when they first appeared on the Russian stage.

With the failure of *The Seagull* in its St Petersburg performance in 1896, barbed comments directed at Chekhov's attempts to reproduce life on stage started to appear in the Russian press. Voiced in particular by conservative theatregoers favouring the *scènes à faire*, curtain lines and 'messages' of the well made-play, the criticism intensified after the success of *The Seagull* at the MAT in 1898 and Chekhov's appointment as its house playwright. Burenin, a former colleague of Chekhov's at *Novoe Vremya* (*New Times*), and himself a well-established playwright and writer of verse, declared Chekhov to be 'the minstrel of hopelessness'.[5] The general air of muted despondency associated with Chekhov's plays was further propagated by the style of the productions at the MAT. As staged by Stanislavsky, Chekhov's attempts to reproduce real life on stage found naturalistic expression in the form of attenuated pauses and authentic sound effects such as birds singing and crickets chirping. Chekhov himself registered his objections to what he saw as misinterpretations of his dramatic intentions. His protests were in vain; the elegiac mood created appealed to the patrons of the MAT, the cultivated merchant class and the intelligentsia, and helped to 'sell' his plays. Translated into English, he emerged as the playwright of lyrical elegies and 'the voice of twilight Russia'.[6]

At the time of his death on 15 July 1904, Chekhov was still a shadowy literary figure in England as well as in America. Still, a year later, in 1905, a company led by Paul Orlenev and Alla Nazimova arrived in New York, bringing with them a repertoire that included Ibsen's *Ghosts* and *The Seagull*. In Chekhov's play, Arkadina and Trigorin, a popular actress-writer couple, are so oblivious to the needs of others that they make innocent victims of Konstantin, Arkadina's son, and Nina, a young actress infatuated with Trigorin. Orlenev, who had managed to get *Ghosts* past the Russian censors for his love of the part of Oswald in Ibsen's play, now proclaimed that he was to 'make suffering fashionable in America'.[7] On 22 December, *The Seagull* was performed in Russian with a synopsis provided for the occasion. What struck the reviewers about the performance was the co-ordination and unity of the Russian acting which, according to the *New York Sun* at the time, 'it has in common with all the best European acting, but which is as yet rare in this country'.[8] In a sense, this can however, only be described as a false start since no further practical interest was aroused: *The Seagull* was not to be performed in English in New York until 1916. It did, however, reach the Royalty Theatre in Glasgow on 2 November 1909, the first Chekhov play to be performed in English translation in the UK. The translation was by George Calderon who also directed the play. Calderon, who had lived in St Petersburg from 1895 to 1897, was a playwright himself, profoundly interested in new European drama. He is reputed to have brought his own creative touch to the translation, and in the preface to his own version of *The Seagull* for Peter Hall's production at the Old Vic in the spring of 1997, Tom Stoppard refers to Calderon's translation as having been singled out by Russians as 'the closest to the original in letter and spirit'.[9]

Before the opening of *The Seagull*, Calderon had given a lecture on Chekhov's work, which might have helped to shape the critics' surprisingly positive responses, willingly attributing any puzzling features to the play's 'Russianness'. However, while *The Seagull* may have succeeded in Glasgow, there was little hope of it being considered for a transfer to a London stage. Instead *Medved* (*The Bear*, 1888) a one-act farce, was the first Chekhov play to face a London audience in a professional theatre. It ran from 13 to 20 May 1911 at the Kingsway Theatre. Again, the play's 'foreignness' resonated in the press, the *Morning Post* commenting on 'the application of the methods of conventional English farce to a work possibly conceived in a quite different spirit'.

In 1923, twelve plays by Chekhov were published in two volumes in translation by Constance Garnett. It is not known when Garnett translated the plays but, like Calderon's translation, they seem to have been available in manuscript form during the first decade of the century. Bernard Shaw, a friend of Garnett, finally succeeded in persuading The Incorporated Stage Society to put on her translation of *Vishnyovyi Sad* (*The Cherry Orchard*, 1904). The play opens on the spring morning of Ranveskaya's arrival at her estate and closes with her return to Paris, precipitated by the sale of the estate including its cherry orchard. It was performed on Sunday 28 and Monday 29 May 1911 in a production described by Bernard Shaw to Constance Garnett as 'the most important in England since that of *A Doll's House*'.[10] Unfortunately, Shaw's enthusiasm was not shared by audiences. Containing a considerable proportion of the intellectual elite of Edwardian London, they appear to have been so bored by the production that almost half left the theatre before the final curtain. The general opinion was that the actors did not know what they were doing, yet the reviewers did not put the blame on them, or on the director. Instead it was more or less felt to be the fault of the 'Russianness' of the play. According to *The Times* on 30 May 1911:

> The fact is, when actors are set to present alien types which they have never seen and which they can only imagine from the necessarily imperfect indications of a translation, they are bound to produce grotesques.

The difficulty for English actors in portraying Russians appears to have continued in the next Chekhov production presented by the Incorporated Stage Society at the Aldwych Theatre on 10 and 11 May 1914. In *Dyadya Vanya* (*Uncle Vanya*, 1896) Chekhov made use of a theme not unlike that of *The Seagull*, as Serebryakov, a retired professor and Yelena, his beautiful twenty-seven-year-old wife, return to the family estate for a visit to its less fortunate inhabitants, only to leave them once again to pick up the pieces of their shattered lives. By now Uncle Vanya and Astrov are both in love with Yelena, while Sonya's secret love for Astrov has been shown to be unrequited.

Many of the London reviews of the play echoed the sentiments expressed by the *Daily Chronicle,* which on 12 May 1914 declared that this was 'not a play that suits the practical optimism of our English temperament'. According to the *Daily Express*, the spirit of the English was simply not attuned to the 'grey, hopeless, depressing picture of Russian middle-class life'. And on 23 May, the *Academy* voiced the view that the play 'belonged to a world apart from ours, to a state of mind as foreign to that of Western or Southern Europe as it is possible to find'. With World War I casting its shadow over the production, some critics also decried the play's 'lack of action'; the only character with whom they were able to feel any rapport was Sonya. 'For Sonya,' wrote the *Times* on 12 May, 'and Sonya alone does something.' For similar reasons, concern at the time was being voiced in the American press about *The Seagull* and Konstantin's vacillations. With Russia a potential ally in the war, a number of critics found 'pussy-footers' like Konstantin setting a dangerously feeble example to contemporary youth. As a critic in the *New York Herald Tribune* on 24 May 1916 wrote:

> Theodore Roosevelt would undoubtedly be intensely annoyed by *The Seagull*, but fortunately the Russia of the day's cablegrams is so far from the Russia of *The Seagull* that it is doubtful if the play will continue to be nationally true when the war is over.

A few years after World War I, the first English language production of *Tri Sestry* (*Three Sisters*, 1900) took place. In this play, the last of Chekhov's 'major' plays to reach Britain, the arrival of the army and its subsequent departure from a small provincial town leaves an indelible mark on the lives of Olga, Masha and Irina. The play was staged on 7 and 8 March 1920 at the Royal Court Theatre, and on 19 March received the following, crucial notice in the *Atheneum*:

> It makes no difference that the scene is laid in a provincial Russian town in an environment fantastically unlike anything of which we know... The fundamental truthfulness is always there, and even in the moment of almost farcical exaggeration we recognise the features of life as we have lived it.

Chekhov's world had started to become part of the English consciousness.

For the intelligentsia, the war had brought about a loss of interest in the social issues made popular by Ibsen's plays; instead they now turned to Chekhov. To those who regarded the Russian Revolution and Soviet egalitarianism as symbols of a new world order, Chekhov became either a prophet of that order as in *The Cherry Orchard* or a chronicler of decadent bourgeois provincialism as in *Three Sisters*. On 25 May 1925, the Oxford Players' production of *The Cherry Orchard* opened at the Lyric Theatre, Hammersmith, with John Gielgud as Trofimov. One month later, on 22 June, the play transferred to the Royalty Theatre, arguably helped more by the vogue for things Russian than the production itself.

During the 1920s, the staging of Chekhov's plays also gained in popular appeal owing to the arrival in England of Theodore Komisarjevsky, a Russian émigré director reportedly highly amused by the 'highbrow' seriousness with which Chekhov's work was treated on the English stage. Deciding that the English needed a different Chekhov, Komisarjevsky had Trigorin, Tusenbach and Trofimov played as romantic leads. In addition, he emphasised the pauses, soaking the stage in moonlight or shadowy silhouettes resulting in 'an almost underwater atmosphere'.[11] Lifting Chekhov out of his previous English gloom,

Komisarjevsky's production for the Stage Society of *Uncle Vanya* on 27 and 28 November 1921, translated by Constance Garnett, was a considerable success. Four years later, on 7 and 8 December 1925, Komisarjevsky directed *Ivanov* (1887) for the Stage Society at the Duke of York's Theatre. The first performance of the play in English, it was greeted by the critics with considerable interest. With great praise bestowed upon the direction, Komisarjevsky now moved on to directing the rest of the ongoing Chekhov season at Barnes, and on 23 December 1925, a recast *Ivanov* opened a series of Chekhov productions which were to hold a legendary place in British theatrical memory. Shortly after *Ivanov*, on 16 January 1926, Komisarjevsky's production of *Uncle Vanya* opened, followed on 16 February 1926 by *Three Sisters*, with John Gielgud in the role of Tusenbach.

Although by 1929 popular with the intelligentsia, it was not until a third phase, extending from 1930 to 1945, that Chekhov's plays in English translation became firmly established in the dramatic canon and moved from being the exclusive property of an intellectual elite to popular masterpieces. Actors, for whom Chekhov's plays had always held an appeal, now returned to his work after becoming established as cinema or stage idols, and the public followed. The period also saw stage directors of repute, both in England and America, leave their mark on some memorable Chekhov productions, such as the 1930 *Cherry Orchard* at the Old Vic directed by Tyrone Guthrie. The battle for acceptance as part of the theatrical canon had been won and Chekhov was sitting increasingly securely on his 'classical' pedestal.

The view of Chekhov as the 'voice of twilight' and the set of early notions associated with the epithet 'Chekhovian' carried over into the latter half of the twentieth century. The first student role of actor and writer Peter Ustinov was that of Waffles in *Leshy* (*The Wood Demon*, 1889), a production that he later referred to as 'all twilight impression'. Ustinov continued to reinforce this view in the comic review *Swinging the Gate*, where, in the role of a Russian professor jealous of Chekhov's success, he appears 'so academic that the need for mystery totally escaped him'.[12] Convinced that Chekhov was equivalent to 'mystery', it was Ustinov's belief that:[13]

> His plays are not so much dialogues as many intertwined monologues,
> plays in which people talk far more than they listen, a technique which
> illuminated all the bittersweet selfishness and egotism in the human heart,
> and made people recognise, if not themselves, at least each other.

During the latter part of the twentieth century, the popularity of Ustinov's 'bittersweet' Chekhov of 'intertwined monologues' has steadily increased to the point that Chekhov in translation now ranks second only to Shakespeare in the number of English-speaking performances staged. As a partial explanation of his ever-growing popularity, it has been suggested that successive English translations of his plays have been instrumental in transforming his description of the human condition into an account of 'the plight of the middle classes'. As in the case of the early MAT performances in Russia, appreciatively embraced by moneyed theatre audiences, present-day Chekhov productions in translation are primarily aimed at members of the English middle classes. Aware of the way Chekhov has been appropriated by predominantly English middle-class theatregoers, British playwright Trevor Griffiths has tried to redress the balance in his own version of *The Cherry Orchard*. The first extract that follows is a faithful translation by Elisaveta Fen,[14] followed by an example of Griffiths' attempt at 'de-bourgeoising' Chekhov. The subject is the incapacitation of the Russian intelligentsia:

TROFIMOV: They all look very grave and go about with grim
   expressions on their faces, and they only discuss important matters
   and philosophise. Yet all the time anyone can see that our work-
   people are abominably fed and have to sleep without proper beds,
   thirty or forty to a room, with bed bugs, bad smells, damp and
   immorality everywhere.

TROFIMOV: Of course, they can look as grave as anyone and talk about
   important matters and make metaphorical speculations with the
   best, while all around them, right beneath their eyes, the workers eat
   scraps of rancid meat and sleep on bare boards thirty or forty to a
   room. Bedbugs, shit, leaking roofs, moral degradation.

The Anglicisation of Chekhov has, according to Susan Bassnett, reached the point where

English translations of Chekhov have established a conventional way of
reading his works that has resulted in a major shift of meaning and an
alteration of the ideological basis of Chekhov's thinking. The acculturation
process has domesticated the Russian writer and shifted the focus away
from the Russian-bound aspects of his work. What we have, therefore, is
not a Russian but an English Chekhov, and it is this playwright, invented
through the translation process, whose work has entered the English
literary system.[15]

Today's Chekhov on the English stage has become so Anglicised that 'English Chekhov' has even been turned into an export product. At the international congress *Theatre and Text* in 1996, Howard Barker represented new British drama with his own *Uncle Vanya* and, a year later in 1997, David Hare represented Britain with *Ivanov* at the Moscow Arts Centre.[16] Nor does interest in Chekhov seem to be lacking among the younger generation of British playwrights who find in his plays themes of immediate application to their own situation. In the opening and closing scenes of *Shopping and Fucking*, Mark Ravenhill has Lulu express her yearning for a different life by reciting Irina in *Three Sisters*:[17]

> LULU: One day we'll know what all this was for, all this suffering, there'll be no more mysteries, but until then we have to carry on living...we must work, that is all we can do. I'm leaving by myself tomorrow, I'll teach in a school, and devote my whole life to people who need it. It's autumn now, it'll soon be winter, and there'll be snow everywhere but I'll be working...yes, working.

Paradoxically, given his present status in the English speaking world, Chekhov himself made little attempt to encourage translation of his work. With Russia not party to international copyright treaties, there was little financial inducement. He also believed that his characters had little in common with the English. This, combined with the initial lukewarm interest of English critics and theatres in contrast to those in Germany and Central Europe, resulted in English being one of the last major languages into which Chekhov's work was translated.[18]

While the quality of some of the early translations was not of a high level, from 1916 a comprehensive, 13-volume set of Chekhov's stories began to appear in translation by Constance Garnett (1861–1946), also, as we have seen, the translator of some of Chekhov's plays. As a translator of the old school, Garnett, like Archer, appears to have been an early adherent to Stoppard's 'ledger principle' (see Chapter 1). Below is a passage translated by Garnett, followed by a slimmed down version:[19]

> But in this case there was still the diffidence, the angularity of inexperienced youth, an awkward feeling and there was a sense of consternation as though someone had suddenly knocked at the door.

> But here was all the shyness and awkwardness of inexperienced youth: a feeling of embarrassment, as though someone had knocked on the door.

Garnett often reproduces Russian syntax and vocabulary literally, producing a translation that is faithful to the original text rather than performance-friendly. This is a characteristic shared not only with Archer, but also with a number of other early twentieth-century translators of modern drama into English. It was to take until the influence of modern linguistics in the latter part of the twentieth century, before the differences between spoken and written language and the prescriptive notions of 'good' and 'bad' English were explored systematically and replaced by a more objective, descriptive approach to language. As a result, it is not surprising that while William Archer has been criticised for writing in Victorian English, Garnett has also at times been described as writing in a timeless nineteenth-century language. Of greater importance, however, is the claim that Garnett often misses out on Chekhov's humour, as well as his literary allusions and references to folklore present in his original Russian text. Lack of awareness of these aspects does not, however, seem to be a problem confined to Garnett. According to F K Bristow, a comparison of nine renditions of a Russian proverb shows only the one by Ronald Hingley clearly conveying the point intended by Chekhov. The proverb is used early in *The Cherry Orchard* by Lopakhin who equates both his character and situation 'with a pig's snout in a row of bakers' stalls'. In chronological order from 1912 to 1966, the year the list was compiled, the following suggestions were available:[20]

CALDERON	a silk purse out of a sow's ear, you might say
GARNETT	like a pig in a bun shop
YOUNG	like a pig rooting in a pastry shop
YARMOLINSKY	a pig in a pastry shop, you might say
MAGARSHACK	like a jackdaw in peacock's feathers
CORRIGAN	like a crown in peacock's feathers
DUNNIGAN	like a pig in a pastry shop
HINGLEY	*barging in like a bull in a china shop* [italics added]
GUTHRIE	talk about a pig in clover

While during the first part of the twentieth century translation of Chekhov's works was the exclusive domain of linguists, the last few decades have seen a number of British playwrights engaged in preparing new versions of his plays for performance on the stage. If the playwright commissioned to do the work has no knowledge of Russian, the new version is based on a translation of the original. Increasingly the name of the originator of this translation is being acknowledged.

In the introduction to her version of *The Seagull*, Pam Gems demonstrates, using one of Masha's lines, the different options available to the playwright working from an already provided translation of the original:[21]

MASHA: Speak to my father yourself. I am not going to. Spare me, please.

But, Pam Gems asks, who is Masha – a plain speaking girl with some social status, and therefore might say instead:

> MASHA: Please be good enough to speak to my father yourself. Do not, pray, request me to do it.

Or she might possibly say:

> MASHA: Do not involve me if you please. I suggest that you give my father the message yourself.

Or she might even say:

> MASHA: Be good enough not to ask me. Please tell my father yourself.

Pam Gems considers all of these translations to be adequate enough renditions. The problem is that when spoken on the stage they do not convince us that Masha uttered them. Instead, Pam Gems gives Masha yet another version of the line:

> MASHA: Speak to him yourself, I'm not going to…honestly.

Pam Gems' preference for the last line may be explained by a closer look at the way speech is processed in tone groups in English. A short stretch of speech spoken with a single intonation contour is found in for instance:

⌐‾‾‾‾‾‾‾¬
What time is it? [22]

Thus Pam Gems' line naturally forms three tone groups:

⌐‾‾‾‾‾‾‾‾‾‾¬ ⌐‾‾‾‾‾‾¬ ⌐‾‾‾‾‾¬
Speak to him yourself, I'm not going to…honestly.

This in turn makes the line fit in more naturally with the way speech is processed in English, giving it a familiar feel to the actress in the role of Masha.

In the 1950s, the Armed Forces Joint Service Courses produced competent Russian translators including the playwright Michael Frayn, fitting the bill of the playwright combining dramatic skills with knowledge of the foreign language. Below is Michael Frayn's translation of the exchange between Masha and Medvedenko, the well-known opening lines of *The Seagull:*

> MEDVEDENKO: Why do you always wear black?
> MASHA: I'm in mourning for my life. I'm unhappy. [23]

In her translation of the opening lines in *The Seagull*, Pam Gems' rearrangement of sentences and sentence elements continues to show her linguistic awareness of ease of utterance for actors:

> MEDVEDENKO: You're always in black. Why?
> MASHA: Because I'm unhappy. I'm mourning for my life. [24]

In his discussion of his 1997 version of *The Seagull* for Peter Hall's Old Vic production, Tom Stoppard sums up the written text versus performance approach by first posing the question: for whom is the translator working? He then provides his own answer: the translator is working for the actor. Stoppard commends Pam Gems for her English version of the opening lines of *The Seagull*, acknowledging that his own intuitions would have led him to the same English rendition. Confronted with the problem of turning a line containing the Russian word meaning 'antediluvian' into an actable English equivalent, Stoppard also pays his respects to Frayn. Actors are more likely, Stoppard acknowledges, to welcome Frayn's line, 'You *keep* as*k*ing me about people who *c*ame out of the Ar*k*' with its series of recurring 'k' sounds than Stoppard's own 'f' series in '…people *f*rom be*f*ore the *F*lood.[25]

While dialogue in translation needs to be actable, lines couched in too familiar a form of English may miss the target. If, for instance, the language of Chekhov's characters were to be too closely associated with the English as spoken in the Home Counties, connotations may be evoked unintended by either playwright or director. Some Irish playwrights have tried to solve this problem by changing the setting of Chekhov's plays to Ireland, which enables them to use Hiberno-English as a linguistic alternative to standard spoken English. English as spoken in Ireland is a distinctive form of speech which reflects the influence over many centuries of cohabitation with the Irish language as well as having developed at a different pace and in different ways from the speech of mainland England. In his translation of the opening lines of *The Seagull*, Thomas Kilroy's version staged at the Royal Court Theatre in 1981 shows the influence of spoken Hiberno-English:

> JAMES: And why is it that you're always wearing black?
> MARY: It's because I'm so sad. Black is for sadness.[26]

Joseph Long points out that modelled on the Irish, Hiberno-English is rich in verb forms which serve to express diverse aspects of verbal action, such as the durative or the habitual. In the line Kilroy gives Medvedenko, here James, the continuous present is used to mark a habitual aspect, i.e., 'you're always wearing black', quickening the pace in comparison with the more standard 'Why do you always wear black?' [27]

Shortly afterwards, Kilroy has Masha, now Mary, use the continuous future, as, looking towards the platform, she says:

> MARY: We'll soon have the play starting…[28]

Again, Hiberno-English differs from Standard English:

> MASHA: (*Looking round at the improvised stage.*) The show will be starting soon. [29]

Another construction widely used in Hiberno-English is the type of question formation used by James, 'And why is it…', as well as Masha's answer 'It's because…'. When for example Dr Hickey, Chekhov's Dorn, is offered flowers, he exclaims: 'Ah, now, is it for me they are…?'[30] Through this consistent use of linguistic features characteristic of Hiberno-English, Chekhov's *Seagull* becomes an Irish *Seagull*. While set in the period of time for which it was originally written, the play is transported to another geographical setting with the language used in the translation contributing to the overall process of its 'Hibernisation'. In this way, a distance from the text is maintained, which avoids false cultural associations and, at the same time, allows the nuances of the original to emerge.

An important aspect of Chekhov's impact on modern drama is his use of dialogue and the way he succeeds in conveying the feelings that lie hidden beneath the words. Not only have English playwrights assimilated Chekhov's ideas; in the case of dramatists such as Harold Pinter, Chekhov's pauses, silences and undercurrents of meaning[31] have been further developed. Here is an example from *The Birthday Party*:

> STANLEY: You know what? To look at me, I bet you wouldn't think I'd led such a quiet life. The lines on my face, eh? It's the drink. Been drinking a bit down here. But what I mean is…you know how it is…away from my own…all wrong, of course…I'll be all right when I get back…but what I mean is, the way some people look at me you'd think I was a different person. I suppose I have changed, but I'm still the same man that I always was. I mean, you wouldn't think, to look at me really… I mean, not, really, that I was the sort of bloke to – to cause any trouble, would you? (*McCANN looks at him.*) Do you know what I mean?[32]

In the case of Pinter's writing, directors seem to have little doubt about the importance of the presence of pauses in his writing. Here is Peter Hall on the subject:

> [T]he first thing I say to actors when we're beginning a Pinter play is, 'Look, don't mislead yourselves into thinking that if there's a pause there, there shouldn't be a pause there, or, if there's a silence, there shouldn't be a silence, because there should. Our job is to find out why. And don't, in order to make it comfortable, turn a full stop into a comma, or break it up in a colloquial way different to the way he's written it.'

And on the importance of the difference between Pinter's use of pauses and silences and other forms of punctuation, Peter Hall has the following to say:

There is a difference in Pinter between a pause and a silence and three dots. A pause is really a bridge where the audience think that you're this side of the river, then when you speak again, you're the other side. That's a pause. And it's alarming often. It's a gap, which retrospectively gets filled in. It's not a dead stop – that's a silence, where the confrontation has become so extreme, there is nothing to be said until either the temperature has gone down, or the temperature has gone up, and then something quite new happens. Three dots is a very tiny hesitation, but it's there, and it's different from a semicolon, which Pinter almost never uses, and it's different from a comma. A comma is something that you catch up on, you go through it. And a full stop's just a full stop. You stop. [33]

Peter Hall's comments clearly show the importance of different types of punctuation in the plays by Harold Pinter. But while the significance of dots and pauses in the plays by Pinter is acknowledged, their presence in the work by European playwrights in English translation is not always met with the same degree of attention. Chekhov makes frequent use of pauses within as well as at the end of sentences. Crucially important, they may for example serve to indicate that a character is unwilling to reveal something for emotional reasons or that someone, due perhaps to lack of education, is unable to put their emotions into words because they are simply not at their disposal. How then do translators deal with this problem when transferring Chekhov's dialogue from Russian into English? A comparison of different translations of an extract from the beginning of Act 2 of *The Cherry Orchard* yields some interesting observations:[34]

Chekhov:

DUNYASHA: (Smushchenno.) *Khorosho...tol'ko snachala prinesitye mnye moyu tal' mochku... Ona okolo shkapa...tut nyemnozhko syro...*
YEPIKHODOV: *Khorosho-s...prinesu-s... Teper' ya znayu, chto mnye delat' s moim revol'verom...*

English translation:

DUNYASHA: (*Embarrassed.*) All right...only first fetch my cloak... You'll find it by the cupboard...it's rather damp here...
YEPIKHODOV: Very well, ma'am...I will, ma'am... Now I know what to do with my revolver...

Elizaveta Fen:

DUNYASHA: (*Embarrassed.*) Very well then...only will you bring me my little cape first... It's hanging beside the wardrobe. It's rather chilly here...

YEPIKHODOV: Very well, I'll bring it... Now I know what to do with
my revolver.

Michael Frayn:

DUNYAHSA: (*Embarrassed.*) All right – only first fetch my cloak. You'll
find it by the cupboard. It's rather damp here.
YEPIKHODOV: Now I know what to do with my revolver.

Ronald Hingley:

DUNYASHA: (*Embarrassed.*) Very well then, only first go and get me
my cape. You'll find it in the cupboard or somewhere. It's rather
damp out here.
YEPIKHODOV: Oh certainly, I'm sure. At your service. Now I know
what to do with my revolver.

In Elizaveta Fen's translation, virtually all the ellipses are observed. Michael
Frayn, on the other hand, appears to have gone for a middle-of-the-road approach,
omitting all pauses, except in one instance providing a single dash. In Ronald
Hingley's version all ellipses have been eliminated. Since Fen's translation
strategy in general is one of not straying too far from the original, her approach
seems likely to have been dictated by faithfulness to the source text. The
factors influencing the choices made by the other two translators can only be
surmised. Eliminating the ellipses undoubtedly makes the translation appear
less foreign but then Michael Frayn is painstakingly faithful in other aspects
of his rendering of the Russian text into English. A possible explanation might
be that pauses, interruptions and tailings-off used in order to point to underlying feelings and reactions might seem too 'foreign' a convention in a play
text intended for English speaking actors, an impression further supported by
Michael Meyer's observations with respect to Strindberg. The translation by
Peter Gill, another English playwright/director, for the production at the
Riverside Studios in 1978, and in a revised version performed by the RSC at
the Swan Theatre in 1995, would support an interpretation that ellipses,
Pinter apart, do not feel comfortable to English actors:

DUNYASHA: Oh, yes. Would you get my shawl first. It's by my
cupboard. It's getting damp. Would you?
EPIHODOV: Your shawl. Of course. Certainly. I'll go now. Don't say
another word. Where's my revolver? Oh, here it is. Yes, well I'll be
needing that.[35]

In contrast, David Mamet, one of the foremost American exponents of
present-day Chekhovian style of dialogue, uses a mixture of repetitions,
insertions and ellipses:

DUNYASHA: (*Sighs.*) Alright. Alright. Get me my, but get me, my scarf, will you. By the door. It's getting...

YASHA: 'Endless misfortune.' Between you and me...

YEPIKHODOV: Yes Ma'am. Yes I will. Yes I will...and now: Where's my revolver...[36]

As indicated by Peter Hall in his discussion of Pinter's use of dots and pauses, their existence is undoubtedly of importance to a director. They may, however, not always be in the best interest of the actors, in whom their presence may bring out less than emotionally subtle interpretations of their parts (see Michael Meyer, Chapter 5), and translators, in particular if they are also directors, may view an adjustment of punctuation in order to lower the emotional temperature as part of the process of Anglicisation (see also translation of Italian and Spanish drama in Chapters 7 and 8).

On 1 January 2000, the worldwide press reported Boris Yeltsin's decision to resign from his post as president of Russia. His resignation speech addressing the Russian people was translated into a number of different languages. A sample paragraph from the translation of Yeltsin's 'I Have Made a Decision' in the *New York Times* shows a display of emotion pitched at a level unlikely to be found in a speech made by an American president or an English prime minister:

> Today it is important for me to tell you. The pain of each of you has called forth pain in me, in my heart. Sleepless nights, tormenting worries – about what needed to be done, so that people could live more easily or better. I did not have any more important task.

And Yeltsin concludes:

> Bidding farewell, I want to tell each of you: Be happy. You deserve happiness. You deserve happiness and calm. Happy New Year! Happy New Century, my dear ones!

Although western politicians are no strangers to the use of superlatives, they would be less likely to verbally convey the emotions expressed in Yeltsin's speech. In translation into English, Russian volubility which may express itself in rapid transitions from 'laughter to tears', can at times come across as overemotional.[37] Being over-effusive about life or talking idealistically or hopefully about the future seems to constitute a potential source of embarrassment in an English-speaking context, not infrequently resulting in difficulties for directors, actors and audiences with Chekhov characters such as Vershinin,

Tusenbach or Trofimov in translation. According to John Cleese, in an interview:

> The English are not terribly good at taking things seriously... Qualities that are elsewhere esteemed – the ability to make money, the possession of a first-rate intellect, any kind of emotion – are in Britain regarded as regrettable flaws. The well-bred Briton is allowed only two emotional attributes – modesty and a sense of humour.

The ponderousness of many Russian texts in translation is hardly compatible with this modesty to which the English aspire, often resulting in suppressed audience laughter, as in *The Cherry Orchard* at Anya's 'good-bye, house, good-bye old life' and Trofimov's 'And welcome, new life'.[38] Given these differences between Russian and English moods and manners, what then is the explanation of the success of 'English Chekhov'?

In evoking the past in order to envisage a different and better future, Chekhov seems to have succeeded in striking a universal chord, in expressing an emotional need which continues to manifest itself in new adaptations of his work throughout the world, often revealing as much about the country in which they have been adopted as they do about Chekhov and Russia. In England, looking forward to the past developed into a more pronounced sentiment in the period following World War II. This was a time when the English would look back to their pre-war days, to the glorious days of turn-of-the-century England. Even John Osborne's *Look Back in Anger*, in itself a rejection of Edwardian nostalgia, ends up describing in nostalgic terms the very sentiments it purports to reject:

> The old Edwardian brigadiers do make their brief little world look pretty tempting. All home made cakes and croquet, bright ideas, bright uniforms. Always the same picture: high summer, the long days in the sun, slim volumes of verse, crisp linen, the smell of starch. What a romantic picture.[39]

Added to the nostalgia, the sense of isolation suffered by the inhabitants of Chekhov's world has also helped to foster the now well-known Chekhovian mood of elegy. Although frequently interpreted in English translation as a purely philosophical concept, for Chekhov's original characters Russia's size makes geographical isolation a real and concrete concept.[40] When Irina in *Three Sisters* complains of boredom it is because of the nature of provincial life, not helped in winter which tends to curtail social life, factors affecting everyday English life to a much lesser degree. To the rural dwellers of northern Europe, accustomed to fighting a more unaccommodating climate, they are, however, only too familiar.

Given the rapid changes taking place during the twentieth century,

Chekhov's plays have increasingly served as a dramatic vehicle for expressing the conflicting forces between present, past and times to come. 'The Cherry Orchard' writes Robert Brustein, 'is like a sponge in the way it picks up the juices of the environment in which it is produced, like a barometer in the way it records the social-aesthetic pressures of current times.'[41]

The wistful, nostalgic aspect of Chekhov's plays and, to many Russians, their over-emphasis on 'fantasising' have been ascribed in part to factors related to translations and partly to factors related to differences in linguistic structure between Russian and English. In the extract below, to take just one example, Uncle Vanya paints a picture of 'what could have been':

> UNCLE VANYA: I first met her ten years ago at my late sister's. She was seventeen and I was thirty-seven. Why didn't I fall in love with her then and propose to her? It *would have been* the easiest thing in the world! And now she *would have been* my wife... Yes... We *would have woken up* together from the storm. She *would have been* frightened by the thunder, and I *would have held her* in my arms and whispered, 'Don't worry, I'm here'. What a marvellous thought. [italics added] [42]

In Russian, the conditional tense corresponding to '*would have been* the easiest thing', 'now she *would have been* my wife' etc., is simply expressed through the use of *by*, one small word placed either before or after the main verb in the past tense, to indicate that the action is unreal or imagined. Translation of the passage into English, reproducing dutifully every occurrence of the conditional marker, results in an abundance of 'would be' and 'would have been'. This in turn means using considerably more words than in Russian in order to express the conditional, that is the 'fantasising' aspect of Uncle Vanya's speech. While the same sentiment is expressed in both languages, the use of only one form of the conditional makes the 'if only' aspect hammered home relentlessly in English.

In similar fashion, the translation of the future tense can also result in the repeated use of the same verb form in translation between Russian and English. In Russian, the 'future perfective' is used to describe a completed action, while the 'future imperfective' serves to indicate an unfinished, continuous or repeated action. However, only the 'future imperfective' is expressed through the use of the modal verb *budu*, as in *ya budu rabotat*, which is used in a similar way to the English use of modals, as in 'I *will* work'; the 'future perfective' conjugates without the use of a modal verb, as in *ya prorabotayu*.

Returning now to *Three Sisters* and to Irina's speech quoted by Ravenhill, a closer study of the text shows that there are altogether eight instances of separate verbs pointing to the future, such as 'there'll be', 'I'm leaving', 'I'll be working' etc. in the English translation:

> One day *we'll know* what all this was for, all this suffering, *there'll be* no more mysteries, but until then *we'll have to* carry on living...we must work, that is all we can do. *I'm leaving* by myself tomorrow. *I'll teach* in a school, and devote my whole life to people who need it. It's autumn now, *it'll soon be* winter, and *there'll be* snow everywhere but *I'll be working*...yes, working. [italics added] [43]

In the Russian original, a number of the verb forms used are in the 'future perfective', expressed only through the use of a prefix to the verb. In English, on the other hand, the use of the modal results, through its repeated use, in focusing attention more relentlessly on the notion of trying to escape the present and fleeing into the future.

A further difference between the Russian verbal system and that of English may also account for the switch from plain factual assertion in the original to a more elevated stylistic variant in English translation. In certain situations in Russian, forms of the verb 'to be' may be left out. When for instance, in *The Seagull*, towards the end of Act 3, Arkadina tries to leave in order to remove her lover from the dangerous proximity of young Nina, Trigorin says in a word-for-word rendering from the Russian:

> TRIGORIN: So to go. Again carriages, stations, buffets, chops, conversations.

In translation into English, however, the grammatical requirements necessarily result in Trigorin's observations appearing in more embellished form.

Pam Gems:

> TRIGORIN: So, we're on the move again...railway stations, refreshment bars, mutton chops and conversation... [44]

Tom Stoppard:

> TRIGORIN: So – off on our travels again. Railway carriages, railway stations, railway cutlets...conversations in compartments... [45]

Stephen Mulrine:

> TRIGORIN: So, we're off again? More railway carriages, stations, buffets, veal cutlets, conversations... [46]

Peter Gill:

> TRIGORIN: So we're ready to go then. More railway carriages, more stations, more station buffets, more mutton chops, more conversations... [47]

It is not difficult to see here how different translators have grappled with Trigorin's line, trying to make it roll off the English actor's tongue more easily. Stoppard chooses to make repeated use of 'railway' and, characteristically, cannot resist an attempt at comic relief in joining 'railway' and 'cutlet'. He also helps the last noun, 'conversation', to go down more easily by combining it alliteratively with 'compartment'. In dialogue, however, the effect in English is not so much of characters engaging in conversation as of offering their individual views about life, while inhabiting parallel worlds, 'from which they now and then emerge, give names to a couple of things, and dive away again, behind dots and dashes, leaving their sentences incomplete'.[48] This particular form of verbal exchange characteristic of Chekhov translation appears to have developed into a style of its own, leaving its mark on the work of English writers. J B Priestley openly acknowledged that he set about to recreate, in his use of English syntax, the effect of people as 'fish swimming in different coloured bowls'.[49]

However, not all syntactic differences between Russian and English have succeeded in making an innovative contribution to English literary language. In three of Chekhov's four major works, the title, the very first words to meet the translator's eye, presents a significant obstacle in translation. As Russian does not make use of articles such as 'the' and 'a(n)' in English, *chaika* may be interpreted either as 'a seagull' or 'the seagull', *vishnevyi sad* either as 'a cherry orchard' or 'the cherry orchard' and *tri sestry* either as 'three sisters' or 'the three sisters'. In the last case, this ambiguity is reflected in the different choices of an English title by translators. In addition to the more commonly found *Three Sisters*, there are also examples of *The Three Sisters*, as for instance David Mamet's 1990 version. The problem here is that the function of the 'the' in English is to pinpoint a noun or nouns as referring to something specific. As a result, if the article 'the' is used as in *The Three Sisters*, the finger points more specifically to three particular sisters stifling in the dreariness of provincial Russia, whereas the absence of the article helps to widen the application, extending the feelings of boredom to express a more universal longing away from the here and now. In the case of *Chaika*, a translation as *The Seagull* also leads to loss of universality and in this case tends to reduce the symbol to a specific seagull. When, for example, just before the curtain goes down in *The Seagull*, Nina applies the epithet *chaika* to herself, is she referring to *the* bird that had been shot two years previously or to the general vulnerability of *an* innocent bird such as herself who has ended up in the

141

firing line of a self-centred cynic such as Trigorin. The answer is likely to be that Chekhov had *both* in mind, but as nouns in English need to be preceded by articles, the ambiguity of the Russian cannot be retained in English translation. Instead English translators must make a choice resulting in different, individual solutions. For example, Pam Gems:

> NINA: I'm so tired…I just want to rest…rest! (*Raises her head.*) *The* seagull, that's me…no, that's not right. I'm *an* actress. Well – yes.

Nina then proceeds to describe Trigorin's lack of interest in the theatre and how this overall cynical approach made her lose faith in her own ability to act. She continues:

> NINA: Me – *the* seagull. No, that's not right…remember, you shot *a* seagull? A man comes by and destroys it, just for idleness. An idea for a short story…no, that's not right…[50]

In Tom Stoppard's version, the reference to the bird is also kept in the definite form.

> NINA: If only I could rest – I need rest! I'm *the* seagull – but I'm not really, I'm *an* actress. Yes.

And, later, after she hears the sound of Arkadina's and Trigorin's laughter:

> NINA: *The* seagull. No, that's *not* me… You remember how you once shot *that* seagull? A man happened to come along and see her, and having nothing much to do, destroyed her? Idea for short story… Wrong story, though.[51]

Peter Gill on the other hand chooses to use the indefinite article 'a' in both instances.

> NINA: I'm so tired. If only I could rest. (*Raising her head.*) I'm *a* seagull. No. That's not it. I'm *an* actress. Oh, well.

Later on Nina continues:

> NINA: I'm *a* seagull. No, that's not it. Do you remember when you shot *a* seagull? 'By chance, a man comes along and, for want of anything better to do, he destroys her'. A subject for a short story? That's not it.[52]

Here Chekhov has used the syntactic resources of Russian to great dramatic effect; the conditions of a particular situation or person may be interpreted as applying to the particular and, at the same time, the universal. In English, on the other hand, the need for articles and the necessary choice between the definite and the indefinite tends to stifle open-endedness and with it the ambiguity that gives life to drama.

A further problem facing the Chekhov translator is the extensive use of diminutive forms in conversational Russian in order to show a higher degree of personal and emotional involvement in what is being said. These diminutives have their roots in colloquial language, in particular the folk idiom, from which they have spread into literary language. In English, however, the process of 'diminutivisation' is normally only used to indicate a reduction in size as in 'booklet' from 'book' or 'kitchenette' from 'kitchen': the number of commonly used diminutive forms in English, excluding proper names, is limited. By comparison, the number is very much larger in Russian. Out of 25,000 of the most frequently used Russian words, more than a thousand nouns and adjectives are or can be used in the diminutive.[53] In addition to indicating size, these diminutive forms fulfil a number of other functions in Russian: they may be used by a speaker to express certain feelings towards the person who is being addressed or towards the subject spoken about. In this way, a range of subtle feelings such as tenderness, affection or admiration may be expressed. Moreover, they may also be used to indicate adverse reactions such as disparagement, irony or condescension. While most diminutive suffixes are associated with positive emotional attitudes, only a few are exclusively associated with the expression of negative feelings. However, diminutives with one and the same suffix may sometimes have either positive or negative shades of meaning. (For a discussion of diminutives presenting similar problems in translation from Spanish, see Chapters 7 and 9.)

Another difficulty relating to diminutives facing the translator is the escalating degree of expressiveness that they may convey. For example, while the diminutive ending *ka* attached to the Russian word for 'book', *kniga*, resulting in *knizhka*, can express a nuance of scorn, the use of *-onk-* (that is, *knizhonka*) also shows a personal interest in the subject. Diminutives of the highest degree of expressiveness lose their connection with the meaning of simple diminutives and serve as a means to express positive emotions, much used when referring to food and drink, and inseparably linked to the accompanying use of emphatic intonation. In the case of drama, diminutive forms provide a powerful tool for playwrights to reveal a range of different aspects of their characters' personalities. In addition to emotional attitudes, excessive use of diminutives may be a marker of low social status, limited education or just poor taste.

In translation into English, the subtle shades of Russian diminutives are usually conveyed through the use of nouns and adjectives. But while the number of diminutive suffixes that can be used for the purpose of expressing emotional attitudes to other humans or objects in Russian are many and varied, equivalent words and expressions are less numerous in English. As a result, what frequently emerges in English translation is a less original word or colourful expression. Conversely, straining to ensure that the original meaning is preserved at all costs and manifested in the translation, that is, applying Stoppard's 'ledger principle', may result in an equally strained translation.

Examples of blandness in the translation of Russian diminutives are often found in the English rendering of endings used to express love and affection. Act 1 of *Uncle Vanya* opens with Marina, the old nurse, offering some tea to Astrov. Addressing Astrov, Marina uses the word *batyushka* containing the suffix *–shka*, a term in Russian used to address a venerable older male person. In translation into English, however, options are more limited, mostly centring on variations on the theme of 'dear'. In Elisaveta Fen's translation, Marina opens the play with the following line:

MARINA: Drink it, dearie. [54]

Pam Gems' National Theatre version does not differ greatly:

MARINA: (*Proffers tea.*) Here you are, my dear. [55]

When Astrov declines her offer, Marina proceeds to raise the ante, this time offering him some vodka. In the original Russian, she adds a diminutive suffix to the word 'vodka', resulting in her now enticing him to have, in close translation, 'nice little vodka', just as in English a motherly female might offer 'a nice cup of tea'. But while the phrasing in Russian points to Marina's maternal feelings towards Astrov, mixed with her attitude towards vodka, little indication of these sentiments appears in English translation:

Elisaveta Fen:

MARINA: Perhaps you'd like a drop of vodka?

Pam Gems:

MARINA: Would you like a drop of vodka?

For the translator, the most difficult aspect of the process of 'diminutivisation' in Russian might be the way suffixes can be used creatively, the means whereby individual speakers are free to make up new expressions by drawing on a wide range of words which can be associated with different degrees of affection and intensity. When for instance, in Act 2 of *The Cherry Orchard*, Dunyasha and Yasha, the two servants, engage in affectionate conversation, Yasha kisses

Dunyasha, calling her what in translation from the Russian amounts to 'little cucumber/gherkin'.

The use of 'gherkin' as an endearment in Russian is likely to be more closely associated with something nice to eat, in particular when pickled and served with vodka, rather than the vegetable as such. However, such pleasant connotations are less readily available to English speakers, and a look at some translations of Dunyasha's epithet reveals obvious reservations on the part of the translators to use a reference to a vegetable as a term of endearment. In Elisaveta Fen's translation the vegetable has turned into a fruit and Dunyasha is referred to as 'little peach',[56] while in Michael Frayn's version Yasha says to the chambermaid, 'Real country pippin, aren't you?'[57] Robert Brustein, basing his adaptation on George Calderon's translation, follows Fen and lets Yasha tell Dunyasha that 'you're a real peach'.[58] David Mamet, on the other hand, prefers the use of a vegetable reference although rejects 'gherkin' and instead settles for 'My little cabbage',[59] while Trevor Griffiths remains faithful to the original Russian image and lets Yasha call Dunyasha his 'little cucumber'.[60]

The practice of making up new terms of endearment out of nouns and adjectives in Russian is matched by the numerous variations on names which Russians use when addressing one another. Working between Russian and English, the translator is often faced with the task of trying to find English equivalents for the wide range of variations on names created by the addition of suffixes.

In order to signal an emotional stance towards the person addressed, Russian speakers can draw on a wide range of suffixes, which they can attach to proper nouns. Whereas a particular set of diminutive endings are commonly used among members of the family, other circumstances warrant a different kind of suffix. In *Three Sisters* only the nurse Anfisa refers to Irina as Irinushka and Olga as Olyushka. Anfisa has worked for the family for thirty years, looking after and helping to bring up the three sisters since the days they were born. Such is the sisters' bond with Anfisa that when Natasha, their sister-in-law, suggests that Anfisa must leave, Olga reacts strongly. The intimacy of their relationship is shown by Anfisa's use of the diminutive forms of the three sisters' names. Although in translation into English, different terms of endearment may be used, successful renderings of the degree of emotional depth in the original is a less straightforward task.

Before the revolution, at the time Chekhov was writing, the choice of names that could be given to a Russian child was limited to a list of saints' names that had been approved by the Eastern Orthodox Church. Each saint had his or her day on the calendar and those who had been named after a particular saint celebrated this day, their name-day, as well as their birthday. Name-days were viewed as a collective social occasion, while birthday celebrations tended to be viewed as more personal or individual. When *Three Sisters* opens Olga is telling us that 5 May is Irina's name-day. Given the lack of attention paid to English name-days, many translators have chosen to turn Irina's name-day into a birthday, as for example the American translator Richard Nelson:

> OLGA: One year ago on this very day, May fifth, – on your birthday, Irina – Father died.[61]

David Mamet also opts for this solution:

> OLGA: Well. I'm going to tell you. It's funny the way time does pass. Here we are. The same day. One year later. Irina. And the anniversaries. Irina's birthday and the day of Father's death.[62]

This is also the solution chosen by Brian Friel:

> OLGA: It's hard to believe it's only a year since Father's death, isn't it? Twelve months to the day. The fifth of May. Your birthday, Irina.[63]

In his American translation, Lanford Wilson, on the other hand, prefers to remain faithful to the original concept, reminding the audience that they are watching a foreign play:

> OLGA: Father died a year ago today, May fifth, your Saint's Day, Irina.[64]

The given name in Russian may also be used in combination with a patronymic, which is formed from the father's given name to which endings are added. If, for example, a woman's given name is Anna and her father's name is Ivan, in polite and respectful conversation, she may be addressed as Anna Ivanovna. In Elisaveta Fen's translation, as Chebutykin enters the drawing room of the three sisters, Irina greets him as Ivan Romanych, a shortened colloquial form of Romanovich:

> IRINA: Ivan Romanych, dear Ivan Romanych![65]

Brian Friel, on the other hand, goes for full Anglicisation, turning Irina's line into an alliterated version:

> IRINA: Dear, darling, dopey Doctor![66]

Retaining the Russian form of address in English translation has the advantage of reminding the audience that they are watching a foreign play, of anchoring the action on stage more firmly in the setting in which it takes place. The disadvantage, however, in repeated uses of name and patronymic is the burden it places on the actors in remembering and pronouncing correctly foreign words. This seems to be the reason underlying Stephen Mulrine's decision to simplify the use of first name and patronymic, the Russian polite mode of address in his translation of *The Seagull*.[67] The acculturation of Russian names on stage may also be motivated by concern for theatre audiences, facilitating comprehension of plot. The problem of committing to memory Russian names in their varying degrees of complexity was an aspect of Russian plays in English translation that met with early unfavourable critical reactions. According to the American critic George Jean Nathan, Russian drama meant a stage 'inscrutably occupied by Mishka Vaselenovitch Klooglosevtloff, a retired professor…and a heterogenous and very puzzling assortment of Pishkins, Borapatkins, Sergius Vodkaroffs, Abrezkoffvitchs and Olthidors, all of them in whiskers'.[68]

At the time in which he wrote, Chekhov was surrounded by seemingly unlimited expanses of unspoilt wilderness, and in his plays references to birds, animals, trees and forests figure prominently. In contrast, in the UK in the 1950s, Chekhov's keen awareness of the environment was bound to fall easy prey to satirists. In 1956, a skit in *Punch* sending up *The Seagull*, included stage directions for a ballet to be performed with a motley crew of 'lions, eagles, partridges, antlered deer, geese, spiders, starfish, cranes, [and] cockroaches'.[69]

Chekhov's knowledge of fauna is matched by his close familiarity with flora. The environmental awareness of Astrov, the local doctor in *Uncle Vanya*, includes ecological insights and an astute understanding of the importance of 'sustainable development'. Concerned about the future and the lack of planning, Astrov plants new forests and does not eat meat. Not happy in his personal life, he is well aware of the importance of work and the need for his medical services. 'It's odd,' he comments to Yelena in the words of Pam Gems:

> ASTROV: You turn up here with your husband and we have to drop
>   everything, those of us who were doing something useful,
>   creative…to dance attendance on you, and your husband's gout –
>   you've infected the lot of us with your idleness. I've done nothing for
>   a month except think about you. People have been ill, the peasants
>   are grazing their stock in my new woods, I'm losing all my young
>   trees![70]

Astrov's attitude to his work, wildlife and forests echoes the Old Testament and the story of the Creation. Man, created in the image of God, is to fill the earth, to rule over the fish in the sea and the birds in the sky. Thus, to the questions 'Who is man?' and 'What is he doing on this earth?' Chekhov appears to give the answer that man is by nature creative, finding in his work an expression of his identity. This is, in a sense, his 'language', the means whereby he communicates not only with other humans, but also with the natural environment in which he exists. And the closer in touch he is with his work, the greater the ease with which he is able to understand and communicate with man as well as flora and fauna. While Astrov combines hard work with his interest in the environment, Yelena does not share his concerns and she soon gets bored with Astrov's company. As he warns her of the impending threat to the environment and the worrying transformations that have already taken place during the last fifty years, her mind starts to drift and she loses interest.

Reflecting his ecological concern, with its link to humanitarian and creative work, Chekhov uses gardens, orchards, individual trees, such as birches, and forests as images to signal impending changes and warnings for the future. 'All Russia is a garden,' begins Trofimov's speech in *The Cherry Orchard* about his intimations of what the future will bring. And in *Three Sisters*, Natasha, catapulted through marriage into a class and world different from her own, first wreaks havoc on the inhabitants of that world, then proceeds to turn her attention to the world outside. 'So tomorrow I'll be alone here,' she says and sighs. Then she continues, in Elisaveta Fen's translation:

> NATASHA: I'll have this fir-tree avenue cut down first, then the maple
> tree over there. It looks so awful in the evenings.[71]

Perhaps not surprisingly, Chekhov's attitude to the relationship of man to nature makes his characters approach their environment as if it were invested with a human spirit, which at times creates problems for translation into English. In *Three Sisters*, before leaving for the duel in which he is to be killed, Tusenbach, in his farewell to Irina, uses tree imagery to foreshadow what is going to happen (Elisaveta Fen's translation):

> TUSENBACH: I feel as if I was seeing those fir-trees and maples and
> birches for the first time in my life. They all seem to be looking at me
> with a sort of inquisitive look and waiting for something. What
> beautiful trees and how beautiful, when you think of it life ought to
> be with trees like these!
> (*Shouts of 'Ah-oo! Heigh-ho' are heard.*)
> I must go, it's time... Look at that dead tree, it's all dried up, but it is
> still swaying in the wind along with the others. And in the same way, it
> seems to me that if I die, I shall still have a share of life somehow or
> other. Good-bye, my dear...[72]

Invested with near-mortal life, trees at times receive epithets more commonly associated with humans. In an earlier exchange in *Three Sisters*, Olga complains to Vershinin about the cold and the mosquitoes in the provincial town where they now live. Vershinin, however, is less critical. In Elisaveta Fen's translation:

> VERSHININ: Really? I should have said you had a really good healthy climate here, a real Russian climate. Forest, river…birch-trees too. The dear, unpretentious birch-trees – I love them more than any of the other trees.[73]

Other, less faithful translations, all show signs of having done battle with Vershinin's delight in 'unpretentious birch-trees', while arriving at different solutions. First Lanford Wilson's version:

> VERSHININ: What? This is good strong, Slavic climate. The forest, the river, the birches; all these wonderful chaste birches, they're my favourite tree.[74]

Another American playwright, Richard Nelson, prefers a different set of attributes:

> VERSHININ: What do you mean?! You have here a fine, healthy Russian climate. You have a forest, the river…and the birches. Those dear modest birches; they're my favourite trees.[75]

Aiming for the greatest possible naturalism in speech, David Mamet reorganises the original into more manageable chunks:

> VERSHININ: *Oh* no, *oh* no. A good and healthy Slavic climate. The *forest*, the *river*, the *birches* you have! Which, to me, are, in their modest selves, most beautiful trees. [76]

Finally, Brian Friel's vernacular version refers to 'silver birches' in the form of a question no Russian would be likely to ask:

> VERSHININ: Cold? You have the ideal Russian climate here. And you have the forest and the river and – those are silver birches over there, aren't they? Gentle, modest birch trees; they're my favourite. [77]

To a greater or lesser extent, these versions all attempt to achieve in translation a more distanced approach to Vershinin's beloved birch trees, toning down the emotionality conveyed in Fen's unadapted translation. In Russia, as in other parts of Europe, communing with nature is commonly accepted as a natural need for man. In translation into English, however, translators appear to have sensed that a faithful rendering would have resulted in too foreign a feel and have attempted to find other solutions. A similar instance occurs at the end of the play. The regiment is now about to leave and Second Lieutenant

Rode has come to pay his respects. Taking his leave, he addresses himself not only to Tusenbach and Irina but also to the trees and the echo. In Elisaveta Fen's translation:

> RODE: (*Glancing round the garden.*) Goodbye, trees! (*Shouts.*) Heigh-ho!
> (*A pause.*) Good-bye, echo! [78]

Both Brian Friel and David Mamet have opted for less faithful renderings:

> *Brian Friel:*
>
> RODDEY: (*Going round garden.*) Good-bye, trees (*Shouts.*) Good-bye!
> ECHO: Bye – bye – bye...
> RODDEY: (*Shouts.*) Good-bye. Echo.
> ECHO: Echo – echo – echo...[79]

> *David Mamet:*
>
> RODE: Farewell. Trees, Farewell. Air, farewell, Echo...echo...farewell...[80]

Although the sentiment may still remain foreign, Friel and Mamet as playwright/translators have both chosen to embellish on the original, and in so doing tried to increase the scope for the actor to convey the 'otherness' to English-speaking audiences of Roddey/Rode's attitude to the world around him.

Using Astrov in *Uncle Vanya* as a mouthpiece, Chekhov expressed his concern about the future of the Russian forests and his uneasiness about the destruction of ecosystems. Showing a grasp of the principles of ecology decades before the term entered everyday use, Chekhov is not infrequently referred to as a proto-environmentalist. 'In the twentieth century the preservation of nature has long been and will be more and more the measure by which the moral potential of each person is tested,' A P Chudakov writes,[81] and, according to Simon Karlinsky, Chekhov 'was the first in literature who included the relationship of man to nature in his sphere of ethics'.[82]

It was not only in his environmental concerns that Chekhov was ahead of his time. Over a century ago, he showed in his role as a physician an awareness of what is now well known: laughter is an important weapon in fighting illness. In a letter to Nicolai Leykin dated 20 May 1884, Chekhov wrote: 'First of all, I'd get my patients into a laughing mood, and only then would I begin to treat them.'[83] So too in his writing, Chekhov's humour centred on 'the sad comicality of everyday life', a juxtaposition of the two opposing notions of 'sad' and 'comical'.

At the time, however, Chekhov's form of humour was sufficiently far removed from more traditional notions to make him a sitting target for parody. Even in Russia, Burenin failed to see the ironic twist in Chekhov's depiction of his self-pitying characters. Equally if not more scathing about Chekhov's lack of humour was Boris F Geyer. In *The Evolution of the Theatre* (1910), a potted history of Russian drama, Geyer's Chekhovian pastiche, *Petrov*, figured Lidya Petrovina, a black-clad, moonstruck romantic:

> All last night the old lindens were rustling in the garden...the old lindens... That have seen so many tears and sorrows... When we moved here it seemed to me that we had been buried in a grave...a grave... Moscow... Oh if only I might see Moscow again...
> (*Sits, burying her head in her hands.*)
> Moskva...Moskve...Moskvoy...[84]

Letting Lidya Petrovina inflect the case endings of Moscow as if memorising a grammatical paradigm, Geyer successfully undercuts the potential pathos of her lines. Also, by not acknowledging Chekhov's awareness of the failings and weaknesses of his characters, the pastiche successfully helped to reinforce all the standard Chekhovian misconceptions.

From the start, the English-speaking world tended to view Chekhov's characters as more than slightly idiosyncratic, their strange behaviour resulting from Slavic melancholy or depression. In 1933, early satirical reflections on the Russian playwright's work were voiced in an attack on new European drama in the Abbey Theatre's production of Lennox Robinson's *Is Life Worth Living* (also known as *Drama at Inish*). During the visit of an acting troupe with a repertoire including Ibsen, Strindberg, Tolstoy and Chekhov, the inhabitants of a small Irish seaside resort begin to show a number of disconcerting symptoms. They suffer severe bouts of depression, enter into suicide pacts, leap off piers and purchase weed killer to rid themselves of decrepit relatives. Only with the closure of the theatre and the arrival of a circus company is normal life restored. As summed up by theatrical journalist A E Wilson, the hallmarks of Chekhov and Russian theatre were 'introspection, morbidity, death and depression'. The common wisdom on Chekhov, according to Wilson, was that he 'simply assembles a lot of melancholy characters on the stage, distributes a few grievances among them, adds a suicide or two and leaves them to worry the thing out to the bitter end'.[85]

The notion of Chekhovian gloom and inconsequentiality was further nourished by Peter Ustinov in *The Love of Four Colonels* (1953).[86] In this post-war comedy, a four-power commission consisting of a French, British, American and Russian colonel are tempted by the Wicked Fairy Carabossa to seduce the Sleeping Beauty in her German Palace. In a play-within-a-play scene, the Russian colonel appears on stage sitting on a swing, busily knitting a jumper, and watching the 'Beauty' play croquet, when a shot rings out:

> BEAUTY: What was that?
> IKONENKO: A wood-man felling a birch tree.
> BEAUTY: It sounded to me like...
> IKONENKO: It was raining in Kharkov last Friday. I know because Grischa left her umbrella at the barracks.
> BEAUTY: Ever since Papa died I have never carried an umbrella. There were so many at the funeral...
> IKONKENKO: Was it raining?
> BEAUTY: No... (*Pause. Ikonenko looks at knitting.*)
> IKONKENKO: Now I have dropped a stitch, and must undo it all. (*Does so.*)
> BEAUTY: (*Rises, crosses D, a step or two.*) I was so looking forward to yesterday.

In 1956, Paul Dehn's satire of *The Seagull* in *Punch* brought another attempt to reduce 'Chekhovian atmosphere' to absurdity. This proposed new musical version of Chekhov's play treated readers of *Punch* to *The Seagull* as if it had been written as a musical by Rodgers and Hammerstein. In *Kitty, Wake!* or *Oklahomov!*, Arkadina becomes Mrs Arkady Brown, her son Konstantin, Con, a choreographer and her lover Trigorin, a gossip writer called Trigger. The exchange between Medvedenko and Masha as the play opens now takes the following form:

> SEM: Whidya always wear black, Mash?
> MASHA: (*Taking snuff.*) I'm in mourning fer my life.
> SEM: O what a beautiful mournin',
> Black as a fishing crow's head
> I gotta beautiful feelin'
> Somebody oughta be dead.[87]

Lampooning Chekhov has fostered the notion of yet another gloom-ridden northern European playwright, with Chekhov joining the ranks of Ibsen and Strindberg. As a result, in preparing new versions of his plays, English playwrights at times feel called upon to inject the humour that is popularly believed to be missing in the original. In the *Guardian* of 13 October 1998, Michael Billington reported on a theatre weekend in Dublin which included a visit to *Uncle Vanya* performed at the Gate Theatre, in a version by Brian Friel (also later used for the 2002 Almeida production):

> One is tempted to ask what is wrong with the old ones, for Friel is not content to surrender to Chekhov but has imposed himself on the material.

Waffles, the cuckolded landowner, is given a series of gags about his excessive sweat and his wife's Germanic lover. Sebryakov, the professor, is a palpably impotent figure lamenting 'this old carcass'. And his wife, Elena, talks of her unsuitability for 'teaching snotty little brats' and running about the countryside in Wellingtons. Friels's version is undeniably funny – but so, I always thought was Chekhov's original.

Chekhov's humour, however, is not always easily discernible, in particular when hidden beneath a layer of translation. Although clearly present in his one-act comedies, the humour in his major plays is less easily revealed. (See Chapter 9 for a general discussion of translation of humour in drama.)

Out of his four major plays, Chekhov subheaded *The Seagull* and *The Cherry Orchard* as comedies, calling *Uncle Vanya* and *Three Sisters* dramas. While in both *Three Sisters* and *The Cherry Orchard* Chekhov shows the paralysis of the cultured elite facing the ominous forces of change, in the latter, his last play, he looks at the problem from a more comic-ironic angle. In 1901 when *The Cherry Orchard* was first beginning to take shape, he wrote in a letter to his wife Olga Knipper: 'The next play I write for the Art Theatre will definitely be funny, very funny – at least in intention'. Stanislavsky, at whom the last comment was probably aimed, chose to interpret *The Cherry Orchard* as a sombre study of Russian life, while Chekhov himself continued to insist that the play was 'not a drama but a comedy; in places almost a farce'.[88]

It also seems likely that there is more of an ironic twist to *The Seagull* than many English-speaking performances would suggest. In *The Seagull*, the first of his major plays, Chekhov deals with the nature of art as seen in the context of theatre. In the play, the 'hero' shoots himself twice (off-stage), the 'heroine' suffers the passion and ecstasy of unrequited love, and, whenever given the opportunity, the majority of the characters show a tendency to deliver grandiose speeches. As in Ibsen's *Hedda Gabler*, it has been argued that the last line of *The Seagull* also gives rise to the possibility of different interpretations. Traditionally viewed as an understatement and translated as 'Konstantin Gavrilovich has shot himself', Dorn's line to Trigorin may also be read to question implicitly the successful outcome of the attempted suicide. The word used by Chekhov is 'shot' and not 'killed', and in English to shoot oneself does not necessarily mean to kill oneself. Also, had Chekhov wished to be completely unambiguous, he could have used *Konstantin Gavrilovich zastrelilsja na smert*, 'Konstantin Gavrilovich has shot himself to death', thus removing any possible doubt.[89]

Arguably, Chekhov may have intended to create some doubt about the outcome of the attempted suicide. Not only had Konstantin attempted once before unsuccessfully to shoot himself, but also Chekhov's characters rarely achieve their desired ends in his plays following *The Seagull*. Vanya misses shooting the hated professor and, in *Three Sisters*, Solyony ends up killing Tusenbach whom he only intended to wound. Thus the last line of *The Seagull* might be viewed as pointing to the ironic gap between aspiration and fulfilment, on, as well as off, stage, nudging the play closer in spirit to the concept of comedy, the description provided by its author.

Once again, the need for care in the translation of the concluding line of a play becomes clear. For the playwright, these are his parting words. It is hardly surprising that they continue to bedevil translators.

Notes

1   H Rappaport in *The Storm* performance programme (Almeida Theatre, 1998)

2   M Slonim, *Russian Theatre. From the Empire to the Soviets* (London, Methuen, 1963), p. 83

3   *Independent*, 27 January 1999

4   R Freeborn, in *A Month in the Country* performance programme (Albery Theatre, 1994)

5   Discussed in L Senelick, 'Stuffed seagulls. Parodies and the reception of Chekhov's plays', *Poetics Today*, 8 (2), 1987, p. 289

6   *Ibid*. p. 294

7   *Current Literature* (1906). Discussed in V Emeljanov, *Chekhov. The Critical Heritage* (London, Routledge and Kegan Paul, 1981), p. 4

8   *Ibid*. p. 5

9   Anton Chekhov, *The Seagull*, version T Stoppard (London, Faber and Faber, 1997), p. v

10 Herbert Farjeon in *The World*, 6 June 1911, p. 853

11 L Senelick, *op. cit*. p. 294

12 P Ustinov, *Dear Me* (Harmondsworth, Middlesex, Penguin, 1979), pp. 107–8, 122–3. Discussed in L Senelick, *op. cit*. pp. 294–5

13 *Ibid*. P Ustinov, p. 113, in L Senelick, p. 295

14 First extract: Anton Chekhov, *Plays* (*Ivanov, The Seagull, Uncle Vanya, Three Sisters, The Cherry Orchard, The Bear, The Proposal, A Jubilee*), trans. and intro. E Fen (Harmondsworth, Middlesex, Penguin, 1959), pp. 363–4. Second extract: Anton Chekhov, *The Cherry Orchard*, adapt. T Griffiths and trans. Helen Rappaport

(London, Faber and Faber, 1989), p. 26. Discussed in Michael Billington, 'Villains of the piece', *Guardian*, 9 November 1984

15 S Bassnett, 'Still trapped in the labyrinth: further reflections on translation and theatre', in S Bassnett and A Lefevere (eds.) *Constructing Cultures* (Clevedon, Multilingual Matters, 1998), p. 94

16 Discussed in S Klimenko, 'Anton Chekhov and English nostalgia', *ORBIS Litterarum. International Review of Literary Studies* 56, (2), 2001, pp. 122–3

17 *Ibid.* p. 123

18 D Rayfield, 'Chekhov', in P France (ed.), *The Oxford Guide to Literature in English Translation*. (Oxford, Oxford University Press, 2000), p. 598

19 *Ibid.* p. 598

20 E K Bristow, 'On translating Chekhov', *Quarterly Journal of Speech* 52, 1966, pp. 290–4

21 Anton Chekhov, *The Seagull*, version Pam Gems, National Theatre (London, Nick Hern Books, 1994), pp. v–vii

22 J Aitchison, *The Articulate Mammal. An Introduction to Psycholinguistics*, 3rd edition (London, Unwin Hyman, 1989), p. 253

23 Anton Chekhov, *Plays (The Seagull, Uncle Vanya, Three Sisters, The Cherry Orchard)* trans. M Frayn (London, Methuen, 1988), p. 59

24 *The Seagull*, version P Gems, *op. cit.*

25 *The Seagull*, version T Stoppard, *op. cit.* p. vii

26 J Long, 'An Irish Seagull: Chekhov and the new Irish Theatre', *Revue de Littérature Comparée* 4, 1995, p. 414

27 *The Cherry Orchard*, trans. M Frayn, *op. cit.* p. 59

28 J Long, *op. cit.* p. 415

29 *The Cherry Orchard*, trans. M Frayn, *op. cit.* p. 59

30 J Long, *op. cit.* p. 415

31 M Esslin, 'Chekhov and the modern drama', in T Clyman (ed.) *A Chekhov Companion* (Westport, Conn., Greenwood Press, 1985), p. 145

32 H Pinter, *Plays 1* (London, Faber and Faber, 1991), p. 34

33 P Hall, 'Directing Pinter', *Theatre Quarterly*, 4 (16), 1974/75, pp. 7, 10

34 Discussed in Anton Chekhov, *The Cherry Orchard*, trans. M Frayn (London, Methuen, 1995), pp. xl–xli

35 Anton Chekhov, *The Cherry Orchard*, version P Gill, from a literal translation by T Braun (London, Oberon Books, 1995), p. 29

36 Anton Chekhov, *The Cherry Orchard*, adapt. D Mamet, from a literal translation by Peter Nelles (London, Samuel French, 1985), p. 28

37 See V Gottlieb, 'Chekhov in limbo: British productions of the plays of Chekhov', in H Scolnikov and P Holland (eds.) *The Play out of Context. Transferring Plays from Culture to Culture* (Cambridge, Cambridge University Press, 1989), p. 165

38 V Gottlieb, *ibid.* p. 165

39 Discussed and quoted in S Klimenko, *op. cit.* p. 121–37

40 V Gottlieb, *op. cit.* p. 165

41 Anton Chekhov, *The Cherry Orchard*, adapt. R Brustein, from a translation by George Calderon (Chicago, Ivan R Dee, 1995), p. 5

42 Discussed in S Klimenko 2001, p. 126

43 S Klimenko, *op. cit.* p. 123

44 *The Seagull*, version P Gems, *op. cit.* p. 52

45 *The Seagull*, version T Stoppard, *op. cit.* p. 67

46 Anton Chekhov, *The Seagull*, trans. and intro. S Mulrine, (London, Nick Hern Books, 1997), p. 48

47 Anton Chekhov, *The Seagull*, adapt. P Gill, from a literal translation by H Molchanoff (London, Oberon Books, 1999), p. 60

48 S Klimenko, *op. cit.* p. 128

49 S Klimenko, *op. cit.* p. 128

50 *The Seagull*, version P Gems, *op. cit.* p. 75 (author's emphases)

51 *The Seagull*, version T Stoppard, *op. cit.* pp. 68–9 (author's emphases)

52 *The Seagull*, trans. P Gill, *op. cit.* pp. 82–3 (author's emphases)

53 B V Bratus, *The Formation and Expressive Use of Diminutives. Studies in Modern Russian Language*, 6 (Cambridge , Cambridge University Press, 1969), p. 2

54 *Uncle Vanya*, trans. E Fen, *op. cit.* p. 187

55 Anton Chekhov, *Uncle Vanya*, version Pam Gems, National Theatre (London, Nick Hern Books, 1992), p. 5

56 *The Cherry Orchard*, trans. E Fen, *op. cit.* p. 356

57 *The Cherry Orchard*, trans. M Frayn, *op. cit.* p. 25

58 *The Cherry Orchard*, adapt. R Brustein, *op. cit.* p. 29

59 *The Cherry Orchard*, adapt. D Mamet, *op. cit.* p. 28

60 *The Cherry Orchard*, adapt. T Griffiths, *op. cit.* p. 20

61 Anton Chekhov, *Three Sisters*, adapt. R Nelson, from a translation by Olgo Lifson (New York, Broadway Play Publishing, 1991), p. 1

62 Anton Chekhov, *The Three Sisters*, adapt. D Mamet, from a literal translation by V Chernomordik (New York, Grove Press, 1990), p. 1

63 Anton Chekhov, *Three Sisters*, trans. B Friel (Loughcrew, Ireland, The Gallery Press, 1981), p. 11

64 Anton Chekhov, *Three Sisters*, trans. L Wilson (Lyme, NH, Smith and Kraus, 1984), p. 3

65 *Three Sisters*, trans. E Fen, *op. cit.* p. 252

66 *Three Sisters*, trans. B Friel, *op. cit.* p. 15

67 *The Seagull*, trans. S Mulrine, *op. cit.* p. xvi

68 G J Nathan, *Since Ibsen: A Statistical Historical Outline of the Popular Theatre since 1900* (New York, Alfred A. Knopf, 1939). Discussed in L Senelick, *op. cit.* p. 292

69 P Dehn, 'Oklahomov!', in B Lowrey (ed.), *Twentieth Century Parody American and British* (New York, Harcourt Brace, 1958), p. 214. Discussed in L Senelick, *op. cit.* p. 296

70 *Uncle Vanya*, version P Gems, *op. cit.* p. 62

71 *Three Sisters*, trans. E Fen, *op. cit.* p. 328

72 *Ibid.* p. 321

73 *Ibid.* p. 259

74 *Three Sisters*, trans. L Wilson, *op. cit.* p. 13

75 *Three Sisters*, adapt. R Nelson, *op. cit.* p. 11

76 *The Three Sisters*, adapt. D Mamet, *op. cit.* p. 13

77 *Three Sisters*, trans. B Friel, *op. cit.* p. 96

78 *Three Sisters*, trans. E Fen, *op. cit.* p. 312

79 *Three Sisters*, trans. B Friel, *op. cit.* p. 96

80 *The Three Sisters*, adapt. D Mamet, *op. cit.* p. 88

81 A P Chudakov, *Chekhov's Poetics*, trans. E J Cruise and D Dragt (Ann Arbor, Michigan, Ardis, 1983). Discussed in J Malcolm, *Reading Chekhov. A Critical Journey* (London, Granta Books, 2003)

82 S Karlinsky and M H Heim, *Anton Chekhov's Life and Thought: Selected Letters and Commentary*, trans. M H Heim, pp. 49–50. Discussed in J Malcolm, *ibid.* and Karlinsky, selection, introduction and commentary by Karlinsky (Evanston, Illinois, Northwestern University Press, 1973)

83 V Gottlieb, *Chekhov and The Vaudeville. A Study of Chekhov's One-Act Plays* (Cambridge, Cambridge University Press, 1982), p. 11

84 Discussed in L Senelick, *op. cit.* p. 291

85 A E Wilson, *Theatre Guide. The Baedeker of Thespia* (London, Methuen, 1935). Discussed in L Senelick, *op. cit.* pp. 291–4

86 P Ustinov, *The Love of Four Colonels* (New York, Dramatists Plays Service, 1953), p. 54

87 P Dehn, 'Oklahomov!', L Senelick, *op. cit.* p. 296

88 Discussed in R Brustein, 'Foreword' to Chekhov: *The Major Plays.* (*Ivanov. The Seagull. Uncle Vanya. The Three Sisters. The Cherry Orchard*), trans. Ann Dunnigan (New York, Signet, 1964), p. xxi

89 Discussed in C Strongin, 'Irony and theatricality in Chekhov's *The Seagull*', *Comparative Drama* 15 (4), 1981, pp. 366–80

Chapter 5

AUGUST STRINDBERG

ALTHOUGH THERE HAD LONG BEEN a tradition of theatre in Sweden, to a large extent it was dominated by foreign imports; in 1844, Swedish drama was likened to a 'delicate, newly planted flower'.[1] There was the occasional drama on historical themes such as the play by Johan Börjesson (1790–1866) about the Swedish regent, *Eric XIV* (1846), but the prevailing theatrical fare consisted of vaudevilles, based on the French and Danish model, as well as imported European plays in translation. Among the playwrights translated at the time was Shakespeare: the first two volumes of Shakespeare's plays in translation into Swedish by Karl August Hagberg (1810–64) appeared in 1847, and were followed successively by further volumes until the twelfth and last in 1851.

At the time, interest was focused on France. On the Swedish stage, the work of playwrights from the Scribean school of the well-made-play with its tightly constructed plot was followed by Émile Augier's prose plays, the *pièces à thèse* by Alexandre Dumas *fils* and satirical comedies such as *La Famille Benoîton* by Victorien Sardou.

French comedies and thesis plays had an impact on Swedish theatre not only through their staging in translation but also indirectly via the work of Bjørnstjerne Bjørnson and Henrik Ibsen. Both Norwegian dramatists were clearly influenced by the themes and techniques of French playwriting, and the publication of a new play from their pen was eagerly awaited in Sweden. Ibsen's play *Brand* (1866) was staged in Sweden in the 1880s, even before it reached the Norwegian stage. At first the critical response was muted, but reservations soon gave way to acceptance, largely due to the efforts of Georg Brandes, whose Copenhagen lectures on current trends in European literature helped place Ibsen's work in an overall European framework.

Brandes and his call to contemporary writers to step out into the real world exercised an early influence on the work of August Strindberg (1849–1912). In his first masterpiece for the stage, *Mäster Olof* (*Master Olaf*), published in 1881, about Olavus Petri, the Father of the Swedish Reformation, Strindberg set out to write a tragic, historical conflict in the style of his time. In so doing he created a revolution in the language used on the Swedish stage. Out went the flowery, literary style characterising Swedish drama at the time, with its stylised, elegantly structured sentences incorporating numerous subordinate clauses: the language that Strindberg now introduced in his drama was Swedish as spoken outside the theatre. However, in spite of Strindberg's status as an innovator of Swedish language and literature and one of the founders of modern drama, by comparison with Ibsen there is considerably less evidence that 'English Strindberg' has as yet fully arrived.

On the whole, the failure of the work of August Strindberg to succeed to the same degree in translation into English as Ibsen may at least partially be explained by the versatility of his talent. Unlike Ibsen – who left a body of plays many of which were concerned with social issues meeting the demand of the day for public debate – Strindberg tried his hand at several literary genres as well as taking an active interest in a number of different fields. In addition to plays, he wrote novels, short stories and poetry, while contributing to discussions of the day on different subjects including scientific issues of topical interest. A keen photographer and a painter, with his artwork exhibited at Swedish national museums, Strindberg's interests also included the visual arts. Frequently forgotten too is the intention behind much of his writing: just as Shakespeare's *Romeo and Juliet* is meant for a wider audience while *The Tempest* is not, some of Strindberg's writing was never intended to be read by the public at large.[2] Even the plays that English audiences are familiar with, such as *Fröken Julie* (*Miss Julie*, 1888), *Dödsdansen* (*The Dance of Death*, 1901) and *Fadren* (*The Father*, 1887), often emerge in English translation shrouded in the angst-ridden gloom with which the name of Strindberg has been associated, bereft of the lightness of touch and deft subtlety of the Swedish originals.

The failure of Strindberg's work to be fully understood and appreciated in English is closely linked to the problem of recreating in translation his forceful, free-flowing, seemingly unrestrained use of language. Credited with having revitalised the Swedish language, the nuances of Strindberg's writing remain difficult to capture even in Danish and Norwegian, let alone less closely related languages.

However, not only did Strindberg's use of language present problems to early translators of his work, many of whom were first or second generation Swedish-Americans with few literary qualifications for translating his work, he also failed to attract the attention bestowed upon Ibsen by the virtually bilingual (possibly also bicultural) William Archer. Instead, Strindberg had to follow the traditional route usually available to Scandinavian playwrights: entry to Europe via Germany, where, unlike English-speaking countries, more or less everything that he ever wrote, literary as well as non-literary, is now available in translation. During Strindberg's lifetime, German productions of his plays were frequent, the result of the untiring work of Emil Schering (1873–1951), the translator of the *Collected Works* that appeared in German between 1902 and 1930. Having attended the opening in Germany in 1893 of Strindberg's play *Fordringsägare* (*Creditors*, 1890), the twenty-year-old Schering decided that he would devote his life to Strindberg.

> I wrote a letter to Strindberg and told him that I would like to translate everything that he had written into German and publish it. I did not know a word of Swedish [...]. I immediately started to take lessons in order to learn Swedish. I sacrificed academic and literary ambitions for the sake of my new ideal.[3]

However, while William Archer learnt Norwegian at a very young age, Schering never appears to have gained sufficient mastery of Swedish to grasp fully, let alone reproduce, Strindberg's innovative use of language. It might arguably have taken a German writer of some literary standing to do full justice to Strindberg's writing: Schering's translations contain mistakes of such an elementary nature that they continue to provide German actors and directors of Strindberg's work with a source of amusement. For example, in his translation of the Swedish place name *Husqvarna*, a small town in the south of Sweden, Schering's literal approach led him to detect a compound resulting in a German rendering of *Hus* as 'House' and *qvarna* as 'mill', yielding *Hausmühle*, in English the equivalent of the novel and intriguing concept of 'House mill'.[4] In some instances Strindberg himself had to come to his translator's rescue and lend a helping hand.

Although Strindberg's reaction to Schering's mistranslations appears to have been one of benevolent amusement, Schering's failure to deduce from the context that his translations contained inaccuracies raises serious doubts about other aspects of his ability as a literary translator. His shortcomings, his often slavish attempts at word-for-word renderings of Strindberg's writing, have been viewed as the result of the method, in common practice at the time, of using translation as a form of language teaching and methodology. Schering simply followed the principles of language teaching in use in the mid-1880s. Translation from Latin into German had taught him to translate word-for-word, to render scrupulously and faithfully the original text in the target language in order to show that he knew 'the meaning' of the words in the foreign language. Although clearly less fluent in Swedish than Archer in Norwegian, Schering was equally insistent that every word of the original text must be faithfully reproduced in translation in order to make possible direct access to the author, allowing the audience to experience the unique features of the translation as unique qualities in the author's writing.[5] Choosing between Schleiermacher's options (see Chapter 1), the audience or readers were clearly to be taken to the text rather than the text to the audience/reader.

Schering was, however, not altogether consistent in this approach. Anticipating that Strindberg's choice of words and expressions might occasionally cause offence, he unhesitatingly replaced them with other more neutral turns of phrase, making the dramatist's characters use a much more educated language than they did in the original. A further factor influencing Schering's translations was the way the German language was taught in school at the time, according to which sentences should be short, words of foreign extraction should be avoided and the use of German was to be cultivated and measured. As a result, the language of 'German Strindberg' became more abrupt, blander and more conventional; it also became 'depersonalised' and, in the process, lost much of its forcefulness. Gone were the characteristic style, the wit, the irony and the satire. Nevertheless, German audiences, who were unfamiliar with the original, did not react to the deformation of Strindberg's language. They liked the plot and the stories, while at the same time experiencing Strindberg as 'Nordic', which was much in vogue at the time. For translators working in other languages, however, who had to use Schering's translations as the basis for their own interpretations of Strindberg, confusion and bewilderment as to the style and meaning of the original must inevitably have resulted in misinterpretations and mistranslations. And in the case of successive translations into other languages, it is not difficult to imagine the distortions likely to have accumulated by the time the text reached the third or fourth language for translation.

Aware of the process of successive translation to which his plays were subject, in a letter written in 1894, as his international career was starting to take off, Strindberg reportedly amused himself by hypothesising about the future of *Leka med Elden* (*Playing with Fire*, 1893) and *Bandet* (*The Bond*, 1892), two of his plays soon to be translated. The German translations, Strindberg speculated, were likely to form the basis for the Italian version which in its turn would be used by the French translator to produce a French translation which, when completed, was likely to provide the text from which the English translator would work. What would happen, Strindberg mused, if, at that point, someone had the bright idea of translating the English text into Swedish, and what would the legal position be with respect to the copyright of his own original?[6]

Although Emil Schering's translations left him open to criticism, his overall commitment to Strindberg and his work is beyond doubt. By ensuring that Strindberg benefited from the royalties that were his due following performances of his work at times when the going in his own country was less good, Schering helped to secure an income for the Swedish playwright. It is a moot point whether Schering's efforts in championing the cause of Strindberg and his attempts to introduce him as a European playwright were in the long run outweighed by his, at times, less-than-perfect German renderings of Strindberg's plays, which in successive translations into other languages helped to perpetuate misconceived notions of his work.

While some of Strindberg's plays travelled from Swedish into English via German, others took an alternative route. Although the first known staging of a Strindberg play in New York was a guest performance in German by a company from St Petersburg in 1905, with the famous Russian actress Alla Nazimoff as Miss Julie, the playwright's popularity in Germany would, on occasion, also result in the staging of his plays by German immigrant theatre, in particular The Irving Place Theatre in New York.[7] Further help in introducing Strindberg on American stages came from Scandinavian immigrant theatre. From 1912 to 1914, the Strindbergians, an organisation of approximately forty members, were active through lectures and study circles as well as staging Strindberg's plays. In co-operation with Maurice Brown's Intimate Theatre, *Creditors, Den Starkare* (*The Stronger*, 1890) and *Påsk* (*Easter*, 1900) were staged in 1913 and, in 1914–15, with the support of the Scandinavian Socialist Club, *Paria* (*Pariah*, 1889) and *Pelikanen* (*The Pelican*, 1907). Prominent among the names of early Scandinavian American translators is that of Edwin Björkman (1866–1951). Granted the rights to translate the playwright's work after having written to him from the United States, Björkman translated 24 of Strindberg's plays between 1912 and 1916, which were published in a series of five volumes attracting the interest of, among others, the young Eugene O'Neill and Sean O'Casey.

In England, however, there were no Strindbergians campaigning to get Strindberg's plays onto the English stage, no dedicated followers like the Ibsenites advancing his cause. Nor does Strindberg appear to have helped his own cause when those who did show an interest in his work took the time and trouble to look him up in Stockholm. In March 1906, Edward Gordon Craig, the stage designer and director, visited Stockholm but failed to establish a rapport with the dramatist. Strindberg was familiar with Craig's *The Art of the Theatre* (1905), which had been brought to his attention by Emil Schering, but communication between the two does not appear to have been conducted with ease. In a letter of 11 March, written to Harriet Bosse, his third wife, Strindberg described the meeting:

> Craig was here. We didn't understand each other; then I sent for [Henning] Berger to talk English and help him. I do not know the result.[8]

Having lived in France and in German-speaking parts of Europe, Strindberg spoke both French and German but very little English. His failure to interact with Craig however appears to have been only partly due to linguistic factors. In a radio broadcast fifty years later, Craig recalled his meeting with Strindberg, commenting that during the entire duration of his visit, Strindberg did not laugh or smile. 'Have you got any friends in Stockholm?' Strindberg asked Craig and, upon receiving a negative answer, he volunteered the information: 'Nor do I'.[9]

Two years later, Bernard Shaw, keen to find out more about Strindberg's work, decided to travel to Stockholm to meet him. Accompanied by his wife, Shaw met Strindberg at his Intimate Theatre in Stockholm in July 1908 in order to attend a morning performance of *Miss Julie*, which had been arranged in their honour. Never a master of diplomacy at the best of times, Strindberg appears not to have taken kindly to the small talk of Shaw's wife Charlotte, and resorted to cutting short the meeting on the grounds of ill health. Shaw later wrote to Archer:

> After some conversation consisting mainly of embarrassed silences and a pale smile or two by [August Strindberg] and floods of energetic eloquence in a fearful lingo, half-French, half-German by G B S, A S [Strindberg] took out his watch and said, in German: 'At two o'clock I am going to be sick.'[10]

Accepting the delicate hint, the visitors hastily withdrew.

Strindberg's disillusionment and disappointment with his fellow Swedes were in no small measure the result of the reaction to *Giftas* (*Getting Married*), a collection of his stories on the subject of marriage (1884–6). Although the volumes dealt with many different kinds of marriage, one story, entitled *A Doll's House*, is the account of a wife who, under the influence of a friend, decides to leave her husband only to return to him in the end. Although Strindberg was fully aware that this reversal of Ibsen's doctrine would not pass unnoticed among Swedish feminists, he was nevertheless not prepared for the publication of *Getting Married* to result in the threat of a trial for alleged blasphemy. Legal proceedings were eventually dropped, but having alienated Swedish conservatives with his socialism and liberals with his anti-socialism, Strindberg had landed himself in a difficult situation, added to which publishers, wary of the cost of legal action, were now getting cold feet. Faced with the reluctance of Swedish publishers to publish his books and theatres to stage his plays, he decided to look outside his own country. There was interest in his work in Copenhagen but, above all, he hoped to be able to have his plays performed in French, the *lingua franca* of educated Europeans at the time.

Strindberg had studied French at school and continued to read French literature during his student days at the University of Uppsala. After leaving Sweden in September 1883 in order to live abroad, a sojourn that was to last for a decade and a half, the Strindberg family spent the first few years in French-speaking Europe. The first six months were spent in Grez-sur-Loing, 80 kilometres south of Paris, then in Passy and Neuilly, just outside Paris. The family then moved to Switzerland before returning to France for another couple of years.

It was in Switzerland that Strindberg decided to resume his formal instruction in French, taking private lessons and writing off to Sweden to obtain specialist dictionaries. From all accounts he appears to have been making good progress and, in April 1884, he reports to his painter friend Carl Larsson in a letter full of confidence that 'in a year I'll be writing in French! I know that everyone thinks it's impossible but I've read and written in French for twenty-five years.' A couple of weeks later, he is even more optimistic, now feeling that it would only take a year before he will become what he calls a 'French-Swiss writer'. Thanks to French he now had in his possession a 'deadly shot-gun' that he could use against his countrymen who had decided to 'take up arms against him', a weapon which he had previously refrained from using, 'out of a misguided sense of patriotism'! Now he is going to write in French while his critics in Sweden may have 'the pleasure of translating his works into Swedish!' In characteristic Strindberg fashion, the letter is splattered with exclamation marks, revealing the writer's disappointment with the country that he feels has let him down.[11]

Following the opening of the Théâtre Libre in Paris in 1887, its founder André Antoine issued invitations to European writers to submit their work to be considered for performance at his theatre. Responding to this call, during the summer of 1887, six months after it was written, Strindberg set out to translate *The Father* into French, his play about the power game between the sexes with the man as the loser, the first in a series of works about marital conflict. He next turned his attention to the translation of *Creditors* – where the happiness of a married couple is endangered by the return of the woman's first husband – almost immediately after having completed the Swedish version in August 1888. The French version of *The Father* was then sent off to André Antoine, together with a French translation of *Miss Julie*, commissioned from the translator who had previously translated *Getting Married* into French. During this period, Strindberg also wrote directly in French, *Le plaidoyer d'un fou* (*A Madman's Defence*, 1895), a prose work portraying the continued husband-wife conflict. He also translated *Drömspelet* (*A Dream Play*, 1902) into French, probably during the spring of 1902.

In his French translations, Strindberg effected what he felt to be the necessary adjustments to turn the Swedish originals of *The Father* and *Creditors* into *Père* and *Créanciers* in order to ensure a successful transition from the page to the French stage. Moving from the specific to the generic, he replaces place names with the idea of what they represent, turning references to the coastal town of Lysekil on the Swedish west coast into the more anonymous *'aux bains de mer'*. On the whole, Strindberg appears to have been willing to acculturate his own plays to a considerably greater extent than have translators of his plays of more recent times.

Strindberg's self-translation had two obvious advantages: by not employing a translator he could save money and, at the same time, he prevented his Swedish texts from becoming bland and depersonalised in French translation, losing his own, personal imprint. Thus, in spite of the occasional inaccuracy such as the incorrect use of conjugation or vocabulary, Strindberg succeeded in safeguarding the power and style of his original Swedish writing. As a result, it has been suggested that his work still lives on in France, due at least partly to the retention of its original spirit preserved by his efforts at self-translation.[12]

Following the 'formula' proposed by Zola, Strindberg was convinced that he had written an important naturalistic tragedy and duly dispatched a copy of *Père*, together with a letter asking for comments from the French writer. In spite of Strindberg's assurances, however, as to the naturalistic nature of his play, Zola was quick to realise that it was considerably less naturalistic than

Ibsen's *The Wild Duck* or Chekhov's *Three Sisters*, and the acknowledgement that Strindberg received from the pioneer of naturalism on stage was not as enthusiastic as he had hoped. On 15 September 1887, *The Father* had its world premiere in Copenhagen where it was favourably received despite the unflattering reviews following its publication two months earlier in Sweden. On 12 October 1890 it opened in Berlin, at the Freie Bühne, a small theatre modelled on Théâtre Libre in Paris, the first of many German productions.

Although *Père* marked Strindberg's breakthrough as a European dramatist, its French premiere only took place after Parisian theatre audiences had seen both *Miss Julie* and *Creditors*. The play opened on 13 December 1894 at Lugné-Poe's Théâtre de l'Œuvre and became Strindberg's first real success in the city on which he was now pinning his hopes for an international career. While the younger generation of Parisian critics greeted *Père* as the first real success for Scandinavian drama on the French stage, others reserved judgement. '*Vraiment, les Suedoises sont-elles si terribles!*' ('Are Swedish women really that bad?') – was the comment that echoed through the French press.[13] This somewhat over-simplistic interpretation of Strindberg's depiction of marital power games would seem to suggest that even in Strindberg's own version, some of the subtlety of the original failed to travel into French.

In *The Father*, Strindberg portrays the prolonged battle between the Captain and his wife Laura, in particular the conflict arising from the difference in their approach to the education of their daughter Bertha. While the Captain – referred to without a name throughout to emphasise the universality of the role of the male *vis-à-vis* that of the female – wants Bertha to become a teacher, his wife would like to see her daughter follow what she considers to be her more artistic leanings. Lacking any real power, Laura resorts to cunning, planting the seed in the Captain's mind that the father of a child can never know beyond a doubt if he is the true father (or rather at the time of Strindberg he could not). All too susceptible a victim, the Captain loses control and throws a burning oil lamp at his wife, further reinforcing the concerns that Laura has already expressed about her husband's state of mind. The play concludes with the defeat of the male at the hands of the female when the Captain, having suffered a stroke, is cajoled into a straightjacket by the old Nanny.

In order to discuss a planned English production of *The Father*, in the early summer of 1893, Strindberg and his second wife Frieda Uhl embarked upon the two-and-a-half day long sea journey from Hamburg to Gravesend. Although Strindberg was not happy to visit a country where he could barely understand and speak the language, his wife was fluent in English, having studied at a London convent school four years earlier. There was, however, more than one reason motivating Strindberg's visit to England. In addition to the plans of J T Grein to produce *The Father*, following *Ghosts*, which his Independent Theatre Society had staged the previous year, William Heinemann had broached the subject of publishing Strindberg's novels in English. Both projects however proved to be abortive. During the time of the visit of the Strindberg couple, Grein was not even in London and, as a result, Strindberg never got the opportunity to meet the patrons of Grein's Independent Theatre, such as Bernard Shaw, Oscar Wilde, Henry James or Thomas Hardy, with whom he might have been able to converse in French or German. Nor did he meet William Archer and Edmund Gosse, Ibsen's campaigners and translators, whose knowledge of Norwegian would have enabled them to understand Strindberg's Swedish.[14] Even if the circumstances had been more propitious, it seems doubtful that the ardour with which the Ibsenites were championing the cause of their Norwegian master would have been extended to include yet another Scandinavian playwright with limited respect for the decorum of Victorian society. Although Voltaire's famous words '*C'est du Nord aujourd'hui que nous vient la lumière*' at the time were frequently quoted throughout Europe, it seemed that England was unwilling to accept more than one Nordic source of light, and Ibsen had got in there first.[15]

Instead, it was not until 1899 that *The Father* was published in English translation by Nelly Erichsen. Nor was it to be the first Strindberg play to reach the English stage. In 1906 *The Stronger* was staged in London, while it took until 24 July 1911 for *The Father* to be produced at the small Rehearsal Theatre in Maiden Lane where it played for two performances. It was dismissed by the press out of hand, with critics deploring the theatre being used for the portrayal of depressive and brutal aspects of human nature, decrying its author as 'the most pessimistic of all living pessimists'.[16] Strindberg had embarked on the route as the prophet of 'doom and gloom', or 'madman' and 'bedevilled viking', epithets still in currency close to a century later.

Strindberg's next, naturalistic play, written in 1887, the year after *The Father*, was *Miss Julie*, his internationally best-known and most frequently-staged play, and by many considered to be his masterpiece. Miss Julie is the aristocrat whose high-ranking birth has led some translators to call her and the play *Lady Julie*.[17] In her sexual encounter with Jean, her father's valet with his strong appetite for life and the absence of a 'code of honour' to restrain him, Julie is doomed to go under. Her fall, under the magic spell of Midsummer, is irredeemable, forcing her, as she leaves the kitchen into which she has disastrously 'descended', to reach for the razor, while Jean is able to resume his servant's duties as well as his relationship with Kristin, the cook who is also his social equal. Too outspoken and explicit, *Miss Julie* initially met with outraged reviews in Sweden and could only be performed outside the country. The world premiere took place on 14 March 1889 at the Danish Student Association in Copenhagen with Strindberg's wife Siri von Essen in the role of Julie, after, at the very last moment, censorship had intervened to stop the planned performance at the Dagmar Theatre. In 1892, the Freie Bühne in Berlin was the first theatre to venture a public performance of *Fräulein Julie*, directed by a young Max Reinhardt, and when, in 1904, it played again in Berlin it had a highly successful run. A year later, in 1893, *Mademoiselle Julie* opened at the Théâtre Libre in Paris, in a production that Antoine described in his memoirs as *'une enorme sensation'* fulfilling Strindberg's dreams of being the first modern Swedish playwright to be staged in the European theatre metropolis.[18]

Although many French critics felt that *Mademoiselle Julie* could have been less outspoken, it made Strindberg's name known in Paris: interviews in leading newspapers attracted attention to his work and helped to pave the way for the productions of *Créanciers* and *Père* that followed, and his short-lived period of glory as a literary star in the French capital. In Strindberg's own country, on the other hand, it was to take until 1906 before a Swedish actress could be found willing to take on the part of Miss Julie. The same year, on 3 January, *Miss Julie* opened in St Petersburg, having first toured the provinces. As in Sweden, the censor intervened, demanding alterations to the text. In the case of the Russian production, however, the censor was less concerned with the outspokenness of the play than with the inequality in social status between Miss Julie and Jean: the changes asked for were designed to promote Jean to a higher, more clearly defined managerial position, more equal in status to that of Miss Julie.[19]

In England, theatre audiences first had an opportunity to see *Miss Julie* in the spring of 1912 at The Little Theatre in London, in a translation not based on the Swedish text, but on a German version, translated by Emil Schering. On the whole, the critics were bewildered by the play, finding Strindberg's view of life 'distorted and a waste of imaginative power'.[20]

While the initial inspiration for the content and setting of *Miss Julie* appears to have been the Strindberg family's stay at Skovlyst, a rundown mansion near Copenhagen, for the conflict between Miss Julie and Jean Strindberg drew on the marital tension with his wife Siri von Essen. Although interspersed with occasional bouts of harmony, their relationship had begun to deteriorate and, on 24 March 1891, they were granted a legal separation: Siri was given custody of the children, with Strindberg agreeing to pay 100 crowns per month in child support. For Strindberg as a writer and artist, the effect of the divorce was immediately noticeable. In the seven plays he wrote between 1891 and 1892 his characters are less complex and multidimensional than both Miss Julie and the Captain in *The Father*. In an attempt to repair his artistic as well as his financial situation, Strindberg now tried to return to his painting, but here too he was ahead of his time and it was to take almost a century for the originality of his bold seascapes to attract attention. Acutely aware of the need for artistic renewal, Strindberg once again contemplated exile and, on 30 September 1892, he boarded an express train leaving Stockholm for Berlin. Here, on 7 January 1893 at a literary reception, he met the 20-year-old Frieda Uhl who became his second wife. But this marriage too was doomed to failure, prompting Strindberg to leave Germany. In August 1894, he arrived in Paris, after a journey beset with misadventures, ominously foreshadowing the course his life was now about to take.

The crisis that Strindberg experienced after he parted from Frieda Uhl lasted until June 1897 and is documented in *Inferno* (1898), a prose account of what he went through. Following this period of severe depression, Strindberg created the trilogy *Till Damaskus* (*To Damascus*, 1900–4), often viewed as the start of expressionist drama, with characters and settings representing symbolic projections of the poet's consciousness. While waiting for *To Damascus* to open in Stockholm in the autumn of 1900, Strindberg was also busy writing two new plays, *Easter* and *The Dance of Death*.

The first one of these two plays is a modern-day passion play, starting on Maundy Thursday and concluding on the eve of Easter, as seen through the eyes of a family living in a small provincial town in Sweden. In 1889, Strindberg's sister Elisabeth had started to show signs of mental imbalance, which he captured in his portrayal of Eleonora, the delicately balanced young woman of *Easter*. But while the last act, on Easter evening, starts with a cloudy sky, it concludes in bright spring sunshine. The 'crime' unwittingly committed by Eleonora in removing a flower from the florist's shop has been resolved, her brother Elis has been reconciled with his fiancée Kristina, the money owed by the family no longer constitutes a threat to their welfare, and everyone is now looking forward to a summer in the country.

Over the years, Sweden has seen many productions of *Easter* in spite of the problems the play presents, largely due to the difficulty of casting for the ethereal, delicately-drawn character of Eleonora. The critical reception to English-language productions of *Easter* seems to lend further evidence to the inherent problems of the part. In 1921, an early production of *Easter* that took place at the Victoria Theatre in London was viewed favourably. In 1924, however, a staging of the play at the Pax Robertson Salon, a small experimental theatre, was less positively received. On this occasion Eleonora was turned into an angel, dressed in white and the flower, the all-important daffodil, symbolising sun, light and happiness, was replaced by a white lily. Nor does the production seem to have been helped much by the translation by Edwin Björkman, which left the actors wrestling with a multitude of American terms and expressions. During the 1927–8 theatre season the play was also performed at The Oxford Playhouse as well as The Arts and Theatre Club in London, without attracting noticeable interest. Two decades later, in June 1948, a student theatre group from the University of Uppsala visited England, presenting guest performances of *Easter* in Swedish as well as in English. Commenting on the choice of play for these guest performances, a leading Swedish newspaper expressed surprise; the play, it felt, must have made a 'close to bewildering impression' on English audiences due to its 'unremittant, heavy feel', accustomed as they were to 'always having some light-spirited episodes interwoven into even the most tragic drama'.[21]

With *The Dance of Death*, the second play written in 1900, an uncompromising unmasking of a stagnant, destructive marital situation, Strindberg returned to the naturalistic drama with its classical unities. *The Dance of Death* depicts a marriage made in hell, between Edgar, an artillery captain, and his wife Alice as they approach their silver anniversary. Isolated in their fortress home on an island, the monotony of their life is temporarily broken by the arrival of Kurt, Alice's cousin, who is immediately seized by both parties as confidant in their marital struggle. But the attempts made by the couple to inflict emotional injury on each other all prove to be empty threats, and the play ends as it started with no change in sight, and Edgar and Alice awaiting their impending anniversary.

At the time that he wrote the play, Strindberg's financial position was somewhat parlous, which made him heed Schering's warning that he found the play too pessimistic. Increasingly dependent on his German royalties, Strindberg wrote a sequel, *The Dance of Death Part II*, which had a more optimistic ending. However, the sequel never matched the quality of the original, and the two are rarely staged together in Sweden.

Outside Sweden, *The Dance of Death* was to become one of Strindberg's most frequently-staged plays. The world premiere took place at the end of September 1905 in Cologne, and the Swedish opening of Part l on 8 September 1909. It was performed in the United States as early as 1912 by Th. Lister's Travelling Theatre Company, and again in New York in 1920, 1935 and January 1948 as *The Last Dance*, a version in three acts. Adapted by Peter Goldbaum and Robin Short, their approach was made clear in an interview in which the two adapters pointed out that they saw no reason why Strindberg merited treatment as 'a sacred cow'.[22] The critical reception after the opening at the Belasco theatre was not favourable, and after eight performances the production closed. In 1960, a shortened version of the play was put on at the small Key Theatre in New York. The play also had an impact on the writing of American playwright Eugene O'Neill. In England, *The Death Dance* Parts I and II were staged November–December 1924 by The Sunday Players in London, an experimental club theatre which played on Sunday nights when the Sunday laws would otherwise prevent public theatre performances. Again, comments in the Swedish press on the event provide an insight into early and lasting reactions to Strindberg on the English stage:

> But the English theatre audience goes to the theatre in order to be enter-
> tained. Getting agitated and, excited and, in the swirl of emotions, lose
> both sense and sensibility are viewed as *a lack of culture*... The audience
> also tried its hardest to treat the ill-matched couple with a sense of humour...

The reviewer then proceeds to compare the English reaction to the play with that of a German audience at a performance at the Grosses Schauspiel-Haus in Berlin, 'where the audience screamed and applauded in turn, reaching its culmination with a woman having to be carried out of the auditorium suffering an attack of hysteria'. The difference between the two reactions was, the reviewer concludes, 'immense'.[23]

The play following *The Dance of Death* was *A Dream Play*, often referred to as Strindberg's most remarkable dramatic creation. Completed in 1901, this was Strindberg's favourite play: he used to refer to it as 'my most beloved drama, the child of my greatest pain'.[24] *A Dream Play* had its world premiere in Stockholm on 17 April 1907, with Harriet Bosse, the young Norwegian actress to whom Strindberg was now married, in the role of Indra's daughter who steps down to earth in order to watch first-hand the plight of the human condition. She first sets free the Officer imprisoned in the Growing Castle, only to have to see him wait as the years pass by for his beloved Victoria, the opera singer who never appears. She also meets and marries the Lawyer, defender of the poor and, finally, the Poet, before she returns to her heavenly father carrying with her the lament of mankind.

With its swift scene changes, *A Dream Play* might be Strindberg's most technically demanding play and, not unexpectedly, when it first opened, it ran into technical difficulties. Most of the critics, however, realised the unique qualities of the play, which contained many details from Strindberg's own life. In 1921, almost a decade and a half later, the play was staged at the Royal National Theatre in Stockholm, directed by Max Reinhardt, following his German production of the play in 1916. Technical developments in the theatre had now taken place, vastly facilitating the production. In France, *A Dream Play*, entitled *Le songe*, reached the Parisian stage in June 1928 at the Théâtre Alfred Jarry, directed by Antonin Artaud. The play was performed in New York in 1925 by the Provincetown Players, a company closely associated with Eugene O'Neill and his work, in a production that attracted considerable attention but also an equal amount of consternation and confusion. It was performed in London in June 1957 in a production making use of a text that had been considerably cut, including the prologue. In the programme for the performance, Strindberg was given an introduction as the first surrealist dramatist on stage, thus anticipating audience bewilderment at less easily-comprehensible aspects of the production, and asking for suspension of disbelief under the general banner of advanced surrealism.

The final contribution to modern theatre made by Strindberg was his chamber plays, written during 1907. These are bold, experimental dramas, linked to the establishment of his Intimate Theatre in Stockholm, where he attempted to put into effect his pioneering ideas about theatre. These ideas were put forward in open letters to the theatre in which he attempted to outline a programme of modern theatre, characterised by atmosphere and setting, less dependent on fully-defined characters who instead often appear as symbolic representations, at times reduced to a set of deformed human features. Language no longer remains fully logical and coherent, as if it has ceased to be an adequate instrument to relay a meaningful portrayal of the real world. This distaste, contempt and fear of life that Strindberg was now experiencing was clearly conveyed in the third of his chamber plays, *Spök-sonaten* (*The Ghost Sonata*), which he completed on 8 March 1907.

In *The Ghost Sonata*, the naïve young student who, in the end, is forced to see life for what it really is, is introduced to the inhabitants of a patrician house in Stockholm. There he meets the Colonel of noble birth who turns out to be neither a colonel, an aristocrat, nor the father of his daughter. His wife, once a beautiful woman, is now a shrunken mummy who harbours the belief that she is a parrot. Her daughter, who languishes in solitude in the 'Hyacinth Room', is slowly pining away, suffering from some form of life-threatening disease. The real father of the Colonel's daughter is, however, the Mummy's wealthy ex-lover, the eighty-year-old Hummel, a cripple confined to a wheelchair. Attending the 'customary ghost supper' at the Colonel's, Hummel takes the opportunity to reveal to the assembled wax cabinet of monsters the truth about 'this wonderful home, where beauty, education and wealth combine'. Nor is the next generation of 'inhabitants' spared Strindberg's pessimism. The Colonel's daughter and the Student who have found each other in the 'hyacinth room' are brought back to everyday reality by the grotesque Cook, and the drama, a black-humoured grimace at life on earth, concludes with the Student reading a hymn to the sun over his dying beloved.

When *The Ghost Sonata* premiered on 21 January 1908 at the Intimate Theatre in Stockholm, it did not receive favourable reviews; eight years later, however, when Max Reinhardt's German production of *Gespenstersonate* was staged in Sweden, the reception of the play was dramatically different. If ever doubt had been cast on the veracity of Strindberg's pessimistic worldview, the atrocities of World War I had now proved his lack of faith in human nature to be well founded.

In the autumn of 1941, the 23-year-old Ingmar Bergman directed *The Ghost Sonata* in Stockholm; he was to return to this play on more than one occasion, including a production at the Royal National Theatre in Stockholm in the spring of 2000. As *La Sonate des spectres*, the play reached the Théâtre de l'Avenue in Paris in the spring of 1933. Nine years prior to the French production, New Yorkers had had the opportunity to see *The Spook Sonata* in a memorable performance presented by the Provincetown Players. The production received considerable attention, with the daily press puzzled and irritated, and theatre magazines buzzing with enthusiasm. Together with the Provincetown Players' production of *A Dream Play* in 1924, this staging of *The Spook Sonata* is one of the most important Strindberg productions in the United States. In London, *The Spook Sonata* played at the Globe in the Strand in 1927, directed by J B Fagan. Although the production was reportedly excellent, as was the acting – in particular Allan Jeayes as Hummel – the audience was conspicuous by its absence. True to the spirit of critical English approaches to Strindberg, past as well as present, W J Turner of the *New Statesman* summed up the event:

> In *The Spook Sonata* we feel the presence of a man, who, like Swift, had great qualities of intelligence and feeling, but in whom some raw and open wound was the cause of madness and hate.[25]

While at the outset, Strindberg lacked the support in England of an apostle with the commitment of Archer to Ibsen, the attraction for leading actors of the larger-than-life parts of the Strindberg canon helped to bring his work to the attention of wider, English-speaking audiences. In the autumn of 1927, Robert Loraine, war hero, actor and director of note, appeared in the part of *The Father* on the London stage, first at the Everyman Theatre in Hampstead, then at the Savoy Theatre; in both cases the play was a box-office success. Loraine's appearance in *The Father* also helped to prepare for the production of *The Dance of Death* at the Apollo Theatre in London in January 1928 which succeeded in attracting considerable interest and received a favourable critical response in the press. The translation used for the production was, however, grossly distorted, reducing the intensity of the original and making it more socially acceptable through cuts and paraphrasing, resulting in an end product closely resembling melodrama. A formal complaint, promptly delivered by the Swedish envoy in London, only served to increase the success and popularity of the production, as Loraine was quick to capitalise on the controversy and use it to his advantage to obtain maximum publicity for the event.[26]

Similarly, in 1967, a translation of *The Dance of Death* by C D Locock was brought to the attention of London theatregoers through the bravura performance of Laurence Olivier at the National Theatre. And in November 1979, Denholm Elliot, another star of the London stage and television, took the part of the Captain in *The Father* against Diane Cilento's Laura in a 'version' directed by Charles Marowitz. In all of Strindberg's plays, however, linguistic as well as cultural aspects of his writing have placed obstacles in the way of easy transfer into English.

Among the linguistic problems to be overcome by the Strindberg translator is his innovative use of language, far from easy to capture in English. When, for instance, Strindberg engages in word games in Swedish, the elegance and economy of the original are often lost in translation as may be illustrated in an exchange between Jean and Kristin in *Miss Julie*. On this occasion, Jean is berating his fiancée Kristin for not showing proper respect for Miss Julie. Jean starts by using the verb '*missakta*' (to show disrespect for): this lacks a one-word equivalent in English, as 'disrespect' is much more commonly used as a noun than as a verb. Kristin's answer contains the noun '*aktning*' (respect), which in turn enables Jean to respond reverting to the word he initially used:

JEAN: *...och för samma sak som du **missaktar** henne nu borde du **missakta** dig själv.*

JEAN: ...and for the same thing that you **feel disrespect for** her now you ought to **feel disrespect for** yourself.

KRISTIN: *Jag har alltid haft så mycket **aktning** för mig själv – – –*

KRISTIN: I have always had so much **respect** for myself

JEAN: *– att du kunnat **missakta** andra*

JEAN: – that you've been able to **feel disrespect for** others[27]

In three recent translations, the translators have solved the problem of Strindberg's word play in their own individual ways. In all cases, however, the elegant playfulness of the original is lost.

Helen Cooper:

JEAN: ...and for the same reason that you *despise* her, you should *despise* yourself.
CHRISTINE: At least I've always had enough *self respect* not to...
JEAN: To *despise* others! [28]

Frank McGuiness:

JEAN: ... Miss Julie is your mistress. You *spit* on her now but you might *spit* on yourself for the same reason.
KRISTIN: I've always had enough *respect* for myself
JEAN: Enough to *spit* on others.[29]

Gregory Motton:

JEAN: ...and the same thing you *despise* her for now, you ought to *despise* yourself for.
KRISTIN: I've always had sufficient *self-respect* to – – –
JEAN: – To be able to *despise* others! – [30]

Other characteristic features of Strindberg's way of writing are equally difficult to recreate in translation, as for example the way his descriptions of inanimate objects often draw upon words traditionally associated with humans. Shoes worn by Strindberg's men and women do not 'crunch' on the gravel under the weight of their wearers, they 'scream'. Characters do not just 'cast glances'; they 'cast grenades'. They do not 'deliver their lines', they 'fire them off', and even when perfectly calm, they have a tendency to 'gush' and 'grunt' or express themselves through the use of highly evocative verbs. Coupled with Strindberg's fondness for incorporating into his writing swiftly associated images, often in rapid succession, the resulting effect in Swedish is that of an intentionally grandiose style. Breaking with previously accepted literary traditions was the hallmark of the circle to which Strindberg belonged and which he portrayed in *Röda Rummet* (*The Red Room*, 1879), his breakthrough novel. Members of this bohemian group of artists took a pride in having created their own style of writing, using a language free from pat phrases and clichés. Credited with having revitalised the Swedish language, Strindberg not only introduced the use of the vernacular into the written literary language but also intentionally set about to break the rules of Swedish syntax. However, while his novel use of language may have the desired effect of making a Swedish reader sit up and take notice, in translation into English the result is different. Instead of appearing interestingly innovative, Strindberg's linguistic neologisms often emerge in translation as stylistically awkward or, if corrected and adjusted to conform to the rules of English grammar and syntax, as bland and lacklustre. When, for instance, Miss Julie and Jean reappear on stage, following their sojourn in Jean's bedroom, Jean turns to Julie (Strindberg, p. 157):

> JEAN: ...*men tror ni att en person i min ställning skulle ha vågat kasta ögonen **upp** till er om ni ej själv utfärdade inbjudningen.*

In a close translation, Jean says:

> ...but do you think that someone in my position would have dared
> cast his eyes **up** on you if you had not yourself issued the invitation?

Here Strindberg has taken the expression *kasta ögonen på någon* (cast your eyes on someone) and slightly altered it into 'cast your eyes *up* on someone', the addition of 'up' capturing the difference in social position between Jean and Miss Julie. Wisely, translators have refrained from transferring this word for word into English, but the price paid for this decision is giving Jean a line which is blander and considerably less original than its Swedish counterpart. In Peter Watts' translation the stock phrase 'look at' replaces Strindberg's neologism while, in compensation, emphasis is placed on *you*:[31]

> JEAN: ...but do you think anyone in my position would have dared to as
> much as look at you unless *you* invited him?

Similarly, in the translations by Helen Cooper, Frank McGuiness and Gregory Motton, other lengthier renditions have been chosen to convey the meaning of the original.

Helen Cooper (p. 25):

> JEAN: ...But do you really think that a man in my position would have
> dared *to even wink at you* unless invited to?

Frank McGuiness (p. 35):

JEAN: ...But do you really believe a man in my position would have
dared *to look at you* unless you offered the invitation yourself?

Gregory Motton (p. 121):

JEAN: ...but do you think anyone in my position would have dared so
much as *to lift his eyes to you*, if you didn't invite it!

Another linguistic device frequently used by Strindberg, is to take a well-known expression and by a slight alteration, give it a new and unexpected, linguistic twist. Painting a vivid picture to Miss Julie of their future life together by Lake Como, Jean draws on his experience as a *sommelier* in Switzerland: he now sees the two of them, 'job sharing' (Strindberg, p. 149):

JEAN: – *jag skall salta notorna och ni skall sockra på dem med ert
vackraste leende* –

I shall salt the bills and you shall put sugar on them with your most
beautiful smile –

While in Swedish '*salta*' (to salt, to put salt on) also means to 'fiddle' or 'cook', a commonly known expression, the construction following, containing the contrasting verb '*sockra*' (to put sugar on), is a Strindberg innovation. In Swedish, the resulting line is not only witty but also says something about both Jean and Miss Julie: it reinforces the impression we already have of Jean's lack of moral fibre, while at the same time telling us that Miss Julie's main function in life is, and will remain, to smile and look pretty. While this information may be conveyed in Cooper's and Watts' translation, it is at the expense of the loss of elegance and wit:

Helen Cooper (p. 21):

JEAN: I'll fiddle the bills and you'll cover up with your sweetest smile.

Peter Watts also interprets the meaning of Jean's statement correctly but offers a less elegant solution:

Peter Watts (p. 95):

JEAN: And I'd cook the bills, too, and you'd sugar them with your
sweetest smiles.

Both Frank McGuiness' and Gregory Motton's versions of Jean's line, on the other hand, stay very close to the original, retaining the polarity salt/sugar. The question remains, however, if the translation makes it clear to an English audience exactly what it is Jean is planning to do with the hotel bills:

Frank McGuiness (p. 30); *Gregory Motton* (p. 117):

JEAN: ...I'll salt the bills and you'll sugar them with your sweetest smile.

Stock expressions, made novel-sounding and amusing through innovative additions or through their unexpected use in new contexts, abound in Strindberg's writing. Not surprisingly they often defy the translator, who is forced to settle for everyday, blander expressions. Almost immediately following the discussion between Jean and Miss Julie about their planned departure for Lake Como, they have another exchange. Here again Jean, the temperamentally more energetic of the two and to whom Strindberg tends to give his linguistically more creative expressions, uses a stock phrase which he imbues with new life. Jean now talks about the advantages of a country being a republic, like Switzerland (Strindberg, p. 150):

> JEAN: *Kom till ett annat land bara där det är republik, och man står på näsan för min portiers livré –*
>
> Just go to another country, a republic and one will stand on one's nose for my porter's livery –

In Swedish 'standing on one's nose' is a commonly-used expression to describe someone falling over, but here Strindberg uses it with the additional sense of someone showing excessive respect: Jean envisages everyone not only bowing to him but bowing so low that they will fall flat 'on their noses'. In translation into English, Peter Watts settles for 'bow and scrape' and Helen Cooper for 'grovel' as does Frank McGuiness, while Gregory Motton chooses 'crawl'.

Peter Watts (p. 96):

JEAN: But if you'll only come abroad – to a country where there's a republic, and then they'll bow and scrape to my porter's livery –

Helen Cooper (p. 21):

JEAN: Come to another country with me, a republic where *they'll* grovel for *me* in my porter's livery.

Frank McGuiness (p. 30):

JEAN: We'll go to another country – a republic – they will grovel before me in my servant's uniform.

Gregory Motton (p. 118):

JEAN: Just come to another country, to a republic, and they crawl before my porter's livery.

The sense is there but part of the image is gone and with it, the liveliness of the original: 'bow and scrape', 'grovel' and 'crawl' are all frequently used in English and, as a result, fail to achieve the effect of Strindberg's play on a well-known phrase.

Strindberg's use of emotive verbs and adjectives, his intentional use of grandiose means of expression in stark contrast to the more frequently understated English mode, as well as his innovative use of style and vocabulary, are some of the many reasons why his plays often suffer a high degree of translation loss when transferred into English. In addition, Mary Sandbach, translator of a number of Strindberg's novels into English, has pointed to an aspect of word formation in Swedish as another problem in Strindberg translation. In addition to the process of forming transparent compounds by putting two words together in order to create a new one, as is commonly found in Ibsen, Strindberg makes imaginative use of a method which entails turning verbs into nouns in order to describe an action or a process. This nominal use of verbal constructions is an important ingredient in Strindberg's way of writing, often the means whereby he achieves his characteristic 'fast-paced action' tempo. Using an example from her translation of *Getting Married*, Mary Sandbach discusses two innovative constructions, translated faithfully into English as 'shawl-putting-on' and 'botee-buttoning' which are used by Strindberg to comic effect in a description of the early, attentive stages of courtship. For the purposes of translation, however, these novel Strindbergian creations need to be converted. But, while 'helping her on with her shawl and buttoning her botees' is semantically correct, the paraphrasing results in an inevitable loss of immediacy and economy in English translation.[32]

In Strindberg's work, as in that of playwrights writing in other languages, each character speaks in his or her own distinctive voice. In *Miss Julie*, Jean's use of language is often more imaginative than Kristin's and, in addition, contains a fair sprinkling of French loanwords which he uses with the clear intention to impress. The effect is often comical, a humorous aspect too often lost in translation into English, where many words originally borrowed from French no longer stand out as foreign. (See Chapter 2.) When, for instance, Jean talks to Kristin in Swedish about Miss Julie's '*projekt*', the word has an unexpected, out of the ordinary sound in the context in which it is used, lost in English translation where 'project' is not likely to be perceived as French and hence no longer has a 'foreign' feel to it. In contrast, at other times Jean's language is less precise, revealing his lack of formal education. On these occasions his use of language resembles that of Kristin, pointing to their shared background as well as their lack of confidence as servants who, in talking about their superiors, become overly verbose in an attempt to be more polite and accommodating. The loss in translation of the distinctiveness of a character's voice may often be compensated for by the use of dialect. In his portrayal of Jean in the 2000 Haymarket production of *Miss Julie*, Christopher Eccleston's decision to draw on a northern English dialect did much to set his valet's language apart from that of his mistress. (For further discussion of the use of dialect in translation, see Chapter 9.)

In *Miss Julie*, Strindberg's use of Swedish to achieve dramatic effect includes consistent switches between formal and informal pronouns of address in order to mirror the swings in mood and emotions of his characters. (See also Chapters 2, 7 and 9.) Commenting on Jean dancing with Miss Julie, Kristin addresses him in the third person singular, a custom not infrequent in Sweden at the time, assuring him that she does not mind (Strindberg, p. 127):

> KRISTIN: *Inte! – Inte för så lite, det vet **han** nog; och jag vet min plats också...*

> KRISTIN: Not for so little, **he** knows that; and I know my place too...

As soon becomes obvious, Jean has social ambitions. He has worked abroad and is able to converse with Miss Julie in French. Taken by surprise, she is impressed and enquires where he learnt to speak French. She uses *ni*, the formal pronoun of address in Swedish (Strindberg, p. 128):

> (*Jean enters in black tails and a black bowler hat.*)
> FRÖKEN: Très gentil, monsieur Jean! Très gentil!
> JEAN: Vous voulez plaisanter, madame!
> FRÖKEN: Et vous voulez parler français! *Var har **ni** lärt det?*
> Where have **you** learnt that?

Later, when the two return from Jean's bedroom to reappear on stage, Jean, still aware of the social gulf between them, addresses Julie with the formal *ni*. Forcibly reminded of reality, she understandably reacts and implores him to use the informal *du*. But he can't (Strindberg, p. 150):

> MISS JULIE: (*Blygt, sant kvinligt.*) **Ni**! *Säg **du**! Mellan oss finns inga skrankor mer! – Säg **du**!*

> MISS JULIE: (*Shy, genuinely feminine.*) **Ni**! Say ***du***! There aren't any barriers between us any longer! – Say ***du***!

JEAN: (Plågad.) *Jag kan inte! – Det finns skrankor mellan oss ännu, så länge vi vistas i detta hus –*

JEAN: (*Pained.*) I can't! There are still barriers between us, as long as we stay in this house –

Another feature that Strindberg's writing shares with Ibsen's, is the use of the polarity effect. While Miss Julie dreams that she is sitting on top of a pillar, trying to fall *down*, Jean imagines himself climbing *up* a high tree. This clear-cut either/or aspect of Strindberg's writing, where imagery is expressed as a series of uncompromisingly opposed extremes, is fundamentally unfamiliar to English audiences. As Michael Meyer has pointed out, there is much in the character of Miss Julie that may be viewed as deeply un-English:

> In the Swedish theatre, as in the German, the unforgivable sin is to underact. In England, it is to overact; how often have we not seen our best actors, when faced by the peaks of Othello and King Lear, take refuge in gentlemanly underplaying or the evasiveness of theatrical fireworks? It is no coincidence that the only two actors who have fully succeeded in Strindberg in England, Robert Loraine and Wilfrid Lawson, have been actors of most un-English, one might almost say continental vehemence, and consequently difficult to cast in roles of ordinary human dimensions. For a parallel reason there has never yet [...] been an adequate Miss Julie in England.[33]

These observations seem to imply that potentially melodramatic interpretations of Strindberg's larger-than-life characters are inherent in the parts as written, unrelated to whatever might have been lost or added in translation.

Following the opening of the 2000 production of *Miss Julie* in London, critics responded to Jean's confessions to Miss Julie that he had been in love with her from an early age with a measure of incredulity. How could this be true? With a well-established (although not always well-founded) reputation for overstatement, here was further evidence, it would seem, of Strindberg, the melodramatic playwright. However, the whole point of Jean's avowals of love is that we are not supposed to know whether Jean is lying or telling the truth, whether or not his childhood love for his mistress is a tale born of the moment. Jean's avowals of love offer an example of what Egil Törnqvist has called 'unreliable narration':

> A narrator is unreliable when s/he consciously or unconsciously provides incorrect information (active unreliability) or when s/he is withholding important information (passive unreliability). Here 'unreliability' does

not necessarily carry negative overtones, implying that a character may be unreliable in other, negative respects usually associated with the use of the word. Here it simply means that a character is 'unreliable' in the sense described because s/he has his/her own good reasons.[34]

Unreliable narration is found in several of Strindberg's plays, one example being the exchange between Laura and her husband in *The Father*. Having been given medical advice that she must, at all costs, try to avoid giving him cause for suspicion that he is being observed for signs of madness, Laura promptly sets about doing just that by sowing the seeds of doubt in his mind that he is not the father of his daughter Bertha. What the audience cannot be sure of however is whether this is true or not:

> We may guess that the Captain's doubt about his fatherhood is a fixed idea, with no basis in reality, but nothing in the play contradicts the opposite interpretation. We grope for the reality of the play in the same way that the Captain himself gropes for the truth among the mists surrounding him.[35]

It seems likely that Laura would not be inclined to admit as readily to adultery if this were *true*. Instead Strindberg, having read his Shakespeare (see Scene 5 and the quotation from Shylock in *The Merchant of Venice*: 'Does not a man have eyes?'), is more likely to have intended Laura to be operating on the level of Iago, sowing the seeds of doubt in Othello's mind, and foreshadowing the eventual humbling of the Captain.[36]

Corroborating the impression that Laura is trying out her hypothesis to dramatic effect is the language that Strindberg makes her use in the discussion with her husband when she sows the seeds of doubt about Bertha's true father. At this point, she delivers her lines in a declamatory style, in a language different from the one she has used immediately before. This shift has been captured in the translation by Richard Nelson:

> LAURA: You don't know if you're Bertha's father.
> CAPTAIN: I know it.
> LAURA: You can't. No one can.
> CAPTAIN: You're joking.
> LAURA: No. It's only what you taught me yourself. How can you ever know if I've been unfaithful to you?
> CAPTAIN: You are capable of many things, just not that. And if you were, you wouldn't be talking about it.
> LAURA: What if I was ready to give up everything, to be thrown out, despised, all of it, just for the right in choosing how my child is brought up? What if I was willing to tell the world that Bertha is mine, but not yours. What if – [37]

In Nelson's translation, Laura's 'What if –' hypothesising, with its elevated, somewhat melodramatic choice of vocabulary, contrasts markedly with the more mundane linguistic register in which she has spoken up to this point. This, however, is not as clearly captured in Peter Watts' translation, nor in John Osborne's adaptation (emphasis added):

Peter Watts (p. 43):

LAURA: Simply that you don't know that you are Bertha's father.
CAPTAIN: Of course I know!
LAURA: No one can tell, so you certainly can't.
CAPTAIN: Is this a joke?
LAURA: No, I'm simply applying your own *doctrine*. Besides, how do you know that I haven't been unfaithful to you?
CAPTAIN: I can believe a lot about you, but not that. Nor do I believe that you'd talk about it if it were true.
LAURA: Suppose I were ready to put up with anything, to lose my home and my good name, for the sake of keeping my child and bringing her up. Suppose I was telling the truth just now when I said Bertha was my child and not yours. Suppose –

John Osborne (p. 19–20):

LAURA: Only that you cannot know whether or not you are Bertha's father.
CAPTAIN: Of course I know.
LAURA: You can't know. Neither can anyone.
CAPTAIN: Is this some joke?
LAURA: No. I'm simply following your own *doctrine*. Besides, how do you know that I haven't been unfaithful to you?
CAPTAIN: I can believe a lot of things about you, but that's not one of them. And if it were true I'm certain you'd never own up to it.
LAURA: Well, think on this: what if I were prepared to put up with anything, humiliation, losing my reputation, my home, anything for the sake of holding on to my child and bringing her up? What if I were just telling the truth when I said Bertha was my child and not yours? Suppose – [38]

Unlike the versions by Watts and Osborne, Nelson's translates the Swedish word 'lärdomar' (learning, knowledge) as 'It's only what you taught me yourself', which accurately captures Laura's sarcastic reference to her husband's interest in the scientific debate at the time. The Captain is a scientist and part of his mounting frustration is attributable to his failure to receive the books that he needs to further advance his reading in the fields of Darwinism and the new discoveries made during the latter part of the nineteenth century. Later in the play we learn that his suspicions are in fact well-founded: the women in his household do not share his keen interest in new thinking and ideas, and as it turns out, the eagerly awaited books have not arrived due to his wife's intervention.

Part of the problem in the translations by Watts and Osborne is linked to their choice of the word 'doctrine' as used by Laura immediately before she starts baiting her husband. In choosing the word 'doctrine,' Osborne and Watts seem to have sought and found a one-word equivalent to the original Swedish word. This decision however leads to two problems. First, it creates an impression of Laura as being more educated and widely read than she is in the original. One of the reasons why the Captain wants his daughter to be educated away from the home is his fear that she would otherwise remain ignorant of the new age now dawning and prove susceptible to the superstitions widely held among the less well educated. Second, the use of 'doctrine' immediately preceding the 'What if –' hypothesising speech that Laura delivers soon afterwards tends to pre-empt the effect of what is to come which requires a change in linguistic register. Motton's solution is to use the word 'teaching' (p. 50):

> LAURA: You don't know if Bertha is your child!
> CAPTAIN: Don't I?
> LAURA: No, you can't know what no one can know!
> CAPTAIN: Are you joking?
> LAURA: No. I'm only using your own teaching. Besides, how do you
> know I haven't been unfaithful?
> CAPTAIN: I could believe many things about you, but not that, and
> neither do I believe you would tell me if it were true.
> LAURA: Imagine if I were prepared for anything, even to be cast out,
> despised, to keep control over my child, and that I'm telling the truth
> when I say: Bertha is my child, but not yours! Imagine...

While a Swedish reader of Strindbergian drama containing 'unreliable narration' might be able to sense that a change in discourse also means a change in emotional exchange, stylistic nuances which serve as indicators of these changes are only too easily lost in translation. Returning now to *Miss Julie*, linguistic markers are obviously not the only means which Strindberg uses in order to indicate that Jean's assurance of his childhood feelings for Miss Julie might be fictitious. From other aspects of his behaviour – he freely helps himself to his Lordship's vintage wine for instance – we know that his character is not unflawed. On stage, however, language plays as important a part as action. If in translation 'unreliable narration' emerges as ordinary narrative, part of the overall design of the playwright's original work has not been given expression, inevitably resulting in the loss of some of the impact of the original.

Jean is however not alone in giving us good grounds for suspicion that he might be economical with the truth. In the case of Julie it has been suggested that 'we never know for sure how much of Julie's personal accounts is make-believe, how much is recollection coloured by the present and how much is reasonably accurate retelling of childhood memories'.[39] Unlike Jean who, when he no longer feels the need to impress Julie, openly admits that it was 'just talk', there is nothing overtly stated in the text telling us that Julie's recollection of her childhood might not tally with the facts. Still, it is not possible to be completely sure that she is telling the truth since earlier on she has been caught lying about her broken-off engagement. When Jean confronts her saying that it was her fiancé who broke off the engagement, Julie is unable to accept the truth and accuses her fiancé as well as Jean, the messenger, of lying when it is of course Julie herself who is now lying. This is corroborated by an earlier exchange between Jean and Kristin where we learn of the events that she witnessed in the stable yard: it was in fact Miss Julie's fiancé who walked off and left her.

What Strindberg is trying to do here is to allow the audience to experience the contradictory signals often experienced in real life. We may have a sense that someone is lying, but not be fully aware what their reasons are for doing so. Failing to understand it all at the time, we might recall the incident much later when the reasons prompting the lies are better understood. This means, however, that the actor must be able to convey that 'hollow' sound which often accompanies 'unreliable information', which in turn presupposes an understanding that this is an aspect of the text in the first place. And, the subtler the signals are expressed in the source language, the more likely it is that they might be missed in translation, resulting in a flattened text bereft of a level found in the original. To quote Strindberg himself on the subject of dialogue:

> I have avoided the mathematical, symmetrically constructed dialogue of French drama [...] allowing the brain to work irregularly as it does in real life where in a conversation a subject is rarely completed but instead one brain responds to the stimulus received from the other speaker.[40]

In order to signal the crosscurrents beneath the level of the spoken word, Strindberg's dialogue is broken up by dashes, dots, question and exclamation marks. Sometimes this is a device used to indicate that a character may say one thing but think something else. When, for instance, Jean and Julie emerge from Jean's room, knowing that they now have to face the music, Jean's characteristically male approach to the problem is to embark upon a plan of action, which includes leaving Sweden and travelling south, to Lake Como. He even goes as far as to consult a timetable for information on the departure times of trains bound for the Continent. Julie, on the other hand, listens absent-mindedly, only concerned to hear Jean tell her that he loves her. Finally she plucks up her courage (Strindberg, p. 149):

> FRÖKEN: *Allt det där är bra! Men Jean – du skall ge mig mod – Säg att du älskar mig! Kom och omfamna mig!*

> MISS JULIE: All that is well and good. But Jean – you must give me courage – Tell me that you love me! Come and embrace me!

Here the dashes interspersed in Miss Julie's response to Jean seem to suggest a lack of faith in her own words, which are being formulated increasingly slowly.

Another famous exponent of the practice of using punctuation to signal underlying emotions and unco-ordinated thought processes is, as we have seen, Chekhov. However, Strindberg's work is characterised by a wider range of different types of punctuation, which are used to serve a variety of purposes. Often completing his plays within a very short period of time, Strindberg was frequently inconsistent in adhering to his own highly idiosyncratic system. While in Miss Julie's pleading with Jean, the dashes may be suggestive of one interpretation, in other contexts they may serve a different purpose; and, on yet other occasions, they may be used to indicate simply that a speaker has been interrupted.

Strindberg's use of ellipses is equally inconsistent. While three dots at the end of a line may indicate a pause in the dialogue as *points suspensifs*, they may also show that a character has been interrupted in the middle of a sentence.[41] When in *The Father* Laura first introduces the idea to the Captain that he might not be Bertha's father, in the original her second 'What if –' speculation is concluded by three dots. In this and several other exchanges, the three dots indicate the speed of the dialogue, that one of the speakers does not have the time to conclude his/her sentence. The liveliness of Strindbergian dialogue is, however, at times also reinforced by the use of question marks and, above all, exclamation marks, the use of which varies greatly from the way they are likely to be used in dramatic texts written by English playwrights. At times their function is to serve as a form of stage direction. In *Miss Julie*, this is clear when an exclamation mark concludes a line such as (Strindberg, p. 155):

> FRÖKEN: (På knä med knäppta händer.) O Gud i himmelen, gör slut på mitt eländiga liv!

> MISS JULIE: (On her knees with clasped hands.) Oh, God in Heaven, put an end to my miserable life!

Here Strindberg is telling the actress playing the part that Miss Julie is far from calm and composed. Yet, on a number of other occasions, he chooses not to use punctuation as acting directives; instead he provides specific information such as '(Screams.)' or '(Convulsed.)'. Most bewilderingly, perhaps, are lines which seem to be candidates for calm deliverance but which nevertheless are followed by exclamation marks. In Miss Julie this happens on more than one occasion when Jean is speaking, as in his description of the loving couples at Lake Como, often departing from the idyllic retreat not long after they arrive. 'They fall out of course! but the rent has to be paid, nevertheless!' There is some evidence here that, when Strindberg unexpectedly inserts an exclamation mark in the middle of a sentence, within the framework of his highly personal form of punctuation he is showing his own emotional identification with the situation. An example of this intense empathy with what he is describing is found in The Ghost Sonata. At the time that he wrote the play, Strindberg was experiencing considerable problems in getting domestic help. Conversing in the Hyacinth Room with the Young Lady, the Student comments on the apparent wealth of the household. He receives an answer containing two exclamation marks:

> FRÖKEN: Det hjälper inte! om man så har tre!

> THE YOUNG LADY: It doesn't help! even if one has three! [42]

Confirming the impression of Strindberg's personal involvement with the problems of getting good domestic service are other references in the play to inadequate support with everyday chores such as beds having to be remade and maids whose methods of cleaning leave something to be desired.

How then are the vagaries of Strindbergian punctuation dealt with in translation? Michael Meyer settles for the following approach:

> What about punctuation? It is, I think, accepted that a translator may legitimately break up a long sentence into two, or join two into one; but what is one to do with for example, Strindberg's repeated use of exclamation marks and three dots? My own feeling is that a translator must have a free hand to excise both. Exclamation marks used as often as Strindberg uses them give a terrible melodramatic effect; and three dots tend to bring out

the worst in any actor – the 'meaningful pause'. Actors nowadays, and readers too, are used to looking for the hidden implication of a phrase; better that a few should miss such an implication rather than saddle the dialogue with something that is as destructive in its way as repeated italics.[43]

In contrast to the approach chosen by Michael Meyer, in his more recent translation of *Miss Julie*, Gregory Motton chooses to replicate Strindberg's punctuation without adjustments to English conventions. Here are Jean and Julie in Motton's translation as they plan to leave the Count's household (Motton, p. 132):

> JEAN: I'll come with you – but now at once, before it's too late. Now this moment!
> MISS JULIE: Get dressed then! (*Picks up birdcage.*)
> JEAN: But no luggage! It would give us away!
> MISS JULIE: No nothing! Just what fits into the compartment.

In addition to linguistic obstacles, social and cultural factors also combine to provide problems for the translation of Strindberg's plays. Some of these concern aspects of Swedish rituals of the past which today are likely to seem as bewildering to a younger Swedish generation as they would to an English-speaking audience. In *The Ghost Sonata*, for example, references are made to the old Swedish ritual of draping white sheets across the windows of a house to indicate bereavement. Overall, this type of translation problem seems to have been handled by translators in three different ways.

1. The source text is faithfully translated into English without comments.
2. The original is reproduced but the translation is annotated and provided with the explanation that the procedure formed part of the Swedish mourning ritual at the time.
3. The explanation is incorporated into the translated text.[44]

While the disadvantage of 1 is that the English reader is not provided with an explanation to something that is bound to seem bewildering, the problem with solution 3 is that it is impossible to tell that the explanation is the work of the translator which might result in even greater problems for the reader. The different approaches are illustrated below:

1. hung with white sheets
2. hung with white sheets* [*Sign of mourning]
3. hung with white mourning sheets[45]

Social and cultural problems in the translation of Strindberg's plays do not differ greatly from those likely to occur in Ibsen's and Chekhov's work, which is not surprising considering their shared north European origin. Strindberg's as well as Ibsen's characters indulge in a glass of *'punsch'*, the arrak-based drink popular in Scandinavia during the latter part of the nineteenth century. At the beginning of *The Ghost Sonata*, the Student mentions the drink by name, asking if he still smells of *'punsch'*, which tells us that the previous night he would have been out drinking with his friends. A comparison of eight translations of Strindberg's play shows two translators opting for the similar-sounding but not similar-tasting English 'punch', three avoiding the trap by referring to the drink as 'liquor', two using the generic 'drinking' and one American translator suggesting 'whisky', a drink that might be popular with present-day American students but unlikely even to have been thought of by Swedish students around the turn of the nineteenth century.[46] (See also discussion of the drink in Chapter 3.)

Like Chekhov's plays, Strindberg's work also reflects his keen interest in nature, and his awareness of flora and fauna informs his novels as well as his dramas. Strindberg, however, is less inclined to resort to the broader and more thematic approach of Ibsen in *The Wild Duck* and Chekhov in *The Seagull*, and instead makes use of more specific symbols. In *Miss Julie*, for example, the symbol of the bird in the cage is an obvious one; it is brutally killed by Jean, foreshadowing Miss Julie's own fate. In some translations this bird is described as a 'siskin', in others as a 'green finch'. The reason for this variation in translation is not difficult to find. In Swedish, the name of the bird is *'grönsiska'*, in a word-for-word translation, 'green siskin'. As no such bird exists in English, translators have been forced to choose between 'green finch', the name of a bigger bird belonging to the finch family, and 'siskin', a smaller bird of the same family, more likely to have been kept in a cage but lacking the reference to the colour green. Although, strictly speaking, 'siskin' would seem a more accurate rendering, referring to the bird as a 'green finch' does not detract from Strindberg's intentions in the original. More questionable, however, is the decision to give the bird a male gender as in Peter Watts' translation. Not only does Miss Julie describe the bird as 'the only living creature that loves me', and we now know Julie's feelings about men, but a reference to the bird as 'he' also makes it difficult for the parallel to be drawn between the two as victims (Watts, p. 111, emphasis added):

> JEAN: All right, give me the little beast, I'll wring its neck.
> MISS JULIA: Don't hurt *him* will you? Don't – Oh, I can't!
> JEAN: Well, I can – let's have it.

While the caged siskin here may be seen to represent a woman unable to shake off her chains, predators such as the eagle, the hawk and the falcon stand for masculinity with its associated attributes of power and incisiveness. It is true that Strindberg at times saw himself as a dove, but this was more likely to happen when he felt under pressure and the victim of an evil world. But he would also use the word *Örnen* (Eagle), his *nom de plume* during university days, to refer to himself in the hope perhaps that some of the strength and power of the bird might rub off on him. Strindberg even went as far as using a quill from an imperial eagle for writing and was frequently photographed pen in hand.[47] Hardly surprising then that Strindberg lets Jean refer to 'the hawks and the falcons' as the 'rulers' soaring high above, while those that they 'rule' have to remain content watching from down below (Strindberg, p. 140):

> JEAN: ...Do you know how the world looks from down there – no, you
> don't! Like hawks and falcons whose backs you rarely see because
> most of the time they're soaring up there!

In Frank McGuiness' version, both predators remain as in the original (p. 23):

> JEAN: ...Do you know what the world looks like from down here – no,
> you don't. You're like the hawk and the falcon. They fly so high above
> you rarely see their backs.

Gregory Motton too stays close to the original (p. 112):

> JEAN: ...Do you know what the world looks like from down there – no,
> you don't! Like hawks and falcons those one hardly ever sees the back
> of because they are mostly soaring about up there somewhere!

In Peter Watts' translation, on the other hand, 'the hawks' remain while 'the falcons' turn into 'eagles' (p. 90).

> JEAN: ...You don't know how the world looks from down below, do you?
> No – of course you don't, any more than hawks and eagles do; and we
> don't see their backs, because they're nearly always soaring up over
> our heads.

In Helen Cooper's translation, the two birds appear as one but in the plural form, 'hawks' (p. 15):

> JEAN: ...Do you know what the world looks like from down here? No,
> you don't you see. Because you see the world from up there –

hovering like great hawks, high above us. What's it like? I've never
flown with the hawks.

A possible reason for Helen Cooper's decision to merge the two birds into
one might have been to reinforce the focus on the hawk image, one to which
Strindberg returns later in the play. Upon their return from Jean's bedroom,
Jean and Miss Julie have the following exchange, now unmistakably sexually
charged (Strindberg, p. 156):

> MISS JULIE: And now you've seen the back of the hawk...
> JEAN: Not exactly the *back*...

In its use of bird symbolism, *The Ghost Sonata* presents problems of even
greater complexity.[48] In this play, the Mummy is using a form of parrot
language, which offers a springboard for a number of allusions familiar to a
Swedish, but not a British theatre audience:

> MUMIEN: (Som en papegoja.) *Vackra gojan! Å Jakob ä där! Kurrrrre!*

> THE MUMMY: (*Like a parrot.*) Beautiful parrot! And Jaco is there?
> Currrrr?

Here the translator is faced with the following problems. The first part of
the line would naturally be translated as 'Pretty Polly' were it not for the fact
that *goja* is also a colloquial Swedish expression for nonsense used in the
context of talking rubbish, which is of course exactly what the Mummy is
doing. In addition, Jacob is not only a well-known name for a parrot in Sweden,
probably derived from *jako*, the generic name for the kind of parrot most
skilled in imitating human language, there is a further dimension to the
reference to Jacob. 'Jacob, where are you' is the name of a form of Swedish
'Blind man's bluff', which draws on the biblical image of the blind Isaac
feeling his son Jacob dressed as Esau. In *The Ghost Sonata* the name is also
likely to refer to Jacob Hummel, the father of the Mummy's child, who has
abandoned her and for whom she is now looking. The likelihood that this
intricate web of references of the original could be transferred into English
with any degree of success would seem slim, possibly one of the reasons why
The Ghost Sonata has made only infrequent appearances on English-speaking
stages.

As in Chekhov's plays, Strindberg's work makes frequent reference not
only to fauna but also to flora. In northern Europe, after many months of cold
and snow, the signs heralding the arrival of spring are eagerly awaited. Among
the first signs of spring are the green shoots of willow trees, used by Strindberg
at the very beginning of *Easter* to set the tone for the play (Watts, p. 124):

> ELIS: (*Looking round.*) The double windows down, the floor scrubbed,

and clean curtains! It's really spring again! They've scraped the ice off the street, and down by the river the willows are out. Yes, it's spring...

In Sweden, as in Russia, intense interest is centred on the birch tree: the reappearance of new green foliage is traditionally linked to the arrival of a warmer, gentler season. Birch trees, sprigs and wreaths interwoven with flowers worn by children on festive occasions during the summer occur repeatedly in the Swedish idylls captured on canvas by Strindberg's friend, the artist Carl Larsson. When towards the end of *The Father*, the Captain, enveloped in a straightjacket, starts reminiscing about spring, it is among the birch trees, representing light, warmth and carefree happiness, that the birds and flowers start to appear. It is doubtful, however, that these deeply-felt emotions expressed by the Captain in the original survive in John Osborne's English adaptation:

> CAPTAIN: ...When you were so young, Laura, and we would walk in the birch woods together, among the cowslips and thrushes. Lovely, so lovely. Just think of it – how pleasing our life was and how it is now.[49]

Through minimal English adjustment of Strindberg's floral imagery, the reliving of the moment is more successfully conveyed in Richard Nelson's version, albeit at the cost of the loss of the birch trees (p. 61):

> CAPTAIN: Laura, when we were young we took walks in the woods, there were primroses, thrushes – that was good, that was good! Life was beautiful then, look at it now.

In Sweden Midsummer Eve is a night of magic, of white light and the fulfilment of dreams. This is the time when Miss Julie steps down into the servants' quarters, fatefully meeting with Jean. Had it not been Midsummer Eve, when the traditional rules governing social behaviour are suspended, Miss Julie would not have been able to invite Jean to dance, nor could she have trespassed onto servants' territory. In fact it may be argued that without the rituals and the enchantment of Midsummer Eve, Strindberg's play could not have been written, as Julie's meeting with Jean would never have taken place. To evoke the atmosphere of the night during which the sun never really sets, Strindberg's stage directions call for the kitchen stove to be decorated with birch twigs, the glass doors to reflect lilac bushes in blossom in the garden, and for a jar resting on the table to be filled with cut lilac. When Miss Julie reminisces about the Midsummers of her childhood she recalls lilacs and birch trees. The very fact that it is on Midsummer Eve that Julie meets her fate, the night of hopes, wishes and promises, is a supreme irony, in itself a sardonic twist impossible to convey in translation. As Julie recalls (McGuiness, p. 49):

> JULIE: The memories would start. I'd remember when I was a child – the church on Midsummer Day was thick with leaves and branches. Birch twigs and lilacs.

As in the case of Miss Julie recalling her childhood, it is not the flowers *per se* which evoke emotions but what they recall and represent: Strindberg uses a wide variety of floral imagery in his plays and novels. In *A Dream Play*, immediately following the prologue showing Indra's daughter descending to earth, the gilded dome of the castle emerges out of a 'forest of giant hollyhocks – white, pink, crimson, yellow, violet'. This, the very first floral image of hollyhocks as the symbol of apparent domestic bliss and happy idyll, may not be too unfamiliar to an English audience. Nor is the next floral image, which occurs shortly afterwards in Act 1 when the courting Officer is waiting at the stage door for his beloved Victoria. Viewed as the original, central core of the play,[50] this scene often elicits the strongest response from the audience, not surprisingly perhaps, considering the number of times Strindberg must have been waiting outside the theatre for Siri von Essen, his first wife, and then, later in life, for Harriet Bosse, his third. Victoria never appears, however, and as the Officer grows older and his hair turns white, the roses in his hand wither and die. But while the image of red roses is well known, Strindberg's stage directions also call for an another flower. Through a gate in the wall a passageway leads to a bright green opening with a giant, blue monkshood. And as the Officer anxiously awaits the arrival of Victoria, failing to find her among the actors hurriedly leaving through the stage door, Strindberg provides him with the following line:

> THE OFFICER: She must be here soon... (*Turning to the stage door attendant.*) The blue monkshood out there. I've seen it since I was a child... Is it the same one?... I remember in a vicarage once when I was seven years old...there're two doves, blue doves underneath that hood...but that time a bumble-bee came and crept into the hood... Got you, I thought and pressed it shut; but the bee stung through it and I cried...but then the vicar's wife came and put some wet mud on it...and then we had wild strawberries and milk for supper... I think it's getting dark already.[51]

The high, rounded hood or helmet of the monkshood seems to have caught Strindberg's imagination in much the same way that the cowslip caught Shakespeare's *in The Tempest*, Act V, Scene 1:

> ARIEL: Where the bee sucks, there suck I;

In a cowslip's bell I lie:
There I crouch when owls do cry

Strindberg's flower, however, according to his own specifications, is an Aconitum, which might grow to the majestic height of close to six feet and must have seemed a towering presence to a seven-year-old. In the northern part of Sweden one variety of this plant, the *Aconitum Septentrionale*, with its lighter blue, purplish flowers is commonly found growing wild in the mountains. Strindberg, however, to judge from the reference to the dark blue colour of the flower, appears to have encountered the *Aconitum Napellus* which, if found in the vicinity of a vicarage, is more likely to be the garden variety. Here Strindberg paints a picture of two doves nesting underneath the helmet or hood of the flower, an image of happiness that matches the initial, blissful state of the Officer, waiting for Victoria. But just as Victoria never appears and the Officer loses the love he thought was his, the happiness of the two doves inside the flower comes to a painful end brought about by a stinging bumble-bee. To this may be added that it is unlikely to have escaped the attention of Strindberg, the scientist, that the monkshood is an extremely poisonous plant, containing the alkaloid aconitine. In the case of the Officer as a young boy, however, there is first some soothing comfort available from the vicar's wife in the form of wet mud to cool the sting. And to make sure the episode had a happy ending, the children finished the day with wild strawberries and milk, every Swedish child's wish come true on a warm summer's evening. For the Officer/author, on the other hand, life's problems are no longer solved quite as simply and he concludes, 'I think it's getting dark already'.

The extent to which translators of *A Dream Play* have been fully aware of the details involved in this floral image is difficult to ascertain. In Meyer's translation the two doves are first described as being 'on it', then 'under that hood'.

> THE OFFICER: Now, she must be here soon. I say! That flower out there, that blue monkshood. I've seen that since I was a child. Is it the same one? I remember in a parsonage, when I was seven – *there are two doves on it, blue doves under that hood* – but once a bee came and crept into the hood. Then I thought: 'Now I have you!', so *I pinched the flower shut;* but the bee stung through it, and I cried. But then the parson's wife came and put wet earth on it – and we had wild strawberries for supper. I think it's getting dark already.[52]

Below is another translation of the same passage, this time by C R Mueller, an American translator:

THE OFFICER: She's sure to come any minute... Madame, that blue
monkshood out there...and *two doves, two blue doves sat there under
the hood – but then a bee came along and flew into the hood* – and I
thought: Now I've got you! And I *grabbed the flower* but the bee stung
me, straight through the petals and I cried – but then the Rector's
wife came and put some moist earth on it. For supper we had wild
strawberries and milk – I think it's already growing dark. [53]

Evert Sprinchorn, another American translator, has tackled the problem
this way:

THE OFFICER: She's got to come along pretty soon... Madame – that
blue flower out there – that monkshood. I remember it from the time
I was a child. Can't be the same one, can it?... It was at the parsonage,
I remember, the minister's house – the garden. I was seven years
old... *Fold back the top petals – the pistil and stamen look like two
doves. We used to do that as children... But this time a bee came –
went into the flower.* 'Got you!' I said. And *I pinched the flower
together*. And the bee stung me... And I cried... Then the minister's
wife came and put mud on my finger... Later we had strawberries
and cream for dessert at supper... I do believe it's getting dark
already. [54]

While Meyer has attempted only a slight adjustment, and added the words
'on it', Sprinchorn has clearly felt the need to expand on the original, perhaps
not altogether a wise decision. Mueller's version, on the other hand,
oversimplifies the complexity of the original; 'I grabbed the flower' might
include closing the helmet of the monkshood but could also just mean grabbing
hold of the stem of the flower.

Strindberg, like Shakespeare, was not a botanist in the strict sense of the
word. Yet both were attracted to flora, Strindberg primarily because of the
variety of shapes and configurations which, to his artist's mind, would trigger
off a chain of associations. In an essay written during the latter period of 1875
about an unfamiliar flower found on the bank of the river Danube, Strindberg's
initial impression was of a violet. However, he also saw features reminiscent
of the orchid family with its gracefully shaped, butterfly flowers. Upon his
return from his botanical excursion he put the flower in water. Floating on
the water's surface, the plant now recalled memories of the leaves of the
water lily. [55] What practising botanists saw as significant details for purposes
of classification was of little interest to Strindberg, the artist, for whom the
importance lay in similarity in form, shape and colour. This triggering of a
chain of associations, set in motion by visual stimuli, is clearly illustrated in
The Ghost Sonata in the exchange between the Student and the terminally ill
Young Lady in the 'Hyacinth Room'. Here, according to the stage directions,

there are 'hyacinths of every colour everywhere': again a clearly intentional choice of flower, as hyacinths at the time of Strindberg had strong associations with funerals (see Chapter 9). The conversation starts with a mention of hyacinths which in turn triggers off more floral imagery, then expands to include other micro- and macrocosmic images:

> THE YOUNG LADY: Now I see – aren't snowflakes also six-pointed like hyacinth lilies?
> THE STUDENT: You're right – then snowflakes are falling stars...
> THE YOUNG LADY: And the snowdrop is a snow star...rising from the snow.
> THE STUDENT: And the largest and most beautiful of all the stars in the firmament, the red and gold Sirius is the narcissus, with its red and gold chalice and six white rays.
> THE YOUNG LADY: Have you ever seen the shallot in bloom?
> THE STUDENT: I certainly have! It too bears its flowers in a ball, a sphere like the globe of heaven, strewn with white stars...
> THE YOUNG LADY: Yes! God, how magnificent! Whose idea was this?
> THE STUDENT: Yours!
> THE YOUNG LADY: Yours!
> THE STUDENT: Ours! – Together we have given birth to something. We are wed...[56]

Seeing similarities in the natural environment forming a cohesive whole, Strindberg's chain of associations progresses with dazzling speed, a further aspect making his writing less than easily accessible even to Swedish audiences. For English theatregoers, also at the receiving end of an additional number of problems of translation, it is not surprising that Strindberg's name has only more recently been linked to audience popularity and box office success.

In late October 2001, the theatre critic of a leading Swedish newspaper delivered a swingeing attack on a recent Broadway staging of *Dance of Death*, in an adaptation by American playwright Richard Greenberg, with Ian McKellen in the role of Edgar and Helen Mirren as Alice. Directed by Sean Mathias, the production was enthusiastically received by New York theatre audiences as well as critics. In contrast, the Swedish review of this interpretation of *Dance of Death* carried the headline 'Strindberg completely misunderstood'. Nevertheless, when the production transferred to the West End, this time with Frances de la Tour taking the role of Alice, the success was repeated. The play opened at the Lyric Theatre on 20 February 2003 in Greenberg's adaptation with the humorous aspects of this parody on the middle-class marriage clearly accentuated.

Later the same year, in the autumn of 2003, another Strindberg play opened to public acclaim in London, this time adapted by British playwright, Patrick Marber.

In *After Miss Julie*, Marber transported Strindberg's play in time and space, moving it from the 1880s to 1945, on the eve of Labour's post-war election victory. In this version, the father of Miss Julie has turned into an aristocrat who has embraced socialism and been elected a Member of Parliament. Michael Grandage directed the production, with Kelly Reilly as Miss Julie, Richard Coyle as Jean and Helen Baxendale as Kristin. Locating the play to an English aristocratic setting, on an occasion as festive and unrestrained as the magical atmosphere of a Swedish Midsummer Eve, Marber successfully overcame the problem of translating this culturally untranslatable event.

The earlier outraged reaction of the Swedish critic to English Strindberg may suggest that the Strindberg that Swedes have learnt to love is not likely to coincide with the Strindberg English-speaking audiences like to see on stage. However, as is true for all great artists, there are sufficient sides to this Swedish dramatist to satisfy more than one party. In the case of Strindberg, taking the audience all the way to the text might be too great a distance. For Strindberg to arrive in full force on the English stage, the text might need to be moved much closer to the audience than has previously been fully realised.

Notes

1   B E Malmströms *Intelligensblad* (1844). Discussed in H Schück and K Warburg, *Illustrerad svensk litteraturhistoria* IV (Stockholm, Hugo Gebers Förlag, 1916), p. 193 (author's translation)

2   Evert Sprinchorn, *Dagens Nyheter*, 12 June 1999

3   H Müssener, '"Det är synd om...": Strindberg och de tyska översättarna', in B Meidal and N Å Nilsson (eds.), *August Strindberg och hans översättare*, Konferenser 33, Kungl. Vitterhets Historie och Antikvitets Akademien (Stockholm, Almqvist & Wiksell International, 1995), p. 25

4   *Ibid.* p. 28

5   Discussed in H Müssener, *ibid.* p. 34

6   B Meidal, 'En klok råtta måste ha många hål!: Strindberg och översättarna', in B Meidal and N Å Nilsson (eds.), *op. cit.* p. 20

7   G Stockenström, 'Strindberg i Amerika 1988', in H-G Ekman, A Persson and B Ståhle Sjönell (eds.), *Strindbergiana* 4 (Stockholm, Atlantis, 1989), p. 87

8   Discussed in M. Robinson, 'Aldrig längre än till Gravesend: Strindberg och England', in B Meidal and N Å Nilsson (eds.), *op. cit.* pp. 120–1

9   M Meyer, *Strindberg: A Biography* (New York, Random House, 1985), p. 466

10 Discussed in M Robinson, *op. cit.* p. 112; author's translation

11 G Engwall, 'Det knastrar i hjärnan. Strindberg som sin egen franske översättare', in B Meidal, and N Å Nilsson, (eds.), *op. cit.* pp. 35–51; author's translation

12 *Ibid.* p. 49

13 G Ollén, *Strindbergs dramatik* (Stockholm, Sveriges Radio, 1961), p. 122

14 M Meyer, *op. cit.* p. 277

15 M Robinson, *op. cit.* p. 111

16 E H Rapp, 'Strindberg biography. Strindberg's reception in England and America: Part A: Strindberg in England', *Scandinavian Studies* 23(1), Feb 1951, p. 9

17 More recently this is the title preferred by Eivor Martinus, whose translations of the play were staged at the Duke of Cambridge Theatre Club, 26 January–20 February 1993 and 3–22 January 1995 at the Finsborough Theatre in London

18 Discussed in G Ollén, *Strindbergs dramatik* (Stockholm, Sveriges Radio, 1961), p. 136 (author's translation here and throughout unless otherwise indicated)

19 *Ibid.* p. 152

20 *Ibid.* p. 152

21 *Ibid.* p. 326

22 *Ibid.* p. 348

23 *Ibid.* p. 350

24 In a letter to Emil Schering discussed in the Introduction to August Strindberg, *A Dream Play: An Interpretation by Ingmar Bergman*, trans. M Meyer (London, Secker and Warburg, 1973)

25 G Ollén, *ibid.* p. 476

26 *Ibid.* p. 351

27 August Strindberg, *Samlade verk, nationalupplaga (27): Fadren, Fröken Julie, Fordringsägare* (Stockholm: Almqvist & Wiksell, 1984), p. 183 (emphasis added)

28 August Strindberg, *Miss Julie*, trans. H Cooper, from a literal translation by Peter Hogg with an introduction by Helen Cooper (London, Methuen, 1992), p. 42 (emphasis added)

29 August Strindberg, *Miss Julie* and *The Stronger*, version F McGuiness from a literal translation by Charlotte Barslund (London, Faber and Faber, 2000), p. 55 (emphasis added)

30 August Strindberg, *The Plays: Volume One* (*The Father, Miss Julie, The Comrades, Creditors*), trans. G Motton (London, Oberon Books, 2000), p. 136 (emphasis added)

31 August Strindberg, *Three Plays* (*The Father, Miss Julie, Easter*), trans. P Watts, (London, Penguin, 1958), p. 99 (emphasis added)

32 M Sandbach, 'Translating Strindberg', *Swedish Book Review* 1, 1985, p. 33

33 M Meyer, 'Strindberg in England', in C R Smedmark (ed.) *Essays on Strindberg* (Stockholm, Beckman, 1966), p. 70

34 E Törnqvist, 'Unreliable narration in Strindbergian drama', *Scandinavica* 38(1), 1999, pp. 61–79

35 G Brandell, *Drama i tre avsnitt* (Stockholm, Wahlström & Widstrand, 1971), translated and discussed in E Törnqvist, *ibid.* p. 78

36 *Ibid.* p. 65

37 August Strindberg, *The Father*, adapt. R Nelson (London, Oberon Books, 1998), p. 29

38 Strindberg's *The Father* and Ibsen's *Hedda Gabler*, adapt. J Osborne (London, Faber and Faber, 1989) (emphasis added)

39 B Steene, 'Alf Sjöberg's film *Fröken Julie*: Too much cinema, too much theater?', in O Bandle (ed.) *Strindbergs Dramen im Lichte neuerer Methodendiskussionen: Beitrage zum IV. Internationalen Strindberg-Symposion in Zürich 1979* (Basel, Helbing und Lichtenhahn, 1981), p. 194

40 L Josephson, *Strindbergs drama Fröken Julie* (Stockholm, Almqvist & Wiksell, 1965), p. 134; author's translation

41 *Ibid.* p. 138

42 August Strindberg, *Samlade verk, nationalupplaga* (58): *Kammarspel, Oväder, Brända tomten, Spöksonaten, Pelikanen, Svarta handsken*, (Stockholm, Almqvist & Wiksell, 1991), p. 219; author's translation

43 M Meyer, 'On translating plays', *20th Century Studies* 11, 1971, p. 49

44 E Törnqvist, 'Att översätta Strindberg. Spöksonaten på engelska', *Svensk litteraturtidskrift*, 39(2), 1976/77, p. 9

45 *Ibid.* p. 9

46 *Ibid.* p. 9

47 G Brusewitz, *Guldörnen och duvorna. Fågelmotiv hos Strindberg* (Stockholm, Wahlström & Widstrand, 1989), pp. 194–5

48 E Törnqvist, (1976), *op. cit.* pp. 22–3

49 *The Father* adapt. J Osborne, *op. cit.* p. 49

50 M Lamm, *Strindbergs dramer* II (Stockholm, Albert Bonniers Förlag, 1926), p. 307

51 August Strindberg, *Samlade verk, nationalupplaga* (46): *Ett drömspel* (Stockholm Norstedts, 1988), p. 23; author's translation

52 August Strindberg, *A Dream Play: An Interpretation by Ingmar Bergman*, trans. M Meyer (London, Secker and Warburg, 1973), p. 14 (emphasis added)

53 August Strindberg, *A Dream Play and The Ghost Sonata*, trans. C R Mueller, with selected notes to the members of *The Intimate Theatre* (San Francisco, Chandler Publishing Company, 1966), p. 14 (emphasis added)

54 August Strindberg, *A Dream Play. Selected Plays* (*Master Olof, The Father, Miss Julie, Creditors, The Stronger, Playing with Fire, To Damascus* I, *Crimes and Crimes, The Dance of Death, A Dream Play, The Ghost Sonata, The Pelican*), trans. E Sprinchorn (Minneapolis, University of Minnesota Press, 1986), p. 662 (emphasis added)

55 K-A Kärnell, *Strindbergs bildspråk. En studie i prosatil* (Stockholm, Almqvist & Wiksell, 1962), pp. 250–5

56 August Strindberg, *Five Plays* (*The Father, Miss Julie, The Dance of Death* I, II, *A Dream Play, The Ghost Sonata*), intro. and trans. H G Carlson (Berkeley, University of California Press, 1981), p. 290

Chapter 6
GERHART HAUPTMANN, ARTHUR SCHNITZLER AND BERTOLT BRECHT

AFTER UNIFICATION IN 1871, Germany under Bismarck enjoyed a period of economic growth and social stability. For the theatre, the decade saw two events of particular importance: in 1873 the Meiningen troupe went on tour to Berlin; and, three years later, Wagner staged the first complete programme of his *Ring* cycle in Bayreuth. While at the turn of the century Wagner's work had become the inspiration for symbolist theatre, Georg II, the Duke of Saxe-Meiningen, set in motion the introduction of naturalism on the German stage. In 1889, the Freie Bühne (Free Stage) was formed on the model of Théâtre Libre in Paris, and, under the directorship of Otto Brahm (1856–1912), started to adopt the principles of the French theatre in staging naturalist drama.

Along with Zola's *Thérèse Raquin* and *L'Assommoir*, Tolstoy's *The Power of Darkness*, Ibsen's *Ghosts* and Strindberg's *The Father*, German playwrights were also performed at the Freie Bühne. One such playwright was Gerhart Hauptmann (1862–1946), perhaps best known for drawing inspiration for his work from his native Silesia. During Hauptmann's younger years the discovery of coal seams drastically changed the living conditions of the agricultural workers of the area. This formed the setting for *Vor Sonnenaufgang* (*Before Sunrise*, 1889), Hauptmann's debut play about a group of coal-owning peasants suddenly confronted by wealth beyond their experience. However, the work that was to make Hauptmann's name as a modern European dramatist was *Die Weber* (*The Weavers*), his play based on the real-life uprising of Silesian handloom weavers in the 1840s, which appeared in print in 1892. Considered by theatre historians to be the first socialist play and a founding work of naturalist theatre, *The Weavers* is subtitled 'A play of the 1840s'. Exploitation of the workforce in the cottage industry of weaving had been in existence since the Thirty Years' War (1618–48), but only once, in the summer of 1844, when the weavers of Eulenbirge staged a protest, had there been an attempt at rebellion. The homes of the factory owners came under attack and, for a brief moment, it looked as if the weavers might win. But not knowing what to do with their new-found freedom, they soon lost heart; soldiers were called in, and following some fatal shootings, the weavers returned to work, submitting yet again to their plight. Fifty years later, when *The Weavers* was written, conditions largely remained unchanged and Hauptmann was undoubtedly aware of the contemporary parallels.

As the first of the German naturalist dramas, *Before Sunrise* caused a mild sensation in 1889; in 1892 *The Weavers* aroused a storm. When it was announced that the new year's theatre programme at the Freie Bühne would open with Hauptmann's play, the police authorities banned the performance. Hauptmann went to court, and a year of litigation followed before the Freie Bühne finally won permission to stage the play in February 1893. The play was also a success when Brahm produced it at the Deutsches Theater. But Wilhelm II, who had a box in the theatre, warned Brahm that he would sever all connections with the theatre if preparations for the performance were not curtailed. When the production was announced, the imperial coat of arms was removed and Wilhelm never again set foot in the theatre.[1]

The play, however, was rapturously received and became a literary sensation. In the preceding era, writers who had won prominence were a flowery nationalist school with ideals focused on the re-establishment of the German Empire. For the young literati around Hauptmann, the working classes represented a completely new world which, for their predecessors, had barely existed. And, although Hauptmann's total work comprises more than 40 plays, a number of novels and several epic poems, it is his early realistic plays that remain most alive. This is the sequence of plays stretching from *The Weavers* to *Die Ratten* (*The Rats*, 1911), a play set on the eve of World War I where the rodents of the title turn out to be the forces undermining the fabric of the Kaiser's Germany.

During the course of his long life Hauptmann grew into a national figure. In his speech on the German Republic in 1922, which was the year of Hauptmann's sixtieth birthday, Thomas Mann acclaimed Gerhart Hauptmann as 'the king of the Republic', a truly popular king. For the Germans, Hauptmann was more than just a successful dramatist. The theatrical upheaval caused by *Before Sunrise* has been compared with the 'revolution' triggered in the London theatre in 1956 by John Osborne's *Look Back in Anger*.

Even outside his own country Hauptmann's reputation was such that when approached by Stanislavsky to write a play for the Moscow Art Theatre, Chekhov answered: 'Why don't you ask Hauptmann? He is a far greater playwright than I am.'[2] Nevertheless, while Chekhov's four major plays have become an established feature of the English stage, professional English-speaking performance of a Hauptmann play are rare. To a large extent, the reason why the plays of Hauptmann, the 1912 recipient of the Nobel Prize for

Literature, have only infrequently travelled between German and English is his use of dialect and the problems this causes in translation.

Consistent with Hauptmann's aim to convey socialist ideas in a naturalist setting was the need for *The Weavers* to be written in the language actually spoken in the region, in the distinctive dialect of Silesia. The first version of the play called *De Waber* was written in uncompromising dialect, but once the stage premiere of this version was prohibited Hauptmann set to work on a second dialect-diluted version, now called *Die Weber*, which has remained the text staged in German and the one on which translations into other languages have been based. Thus the standard German version is already a 'translated' approximation of Hauptmann's first, more unrestrained Silesian-dialect play. When transferred yet again, this time into a Standard English medium, Hauptmann's original Silesian in German-language theatre inevitably becomes even more diluted.[3]

The problem of capturing the robustness of the original dialect in English translation is compounded by the fact that the events described took place a long time ago, and unless the language of the characters is in keeping with the period there is the potential danger of anachronism. A further linguistic problem for the translator is Hauptmann's German which is 'masterly handled', and his reproduction of everyday speech with its subtlest nuances 'unsurpassed', including the different mixtures of local dialects, colloquial talk and several layers of High German. In fact, it has been suggested that 'even the most talented and experienced translator with a perfect command and knowledge of German (including not only several dialects but, in addition, various sociolects and idiolects too) will never succeed in rendering Haupt-mann's naturalistic texts entirely satisfactorily.'[4] Part of Hauptmann's talent lies in his ability to imbue all of his characters with distinct, individual voices. 'Each speaks in his own characteristic language with distinctive dialectical inflections, idiomatic peculiarities, syntax, speech rhythm and melody and even gestures.'[5] Hauptmann's plays have been described as not dependent 'primarily on subject matter theme or even location: the stuff of his drama is language'.[6]

Given the problems posed by this degree of linguistic complexity, it is not surprising that Hauptmann's work does not figure prominently in translation into English. Still, if an attempt were to be made to render *The Weavers* into English, in order to avoid misrepresenting the nature of the original German text, it would obviously seem preferable to draw on the use of a non-standard rather than a standard variety of English. Aware that Standard English translation of classic plays written in dialect or vernacular speech often fails to capture the spirit of the original, for *The Weavers*, which was staged in Dundee and Glasgow in November 1997, Bill Findlay opted for a Scots dialect version. As pointed out by Findlay, the particular feature whereby all but the most peripheral of Hauptmann's characters generate and communicate their personalities and shifting social relationships through linguistic variation, is also found in Scottish writing. In a position to draw on a varied linguistic resource embracing Standard English, Scottish Standard English and Scots dialect, Scottish writers are able to style-shift between these different linguistic varieties as they see fit. As a result the numerous linguistic options made use of by Hauptmann can find their match in Scots dialect, offering a number of flexible choices: urban or rural, regional or standardised, historic or contemporary.[7] Shared historical circumstances were also helpful to Findlay in creating common ground between the German original and his Scots version: in the nineteenth century there were obvious parallels between Silesian and Scottish handloom weavers. While in 1840 the number of weavers in Scotland peaked at 84,560, by 1850, as a result of mechanisation, this number had plummeted to 25,000, leading to appalling destitution in subsequent depressions, a situation analogous with Hauptmann's Silesia in the 1840s.

In a play on the theme of worker/management conflict such as *The Weavers*, clear linguistic signals are needed in order to highlight differences in occupation and/or class. To this end, Findlay decided to draw a basic distinction between Scots and English-speaking characters. He then took the process a step further, using a stiff variety of standard English to help reinforce an attitude of inflexibility in some characters and their concern to uphold the status quo as reflected in their reactions to the weavers' action. Unmoved by their plight, Pastor Kittelhaus shows them little understanding or sympathy, which in turn is reflected in his use of pompously correct and sanctimonious English:

> PASTOR KITTELHAUS: When a man has delivered sermons from the
> pulpit fifty-two Sundays a year for some thirty years – and that's not
> counting the Holy Days in the calendar – of necessity he acquires a
> sense of proportion.[8]

In contrast, Surgeon Schmidt is a more sympathetic character who is able to relate to the weavers and their suffering. In order to show that this is his attitude, Schmidt makes use of a more conversational tone, generously peppered with Scotticisms, as for instance when he speaks to the little girl Mielchen:

> SCHMIDT: Here Mielchen, come and have a lookie in my coat pocket.
> (*MIELCHEN does so.*) The ginger snaps are for you – but don't wolf
> them all at once... In fact, I'll have a song first! 'The tod run off...wi
> the bubbly, bubblyjock, bubbly, bubblyjock' ...oh, just you wait, young
> lady![9]

In the case of Dreissiger, the manufacturer, the choice of language was not, however, as clear cut. While seemingly voicing a degree of compassion, Dreissiger retreats to his office, referring the weavers to Pfeifer, his manager. At best he can be described as ambivalent; at worst as hypocritical. Still, for Dreissiger simply to have been English-speaking would have polarised his relationship to the weavers to the point of turning him into a caricature of a capitalist. To avoid creating such a stark black-and-white distinction, Findlay's version has Dreissiger use a Scots similar to that of the weavers while, at the same time, making it sufficiently differentiated and less dense, to leave us in doubt whether he is good or bad, humane or exploitative. First an exchange between Pfeifer, formerly one of the weavers himself, and the weavers, as he is inspecting their cloth, dismissing their efforts:

> PFEIFER: (*To the weaver standing before him.*) If ah've tellt ye wance
> ah've tell ye a hunner times! Yuv goat tae redd up yir wabs better nor
> this! Look at the state o'this claith! Hit's fu o'durt, bits o'strae as
> lang's ma finger...a'kinna muck an fulth.
> WEAVER REIMANN: Ah canna help stoor gittin intil it.
> APPRENTICE: (*Has weighed the cloth.*) The wecht's shoart an a'.[10]

And here is Dreissiger, when the starving weaver laddie faints, in his Scots tempered by English, allowing him to veer between familiarity and superiority:

> DREISSIGER: It's a doonricht disgrace. The bairn's jist a skelf, thurs
> nuthin o'him. Hoo onybody kin ca' thumsels a mither an faither an
> treat thir bairns that wey ah jist don't know – [11]

Through a cruel twist of irony, old Hilse, the only weaver to remain faithfully at his loom, becomes the arbitrary victim of a bullet. Reflecting his individualism in his use of language, in Findlay's version Hilse's conversational Scots is made more restrained than that of the other weavers, and is also suffused with religiosity in the form of references to God, the Lord, the Day of Judgement and vengeance. Through the inclusion in his speech of 'biblical English', sprinkled with Scots items, a language is created, distinctive of someone God-fearing and resigned to the life God has meted out for him, which sets him apart from the other weavers whom he declines to join in their stand against authority. Here, at the opening of Act 5, he recites a family prayer:

HILSE: Our Father, we offer up our thankfulness that in Thy *almichly* grace and goodness Thou have this *nicht* cast your benevolence upon us. We offer our thankfulness too, that this *nicht* Thou have protected us from misfortune. Lord, Thy grace is infinite: we stand here before You, poor *hummle* sinners...[12]

Through the creative use of dialect varieties available in another language, Hauptmann's play, which appears to defy transfer into standard language, has been recreated in translation. What Findlay provides is an imaginative re-creation of the dialect-coloured essence of a little-known text in English, a text which in German, the language in which it was originally written, constitutes the masterpiece of one of the leading European representatives of modern drama.

Not long after *The Weavers* gave rise to police intervention, the staging of another play, also written in German, aroused social concern, although of a somewhat different nature. On 9 October 1895, *Liebelei* (*Flirtation*, 1895), written by the Austrian playwright Arthur Schnitzler (1862–1931) opened at the Burgtheater in Vienna in the presence of an Archduke and an Archduchess. In the play, two unchaperoned girls pay a visit to a bachelor's flat. After the play, the Archduke was overheard expressing his amazement to another member of the audience 'that you should have taken your daughter to see it. Am altogether surprised that they put on such a play at the Burgtheater'.[13]

In spite of breaking with the conventions of the time, *Liebelei* made Schnitzler famous overnight and, at the same time, broke the Burgtheater's resistance towards naturalistic drama. With this production, Schnitzler was acclaimed as a naturalistic revolutionary, even though his ambition to become the 'Ibsen of the Vienna Woods'[14] never quite came to fruition. He did, however, share Ibsen's desire to reveal the truth and, like the 'master', through 'unmasking' his characters, strove to lay bare the truth about the society into which he had been born.

Although Schnitzler reportedly described himself as 'a European Jew of German culture', the world in which his characters move is very recognisably Austrian, more specifically *fin-de-siècle* Vienna. Not only a whirlpool of new ideas, with Freud, Mahler, Wittgenstein, Schoenberg, Klimt and Schiele among those living there at the time, Vienna at the turn of the century, soon to be shattered by impending war, was set on pursuing the pleasures of the senses with a feverish intensity. The world, it was felt, was basically indifferent, and the lack of social commitment and concern was widespread. *Fin-de-siècle*

Vienna was a world characterised by double standards with only lip service paid to moral values: this is the world that Schnitzler put on stage, together with the characters inhabiting it. Born in Vienna, Arthur Schnitzler, who hailed from a family of physicians on his father's side, first studied medicine. Through his father, who treated many of the best known performers of the day, he came into contact with actors at an early age. After qualifying in 1885, Schnitzler spent almost a decade dividing his time between medicine and writing.

In 1922, Freud wrote to Schnitzler, seeing in him a 'doppelgänger' who shared his keen insight into human behaviour:

> Your determinism as well as your scepticism…your awareness of the truths of the subconscious, of the instinctual nature of man, your destruction of conventional cultural certainties, the preoccupation of your thought with the polarity of love and death – all this appeared uncannily familiar to me.[15]

Among Schnitzler's better known plays are: *Anatol* (1893), a series of seven short dialogues portraying different erotic situations and conflicts, to which *Liebelei* (adapted by Tom Stoppard as *Dalliance*) constitutes a large-scale tail-piece; *Der grüne Kakadu* (*The Green Cockatoo*, 1899); *Reigen* (*The Circle-dance*, 1900: more widely known in English as *La Ronde*); *Der junge Medardus* (*The Young Medardus*, 1910); *Das weite Land* (*The Vast Country*, 1911, translated by Tom Stoppard as *Undiscovered Country*), and *Professor Bernhardi* (1912).

On 27 May 1986, Schnitzler's *Liebelei* opened at the National Theatre as *Dalliance*. The play portrays the relationship between Christine, the suburban daughter of a musician, and Fritz, a Viennese *Lebemann*, or young man about town. Fritz has been introduced to Christine by his friend Theodor in an attempt to ensure that Fritz does not get too deeply ensnared in a potentially dangerous liaison with a married woman. Christine's feelings for Fritz are all-embracing and Fritz, too, at some unconscious emotional level, responds to her. Their love affair is, however, cut short by the arrival of the husband of Fritz's mistress, challenging Fritz to a duel in which he is killed. Devastated by the news of his fate, Christine leaves to seek her own death, realising that while Fritz meant everything to her, for him she was nothing but a passing fancy.

Indifference to inequality and double standards were sentiments as familiar at the turn of the century to Victorian England as they were to Vienna, making the transference of Schnitzler's play from German into English a reasonable undertaking in terms of social setting. The psychology of love, the other focus of Schnitzler's attention, also constitutes a subject of universal interest: as a result, we would expect the process of transforming *Liebelei* into *Dalliance* not to present major problems in adaptation. Other versions of the play, in addition to *Dalliance,* are also available in English including *Love Games,* translated by Charles Osborne[16] and *Flirtations,* in translation by Egon Schwarz.[17] An interesting insight into the strategy used by Stoppard to turn Schnitzler's play, written in the 1890s, into a new version for an English audience in the late twentieth century, is offered by a comparison between *Love Games* and *Dalliance.* From this comparison, Stoppard's adaptation emerges charged with a heightened sense of conflict and theatricality. It also tends to introduce word games whenever the opportunity presents itself and to take steps to minimise overt aspects of melodrama.

In his autobiography, written in 1915, Schnitzler described how the idea of the play came to him.[18] During a stroll in the Viennese suburbs, together with another medical student, the two young men started to chat up a couple of girls, quick-witted, uninhibited and full of *joie de vivre.* This is the atmosphere of Act 1, Scene 1, set in Fritz's flat, which sees the arrival of two Viennese *süsse Mädl.* These are two sweet young things from lower-class suburbia, ideal companions for the man about town, wanting to avoid the capitalist transactions of the whorehouse. However, the ominous ringing of the doorbell shatters the atmosphere of the scene. When Fritz opens the door, waiting outside is *der Herr,* the Gentleman, whose arrival evokes echoes of Everyman, of the late Medieval Morality Play, where the High Father of Heaven sends Death to summon every creature to come and give account of their worldly lives. In the case of Fritz, the fate awaiting him is that of death in a duel with his mistress's husband. In an interesting study by Catherine Spencer, three scenes in different English translations have been compared. Having answered the doorbell Fritz returns, ushering in his visitor, elegantly dressed in overcoat and gloves with his hat in his hand. First an extract from Scene 1 in translation by Charles Osborne:

> FRITZ: (*As they enter.*) I must apologise for keeping you waiting –
> please – (*Gesturing to a chair.*)
> THE GENTLEMAN: (*Quite pleasantly.*) Oh, that's all right. I'm very
> sorry to have disturbed you.
> FRITZ: Not at all. Please, won't you – ? (*Again, indicates a seat.*)
> THE GENTLEMAN: I see that I have disturbed you, however. A little
> entertainment, yes?
> FRITZ: Just one or two friends.

THE GENTLEMAN: (*Sitting, still friendly in manner.*) A fancy dress party, apparently.

FRITZ: (*Self-consciously.*) How do you mean?

THE GENTLEMAN: Well, your friends were wearing women's hats and coats.

FRITZ: Ah, yes – (*Smiling.*) – well, there may be lady friends here as well – (*He falls silent.*)

THE GENTLEMAN: Life can sometimes be quite amusing – yes? (*He looks fixedly at FRITZ.*)

FRITZ: (*Holding his gaze for a time, then looking away.*) May I be allowed to ask you to what I owe the honour of your visit?

THE GENTLEMAN: Certainly. (*Calmly.*) My wife has left a veil of hers here by mistake.

FRITZ: Your wife? Here? Left her – (*Smiling.*) Your joke is a trifle peculiar.

THE GENTLEMAN: (*Suddenly rising, very sternly, almost angrily, and standing with one hand on the chair.*) She left it here.
(*FRITZ rises also, and they stand facing each other. THE GENTLEMAN raises his fist, as though he were about to strike FRITZ. In rage and disgust, he exclaims.*)
Oh!
(*FRITZ, on his guard, takes a short pace backwards. After a long pause THE GENTLEMAN continues.*)
Here are your letters. (*He takes a bundle of letters from the pocket of his overcoat, and throws them on the desk.*) I must ask you for those which you have received –
(*FRITZ shakes his head. THE GENTLEMAN says, passionately, and with emphasis.*)
I do not want them to be – found here later.

FRITZ: (*Very sternly.*) They won't be found.
(*THE GENTLEMAN looks at him. Pause.*)
What else do you want from me?

THE GENTLEMAN: (*Sneeringly.*) What else do I want?

FRITZ: I am at your disposal.

THE GENTLEMAN: (*With a cool bow.*) Good. (*He allows his glance to take in the room. As he notices the table laid for supper, the women's hats and so on, a violent expression passes over his face, as though he contained his fury only with the greatest difficulty.*)

FRITZ: (*Noticing this, repeats.*) I'm completely at your disposal. I shall be at home tomorrow morning until twelve.
(*THE GENTLEMAN bows and turns to go.*)[19]

In contrast, in Tom Stoppard's *Dalliance*, the tone of the scene is sharpened from the moment the Gentleman arrives. Whereas, in the original, he is elegantly dressed in overcoat and gloves with his hat in his hand, Stoppard dresses him in an officer's uniform, which succeeds in adding a further element of danger to the conflict, heightening the impending sense of disaster which culminates in the Gentleman's outburst, 'You young know-it-alls...':

> (*FRITZ goes out to the front door. After a few moments the GENTLEMAN enters. He is wearing an officer's uniform.*)
> [FRITZ:] I must apologise for keeping you waiting. Please...
> GENTLEMAN: Not at all. I'm sorry to have disturbed you.
> FRITZ: You haven't at all.
> GENTLEMAN: Oh, but I can see I have. A little gathering?
> FRITZ: Just a few chaps.
> GENTLEMAN: (*Still friendly.*) Sounds a bit dubious.
> FRITZ: (*Awkwardly.*) I beg your pardon?
> GENTLEMAN: They seem to go in for boas and picture hats.
> FRITZ: Oh, yes (*Smiles.*) One or two of them *are* a bit dubious.
> GENTLEMAN: Life can be so amusing sometimes.
> FRITZ: May I make so bold as to inquire to what I owe the honour of this... Why have you come?
> GENTLEMAN: (*Calmly.*) My wife left one of her gloves here...
> FRITZ: Your wife? Here? There must be some mistake.
> GENTLEMAN: My wife left one of her gloves here – a glove like this one...
> (*The GENTLEMAN slaps FRITZ on the face with the glove. FRITZ takes a step back. Pause.*)
> Well? I said – well? A Yellow Dragoon.
> (*FRITZ snaps to attention.*)
> FRITZ: I am at your disposal.
> GENTLEMAN: And I shall dispose of you.
> (*The GENTLEMAN produces a bundle of letters.*) Here are your letters. I must ask you to give me those you have received. I wouldn't want them to be found here...afterwards.
> FRITZ: They won't be found.
> (*FRITZ stares at him. Pause.*)
> Is there anything more I can do for you?
> GENTLEMAN: Anything more? That *you* might do for *me*? (*The GENTLEMAN turns to leave, then changes his mind.*) You young know-it-alls...take-it-alls... My box, my table, my – You grab – brag – strut – rut like dogs in the street – and you'll be shot down like dogs.
> FRITZ: I am at your disposal.
> GENTLEMAN: (*Bows coldly.*) Good.
> FRITZ: I am entirely at your disposal. I shall be at home tomorrow until noon.
> GENTLEMAN: Ah about tomorrow. My wife's musical evening.
> FRITZ: Please ask her to forgive me.
> GENTLEMAN: I'm sure she will miss you.
> FRITZ: Perhaps another time.

GENTLEMAN: Yes, perhaps. After all I might miss you too.
(*The GENTLEMAN turns to leave.*)[20]

True to form, Stoppard has not missed the opportunity to enliven the dialogue through the use of additional word games. By giving the Gentleman the line 'Sounds a bit dubious' in reply to Fritz's defensive 'Just a few chaps', Stoppard sets it up for Fritz's later reply when, with a smile, he refers to his friends as 'One or two of them *are* a bit dubious'. In similar manner, the Gentleman's comment 'I'm sure she'll miss you' in answer to Fritz's apologies for his absence from his wife's musical evening prepares the way for the Gentleman's later retort 'After all I might miss you too'.

While the tone throughout has been sharpened, in replacing 'veil' by 'gloves' for the article left behind by the Gentleman's wife, Stoppard also successfully increases both tension and theatricality. In the original, the stated purpose of the Gentleman's visit is to collect the veil, the means whereby the truth has been hidden, in conformity with the baroque and characteristically Austrian literary tradition, with its notions of illusion and reality, theatre and life. In Stoppard's adaptation the focus has been shifted, and the mention of 'glove' now leads to its use as a weapon, foreshadowing further, more fatal wounds soon to be inflicted upon Fritz.

In Act 2, Scene 2, the audience has the opportunity to find out a bit more about the nature of the relationship between Christine and Fritz. Although Christine's suburban background might place her relatively low on the social ladder, she is in many respects culturally superior to Fritz who fails to recognise a bust in Christine's room as the composer Schubert. Christine is no ordinary 'sweet young thing' and, unlike Mitzi in her relationship with Theodor, is not playing the game according to the rules: she is far too emotionally involved with Fritz. Fritz, on the other hand, comes from a world so distanced from the immediate realities of feeling that for him genuine emotions appear to be nothing but childishness. This social and emotional gulf between Christine and Fritz is illustrated in Schnitzler's original play through Fritz's use of the German word *Kind* (child) when he addresses Christine. In Stoppard's translation, the use of additional adjectives turns *Du Kind* into the imperious yet affectionate 'you funny little girl', capturing successfully Fritz's contradictory emotions towards Christine who he dimly senses might be able to meet what he vaguely acknowledges as an unfulfilled need in himself.

Originally, Schnitzler had planned *Liebelei* to be a *Volksstück*, a dialect folk play, a genre primarily intended for the less-educated sections of the theatregoing public. From the 1830s onwards, the *Volksstück* enjoyed widespread popularity, with Vienna and its suburban theatres catering for the workers, artisans, craftsmen and the *petite bourgeoisie*, as its main centre. Although Schnitzler decided against calling *Liebelei* a *Volksstück*, settling instead for the more neutral *Schauspiel* (play), his first choice of title was *Das arme Mädl* (the poor girl). Nevertheless, there remains in the play a lingering note of the sentimentality of the melodrama, often associated with the *Volksstück*, as illustrated by the ending when Christine's father repeatedly states: 'She won't be back', leaving us in little doubt his daughter now feels that she no longer has anything to live for.

Carefully eschewing melodrama, in Stoppard's version the finale of *Dalliance* relocates and moves the original from the Weirings' modest flat to the Josefstadt Theatre where Christine's father plays in the orchestra and Mitzi, no longer Schnitzler's unemployed seamstress, now works as a wardrobe mistress. Learning of Fritz's death and burial, in Stoppard's version Christine's first line does not differ markedly from Schnitzler's original:

> CHRISTINE: I WORSHIPPED HIM. He was God and salvation and I
>   was his day off.[21]

However, in acknowledgement of the time-lapse of close to a century between the play's premiere in Vienna in 1895 and its opening at the National Theatre in 1986, Stoppard has placed his version firmly in contemporary history: no longer are women passively accepting their fate at the hands of men. A far cry from the lovesick and abandoned 'sweet young thing', defeated by life, Christine now reveals an unexpected, underlying strength; turning on Theo, in Stoppard's adaptation she is given the last word:

> CHRISTINE: You shit-bucket, Theo. You fat, ugly, ignorant, lecherous,
>   dirty-fingered God's gift to the female race, your breath stank of stale
>   women when you kissed me, I was nearly *sick!*[22]

And the play ends, as befits an English version, with the original melodrama simply turned into an ironic comment on the peccadilloes of life. On her way out, as she exits, Christine pauses to listen to the words of the song, as sung by the tenor and the soprano, busy rehearsing their duet:

> Sweetheart, won't you dally, do
> Or I'll die,
> Or I'll die for love of you.

The theme of casual erotic encounters to compensate for the lack of more deeply-felt emotional commitment recurs in *Reigen*, Schnitzler's loose series of sexual scenes written in 1900. This play, which provoked an uproar in

Vienna and anti-Semitic riots in Berlin, was considered by Schnitzler himself to be completely unprintable and, not surprisingly, when it opened in Vienna in 1921, the performance was closed down by the police. When, the same year, the first production took place in Berlin, it met with a similar fate: the actors were put through a six-day trial on charges of obscenity. Two years later, a performance was given for friends only in a private home in London, with members of the Bloomsbury Group joining cheerfully in the proceedings. 'The audience felt simply as if a real copulation were going on in the room,' Virginia Woolf commented in a letter, 'and tried to talk to drown the very realistic groans made by Partridge! It was a great relief when Marjorie sang hymns.'[23]

Fifty years after *Reigen* was first written, Max Ophüls turned Schnitzler's sexual daisy-chain into a film called *La Ronde* with a glittering French cast including Gérard Philipe, Danielle Darrieux, Jean-Louis Barrault and Simone Signoret. Following the success of the film, the play also started to become known as *La Ronde*. However, subsequent to the Berlin obscenity trial, Schnitzler had banned all performances of the play in Europe until after his death. In January 1982, just over fifty years after Schnitzler died in 1931, the Royal Shakespeare Company staged a production of *La Ronde*, in a version by John Barton, the director, based on a translation by Sue Davies. And, close to twenty years after the RSC production, Sam Mendes marked the passing of a century since Schnitzler first wrote the play, by staging it at the Donmar Warehouse Theatre. British playwright David Hare was commissioned to do a new English version which was given the name *The Blue Room*, and in which all the characters of the ten scenes were played by two actors, Nicole Kidman and Iain Glen. The play transferred to Broadway and, in the autumn of 2000, returned to the West End, although this time with a different cast.

Unlike his adaptations of Chekhov, Brecht and Pirandello, Hare's reworking of Schnitzler's original follows Ophüls' example by adapting the text with considerable freedom, including relocating the play to the contemporary world. Thus, while the sexual encounters in the scenes in the John Barton/Sue Davies version closely reflect Schnitzler's original, the scenes in *The Blue Room* reveal some changes illustrating Hare's attempt to adjust the play to today's world. In the 1982 RSC production the encounters take place between:

Scene 1	The Prostitute and the Soldier
Scene 2	The Soldier and the Parlour-maid
Scene 3	The Parlour-maid and the Young Gentleman
Scene 4	The Young Gentleman and the Young Wife
Scene 5	The Young Wife and the Husband

Scene 6   The Husband and the Sweet Girl
Scene 7   The Sweet Girl and the Poet
Scene 8   The Poet and the Actress
Scene 9   The Actress and the Count
Scene 10   The Count and the Prostitute[24]

While some changes are dictated by cultural differences between *fin-de-siècle* Vienna and 'one of the great cities of the world in the present day', as Hare describes his setting for *The Blue Room*, others are the result of the hundred-years' time lapse since Schnitzler wrote the ten scenes of the original. A soldier walking the city streets is no longer as frequent a sight and, in *The Blue Room* has been replaced by a cab driver. Parlour-maids and young gentlemen also belong to the past and, as a result, have been turned into a French au-pair with a French accent to boot and a student; the element of implied risk to which reference is made is no longer understood to be syphilis but Aids. Hare also turns Schnitzler's wayward Viennese husband in search of extramarital diversion with a sweet suburban girl into a present-day politician seeking solace with a coke-snorting model. This yields the following constellations of more up-to-date encounters:

Scene 1   The Girl and the Cab Driver
Scene 2   The Cab Driver and the Au Pair
Scene 3   The Au Pair and the Student
Scene 4   The Student and the Married Woman
Scene 5   The Married Woman and the Politician
Scene 6   The Politician and the Model
Scene 7   The Model and the Playwright
Scene 8   The Playwright and the Actress
Scene 9   The Actress and the Aristocrat
Scene 10   The Aristocrat and the Girl [25]

The universal aspect of the play, the link between lack of emotional commitment and never-satiated sexual fulfilment, is well served in *The Blue Room* by all female and male parts being assigned to one actress and one actor. Less successful, however, is Hare's deliberate decision not to anchor the play in a specified place. As a result of relocating Schnitzler's play to 'one of the great cities of the world', Hare also has to refrain from making specific local references. Talking, for instance, about the place where she lives, the Model tells the Playwright that:

MODEL: I've got an apartment. Near the centre.
PLAYWRIGHT: The centre? Really?
MODEL: Someone… Someone found it for me.[26]

In a London-based version, for example, a young woman in the Model's position might typically have been relocated to an apartment in Mayfair, with the flavour of the associated imagery having a stronger impact than the more neutral 'centre'. While the concept of a metropolitan setting is intellectually easy to grasp, its emotional impact is less easily evoked in a no man's land than anchored in the specific. It also seems as if in spite of the attempts to update Schnitzler's play in order to capture a different *Zeitgeist*, to some Hare's new version still emerges as too closely linked to the original. In its critical review of the Royal Haymarket production in the autumn of 2000, the *Sunday Telegraph* felt that the production could not get to grips with 'characters who remain chained to the nineteenth century story-line while performing cunnilingus and snorting cocaine'.[27]

In stark contrast to Schnitzler's naturalistic plays, in which audience empathy is easily evoked for the sad fate or empty life of his characters, stands the work of another German playwright. For Bertolt Brecht (1898–1956), the most frequently performed playwright in translation between German and English, it was crucial to reduce as far as possible the 'empathy on the part of the audience, or between actor and role, performance and audience – a deliberate attempt to prevent the cathartic experience of emotional fulfilment.'[28] What Brecht objected to was a theatre of illusion where the audience was left spellbound, and he reacted to realism, preferring a theatre that teaches and empowers the audience. In the 'epic' theatre of Brecht the actors are less concerned with analysing the psychological complexities of the characters than with the political and social forces that make them into what they are. What epic theatre entails is the actors establishing a link between the role they play and the argument as put forward by Brecht, highlighting the overall concept of the play rather than themselves.[29]

Before Brecht's work was staged in translation into English, three of his plays were presented in German to London theatre audiences during a guest visit of the Berliner Ensemble in September 1956: *Der kaukasische Kreidekreis* (*The Caucasian Chalk Circle*, 1949), *Trommeln in der Nacht*, (*Drums in the Night*, 1922), *Pauken und Trompeten* (*Drums and Trumpets*, 1955) – Brecht's adaptation of George Farquar's Restoration comedy *The Recruiting Officer* – and *Mutter Courage und ihre Kinder* (*Mother Courage and Her Children*, 1949). On 14 August, two weeks before the visit of the Berliner Ensemble, Bertolt Brecht died. His last message to the company, a typed note placed on the notice-board at the Theater am Schiffbauerdamm, was dated 5 August 1956 and headed 'Our London Season':

> For our London season we need to bear two things in mind. First: we shall
> be offering most of the audience a pure pantomime, a kind of silent film
> on the stage for they know no German... Second: there is in England a
> long-standing fear that German art (literature, painting, music) must be
> terribly heavy, slow, laborious and pedestrian.[30]

Brecht's communiqué to his troupe of actors before their impending visit
to the UK shows his first concern to be an issue of language. Ironically,
Brecht might have had reason to feel greater concern had there been plans for
his work to be performed in translation; when plays are presented in an
unfamiliar language, audiences are willing to suspend disbelief, so that guest
performances where foreign actors express themselves in their own language
are often more likely to succeed than an English cast, struggling with a less
than perfect translation. Time was indeed to prove this to be the case: though
the Berliner Ensemble was enthusiastically received by many Londoners in
1956, the inclusion of Brecht's plays into the dramatic canon has frequently
not been helped by English-language versions of his texts.

In addition to Brecht's second concern, that audiences might have
preconceived notions of German art and culture as slow and ponderous, there
was, at the time, a further problem to be overcome: the strong resistance to
things Teutonic, as the inevitable outcome of the two relatively recent world
wars. As a German writer, Brecht was all too easily seen as lacking a sense of
humour or at least irony. A further barrier was created by his political ideology.
Fundamental to Brecht's dramaturgical exploration of the relationship between
the individual and society was his Marxist philosophy, encompassing a set of
ideas unlikely to find easy acceptance with traditionally bourgeois theatre
institutions and theatregoers. In addition to his political leanings his innovative
approach to theatre constituted yet another factor influencing the way his
work was to be perceived in English translation.

Given Brecht's political leaning, not surprisingly it was through the initiative
of amateur socialist groups that his work first became known in Britain in the
mid-1930s. Fired by the cultural renewal following the revolution in Russia,
the Council for Proletarian Art was established in 1924 by socialist theatre
practitioners in Britain. In 1926 it changed its name to the Workers' Theatre
Movement and turned into an umbrella organisation for a number of British
socialist theatre groups. A shared feature of many of these groups was their
rejection of naturalism as a mode of performance and the adoption of an
'agitprop' style of presentation, in large part borrowed from the work of similar
groups in Russia and Germany.

In order to promote his plays and to look for work in the film industry, in
1934 Brecht paid a visit to London. In spite of his failure to find interest in his

plays in London, his work caught the attention of some British socialist groups such as the Manchester-based company Theatre of Action. Founded in 1934 by Joan Littlewood and Ewan MacColl – together the driving force behind the Theatre Workshop after the war – in 1935 the company presented selected scenes from Brecht in their own translation including *Die Rundköpfe und die Spitzköpfe (Roundheads and Peakheads*, 1936), a project on which Brecht had been working between 1931 and 1935.

The 1930s also saw the staging of a Brecht play by the London Unity Theatre, the last pre-war production of a Brecht play in Britain. The Unity Theatre had grown out of the Workers' Theatre Movement, which was disbanded in 1935 when some members joined with others from a group known as the Rebel Players to become the Unity Theatre. By 1937 there were numerous Unity groups throughout the UK engaged in socialist theatre. In September 1938, the London Unity presented the first English-language production of *Die Gewehre der Frau Carrar (Señora Carrar's Rifles*, 1937) based on J M Synge's *Riders to the Sea*. The production was later taken on tour 'to raise consciousness, spirits and money for Spain', in its fight against fascism.[31]

Although the repertoire of British theatre during the early post-war years was dominated by light comedies, whodunnits and imported American musicals, the occasional Brecht play still managed to reach the British stage. In 1950, Stretford Civic Theatre, Manchester, presented Eric Bentley's translation of *The Caucasian Chalk Circle*. Little is known about this production and even fewer details seem to be available from the production of *Der gute Mensch von Sezuan (The Good Person of Setzuan*, 1943), at the Progress Theatre, Reading in 1953.[32] Then, the following year, London theatregoers had the opportunity to see a rehearsed reading of *Mother Courage and Her Children* at The Institute for Contemporary Arts. Two years later, in July 1956, *Mother Courage* was given a production by the Theatre Workshop at the Tor and Torridge Festival in Barnstaple, Devon, with Joan Littlewood as director as well as in the title role of the war-profiteering survivor of the 1618–38 war in Europe. The event was not considered a success, hardly surprising given that Littlewood first dropped out of the role then resumed it 24 hours before the opening performance.[33] The result, according to Kenneth Tynan – an ardent Brecht supporter after having seen the Berliner Ensemble's *Mother Courage and Her Children*, directed by Brecht and Engel in Paris in 1954 – was 'a discourtesy to a masterpiece border[ing] on an insult, as if Wagner were to be staged in a school gymnasium'.[34]

The year in which *Mother Courage* failed to impress Kenneth Tynan and other critics at Barnstaple also saw a revival of the English Stage Company's plans to mount a production of *Die Dreigroschenoper* (*The Threepenny Opera*, 1928). When first approached to direct the production at the Royal Court, actor and director Sam Wanamaker expressed his doubts that 'English audiences could take this'.[35] The critical response to the production, which consisted of polar extremes, confirmed, at least in part, Wanamaker's misgivings. In *The Sunday Times* Harold Hobson described the production as 'one of the most exciting things in London for some time' and expressed his admiration for Brecht's dramaturgy.[36] Other reviewers were less enthusiastic and pointed to shortcomings in the acting resulting from the Brechtian approach, which sharply contrasted with the more understated and favoured English style. However, having left his native America on political grounds to avoid becoming a victim of Senator Joseph McCarthy and the House Un-American Activities Committee, Wanamaker remained convinced that some of the less favourable reviews were unrelated to the artistic shortcomings of the production and more closely linked to an entrenched political antipathy to Brecht's ideas.[37]

Wanamaker's production of *The Threepenny Opera* transferred from the Royal Court to the Aldwych Theatre, critics notwithstanding, and Brecht the playwright was now beginning to become accepted by at least a portion of English theatregoers. Also helping his cause was the new concept of an ensemble theatre, and the welcome awarded the Berliner Ensemble on their visit to London in early autumn 1956 should probably be viewed against the background of the debate about the future of a subsidised English National Theatre, to which the German theatre company and its artistic achievements added further weight.

The very existence of this debate, however, also indicated that times were a-changing. On 8 May 1956 John Osborne's *Look Back in Anger* opened at the *Royal Court*, challenging old values and pointing to changes to come. A month after the London visit of the Berliner Ensemble, in September the same year, with Britain and France engaged in combat against a radical Egyptian government over the Suez Canal, George Devine directed *The Good Woman of Setzuan* at the Royal Court Theatre. Brecht's theatrical tale, written on the eve of the Second World War, is concerned with the good-hearted Shen Te who, to protect herself, has to invent a ruthless male cousin Shui Ta. Peggy Ashcroft, known for her commitment to anti-fascist ideas, took the dual role of Shen Te/Shui Ta. Her interpretation of the part did, however, meet with some unfavourable reviews, at least partly resulting from her performance leaving the impression that 'there was something in Brecht's message that was alien to her...when things are too overtly political in a doctrinaire way she withdraws.' [38] Criticism was also levelled at the direction, possibly an indication of the sheer lack of experience of British critics and audiences in responding to the new radical theatrical form of Brecht. [39]

The English translation also came in for its share of criticism. Eric Bentley, the translator, had worked with Brecht and had translated several of his plays, including *Mother Courage and Her Children, Baal* (1922), and *The Caucasian Chalk Circle*. In his review in the *Observer* of 4 November 1956 of George Devine's production of *The Good Woman of Setzuan*, Kenneth Tynan referred to the translation as 'clumsy', which in turn resulted in a letter to Tynan from Bentley. Reproduced below, Tynan's reply, in particular points 2 and 4, indicates that his expectations of the translator entail considerably more than just transferring the text from German into English.

> Dear Eric,
>
> Thank you for your letter.
>
> 1. I didn't know the epilogue was your idea. It still seems a good one.
>
> 2. I did read the German original but am, of course, no judge of its literary merits. In translation, however, I got an impression of heavy handedness that I had not got from the original. It's perfectly possible, of course, to make a clumsy translation of Racine or Marivaux.
>
> 3. Americanisms. You may be right; I haven't your text to hand. Though why the flier should be Americanised I don't quite understand.
>
> 4. I believe in the inviolable text no more than Brecht. Adaptation is something that should befall all good plays – perhaps, for English audiences, yours doesn't go quite far enough. They resent – and to my mind rightly – the length of the first (and weakest) act. They find many of the asides superfluous. Perhaps I mean excision rather than revision.
>
> In spite of all this I hope you gathered from my review that I thought the play very, very well worth doing.
>
> Yours
>
> Ken T. [40]

Tynan's less than happy reaction to Bentley's translation was shared by John Willett, writer on Brecht and translator of his work. According to Willett:

> Peggy Ashcroft was much too sweet a *Good Woman* and an instantly forgettable bad man; part of the fault there lay in the softness of Bentley's translation, which led me for the first time to make one of my own that would shun the slightly soppy implications of his inaccurate title. [41]

The observations of Kenneth Tynan and John Willett point to a number of obstacles in the translation of Brecht's plays. In the case of the *Good Woman...*, the problems start with the very title, in German *Der gute Mensch von Setzuan*. While in German *Mensch* means a human being, man or woman, with *The Good Woman of Setzuan* associations are inevitably established with feminine virtues. Hence, while the original describes someone irrespective of gender being compelled by social and political forces beyond their control to assume dual identity, the use of 'woman' in the title of the play tilts the balance from the very start. Although this choice may have been dictated by the assumption that an English audience required a central character with identifiable characteristics to empathise with, it clearly contravened Brecht's wish to reduce the degree of emotional involvement on the part of the audience. As a result, more recent performances of the play seem to have opted for the use of 'person' in the title.

Throughout the history of the Anglicisation of Brecht a clear message emerges: the reservations about his ensemble style of work felt by some of the more hierarchical UK theatre organisations with their established pattern of stars and supporting players. This appears to have been one of the misfortunes that beset William Gaskill's Royal Shakespeare Company production in 1962 of *The Caucasian Chalk Circle*, Brecht's play set in the Soviet Caucasus where, through the medium of a folk tale, the concepts of justice, social oppression and revolution are explored. However, despite the final production having been shortened by Peter Hall, and the various problems encountered, the overall response to the play was favourable, moving Brecht in English translation closer to the Berliner model. Just over a year later Laurence Olivier, artistic director of the recently formed National Theatre, invited William Gaskill to join the company. In 1965, Gaskill directed *Mother Courage and Her Children*, with Madge Ryan as Mother Courage and Michael Gambon as Eilif, on the whole a production that was not enthusiastically received. However, not long after, the Berliner Ensemble returned for another visit with performances of *Der aufhaltsame Aufstieg des Arturo Ui* (*The Resistible Rise of Arturo Ui*, 1947), *Coriolan* (*Coriolanus*, 1952/53), *The Threepenny Opera*, *Die Tage der Commune* (*The Days of the Commune*, 1948/49) and excerpts from the Brecht/Weill opera, *Aufstieg und Fall der Stadt Mahagonny* (*The Rise and Fall of the City of Mahagonny*, 1930). Harold Hobson, critic for *The Sunday Times*, now a committed Brecht advocate, described the Berliner Ensemble performances as 'Brecht For Grown-Ups'.[42] Not only was Brecht's theatre beginning to be more easily understood: the social and political changes in progress at the time were soon to bring about a more general acceptance of the political content of his plays, his Marxism and the overt socio-political function of his theatre.

In the late 1960s, the political climate in Europe and the USA provided fertile ground for dissemination of Brecht's ideas. Social and political changes in Britain during the decade, the 'Prague Spring', the anti-Vietnam War movement and the student and worker uprising in Paris now supplied the right cultural context for Brecht's work. In 1973, the first year of its existence, Foco Novo, an 'alternative' British theatre company, produced *Drums in the Night*, adapted by British playwright C P Taylor. The second Brecht play presented by the company, *Mann ist Mann* (*A Man is a Man*, 1927) followed in 1975, again in an adapted English version, this time by Bernard Pomerance, British play-wright and renowned author of *Elephant Man*. *A Man is a Man* has a colonial setting, and, presenting the play in the mid-1970s, writer and director decided to incorporate the recent 'colonial history' of the Vietnam War. Pomerance's adaptation, according to Roland Rees, the director, was 'not unlike demolishing a house, except for the façade. I completely rebuilt the inside.'[43] Three years later, a highly successful production of *Die Mutter* (*The Mother*, 1932), was staged by Belt and Braces, another radical touring company.

Touring companies with a political agenda were not alone in appropriating Brecht's work to produce theatre with a more radical view: regional companies were also finding ways of using Brecht's plays for their own artistic and political purposes. In 1972, Alan Dossor, artistic director of the Everyman Theatre in Liverpool, joined up with John McGrath of 7:84, and together they worked on an Everyman production of *The Caucasian Chalk Circle* subtitled 'a play for Liverpool', acculturating the play to portray the working conditions of the run-down city of Liverpool. Dossor's second Brecht play, *The Good Woman of Setzuan*, followed two years later, also at the Everyman. This time, Dossor enlisted the help of poet/playwright Adrian Mitchell, and together they adapted the text, setting it in the foyer of the Setzuan 'Imperial Hotel', as though the district had been part of the British Empire. Theatricality and an open approach to the text also characterised the Brecht productions at the time of the Citizens' Theatre, Glasgow, another regional company with a radical agenda which, by 1994, had presented 17 of Brecht's plays, the largest number of the German playwright's work in Britain. Dating back to 1969, the artistic policy of the Citizens' Theatre has been to produce British and foreign classics, including a large number of German plays, many translated by Robert David MacDonald. For young directors, the impact of working in the collaborative atmosphere of the Citizen's Theatre proved to be lasting: building on his experience at the Citizens' Theatre, Rob Walker went on to initiate an ensemble set-up at the Half Moon Theatre in the East End of London where, in 1978, he directed a memorable production of *Arturo Ui* with Simon Callow as the evil face of fascism, as well as work by the politically committed Italian playwright Dario Fo (see Chapter 7).

Already figuring prominently among fringe and alternative theatre companies, Brecht now started to move into mainstream repertory theatres. During the 1970s, there were more than 80 Brecht productions staged by provincial British repertories. The price of this popularity, however, was the frequent assimilation into a much blander and depoliticised Brecht, adjustments deemed necessary in order to make him conform more closely to the tastes of the orthodox British theatre world. About this time, Brecht also started to become subsumed under the Royal Shakespeare Company's definition of 'modern classics' which, in addition to their programme of Shakespeare and his contemporaries, were mounted in their smaller venues in Stratford-upon-Avon and London.

As a director of Brecht productions presented by the Royal Shakespeare Company, the name of Howard Davies figures prominently. Davies' first production for the RSC in 1975 was *A Man is a Man* staged at the Other Place in Stratford with playwright Steve Gooch as translator/adapter. Recognising the attempt at reworking the material rather than simply conveying it in its original form, the critical reception acknowledged the morality of the play as more theatrically effective than ever before. Davies also set about finding new ways in which to present the politics of Brecht's writing, settling for an ironic rather than direct style, one more closely in line with an English mode of interpreting Brecht's intentions.[43] The success of *A Man is a Man* encouraged Davies, in 1976, to take on *Schweyk im Zweiten Weltkrieg* (*Schweyk in the Second World War*, 1943) and, a year later, *The Days of the Commune*. While critical opinion was more divided on *Schweyk in the Second World War* than Davies' previous directorial attempts at Brecht, the overall unfavourable reviews for *The Days of the Commune* temporarily seem to have curbed Davies' enthusiasm, making him abandon Brecht until 1984 when he returned with a production of *Mother Courage and Her Children*. In an attempt to match the ideological thinking of playwright with that of translator/adapter, Hanif Kureishi was invited to produce an English version of the play working from a translation of the original. Kureishi and Davies agreed that they wanted to depart from Brecht's wish for audience sympathy rather than empathy and to emphasise qualities in *Mother Courage*, as played by Judi Dench, of warmth and affection. This Anglicised approach resulted in a number of positive reviews, with praise given to Howard Davies by Michael Billington for attempting to jettison 'the museum piece approach to Brecht'.[45] For others, however, culturally closer to 'pure Brecht', Davies' pursuit of Courage's warmth was viewed as defeating Brecht's purpose: 'The so-called warmth [...] that the translator and director wanted to put into the play [...] amounted, as usual, to nothing more than a pandering sentimentalism.'[46] According to Christopher McCullough, the Davies/Kureishi production of *Mother Courage* provided an example of 'an intriguing case of cultural appropriation', whereby 'the work and example of the historical materialist theorist and playwright is accommodated into a humanist concept of unchanging human nature.'[47] Still, Brecht's work is now becoming increasingly accepted among mainstream English theatregoers, not infrequently in productions where Brecht the artist does not keep close company with Brecht the committed socialist.

Unlike the Royal Shakespeare Company, by 1979 the National Theatre had only presented one original Brecht play since its establishment in 1963 – *Mother Courage and Her Children* in 1965 – and two adaptations, *Edward II* in 1968 and *Coriolanus* in 1971. It was not until the move to the South Bank in 1979 that Peter Hall, its artistic director, decided to stage *Leben des Galilei* (*The Life of Galileo*, 1939), Brecht's play about a scientist's social and ethical responsibility, as the brilliant Galileo is forced to choose between his own life and his life's work when confronted with the demands of the Inquisition. Underlying the choice of the play appears to have been the feeling that *The Life of Galileo* was a play that resembled more traditional plays more than the rest of the Brecht canon.[48] Brecht, it would seem, was now being viewed 'as a modern classical writer whose work had a place in the programme of the National Theatre if only it could be made to appear more like that of other playwrights'.[49] In addition, the play had a clearly-defined male lead, a fact which may also have helped to place it in the category of plays attractive to English actors and producers. Accounting for the lack of enthusiasm for Brecht's work as due to the Teutonic heaviness associated with his plays in English translation, Peter Hall decided to commission a new version, and approached the British playwright Howard Brenton, who was known to be sympathetic to Brecht's political ideology. Lacking knowledge of German, Brenton produced an English version from a translation of Brecht's play. Michael Gambon took the part of Galileo, and the task of directing the play was offered to John Dexter. But although John Dexter declared himself pleased with the end result, and the role of Galileo brought Michael Gambon several 'Best Actor of 1980' awards, the actor acknowledged the difference between the approach of the

National Theatre and the Brechtian requirement of collaborative ensemble work.[50] Although less than fully Brechtian, the production was viewed as successful, resulting in one critic concluding that 'Dexter's great *Galileo* took the curse off Brecht in Britain',[51] breaking the anti-Brecht prejudice that had persisted among British audiences until 1980. Further evidence of an easing of the resistance to Brecht's work at the National followed in 1982 with the production of *Schweyk in the Second World War,* directed by Richard Eyre, with Bill Paterson much praised for his interpretation of the title role. The same year a group of National Theatre actors, under the direction of Michael Bogdanov, took a workshop presentation of *The Caucasian Chalk Circle* on tour before giving it half a dozen performances at the Cottesloe Theatre.

At the cost of diluting his characteristically Brechtian style, during the late 1970s and early 1980s, Brecht's work became familiar on major English stages. His call for social action largely defused in adaptation, his plays started to fit into a middle-class British setting, resulting in 'English Brecht' becoming acceptable not only on the fringe but also on subsidised stages.

During the first half of the 1980s, alternative theatre continued to grow, but the emphasis had now shifted to aesthetic experimentation, drawing on post-modern theories according to which art offers a multiplicity of meanings and the authoritative reading rests with the individual consumer. Interest had now moved to the deconstruction of the written text, the substitution of physical expression for the word and the high profile of music and visual effects; the influence of innovators such as Robert Lepage and Robert Wilson was noticeable. Nevertheless, during the late 1980s and the early 1990s several Brecht productions were staged, that might be interpreted as 'a direct riposte to the each-man-for-himself, weakest-goes-to-the-wall ethic of Mrs Thatcher's sub-Reagan government'.[52] A reaction to the political and social thinking at the time may have been the reason underlying Deborah Warner's decision to direct *The Good Person of Sichuan* for the National Theatre. Seeing it as an important play for the late 1980s and early 1990s, her performance programme for the production contained photographs of cardboard shelters used by the homeless underneath the arches of Waterloo Bridge adjacent to the National Theatre, and pictures of dead bodies littering Tiananmen Square in Beijing following the crushing of the 1989 student uprising. For a translation of the play, Michael Hofmann, a well-established translator of German fiction, was commissioned to produce an English script based on the 'Santa Monica text', Brecht's second version of the play written during his exile in the United States.

Although Warner may have shared Brecht's social commitment, other factors seem to have affected the overall impression of the final production. As the 1943 'Americanised' version of the play had been left unfinished, director and translator decided to add scenes from the other version while excluding scenes such as the Epilogue. Also, in common with many other English actors, Fiona Shaw as Shen Te/Shui Ta did not cherish Brecht's relocated emphasis from role to narrative, preferring a naturalistic involvement with character rather than an ensemble-shared contribution to storytelling. All in all, as Warner admitted, in spite of touches of high quality in the performances, the production proved to be a 'difficult experience with an unhappy company'.[53]

Just over a decade later, the National Theatre offered another Brecht play. On 2 August, 1991, *The Resistible Rise of Arturo Ui*, with Anthony Sher in the title role, opened in the Olivier Theatre, directed by Di Trevis and in a version by Ranjit Bolt working from a translation of the original. As the director put it, 'of all the Brecht plays, this is the one for the moment. The only legitimate political position is to be anti-fascist...'[54]

Illustrating her point with applicable references, on one occasion during the production Ui produced a mirror and a false moustache to transform himself into Hitler, on another he ruffled the hair of a small boy standing near him, exactly as Saddam Hussein had done to a small English boy in full view of Western television cameras during the hostage crisis in the Gulf War.[55]

Although in his review in the *Independent* Irving Wardle praised the comic aspects of the play, criticism of the translation was raised, including a suggestion that the second half of the play was less successful than the first: 'Bolt is wonderful with tightly controlled comic verse but, when the stylistic restrictions are relaxed his powers dry away.'[56] In the *Observer*, Michael Coveney objected to the slogans, slides and music, the historical parallels being 'ponderously spelt out',[57] but others saw 'an energy and a clarity in the storytelling and the creation of the socio-political meaning that combined with a sense of fun that was faithful to the spirit of Brecht'.[58]

According to Anthony Sher, a bolder editing job of *Arturo Ui* might have been helpful to bring out the narrative simplicity as well as the political clarity of the play, an approach that has proved to be effective in contemporary versions not only of Brecht but also of European playwrights of an earlier epoch. In order to provide the cast with greater freedom through a sparser text, for their 1994 production of *The Life of Galileo* the Almeida Theatre commissioned David Hare to prepare an English script. Sharing Brecht's socialist leanings but lacking a knowledge of German, Hare set to work from a translation of the original, seeing it as his primary aim to strip down the text. As well as cutting the text and reducing its theatrical scope, Hare curbed Brecht's occasional overloading of arguments as well as his inclination to provide his own answers to hypothetical objections.

Underlying his decision to strip down the text for a contemporary audience was Hare's belief that in 1994 the political context was dramatically different, not only from the time of Brecht but also from Hare's own early career:

> There is no longer 'socialist drama'. Political theatre now can't rely on the ready-made structure, a common ideology that was understood. So political writing now has in some way to be affirmative about common action, common values. We've got to create a contemporary political theatre out of the wreckage of Thatcherism.[59]

Richard Griffiths, who took the title role, admitted that when he was first approached to take on the part of Galileo, 'his heart sank'.[60] His previous experience of Brecht in translation had led him to fear something inevitably 'heavy and pedantic and grey'. However, the Almeida production of *The Life of Galileo* directed by Jonathan Kent, was on the whole very successful, with Michael Billington's review punningly headed 'Speed of the Hare', giving due praise to Hare's adaptation in which a honed-down text allowed greater attention to be focussed on the political debate within the play.[61]

A shared feature of *The Life of Galileo* and *Mother Courage and Her Children* is the larger-than-life portrait of the protagonists. In 1995, Diana Rigg agreed to take on the role of Mother Courage in a production at the National Theatre. Again Jonathan Kent, the director of *The Life of Galileo*, teamed up with David Hare for a production which opened at the Olivier Theatre on 14 November. This time the reviews were less than fulsome, largely the result of a mixed reaction to Diana Rigg as Mother Courage.

At the beginning of the new millennium, 'English Brecht' is not as much in evidence as he once was, but when he does appear, a balance often seems to have been achieved between the spirit of the German original and the expectations of modern English audiences. The spring of 2000 saw Nancy Meckler's production of *Mother Courage* for Shared Experience performed at the New Ambassadors Theatre, endorsing Brecht's approach of a company collective involvement, adding to the sense that a play is a collaborative event rather than a showcase production. Although the translation by Lee Hall, author of the screenplay for the film *Billy Elliot*, with its lines such as 'Get real, padre,' struck Michael Billington as at times excessively slangy, on the whole the translation appears to have helped to clarify Brecht's underlying intentions. According to Billington:

> The end result is a production that shows we are mad to neglect Brecht: at their best, his plays have a Shakespearean complexity, dealing with the eternal problem of how the individual is to survive in a corrupt, imperfect world.[62]

Such a reference to the Bard would seem to indicate that, from Brecht's first fleeting acquaintance with amateur theatre groups in the 1930s through to the New Ambassadors Theatre in the heartland of London, in 2000, the German playwright has now edged his way into acceptance by the theatre establishment, although perhaps to a lesser degree by the theatre-going public.

The history of the development of 'English Brecht' shows the playwright's work registering swings in popularity like a barometer, reflecting the political climate at a particular point in time. During the politically-conscious 1960s and 1970s, Brecht's political agenda was seized by radical, alternative theatre companies, often retaining the message while adjusting the plays to apply to local issues. On the other hand, during periods when commercially-based theatre in the form of musicals, whodunnits and light comedy reigns supreme, and alternative and fringe theatre groups have more or less been financially squeezed out of existence, Brecht's work figures less prominently on English stages. More closely suited to orthodox theatre tastes, a play like *The Life of Galileo*, which depicts the struggle of a single individual, can be more easily Anglicised than some of Brecht's other, more characteristic, ensemble pieces. According to translator John Willett, one of the problems with Brecht's work is the relative scarcity of opportunity for English actors for ensemble work, with actor training in Britain emphasising the role of the individual as a performer. As a result, it is not surprising that English directors and translators choosing and chosen to stage Brecht productions have often been known for sharing the writer's left-wing sympathies, including an appreciation of the ethos of collected ensemble work. And it is equally easy to understand that English actors not of a left-wing persuasion, accustomed to vying for work through individual star performances, have tended to resist an approach denying them this opportunity.

The resistance to Brecht on the English stage may also be linked to the didactic element inherent in his plays. In the words of Eugène Ionesco, reportedly scribbled by Harold Pinter on the door of the director's office at the Royal Court Theatre: *'Le théâtre de Brecht est le théâtre de Boy Scout'*.[63] At one end of the spectrum there is Pinter disinclined to offer overt explanations for aspects of his work, his characters and settings; at the other, there is Brecht and his epic theatre.

Political factors and the reluctance to trade star performances in favour of ensemble work also seem to have dogged the history of Brecht performances on other European stages. In France, the German playwright's first appearance coincided with the movement towards decentralisation. Absorbed into the ideology of the 'Popular Theatre' at the end of 1951, Jean Vilar opened his season at the Théâtre Nationale Populaire with *Mother Courage and Her Children*. At the time, Brecht appeared to be the touchstone of the popular political theatre to which the proponents of decentralisation aspired, while in the eyes of the established commercial theatre he was synonymous with indoctrination. Still one of the most popular playwrights in the decentralised theatres in 1972, he was the third most performed playwright in France, with 48 productions, trailing behind Molière and Shakespeare, but ahead of Chekhov and Marivaux. In the 1980s, on the other hand, Chekhov had the edge over Brecht, the stage now being viewed as the individual actor's space for his or her own fulfilment. Yet a further change quoted that has taken place is the shift in the intellectual climate, with the loss of the belief that thought is capable of transforming the world.[64]

Brecht's well-known concept of '*Verfremdungseffekt*' (alienation or distancing effect) also appears to have constituted a problem when used in the French as well as the English theatre. This is an anti-illusionistic effect used by Brecht to ensure that the audience will remain active participants and not passive watchers. According to Brecht:

> To alienate an incident or a character means to take from that incident or character what makes it obvious, familiar or readily understandable, so as to create wonderment or curiosity.[65]

Many aspects of Brecht's principle of '*Verfremdung*' or 'V-effect' have now become conventional, such as actors walking on and off stage carrying bits of scenery. Others include the actors stepping out of their roles and addressing themselves to the audience. Yet others are linguistically based, likely to present considerable problems in translation. In fact, the problems start immediately with the difficulty of conveying the exact meaning in translation of '*Verfremdung*'. This German word is often translated into English as 'alienation', which, however, is not free from negative associations. It has been suggested that 'defamiliarisation' or 'estrangement' may give a more accurate sense of Brecht's intentions, or perhaps even 'de-alienation'.[66] The difficulty here concerns the prefix *ver–*, which travels with ease in translation between other Germanic languages, as does the suffix *–ung*, the use of which indicates a process, in the case of '*Verfremdung*', of making something less familiar.

In English, however, where many of the Germanic prefixes and suffixes are no longer productive, new words have instead been borrowed from other languages, in particular from French. This in turn means that prefixes and suffixes in German are not easily matched, with the result that complete words often need to be used in translation. Thus 'distancing effect', an alternative translation using a French loan word, is also less than a perfect solution as it might risk creating the impression that Brecht meant the audience to be detached from their feelings during a performance.[67]

In French, the German concept is usually rendered as '*distantion*' which, as in English, is not a perfect equivalent of the original, having on occasion been interpreted in France as 'a measure of remoteness of the actor from his role and from his character'.[68] As a result, the concept of the distant and detached actor has produced actors condemning themselves to sterility, which erroneously yields a predictable Brecht, a Brecht without surprises.

While Brecht clearly did not intend his work to have this effect on either audience or actors, it is not altogether obvious what he did have in mind, and his proposed concept, particularly in translation, often seems to vary with the interpretation of the beholder. Thus, for Roland Barthes:

> [T]o distance is to cut the circuit between the actor and his own pathos, but it is also, and essentially, to re-establish a new circuit between the role and the argument; it is for the actor to give meaning to the play, and no longer to himself in the play.[69]

According to others such as Brecht's wife, the actress Helene Weigel, the origin of Brecht's approach was purely practical, growing out of his efforts to deal with difficult actors.[70] This view is shared by Peter Hall, who sees Brecht's theories of alienation for actors as making sense only if seen in the light of the heavily sentimental and excessive style of German acting, the prevailing tradition before Brecht.[71]

Still, what was clearly Brecht's intention was for his audience to feel sympathy rather than empathy for the plight of his characters, thus stopping short of total identification and remaining sufficiently clear-headed to bear in mind the political and social forces at the root of the problem. And, as far as acting is concerned, in order for the Brechtian actor to exploit the tension created between the 'cooler' showing of his epic theatre and the 'warmer' experience of more naturalistic forms, Brecht 'builds such juxtapositions into the dramaturgy of his plays so that much of the intended distancing is achieved by the text itself rather than the work of the actor'.[72] To this end, the Brechtian performer is aided not only by the text's wholesale changes in dramaturgical style, but also by the detailed distancing efforts created through the startling use of slang, expletives and linguistic structures that are designed to catch the spectator's ear.

In *Mother Courage and Her Children*, Mother Courage's speech is earthy and strongly coloured by her Bavarian dialect. In an attempt to equate one provincial idiom with another, in his 1983 translation John Willet uses a form of northern English. In the preface to his translation, Willett describes his aim as an attempt to create hard-hitting, even 'vulgar exchanges, as befits life in an army camp, but they are never obscene. For instance, Mother Courage refers to Yvette's VD obliquely as her complaint'.[73]

This 'obliqueness', which is not present in the original, may, however, constitute one of the problems in the translation of Brecht's text from German into English. Characteristically, Mother Courage is more direct in German, where she straightforwardly refers to Yvette's *'Krankheit'*, that is, her 'illness'.

Another example of this form of linguistic 'toning down' is found in Scene 2, when Mother Courage discusses the quality of the beef that the Cook is about to roast, questioning the freshness of the meat. In Willett's translation she suggests:

> MOTHER COURAGE: Put plenty of pepper on it so his lordship the
> general don't smell the pong.[74]

But although perhaps amusing, the word 'pong' does not capture the earthiness of the original:

> MUTTER COURAGE: *Nehmens viel Pfeffer, dass der Herr*
> *Feldhauptmann* **den Gestank** *nicht riecht.*[75]

By the use of 'pong', the immediate physicality of 'stink' or 'stench', which would have been closer to the German, is avoided; the translation becomes more genteel and, as a result, Mother Courage less off-putting. Again, although this might appear an improvement on what would otherwise have seemed a more 'Teutonic' translation, it is also a shift that tends to soften the impact of the line as well as weaken the attempt by Brecht to 'distance' the audience from Mother Courage.

As Willett acknowledges, doing justice to Brecht's deft linguistic tricks in English translation is near impossible.[76] And, as if this would not be enough, there is a further problem. For Brecht's linguistic 'V-effect' to work, the audience has to pay close attention, one of the reasons underlying his decision to use the technique in the first place. In the case of Brecht on the English stage, this poses a number of problems, including making unexpected demands on audiences, in particular in commercial theatres.

Spectator concentration is also required for another closely related reason: Brecht's linguistic manipulations are often aimed at creating a humorous effect. One way in which such humour may be achieved is through the conscious change of part of a well-known phrase or expression. However, for this device to work, the original must be instantly recognisable. For example, 'One small step for a man, a giant *tumble* for mankind' is only amusing if you recognise the original as uttered by Neil Armstrong when he took his first steps on the moon in 1969, using the word 'leap' and not 'tumble'.[77]

So too in translation. For instance, in Scene 8, Mother Courage bemoans the end of the war:

> MOTHER COURAGE: Don't tell me *peace has broken out* just after I
> laid in new stock.[78]

Since it is 'war' and not 'peace' that usually 'breaks out', the unexpected use of a word meaning the opposite produces a startling and jocular effect.

The use of polar opposites intended to make the audience sit up and take notice is a regular feature in Brecht's work. In Scene 3, Mother Courage concludes her exchange with the Chaplain by unexpectedly replacing 'guilty' with 'innocent':[79]

> MOTHER COURAGE: Corruption's our only hope. Long as we have it
> there'll be lenient sentences and even an *innocent* man'll have a
> chance of being let off.

At times, the effect is achieved by simply turning a negative statement into a positive one. Concerned that Kattrin may attract unwanted male attention, in Scene 3 Mother Courage sets about making her daughter less appealing to look at. In doing so, she uses a line in which omission of the negation turns the common phrase 'Don't hide your light under a bushel' into the opposite and unfamiliar:

> MOTHER COURAGE: (*She rubs KATHRIN's face with ash.*) Keep still,
> will you. There you are, a bit of muck and you'll be safe. What a
> disaster. Sentries were drunk. *Hide your light under a bushel*, it says.
> Take a soldier, specially a Catholic one, add a clean face, and there's
> your instant whore.[80]

For humour on stage to produce a laugh, it needs to be instantly grasped, and at times Brecht's use of opposites seems to have made translators wary of the prospect of successfully transferring the German joke into English. This may have been the reason underlying Eric Bentley's decision not to strive for Brecht's 'V-effect' in his translation of this passage:

> MOTHER COURAGE: (*She is rubbing ashes into KATTRIN's face.*) Keep still! A little dirt, and you're safe. When a soldier sees a clean face, there's one more whore in the world.[81]

(For further discussion of humour in translation, see Chapter 9.)

Also difficult to capture in English is Brecht's elegant use of prefixes. When in Scene 2 the Captain addresses Mother Courage's son Eilif, he refers to '**unver**schamte **und ver**dreckte Saubauern'.[82] Here the repetition of similar sounding constructions (*unver-* followed by *und ver-*) would roll off the tongue of a German actor with considerable ease. However, in Willett's translation into English, this turns into 'insolent dung-encrusted yokels'.[83] Although semantically unimpeachable, this line is not likely to be greeted with the same degree of enthusiasm by an English-speaking actor.

In a number of respects, early Brecht translation was afflicted by the same problem as Strindberg and at times Chekhov more than half a century earlier: translators with a knowledge of the target language were not sufficiently familiar with the source language, resulting in translations full of errors of interpretation. In the case of *Mother Courage and Her Children*, the 1941 translation by H R Hays appears to have contained howlers far surpassing those of Schering's Strindberg translations. When for instance in Scene 1 Mother Courage says in German '*Da ist ein ganzes Messbuch dabei, aus Altötting, zum Einschlagen von Gurken*' [84] (there is a whole prayer book there, from Altötting, handy for wrapping cucumbers in), this becomes, in Hay's translation, 'There's a whole ledger from Altötting to the storming of Gurken',[85] where the prayer book has been turned into a ledger and the cucumbers into a town under siege.[86]

Some small consolation may be drawn from the fact that Hays' 1941 version of *Mother Courage and Her Children* was never published in book form: it only appeared in New Directions' semi-annual anthology of avant-garde literature in which the overriding interest was its anti-war message.

More recent Brecht translations have been more attentive to the reception of the translation by the target audience than to the translator and the text. Conscious of translating for an American audience, Eric Bentley ensured in his translation of *Mother Courage and Her Children* that Brecht's text was adjusted for performance on the New York stage; *Käs aufs Weissbrot* (cheese on white bread) was turned into 'cheese on pumpernickel', presumably based on the assumption that an American audience would expect Germans to use pumpernickel as their favourite kind of bread. In the same spirit of making 'the other' seem some more familiar, Bentley changed *in dem schönen Flandern* (in beautiful Flanders), to 'in Flanders fields', evoking associations with World War I, seemingly in an attempt to draw on a more familiar European combat, less historically remote than Mother Courage's Thirty Years' War.[87]

Close to half a century after his death, Brecht translation might have been expected to have transcended the problems of simple misinterpretation. Not so, it seems. Only six years ago, a review by Michael Meyer of recent books by and on Brecht[88] resulted in a flurry among Brecht scholars.[89] The books reviewed by Meyer included John Fuegi's *Brecht and Company: Sex, Politics and the Making of the Modern Drama*, a 732-page work already published in England under the title *The Life and Lies of Bertolt Brecht*. In his discussion of Fuegi's work, Michael Meyer reported his and the author's concern about Brecht's infamous laxity in matters of personal hygiene, quoting unquestioningly the allegation that the young Brecht 'had a habit of urinating into baskets of clean laundry to save going downstairs to the ground floor toilet.' As pointed out by Brecht scholars, including John Willett, Ronald Speirs and Ian Strasfogel, Brecht's alleged time-saving habit turns out to be nothing but a mistranslation: in one of his poems the image used is that of his mother's dripping *laundry*, 'pissing' into the basket downstairs.

Together, translation, criticism and reference works contribute towards creating an image of the dramatist and his/her work which, for those with no knowledge of the original language, is all there is. In the case of Brecht, it would seem that although the plays by Bertolt Brecht now make up part of the English canon, the complete transition of the man and his work from German into English still leaves some loose ends. Hopefully there are changes in sight. With the fall of communism, it is not unlikely that new approaches to Brecht's work are still to emerge. Both Ranjit Bolt and David Hare, the adapters of *Arturo Ui* and *The Life of Galileo* for more recent London productions, attest to the changing attitude of the Brecht estate, in the past actively concerned to safeguard the sanctity of the German playwright's texts (see Chapter 9.) Instead of the overtly specified political commitment, the emphasis may yet move to highlight other forms of conflict acted out in a different theatre of war, while involving equally powerful and corrupt players.

Notes

1   L Lore, 'Hauptmann in his Youth' (New York Herald Tribune Books), 28 February 1932

2   H F Garten, 'A Playwright of Compassion', *The Listener*, 1963, pp. 135–7

3   B Findlay, 'Silesian into Scots: Gerhart Hauptmann's *The Weavers*', *Modern Drama* XLI (1), 1998, pp. 90–104

4   R Grimm (ed.), *Plays by Gerhart Hauptmann* (New York, Continuum Publications, 1994), Introduction, p. xiv

5   W Maurer, *Gerhart Hauptmann* (Boston, Twayne Publishers, 1982), p. 50

6   P Skrine, *Hauptmann, Wedekind and Schnitzler*, (London, Palgrave Macmillan, 1989), p. 19

7   B Findlay, *op. cit.*

8   Discussed in B Findlay, *op. cit.* p. 97

9   B Findlay, *op. cit.* p. 97

10 *Ibid.* p. 98

11 *Ibid.* p. 99

12 *Ibid.* p. 101

13 *Dalliance* performance programme (National Theatre, 1986)

14 C Spencer, *The Translation of Theatre Texts – An Analysis of Translations of Arthur Schnitzler's* Leibelei *into English*, Unpublished MA in Translation, Dublin University, 1996, p. 60

15 *Dalliance* performance programme, *op. cit.*

16 Arthur Schnitzler, *The Round Dance and Other Plays*, trans. C Osborne (Manchester, Carcanet New Press, 1982)

17 Arthur Schnitzler, *Plays and Stories 1862–1933* (*Flirtations, La Ronde, Countess Mitzi or the Family Reunion*), trans. E Schwarz (New York, Continuum Publications, 1982)

18 Discussed in *Dalliance* performance programme, *op. cit.*

19 *Love Games*, trans. C Osborne, *op. cit.* p.188

20 Arthur Schnitzler, *Dalliance and Undiscovered Country*, adapt. T Stoppard (London, Faber and Faber, 1986), p. 22

21 *Dalliance*, adapt. T Stoppard, *op. cit.* p. 52

22 *Ibid.* p. 53

23 Discussed by David Hare in the introduction to *The Blue Room* performance programme (Donmar Warehouse, 1998)

24 Arthur Schnitzler, *La Ronde*, adapt. John Barton, from a translation of *Reigen* by Sue Davies (Harmondsworth, Penguin, 1982)

25 Arthur Schnitzler, *The Blue Room*, adapt. D Hare (New York, Grove Press, 1998)

26 *The Blue Room*, adapt. D Hare, *ibid.* p. 57

27 'The Editor', in *The Guardian*, 13 October 2000, p. 17

28 M Eddershaw, *Performing Brecht. Forty Years of British Performance* (London, Routledge, 1996), p. 14

29 *Ibid.* p. 13

30 B Brecht, *Brecht on Theatre*, ed. and trans. John Willett (London, Methuen, 1964), p. 283

31 C Chambers, *The Story of Unity Theatre*, (London, Lawrence & Wishart, 1998), p. 112

32 M Eddershaw, *op. cit.* p. 44-5

33 *Ibid.* p. 46

34 K Tynan, *Tynan on Theatre*, (London, Methuen, 1964). Discussed in M Eddershaw, *op. cit.* p. 229

35 M Eddershaw, *op. cit.* p. 47

36 *The Sunday Times*, 12 February 1956

37 M Eddershaw, *op. cit.* p. 49

38 M Billington, *Peggy Ashcroft* (London, John Murray, 1988), p. 166

39 M Eddershaw, *op. cit.* p. 54

40 K Tynan (ed.), *Kenneth Tynan's Letters* (London, Minerva, 1994), p. 209

41 J Willett, 'Ups and downs of British Brecht', in P Kleber and C Visser (eds.), *Re-interpreting Brecht: His Influence on Contemporary Drama and Film* (Toronto, Cambridge University Press, 1990), p. 80

42 *The Sunday Times*, 15 September 1965

43 R Rees, *Fringe First: Pioneers of Fringe Theatre on Record* (London, Oberon Books, 1992), p. 58

44 M Eddershaw, *op. cit.* p. 96

45 *Guardian*, 9 November 1984

46 M Van Dijk, 'Blocking Brecht', in P Kleber and C Visser (eds.), *op. cit.* p. 120

47 G Holderness (ed.), *The Politics of Drama and Theatre* (London, Macmillan, 1992), pp. 120, 123

48 J Hiley, *Theatre at Work*, (London, Routledge, 1981), p. 2

49 M Eddershaw, *op. cit.* p. 105

50 *Ibid.* p. 112

51 *Guardian*, 17 September 1981

52 J Willet, 'Ups and downs of British Brecht', in P Kleber and C Visser (eds.), *op. cit.* p. 9

53 M Eddershaw, *op. cit.* p. 129

54 *Ibid.* p. 149

55 *Ibid.* p. 147

56 *Independent*, 11 August 1991

57 *Observer*, 11 August 1991

58 M Eddershaw, *op. cit.* p. 147

59 Interview with M Eddershaw, 11 May 1994, discussed in M Eddershaw, *op. cit.* pp. 154–5

60 *Ibid.* p. 155

61 *Guardian*, 18 February 1994

62 *Guardian*, 29 April 2000

63 R Findlater, *At the Royal Court*, (London, Amber Lane Press, 1981), p. 59

64 B Dort, 'Crossing the desert: Brecht in France in the eighties', in P Kleber and C Visser (eds.), *op. cit.* pp. 90–103

65 B Brecht, *Mother Courage and Her Children*, trans. J Willett, with commentary and notes by Hugh Rorrison (London, Methuen, 1983), p. xxxi

66 P Brooker, 'Keywords in Brecht's theory and practice of theatre', in P Thomson and G Sacks (eds.), *The Cambridge Companion to Brecht*, (Cambridge, Cambridge University Press, 1994), p. 193

67 M Eddershaw, *op. cit.* p. 16

68 B Dort, *op. cit.* p. 96

69 'Seven photo models of *Mother Courage*', *Tulane Drama Review*, 1967, 12(1), p. 44

70 *The Times Educational Supplement*, 8 January 1982

71 M Esslin, 'Brecht and the English theatre', *Tulane Drama Review*, 1966, 11(2), p. 159

72 M Eddershaw, *op. cit.* p. 14

73 *Mother Courage and Her Children*, trans. J Willett, *op. cit.* p. 22

74 *Ibid.* p. 15

75 B Brecht, *Mutter Courage und Ihre Kinder* (Berlin, Suhrkamp Verlag, 1963), p. 21

76 *Mother Courage and Her Children*, trans. J Willett, *op. cit.* p. xxxiv

77 Discussed in R Leppihalme, *Culture Bumps. An Empirical Approach to the Translation of Allusions* (Clevedon, Multilingual Matters, 1997), p. 74

78 *Mother Courage and Her Children*, trans. J Willett, *op. cit.* p. 61

79 *Ibid.* p. 40

80 *Ibid.* p. 44

81 B Brecht, *Seven Plays*, ed. and trans. E Bentley (New York, Grove Press Inc., 1961) p. 284

82 B Brecht, *Mutter Courage und Ihre Kinder*, *op. cit.* p. 22

83 *Mother Courage and Her Children*, trans. J Willett, *op. cit.* p. 15

84 B Brecht, *Mutter Courage und Ihre Kinder*, *op. cit.* p. 26

85 B Brecht, *Mother Courage*, trans. H R Hays (New York, New Directions, 1941), p. 5

86 See André Lefevere, 'Acculturating Bertolt Brecht', in S Bassnett and A Lefevere (eds.), *Constructing Cultures. Essays on Literary Translation* (Clevedon, Multilingual Matters, 1998), p. 110

87 A Lefevere, *op. cit.* p. 111

88 *New York Review of Books*, 1 December 1994

89 *New York Review of Books*, 12 January 1995

Chapter 7

LUIGI PIRANDELLO, EDUARDO DE FILIPPO AND DARIO FO & FRANCA RAME

DURING THE 1860s AND 1870s, Italian drama consisted of melodramas *à la* Sardou, *drames à thèse à la* Dumas *fils*, sentimental historical tragedies, comedies of manners and farces. Few native Italian playwrights were in a position to live from their pen alone, many having to supplement their own efforts by translating French boulevard comedies. 'We have always, and this is the problem,' wrote Fernando Martini in 1888, 'more or less imitated the French.'[1] However, following Zola's quest for naturalism in the theatre, a French influence of a different kind began to exert itself, in particular after 1879 when *Thérèse Raquin* had been seen throughout Italy. By the early 1890s, naturalism, known in Italian as *verismo*, had become the dominant style of dramatic expression.

In the theatre, two popular naturalist currents prevailed. One was regionalism, drawing on characters from the lower socio-economic strata, flavoured by generous use of local colour. The other drew on realistic middle-class drama, concerned with the psychological interplay between the characters within the confines of class interest. While regionalism tended to favour a local dialect or vernacular Italian, middle-class drama was largely written in an educated register. These two types of naturalist theatre were not, however, mutually exclusive. In his Sicilian plays Luigi Pirandello (1867–1936) addressed psychological issues involving a class component; by 1917 he had also made his mark on bourgeois naturalist drama, with drawing-room plays inhabited by the provincial middle class as well as seasoned by a strong Sicilian flavour.

It was not, however, until *Sei personaggi in cerca d'autore* (*Six Characters in Search of an Author*, 1921), that Pirandello became a renowned dramatist. In the play, six characters abandoned by their author arrive during the rehearsal of another Pirandello play, demanding that their story be given dramatic expression. When the play first opened in Rome, it was a fiasco, achieving acclaim only later when it was staged in Milan, Paris, London, Berlin and New York.

Pirandello's experimentalism gradually changed the state of Italian theatre in his day; his plays are often viewed as forerunners of later experiments, including the theatre of the absurd, 'happenings' and performance art. In 1934 he was awarded the Nobel Prize for Literature.

Pirandello's literary output was prolific, including six collections of poetry, seven novels, 14 collections of short stories, 27 full-length plays, 16 one-act plays as well as translations and critical essays. To many English-speaking readers and theatregoers, his reputation as an innovative playwright tends to be associated with *Six Characters in Search of an Author*, although *Ciascuno a suo modo* (*Each in His Own Way*, 1924) and *Questa sera si recita a soggetto* (*Tonight We Improvise*, 1930), the other two plays forming his 'trilogy of the theatre in the theatre', may, if anything, be considered even more theatrically path-breaking.[2]

Nevertheless, for an 'English Pirandello' to emerge, his work, like that of other European playwrights, needed to pass through successive stages of acculturation. In early Pirandello productions the 'Italianness' of the playwright's work was accentuated, only to be successively shed in subsequent stagings of his plays. It has been suggested that this ethnocentric approach to putting the work of Italian playwrights on the English stage can be placed in the context of a wider divide – the gulf between the Anglo-Saxon North and the Mediterranean South. Despite its affiliation with the ancient civilisations of Greece and Italy, by the late eighteenth century perceptions of Italian culture in Britain were also influenced by associations with the Mediterranean South as exotic and somewhat primitive, a land of food and family, love and laughter.[3] In the case of Italian drama on the English stage, this latter image has proved to be lasting.

When, on 10 May 1921, *Six Characters in Search of an Author* opened at the Teatro Valle in Rome, an uproar broke out in the theatre. Using a side door, Pirandello escaped from the theatre amidst jeering and laughing, his daughter clinging to his arm. The overnight *succès de scandale* ensured fame throughout Europe including Britain. In Paris the play was staged in 1923 at the Théâtre des Champs-Elysées, in a production where the six characters arrived on stage in a lift, lowered from above. The production, directed by Georges Pitoëff, became a milestone in the history of contemporary theatre. After his Parisian triumph Pirandello's plays quickly entered the standard repertory of European companies. In Germany, *Six Characters in Search of an Author* was staged in May 1924 in a Berlin production by Max Reinhardt, where the six characters did not arrive in the middle of a rehearsal but were present on a darkened stage from the very start, later to be focused on by a white spotlight. According to one reviewer, this production saw 'Reinhardt give the best evidence so far in his career of his inexhaustibly fertile mind'.[4] Successful performances throughout the world followed, and between 1922 and 1925 *Six Characters in Search of an Author* was translated into 25 languages.

Banned from public performance by the Lord Chamberlain due to its underlying themes of adultery and incest, the play was first staged in London by the private Stage Society in 1922, directed by Theodore Komisarjevsky. In a review of this first foreign production of *Six Characters in Search of an Author* which was subsequently published in *Drama* in 1940, Desmond MacCarthy hailed the play as 'most original', referring to it as an 'experiment in dramatic form'. Two years later, *Enrico IV* (*Henry IV*, 1922), Pirandello's play about a man who becomes the person he is pretending to be, was staged by the Cambridge Amateur Dramatic Club at the New Theatre in Cambridge in an unauthorised translation by two academics. The same year the play was also performed at the Abbey Theatre in Dublin.

When first performed in Italy, on 24 February 1922, the success of *Henry IV*, in combination with Pirandello's international reputation following *Six Characters in Search of an Author*, led to the play rapidly emerging in English translation. In 1923, *Henry IV* appeared in translation by Edward Storer and, on 24 January 1924, the first American production of the play, now called *The Living Mask*, opened at 44th Street in New York. In his review of the premiere, Stark Young pointed to the play's importance as a milestone in world theatre.[5]

The following year saw a personal appearance of Pirandello in London, together with the Teatro d'Arte company, which presented, in addition to *Six Characters in Search of an Author* and *Henry IV*, two more of his plays, all at the New Oxford Theatre. In *Vestire gli ignudi* (*To Clothe the Naked*, 1922), the subject brought up for discussion is the difficulty of establishing the absolute truth of a story, focusing on the struggle of Ersilia Drei, the protagonist, in a pitiless world. In the last of the four plays brought by the Teatro d'Arte company, *Cosí è (se vi pare)* (*Right You Are (If You Think So)*, 1917), a group of well-to-do neighbours are rattled by the behaviour of a new arrival, reflecting Pirandello's use of the stage-life division as a metaphor for the illusion-reality dichotomy of his philosophy. Since the plays were all performed in Italian, the Lord Chamberlain now put no obstacles in the way of a public staging of *Six Characters in Search of an Author*. The same principle appears to have been in operation with respect to plays with Italian-speaking actors, as applied to French plays performed in French on the English stage: a company performing in a foreign tongue was viewed as being on home rather than on English soil and, as a result, was considered to be less of a threat to the moral code of conduct of an English audience (see also Chapter 3). The event, referred to by *The Times* of 16 June 1925 as 'The Pirandellian Season' and enhanced by the presence of the playwright, was generally viewed as a considerable success.

From the critical response, it was clear that *Henry IV* was by far the most popular of the four plays in the Pirandellian season: it has remained one of Pirandello's most frequently performed plays, including a 2004 Donmar Warehouse staging with Ian McDiarmid in the role of Henry in a version by Tom Stoppard. On 20 June 1925, the theatre reviewer for the *Manchester Guardian* referred to the play as a great work, although confessing to an inadequate command of the Italian language. But there were also critical voices. Not everyone was able to transcend the language barrier: by his own admission, lack of understanding of Italian made James Agate of *The Sunday Times* feel not only frustrated but also very nervous. As pointed out by Stefania Taviano, it is difficult to believe that his response to the production would not have been influenced by this frame of mind:

> Let not the Pirandellists rage too furiously together; I speak for myself, not for them […] When the King was absent – for immense periods alas! – the play seemed to me to be one long wilderness of dementia.[6]

Agate's reaction to the play shows little sign of having changed about a month later when *Henry IV* was given an English-language production at the Everyman Theatre in Hampstead in Edward Storer's translation. *Henry IV* is, he declared, 'a pretentious nonsense', and 'the high frenzy for it is largely composed of the feeling that not to enthuse is to be out of the fashionable swim'.[7] Other critical voices expressed similar reservations about the other plays of the Pirandellian season. In a review of *Right You Are (If You Think So)* which appeared in *The Times* of 26 June 1925, epithets such as 'sheer futility' and 'thesis play' echoed past battle cries from the opponents of the Ibsenites' attempts to put the work of the Norwegian playwright on the English stage.

The year of the Teatro d'Arte company's visit to the United Kingdom and the English-language production of *Henry IV* also saw the staging of two other Pirandello plays in English translation. At the Lyric, Hammersmith, Nigel Playfair directed *Right You Are (If You Think So)*, now entitled *And That's the Truth* and translated by Arthur Livingston, while *L'uomo dal fiore in bocca* (*The Man with the Flower in His Mouth*, 1923) was staged at the Playhouse, Oxford, with John Gielgud in the title role and directed by J B Fagan. Of the approximately 300 performances of Pirandello plays in the UK, this one-acter, about a late night conversation between two strangers, where the 'flower' is revealed to be a fatal cancerous growth of one of the men, ranks second only to *Six Characters in Search of an Author* as the Italian playwright's most popular play in England.[8] The following year another production of *The Man with the Flower in His Mouth* took place, this time at the Everyman Theatre and, in addition, two stagings of *Il Piacere dell'onestà* (*The Pleasure of Honesty*, 1918), by the Cambridge Amateur Dramatic Club and at the Abbey Theatre, Dublin.

The same year yet another Pirandello play was staged in English translation: *Right You Are (If You Think So)* as *It's the Truth if You Think It Is* at the Theatre Royal, Huddersfield, the first of a number of Pirandello productions at the West Riding theatre. The following year, the YMCA Theatre in Sheffield put on *Il giuoco delle parti* (*The Rules of the Game*, 1918) as *The Game as He Played It*, in a translation by C K Scott Moncrieff and, at the Royalty Theatre, London theatregoers had a chance to see *Naked*, in Arthur Livingston's translation, directed by Theodore Komisarjevsky.

In large measure due to the touring of the Teatro d'Arte, the 1920s represent the first period of success for Pirandello's work throughout Europe. In the 1920s and 1930s Parisian theatres regularly included Pirandello plays in their programme, not infrequently with performances at more than one theatre concurrently.[9] Pirandello's success in Europe and the Americas, where his work was also shown, has been ascribed, above all, to the impact of *Six Characters in Search of an Author*, in 1998 voted the third best play of the twentieth century.[10] The reputation for being revolutionary and innovative in the theatre also seems to have helped to secure suspension of censorship in England for *Six Characters in Search of an Author*: in May 1928, the play was produced at the Arts Theatre and from there it was transferred for further performances to the Globe Theatre in Shaftesbury Avenue. The concept of 'Pirandellism' was now introduced in reviews, later to be joined by the adjective 'Pirandellian', as a term to describe 'an absurd and ironically unsolvable situation'.[11]

Following the first period of success in the 1920s, interest in Pirandello now started to subside and Pirandello no longer figured prominently on the English stage, with the exception of Yorkshire where, in the West Riding, new work by the Italian dramatist was introduced, unknown to theatregoers in other parts of the country. The manager of the Theatre Royal in Huddersfield, Alfred Wareing, was committed to the idea of forging links with European theatre, having established a strong network of international theatre contacts. On 8 July 1929, *Lazzarro* had its world premiere at the West Riding theatre, the title referring to the biblical figure Lazarus. It formed part of a set that Pirandello labelled 'modern myths' – while *Lazzarro* represented the religious myth, *La nuova colonia* (*The New Colony*, 1928) represented the social myth and *I giganti della montagna* (*The Mountain Giants*, 1937) the myth of art.

The production, which included Donald Wolfit as Diego Spina, was directed by Arthur R Whatmore with the English translation by Scott Moncrieff. It received mixed reviews: the aspect that appears to have attracted most publicity was the competition linked to the premiere to determine an English title for the play.[12] There were over 700 entries, and the title eventually selected for the play was *Though One Rose*, which, however, never seems to have properly caught on, and the play today remains known in English as *Lazarus*. Before his departure from Huddersfield, Wareing also presented, as part of a triple bill, Pirandello's *La vita che ti diedi* (*The Life That I Gave You*, 1923), a production that has been described as '[t]he climax of Wareing's career'.[13]

Apart from a handful of stagings, there is little evidence of documented performances or published translations of Pirandello's plays in the 1930s, a lack of interest that appears to have continued into the next decade. This change in attitude to Pirandello and his work in the UK might be explained by a number of different factors: the state of the British theatre, a change in Pirandello's style and his political association with Mussolini.

The inter-war years represented a period of crisis for the theatre in the UK as for many other European countries: while the 1920s brought about a period of profound social change, the theatre did not undergo similar upheavals. With few innovations and the same playwrights continuing to write before and after World War One, a vacuum was created, into which Pirandello's new, revolutionary theatre was readily absorbed. In the 1930s, on the other hand, the plays increasingly on offer by theatrical managements were light comedies, a theatrical fare rather different from Pirandello's theatre.[14] The decade also saw a change in Pirandello's writing, many of his plays now focussing on new themes such as the isolation and loneliness of single individuals trapped by their fate, as in *Come tu mi vuoi* (*As You Desire Me*, 1930), filmed in 1933 with Greta Garbo and Erich von Stroheim. A further factor accounting for the decline of interest in Britain for Pirandello's work in the 1930s and 1940s might be linked to his support of Mussolini and his fascist regime.[15]

In 1924 Pirandello joined the Fascist Party and, not shying from maximum publicity, released for publication in *L'Impero*, the Fascist newspaper, his letter to Mussolini. In English translation, it started:

Your Excellency,

I feel that this is the most propitious moment for me to declare a loyalty which I have hitherto observed in silence. If Your Excellency finds me worthy to join the National Fascist Party I will consider it the greatest honour to become one of your humblest and most obedient followers.

With utter devotion.[16]

An important, underlying reason for Pirandello's decision to support Fascism was his attempt to obtain funding for the Teatro d'Arte. On 19 March 1925, Pirandello wrote to Mussolini in Rome:

> We are being invited by all countries; All the major theatrical bodies are offering us contracts in South America, in Spain, in Belgium, in France and in Germany. I have given serious considerations to these offers since I propose to accompany the Company abroad where, through conferences and public interviews on contemporary Italian life, I propose to undertake a propaganda exercise for the State, as I did last year in North America.[17]

Pirandello was indeed instrumental in spreading propaganda for the Fascist party during his international tours abroad where the support from Mussolini for the Teatro d'Arte was well known. Still, the relationship between Pirandello and the regime was far from consistently amicable. Pirandello's dream of a national theatre was of limited interest to Mussolini and, in 1928, due to the lack of financial funding, Teatro d'Arte performed for the last time in Italy. By the time he was awarded the Nobel Prize for Literature in 1934, relations between Pirandello and the Fascist regime had deteriorated to the point that the honour bestowed upon him was no longer of any interest to them. Nevertheless, Pirandello's known links with the Italian fascist regime did little to help his popularity as a playwright, and the low ebb of interest in Pirandello's work persisted until well after World War II.

In the mid-1950s, English theatre flourished: it was also a time when an increasing number of foreign companies visited the UK. During the 1953 summer season of the Cambridge Arts Theatre Trust, Peter Hall directed Pirandello's *Henry IV*, which in August moved to the Arts Theatre in London for a two-week season. This was followed three years later, in September 1956, by the visit to London from the Berliner Ensemble with a selection of Brecht plays (see Chapter 6).

After a couple of decades' absence, the Pirandello now returning to the English stage was different from the Pirandello of the 1920s. Coinciding with the British discovery of Brecht and Beckett, at this point in time, the theatre of Pirandello was attracting attention for its philosophical consideration of the human condition, and seen to be related to existentialism and the Theatre of the Absurd. In addition to a large number of Pirandello productions, the 1950s also saw the publication of his plays in English translation. In New York, a volume with the title *Naked Masks, Five Plays by Luigi Pirandello*, appeared in 1952, edited by Eric Bentley. This was followed in 1958 by *The*

Mountain Giants and Other Plays in translation by Marta Abba, the actress who became Pirandello's close confidante and for whom he wrote a number of parts in his plays.

The Pirandello on the English stage in the 1950s proved to be Janus-faced: two decades passed and the late 1970s saw yet another Pirandello. Now, new aspects of Pirandello's work were attracting attention, in Italy as well as in the UK. At this point in time Pirandello was no longer exclusively associated with plays such as *Henry IV* and *Six Characters in Search of an Author*. While from the mid-1970s to the 1980s only two Pirandello plays, *Henry IV* and *The Rules of the Game*, were performed in London's West End, from the late 1980s onwards, Pirandello's later plays, in particular *The Mountain Giants*, were staged on several occasions. At a time when the beliefs and values of previous decades began to be reappraised, Pirandello's plays now lent themselves to interpretation as 'an imaginary alternative to the reality of everyday life',[18] the myths and their symbolic nature reflecting the cultural atmosphere of the time. Among the plays that Pirandello grouped together in the category 'modern myths', in the 1980s and 1990s *The Mountain Giants* in particular was staged on a number of occasions in Britain as well as in other parts of Europe. Now the work of the Italian playwright had come to be viewed from yet another angle: in the 1990s, Pirandello's plays provided an insight into the world of the artist, in a number of respects resembling the rapidly changing world that we inhabit today.[19]

Thus Pirandello on the English stage has appeared in many guises, influenced by the Zeitgeist of different epochs: in the 1920s, as an experimental playwright, in the 1950s, as an early existentialist and in the 1990s as an artist struggling to find an identity in a changeable world. In addition to the multifaceted nature of his work, enabling successive generations of artists to draw inspiration from his plays, boom periods of interest have also been the result of the committed work of individuals determined to bring the playwright onto the English stage. In the 1920s Alfred Wareing, the manager of the Theatre Royal in Huddersfield, was an ardent supporter of the Italian playwright's work. When in 1931 Wareing left Huddersfield, the change was noticeable and interest in Pirandello started to wane. For the second boom period of interest in Pirandello in the 1950s, Wareing's role as promoter of Pirandello was taken over by Frederick May, an academic at Leeds University. In an article in the *University of Leeds Review*, in June 1963, Frederick May acknowledged Alfred Wareing's importance for Pirandello's work, recording 'with gratitude his achievement in presenting the plays of Luigi Pirandello in the West Riding, for his work at the Theatre Royal, Huddersfield… [which] made it possible for there to be a continuing tradition of performance and enlightened acceptance of his dramas'.[20]

A lecturer in Italian, May not only knew the language in which Pirandello wrote but was also an actor and came to play an important role in presenting Pirandello's plays to the anglophone world on stage as well as a translator. Pirandello's theatre developed into one of the main interests of May's life: he was actively involved in several major theatrical productions of Pirandello's plays, in some as translator and director as well as lead actor. Without such intimate knowledge of Italian, the playwright's work and the theatre, considerable odds have often had to be overcome for Pirandello's plays to succeed on the English stage.

In his essay of 1908, *Illustratori, attori e traduttori* ('Illustrators, Actors and Translators'), Pirandello expressed his own doubts about the limits of translation:

> It is like transplanting a tree that has sprung from one soil and flowered in one kind of climate into a soil that is not its own; its foliage and flowers will be lost in the new climate, and by foliage and leaves I mean native language, and by flowers I mean those particular graceful features of the language, its essential harmony, all of which are inimitable.[21]

Like many other dramatists and writers of the period, Pirandello also drew on the distinction between polite and informal pronominal address found in many European languages in order to indicate changes in mood and feeling in the interaction between characters. As in the case of Ibsen and Strindberg (see Chapters 3 and 5) in translation into English, this form of pronominal switching presents a problem of complete 'untranslatability'.

In *Six Characters in Search of an Author*, the change between the formal *lei* or *loro* and the informal *tu* or *voi* is used in different ways. One way is to indicate the difference between the characters in their 'unnatural' state when interacting with the Director, in contrast to their 'natural' state when they are performing a scene. When, for instance, on the occasion that the Father and the Stepdaughter speak to each other directly, as might be expected, they tend to use the informal pronoun of address:

> IL PADRE: *Ma io non narro! voglio spiegargli.*
> LA FIGLIASTRA: *Ah, bello, sí! A modo* **tuo***!* [22]

In English translation by Eric Bentley this reads:

> FATHER: I said – explanations.

STEPDAUGHTER: Oh, certainly. Those that suit **your** turn.[23]

However, when the Father and the Stepdaughter perform their scene in Madam Pace's shop together, they switch to the use of the formal pronouns of address. Here this mode of address emphasises the nature of the scene, that neither knows who the other one is. However, before they act this scene together, the Stepdaughter's role *vis-à-vis* the Father changes by her taking on the role of the Director, issuing directives to the Father. She now uses the formal form of address:

LA FIGLIASTRA: (Al Padre.) *E **lei** faccia l'entrata!*[24]

In English:

STEPDAUGHTER: *(To the Father.)* And **you** can make your entrance.[25]

Here the use of the formal pronoun of address imitates the way in which the Director has spoken to the characters. The element of formality introduced through this use of address not only allows the Stepdaughter to distance herself from the Father, but also helps to invest her with a new power and authority which until now she has been lacking. When, on the other hand, she addresses the Father and the Director at the same time, now in a temper, she chooses the informal form of address:

LA FIGLIASTRA: *Non ci sto! non ci sto! Quello che è possibile sulla scena **ve** lo siete combinato insieme tutti e due, di là, grazie!*[26]

In English:

STEPDAUGHTER: I'm leaving! I'm leaving! You went in that room, you two, didn't you, and [**you**] figured out 'what is possible on the stage'? Thanks very much![27]

This is the only occasion when the Stepdaughter does not use the formal mode of address with the Director, suggesting that the contempt she feels for the Father has got the better of her customary respect for the Director and she addresses both as she would have the Father on his own.

A further obstacle in the way of Pirandello successfully reaching the English stage is the way Mediterraneans have often been represented in English productions. At times, English actors and directors have been inclined to highlight what is perceived as the Latin element which, if over-emphasised, may result in stereotyping. This tendency to accentuate the exuberance of the Latin temperament to the point where it becomes stereotypical seems to have been recurrent ever since Pirandello first made his appearance on the English stage. In her review of the production of *Liolà* (1916), originally written in Sicilian dialect, staged by the New International Theatre in London in 1982, Jennifer Lorch found the 'gelato/spaghetti English' a regrettable 'reflection of the British view of the Italian urban proletariat uneasily absorbed into its culture'.[28]

In addition to Pirandello's work being presented in conformity with commonly-shared views about what is popularly believed to be an Italian way of life, the history of critical evaluation of 'English Pirandello' includes frequent mention of his work as being 'cerebral'. Not always an easy fit with British theatre, Pirandello's plays have become known as offering intellectual debates on matters such as the nature of Life and Art. Employing the naturalistic technique with its reliance on added verbal wit, which dominates the British acting style, many of Pirandello's plays, originally perceived as comedies with fast-moving dialogue broken by moments of internalised debate, often become slow and leaden in English translation.

The lightness of touch which frequently seems to have been lost in translation, is vividly illustrated by the English titles of Pirandello's plays. A note of ponderousness often manages to creep in, as in the case of *Come tu mi vuoi*, the play written for Marta Abba in 1930, in which the Italian title literally meaning 'however you like/want me' in English has been translated as *As You Desire Me*. As Susan Bassnett points out, in Italian the title of the play is a colloquial phrase, casually indicating that the speaker wishes to accommodate the listener but, at the same time, does not really care one way or the other.[29] In English, however, the use of a more formal register in combination with the word 'desire' moves the Italian name of the play from a colloquial to a different stylistic level: the English title gains added weight and with it a note of gravity not present in the original.

A similar problem of translation is found in the title of another well-known Pirandello play. *Cosi è (se vi pare)* deals with the recurrent problem discussed in Pirandello's work of the impossibility of knowing exactly who someone really might be. The Italian, which could be translated approximately as 'That's how it is (if you see it that way)' contains a light, jocular note, not captured in any of the titles under which the play is known in English: *Right You Are (If You Think So)*; *It is So (If You Think So)*; *And That's the Truth*; *It's the Truth if You Think It Is*; *You Are Right, If You Think You Are*. The most recent attempt to capture the spirit of the original Italian is also the shortest. For the London production of the play in the summer of 2003 in translation by playwright Martin Sherman, the title chosen was *Absolutely (Perhaps)*.

The change of mood of a Pirandello play in English even before the curtain rises – the result of the loss of the light touch of the original title – is frequently reinforced by the translation of the Italian dialogue. The inevitably increased verbal load due to grammatical and syntactic differences between Italian, a Romance, and English, a Germanic language, often creates the impression of a 'wordier' and more serious 'English Pirandello' than is his Italian counterpart. At the beginning of *The Life That I Gave You*, Donn'Anna's only son lies dead; here key words such as *'vita'* (life) and *'morte'* (death) and their derived forms are used in ironic juxtaposition. Alone on the stage, at the end of Act II, Donn'Anna utters only one word: *'Vive'*. Whereas in Italian the subject of the verb does not have to be spelt out, the English translation uses three words, 'He is alive'. Thus the dramatic impact of the playwright employing a single key word at an important, conclusive moment is lost, the inevitable result of syntactic differences between the structure of the source and the target language.

Less than successful translations of Pirandello's plays have even been quoted as the reason for the limited knowledge of the playwright's work in the English speaking world:

> Of the plays appearing from 1927 onward, when the great boom period of Pirandello's popularity in Europe and the United States was beginning to fade, little is known, perhaps because in several cases the English translations are so bad as to be unreadable, let alone actable.[30]

Matters were not helped by Pirandello granting the copyright of some of his plays to Marta Abba, including *The Mountain Giants*, his unfinished play, which as a result was available only in the actress's own translation, dated 1958. Although the original period of copyright ended in 1986, fifty years after the playwright's death – thus opening a window for new translations of Pirandello's work – in 1995, after less than a decade, new European legislation extended the period to seventy years, and original copyright restrictions were reinstated.

Susan Bassnett is not alone in pointing to the damage suffered by Pirandello's work in translation. According to William Murray, another of his translators: 'No other playwright has suffered as much in translation as he has, and even in his life time he was well aware of it'. In conversation with a friend, Pirandello went as far as using the now well-known dictum of equating translators with traitors: 'Traduttore, traditore'.[31] He knew that his work had been distorted in translation, to the extent that lengthy speeches had been added and, perhaps even worse, that his mastery of Italian, raised in its simplicity to the level of poetry, had not been captured in translation into English. In *To Clothe the Naked and Two Other Plays* published in 1962, introduced and translated by Murray (1962), a short speech in Murray's translation is compared with a short speech from an earlier, not accredited translation of *The Pleasure of Honesty*. In the earlier translation, towards the end of Act 1, Angelo tells us:

> ANGELO BALDOVINO: I am like a person trying to circulate gold money in a country that has never seen anything but paper. People are inclined to suspect that gold, are they not? It is quite natural. Well, you are certainly tempted to refuse it here. But it's gold, Signor Marchese, I assure you – pure gold – the only gold, by the way, I have never been able to spend, because I have it inside me – in my soul and not in my pockets. If I had it in my pockets –[32]

In contrast to this translation, 'a laboured job, stilted and awkward',[33] stands Murray's own version, more condensed as well as more colloquial:

> ANGELO BALDOVINO: I'm like a man who wants to spend gold in a country where the money is made of paper. Everyone mistrusts such a man at first, it's only natural. You're tempted now to turn me down, aren't you? But it's real gold, Mr Colli. I've never been able to spend it because I have it in my soul and not in my pockets. Otherwise...[34]

Murray's method of translation, whereby sentences are contracted and the language used is turned into colloquial speech, reflects a more general trend further developed over the last few decades in the approach to the Italian playwright's work. More recent Pirandello productions staged by London theatres have been based on new versions by well-established British playwrights. On 7 May 1992, during the period prior to the re-introduction of copyright restrictions, a production of *The Rules of the Game* premiered at the Almeida Theatre, in a new English version by David Hare. However, just over 20 years earlier, the National Theatre had staged the same play, the first performance of which opened on 15 June 1971 at the New Theatre in St Martin's Lane. This earlier translation of the play bore, along with the name of David Hare, the name of another translator, that of Robert Rietty as co-translator. For the Almeida performance, David Hare appears to have set about producing a new version in further keeping with a move towards freeing the language for the stage from the shackles of the page.

Contrary to what is suggested by the title, Pirandello's play deals with the game of role-playing rather than the rules that apply in the game. The title of the play, *Il giuoco delle parti*, translates as 'the game of rules', pointing to the social requirement that must be followed whatever game might be played. Long before the concept of role-playing became familiar through psychological literature, Pirandello, perhaps as the result of his wife's paranoia (she was finally, after 16 years, committed to an asylum) could not help but be aware of the tension between appearance and reality; and that throughout our lives we all, to varying degrees, play conventional roles. To all appearances Leone Gala in *The Rules of the Game* condones the affair between his wife Silia and Guido, accepting the role as that of 'betrayed husband'. His seemingly serene indifference proves to be too much for Silia and, in an attempt to get back at him, she cunningly engineers a duel between her husband and a drunken young man who she claims has assaulted her. At first Leone agrees to settle this point of honour, but as the event draws closer he turns the tables on his wife, forcing his second, no other than Guido, to take his place. Admitting to his intention to mete out punishment on his wife and her lover, Leone drops his adopted mask of indifference and bursts into violent anger against Silia, now appearing in a new unexpected role.

The play opens with Guido making strenuous efforts to attract the attention of Silia who, by her own declaration is 'elsewhere' and 'far away'. Everything else having failed, he moves to kiss her but this only results in Silia leaping to her feet and pushing him away. In Murray's relatively faithful 1962 translation of the play, the following exchange ensues:

> SILIA: Stop it! I said no! No, no, and no!
> GUIDO: Back already? Too bad! I guess your husband was right when he said that what we seek on the outside is really within ourselves.
> SILIA: That's the fourth or fifth time you've mentioned my husband this evening.
> GUIDO: It seems to be the only way I can get you to talk to me.
> SILIA: No, darling, it just makes you even more insufferable.
> GUIDO: Thank you.[35]

In comparison, Hare's new version of the opening scene lowers the emotional temperature by removing the exclamation marks as well as Silia's strongly worded rejection of Guido's advances. Hare also polishes the verbal repartee, letting Silia pick up on Guido's words '…the only way I've found of making…' in order to put her lover down:

> SILIA Stop. Just leave me alone, I've told you before.
> GUIDO: So you're back already. What a shame. Perhaps your husband is right when he says we only really travel inside our own heads.
> SILIA: That's about the fifth time you've mentioned him this evening.
> GUIDO: It's *the only way I've found of making* you talk to me.

SILIA: Guido, it's *a way you've found of making* yourself even more
insufferable.
GUIDO: Thank you.[36]

Overall, the exchange has been made sharper and more economical through
verbal pruning, as in turning '…what we seek on the outside is really within
ourselves' into '…we only really travel inside our own heads.' Hare also takes
care to ensure that what there is of comic potential in the original is more
clearly brought out. For example, here is Murray's translation of an exchange
in which Leone warns Guido of the effects of drinking chartreuse at too late
an hour:

LEONE: At about two o'clock you'll dream you're chewing on a dead
lizard.
GUIDO: (*Grimacing.*) Chewing on a what?
LEONE: A lizard. It's the one sure effect of drinking liqueurs too late
after dinner…[37]

Hare's version, on the other hand, removes the somewhat graphic reference
to 'chewing a dead lizard' and replaces it with the more absurdly comical 'a
lizard stuck between your teeth'. Guido's answer is also more expressive,
heightening the repartee of the exchange:

LEONE: Yes. Well round about two o'clock you'll dream there's a lizard
stuck between your teeth.
GUIDO: (*Disgusted.*) Oh God. Are you sure?
LEONE: Absolutely. That's what happens if you drink liqueur at this
time of night…[38]

In 1987, sixty-five years after the first English translation of *Six Characters in
Search of an Author* first opened at the Kingsway Theatre after initial opposition
from the Lord Chamberlain but with support from Bernard Shaw, the play
was staged by the National Theatre in a 'new version' by Nicholas Wright. In
what appears to have been an attempt to make the play more accessible to
English audiences, what was deemed to be too alien was changed and replaced
by more familiar references. For example, while in the original, the play which
the actors are rehearsing when the six characters arrive is *The Rules of the
Game*, in Nicholas Wright's Anglicised version, Pirandello's play is replaced
by *Hamlet*.

Commenting on the National Theatre production, Giulia Ajmone Arsan
noted that 'the play has been Anglicised', criticising 'the intention to tone
down the exuberance of Latin passion', concluding that the approach could

only be viewed as 'patronising towards the public'.[39] In another discussion of the production, Katherine Worth found that 'the actors hold the audience in a warm, intimate relationship which provides an unusually homey context for the disturbing phenomenon of *Six Characters in Search of an Author*', but she concluded that '[w]hat is clear is that the production has opened up Pirandello's play for popular consumption in the English theatre'.[40] Both of Worth's observations would appear to be correct: while in the original the audience is made to feel somewhat uncomfortable by the playwright having abandoned his characters and left them to their fate, being presented with the rehearsal of *Hamlet*, a play from the 'familiar classic repertoire', helps to save the audience from experiencing this discomfort. It is a moot point whether the gain in accessibility is worth the sacrifice of exactitude. We are back to the question of taking the text home to the reader or the reader abroad to the text.

Two years later, on 7 September 1989, *Man Beast & Virtue*, an English version of Pirandello's *L'uomo, la bestia, e la virtù*, opened in a National Theatre production at the Cottesloe. The original play premiered in Milan on 2 May 1919, taking 'up a traditional *commedia* plot (two lovers, slightly the worse for wear, and a deceived and deceiving husband)'.[41] Again, the English version of the play used for the performance involved co-operation with a professional playwright; it was based on an English translation by Gwenda Pandolfi, serving as a starting point for the work by playwright Charles Wood. Four years later, a production of *The Mountain Giants* followed at the National Theatre, directed by William Gaskill, also the director of *Man, Beast & Virtue*, with, once more, Wood as the adapter. The play opened at the Cottesloe Theatre on 14 July 1993.

In a letter to Marta Abba, with whose name copyright of the play was linked until 1986, Pirandello described the play, as 'the triumph of fantasy, the triumph of poetry, but at the same time also the tragedy of poetry in this brutal, modern world'.[42] In a production directed by Giorgio Strehler, *The Mountain Giants* has been viewed as a milestone in Italian theatre history. As if the play were not in itself sufficiently daunting for an English translator/adapter, a further problem is presented by the need for the play and its characters to be bought to completion (if not, this being Pirandello, to a conclusion), since the death of the playwright left the last act unwritten. According to Charles Wood in the National Theatre performance programme: '[Pirandello] did say how he thought it might come out: he knew what was to happen to his characters and the pass he had brought them to.' Wood went on to reflect on his work on the play:

> It is so brilliantly written that an adaptation is mostly a process of uncovering

meaning and presenting it in speakable English. But it is a process one can never be sure is finished when preparing the play for the stage. The 'version' starts off this process but, in rehearsal, there *are* inevitable moments when recourse is made to the original text (a furtive look at the crib by Mr Gaskill), before taking a chance on my reading being right.

Towards the end of the 1990s, steps were also taken towards further acculturation of another Pirandello play: *To Clothe the Naked*. On 12 February 1998, a new English version by Nicholas Wright entitled *Naked* premiered at the Almeida Theatre with Juliette Binoche as Ersilia Drei. Wright's amendments to the original involved sharpening the dialogue and highlighting humorous elements of the text. At the same time he also adjusted the emotional climate of the world which the play's characters inhabit to a more easily recognisable Anglo-Saxon temperature.

The subject of *Naked* is – what is the truthful version of a story? The ageing writer Ludovico Nota becomes interested in the reasons that have driven Ersilia Drei to attempt to take her own life, and he invites her to his home. Convinced that she has tried to kill herself on account of his having abandoned her, Franco Laspiga turns up on Nota's doorstep in order to make amends. So too does Consul Grotti from whose household Ersilia has been dismissed, following the death of the family's baby daughter. It now emerges that the Consul and Ersilia were lovers and in each other's company at the time of the death of the small child. Surrounded on all sides by men insisting on imposing their own version of events, Ersilia, now desperate, again resorts to taking poison and, this time, she is successful. She dies 'naked', deprived of bourgeois respectability, but, in the eyes of the audience, she does so with dignity.

Wright's version of *Naked*, aimed at the late 1990s, shows much the same technique as that of William Murray in his approach to the updated 1962 translation of *The Pleasure of Honesty* discussed above. Sentences are contracted and language is made snappier. At the beginning of Act 1 Ersilia arrives, together with Ludovico, at his flat. Soon afterwards, Signora Onoria, bourgeois landlady and representative of society at large, appears, carrying a broom and a pile of dirty laundry. After announcing that she has just put 'clean sheets' on his bed, Signora Onoria addresses Ludovico, here in Murray's translation:

> ONORIA: But if it's for – (*She looks at Ersilia and breaks off.*) Mr Nota, I think it's time we reached an understanding. I'll just take these things downstairs and –

LUDOVICO: (*Drily.*) That's *decent* of you.
ONORIA: (*Angrily.*) Who are you to talk about *decency*?
LUDOVICO: Well, I only meant that you ought to get rid of that dirty
    laundry before –
ONORIA: I'm going to get rid of all the dirt around here!
LUDOVICO: What do you mean by that?
ONORIA: I mean that girl, for instance. And you talk to me about
    decency, bringing one of her kind into my house –
LUDIVICO: By God, you keep a civil tongue in your head or I'll –
ONORIA: You'll what? We're going to have this out once and for all! I'll
    be right back! (*She exits hurriedly.*)
LUDOVICO: Dirty-minded old gossip!
ERSILA: (*Dismayed, holding him back.*) No, no, please, I'll go.
LUDOVICO: Not at all! This is my house! [43]

In Wright's version, the play on 'decent'/'decency' finds an alternative in
Ludovico's reference to the dirty laundry as 'disgusting', which in turn prepares
for Signora Onoria to get back at him, using the same word but this time in
relation to Ersilia. In keeping with the times, Wright also streamlines the
dialogue, reducing the number of words in the exchange. Also, in choosing to
comment on, rather than addressing Signora Onoria, he lowers the emotional
temperature of Ludovico's parting comment to his landlady, turning a volatile,
by popular definition Mediterranean, into a more world-weary, arguably more
Anglo-Saxon male. Wright also appears to feel that Ludovico's announcement
'Not at all! This is my house' is too direct for British social intercourse and
requires softening. Having registered the presence of Ersilia, in Wright's version
Signora Onoria and Ludovico now have the following exchange:

ONORIA: Ah. I see. (*To LUDOVICO.*) You and I had better have a talk.
    I'll take these out and then…
LUDOVICO: Quite so! Let's get rid of those disgusting objects.
ONORIA: *Disgusting.*
LUDOVICO: Yes. You said yourself, you wanted to remove them.
ONORIA: What about *that* disgusting object? What about *her*?
LUDOVICO: This young lady is my guest. If you continue to insult
    her…
ONORIA: What if I do? What then?
    (*Pause.*)
    I'll be back.
    (*She goes.*)
LUDOVICO: (*To Ersilia.*) Sad, disappointed creature. She'll come round.
    She'll have to. I'm standing firm on this. My home is yours. Now, if
    you'd…[44]

Throughout, Wright's version also leaves out a multitude of exclamation marks and stage directions indicating extreme emotions, all part of a move towards further Anglicisation of the Italian text, with the aim of making the emotions of confrontation less overt.

The process of acculturation whereby cultural and linguistic features of the original, deemed to be too unfamiliar in translation, are placed within an overall, more familiar English framework, has done much to ease Pirandello onto the English stage. There is, however, a delicate balance that needs to be struck. Increased familiarity also invites the loss of authenticity, and, in the case of translation into English, the risk of eagerly extracting anything that may be interpreted as humorous in order to satisfy the requirement for wit at all cost. To quote Michael Billington in the *Guardian* of 17 February 2001, on a production of *Six Characters in Search of an Author* at the Young Vic:

> But exhilarating as it is to see this seminal work back on a British stage, Richard Jones' ingenious production over-elaborates an already complex work. Stressing its prankishness more than its psychopathology, he turns it at times into an Italian *Noises Off*.

At the start of the twenty-first century, the temptation to emphasise the humour of a foreign play in English translation at the cost of its psychological underpinning is as keenly felt as it was in Pirandello productions of the distant past. According to H Conway, writing in 1955:

> The Arts Theatre came up last night with a novelty well-worth braving the snow and slush to see. Not only a novelty but a revelation – for *The Rules of the Game* shows fellow-playwrights that Pirandello, who happens to be writing in another language, could write a French farce with the best of them.[45]

Ironically, the Italian playwright himself would have been the first to understand the need for humour on the English stage, as revealed in his *Impressions of London*:

> In the theatre, the audience seem to laugh at nothing, but it is not so. It may seem so to a foreigner who has not that special taste for the flavour of words, which is called humour. Humour is the only frivolity which the English allow themselves. It is true that they manage to find some everywhere. And then, instead of frivolity, I think you could call it wisdom.[46]

Not only does the delicate touch of Pirandello's stage language at times defy attempts to extract humour, the overall effect of the poetry of his writing often does not travel in naturalistic English interpretation. Recalling Shelley's

The Defence of Poetry, that the 'plant must spring again from its seed or it will bear no flower', reconstruction may be necessary or, like Shelley's 'violet in the crucible', the delicacy of Pirandello's language is likely to be crushed. Although faithful translations often aim to reproduce the poetry of the original, neither playwright nor cast may be best served by characters on stage declaring for example that they are 'engulfed by the strength of our passions' or 'protected on the outside by the scaffolding of our assumptions'. For the beauty of the original to come to the fore it would seem unlikely that there will ever be an English flower to match the Italian one unless the plant/text springs from its seed again in quite a different poetic form.

In 1981 Eric Bentley posed the question, 'In the matter of Luigi Pirandello, where do things stand?' Bentley then proceeded to provide an answer to his own question: 'For the English-speaking world, Luigi Pirandello remains *terra incognita*'.[47] More recently, however, Pirandello scholars Jennifer Lorch and Stefania Taviano have been more optimistic. Although not sharing the status of Ibsen as an 'Honorary British playwright', as the result of the successful stagings of *The Rules of the Game* in 1992 and *Naked* in 1998, Pirandello's arrival on the English stage has now been proclaimed. 'There is now an English Pirandello: that is better than no Pirandello at all, or even Pirandello on the fringe'.[48]

However, for Pirandello to become English, his plays, like those of other European playwrights, had to pass through successive stages of acculturation, his 'Italianness' gradually ebbing and the universality of his work emerging. The use of stereotypes on stage in relation to Italian drama has been discussed by Stefania Taviano.[49] Taviano is not alone in her view that Italians on the English stage are represented in accordance with a set of preconceived notions as to what is 'Italianness'. Clive Barker has pointed to other, frequently selected characteristics of 'stage' Italians: '[in] British theatre, Italian characters have tended to be viewed as devious, over-emotional, Machiavellian in cunning, or as a source of comic relief'.[50] The plays of Eduardo de Filippo, identified by Eric Bentley as 'more likely...to be the heir of *commedia dell'arte* than any other important performer now living', arguably lend themselves even more easily than Pirandello's work to typecasting influenced by popular English perceptions of 'Italianness'.[51]

The move from realism toward a new theatricalism as embodied in the work of Luigi Pirandello was further energised at the beginning of the twentieth century by the rediscovery of *commedia dell'arte*. Over the years, the popularity of *commedia*, a form of non-literary theatre that stresses the skill of the improvising actor, has been growing, providing diverse entertainments throughout the theatres of Europe. Frequent mention has been made of the influence of *commedia dell'arte* on Pirandello's early work for the theatre, written in dialect and inspired by Sicilian folk traditions and, more recently, the relation of *commedia* to Pirandello's major plays.[52]

The *commedia dell'arte* tradition makes itself felt even more strongly in the work of Eduardo de Filippo (1900–84) who, after the death of Pirandello, took over his role as the leading figure in Italian theatre. A citizen of Naples, at the beginning of the twentieth century De Filippo led his own theatre company, first with his sister Titina (1898–1963) and his brother Peppino (1903–80) until, in 1945, he broke away to form his own group, called simply Il Teatro di Eduardo. Over seven decades, Eduardo de Filippo wrote more than 50 plays for the stage as well as poetry, plays for television and several screenplays, including, in 1964, an adaptation of his 1946 stage play *Filumena Marturano* for the film *Marriage Italian Style*, directed by Vittorio de Sica and with Sophia Loren and Marcello Mastroianni. As in the case of Pirandello, De Filippo's work was first shown on the English stage in the original Italian. When, in 1972, *Napoli milionaria!* (*Naples Millionaire*, 1945) formed part of Peter Daubeny's World Theatre Season, it was presented by Il Teatro di Eduardo in a performance directed by Eduardo, as he was familiarly referred to by Italians. In this production, Eduardo also took the part of Gennaro, who, returning from a German prison camp, finds his wife suspiciously well-dressed and teamed up with a black marketeer, his daughter an aspiring hooker and his son a thief, all uninterested in his stories about his own wartime sufferings.

A year later, in November 1973, the National Theatre invited the Italian opera, film and theatre director Franco Zeffirelli to direct De Filippo's *Sabato, domenica e lunedì* (*Saturday, Sunday, Monday*, 1959). As the title suggests, the action takes place over a weekend, during which the devastating effects are revealed that result from a lack of communication among the members of an Italian family. The play was adapted by Keith Waterhouse and Willis Hall, with a cast including Lawrence Olivier, Joan Plowright and Frank Finlay. A central scene of the play is the Sunday lunch for which, in order to create an authentic Neapolitan atmosphere, Zeffirelli decided to make use of real *ragù*. In addition to the emphasis on the celebration of food as an essential feature of 'Italianness', the key role played by the family in Italy was highlighted through the inclusion in the National Theatre performance programme of a family tree illustrating the relationship between the different members of the Petrione family. Reinforcing popular Anglo-Saxon perceptions of the Italian

South while, at the same time, evoking latent nostalgia for the extended family in English society, the production was a big box-office hit. Its success was, however, in large measure due to the emphasis placed on the humorous aspects of the play, which transformed it into light comedy, leaving its dark underside basically untouched. While in the original the theme explored was the tensions behind the fun-loving face that the Neapolitan puts on to the world, in Zeffirelli's production the comedy succeeded in edging out the tragedy, turning the play into 'the finest and funniest show in London' and 'a warm and lively comedy'. The entertainment value was even further pronounced when, in 1974, the production was transferred to the Queen's Theatre in the West End.[53]

The success of De Filippo's play on the London stage was, however, not repeated when Zeffirelli's production moved across the Atlantic. When on 22 November 1974, *Saturday, Sunday, Monday* opened at the Martin Beck Theatre, the fact that the audience could not only see but also smell the *ragú* gave rise to a variety of comments in the American critical reviews. On the whole it was clear that New York audiences, accustomed to a different form of Italian ethnicity, did not share the ideas about 'Italianness' embraced by British theatregoers.

A similar fate befell *Filumena*, Zeffirelli's second De Filippo production at the Lyric Theatre in London in 1977, when it transferred to New York. In order to gain respectability for herself and her three sons, one of whom is the son of Domenico Soriano (but she has not told them which one), Filumena feigns a deathbed scene. Convinced that she is at death's door, Domenico agrees to marry her, only to witness her miraculous recovery. As with the previous Zeffirelli production, the Italian aspect of the play was emphasised, including the use of mock-Italian accents. Highly successful, the play ran for two years in the West End and won a best play award. Again in an adaptation by Keith Waterhouse and Willis Hall, the cast included Frank Finlay and Joan Plowright, whose interpretation of the part of Filumena earned her a prize for best actress.

In the context of the English-speaking world, however, the use of what Taviano calls 'the accent convention', whereby actors in plays by foreign play-wrights assume accents in order to evoke atmospheric associations of other cultures, runs the risk that one nation's stereotyping is not necessarily that of another. The number of Italian immigrants living in New York have created notions of 'Italianness' for the inhabitants of that city rather different from those popularly held in the UK. As a result, when *Filumena* transferred to New York, where it opened at the James Theatre in New York in February 1980, the American reception of De Filippo's play was no more favourable than that of *Saturday, Sunday, Monday*. One factor blamed for the failure of the production was the use of mock accents:

> The most idiotic of all English theatrical conventions had to be brought in, namely that these Italians in Italy have to speak English with an Italian accent [...] as though they were Italian waiters just arrived in England and trying to communicate with English customers.[54]

Suspension of disbelief in the 'Italianness' of the production appears to have been stretched even further by the inconsistent use of accents by the cast blamed by American reviewers for undermining credibility. While Frank Finlay spoke with an Italian accent, Joan Plowright remained British, the rest of the cast making use of a multitude of American accents, which caused New York theatre critic Walter Kerr to refer to the multi-accented cast as a veritable 'Tower of Babel'.[55] But even more important for the Americans was the play's failure to meet their expectations as to what represented 'Italianness'. Critics decried the lack of 'Latin fervour' and absence of Italian-American notions of sensuality and passion: parallels were drawn between Joan Plowright and Mary Poppins.[56] In contrast, the true notions of Italian womanhood held by American theatregoers were illustrated by the reception of a production of *Filumena* which opened in New York in November 1997, following a successful staging at the Williamstown Theater Festival in Massachussets fifteen months earlier. Unlike the British cast list, a striking feature of the New York performance programme was the preponderance of Italian names. In a review of the production dated 7 November 1997, *New York Times* Theatre critic Wilburn Hampton described Maria Tucci's Filumena as 'the ideal cicerone in her bravura performance', commenting on how she 'captures the heart and soul of Italian womanhood in her own deft translation and interpretation of the wily *bella di notte*, with singularly Neapolitan ideas of family values'.

As in the case of Pirandello in his first English phase, London productions of De Filippo's plays in the 1970s attempted to capture the spirit of 'Italianness' by taking the audience to the original text through the addition of ingredients popularly associated with Italian life and culture. By means of Italian food and drink, animated conversation and mock accents, stereotypical images were created of a different country and its culture as seen through English eyes, often resulting in comic effects. Adhering to this model of adaptation, the translated text is provided with 'a comic set of signs denoting Italianicity', as pointed out by Susan Bassnett in her discussion of British productions of De Filippo's work of this earlier period.[57]

The next decade saw the opposite approach applied to a De Filippo play, whereby his work was brought home to the audience through a process of complete acculturation, to the point where it was relocated to the country of the language of the audience. In this attempt to Anglicise the work by De Filippo, British playwright Mike Stott adapted *Natale in casa Cupiello* (*Christmas at the Cupiello's*, 1931), from a translation of the Italian text. Keeping the focus of the play on the financial and social struggles of a Catholic working-class family, Stott, successful author of *Funny Peculiar*, set the play in Lancashire; De Filippo's close study of Neapolitan family life was relocated and applied as a framework to Stott's own home town. Retitled *Ducking Out*, in reference to the protagonist Len who manages to eschew family crises by retreating into a world of his own, the play opened at the Greenwich Theatre with Warren Mitchell and Gillian Barge, directed by Mike Ockrent; in 1982 it transferred to the Duke of York in the West End. With the slower pace of Mike Ockrent's production, laughter no longer dominated the performance, but De Filippo's reputation as a comic writer was by now well-established and audiences were prepared to take on board that, in addition to comedy, there was a more sombre note to his work. On 17 November 1982 Francis King of the *Sunday Telegraph* was moved to conclude that 'Mr Mitchell and Mr Ockrent have made of [the play] something less immediately amusing but more memorable in the long run'.

Almost a decade later, the same domesticating approach was used to transport *Napoli milionaria!* to Liverpool, the home town of British playwright and adapter Peter Tinniswood. The production for the National Theatre, which opened at the Lyttelton in 1991 and starred Ian McKellen and Clare Higgins, had the actors speaking with Liverpudlian accents and was directed by Richard Eyre. Through the use of dialect rather than standard English, De Filippo's Italian characters were now given a voice of authenticity in translation, accurately reflecting the social origin of the playwright's Neapolitan characters. Shortened sentences also served to help the play to fit into present-day theatrical conventions of stage dialogue which, together with the successful adaptation, helped to edge the work of De Filippo closer towards assimilation and the status of an 'English Eduardo'.

The period of time between these two nationalised productions of De Filippo's work also saw the National Theatre present *Le voci di dentro* (*Inner Voices*, 1948), set in a Naples of 1948, still reverberating from the effects of the invasion of the Allies and the retreat of the Germans, with Ralph Richardson and Robert Stephens, directed by Mike Ockrent and translated by N F Simpson.

In an interview with De Filippo in the *Guardian* of 7 November 1983 preceding the start of the tour of *Inner Voices* to Nottingham and Liverpool, Michael Billington first pointed to De Filippo's contribution to Italian theatre, then to the striking feature of Eduardo's work, that 'he uses the traditional format of family comedy to put his finger on some moral flaw in society; and the notion of the family at war with itself is the invisible thread that links much fine drama from Aeschylus to Ayckbourn'. The combination of comedy and tragedy in the work of the Italian playwright was now becoming increasingly acknowledged. According to De Filippo himself in the interview with Michael Billington:

> At the centre of all my plays lies a conflict between the individual and society. That is to say, my plays stem from an emotional stimulus: reaction to injustice, disgust at hypocrisy, compassion for a person or group of people, a revolt against outmoded laws. On the whole, if an idea has no social meaning or application, I'm not interested in developing it.

Confirming that to be specific is to be universal, De Filippo's plays are firmly anchored in Naples. However, the specific knowledge required to understand fully all aspects of this Neapolitan setting is not granted to everyone, which inevitably results in problems when translating and transferring De Filippo's plays from the Naples of their origin. 'To know and to love Eduardo's plays,' according to Thornton Wilder in a letter to an American student engaged in research into the work of the Italian playwright, 'one must have':

> (a) a relish for dialect and regional speech, for colour and immediacy of language, used for a long time by a portion of society little touched by the over-sophisticated and cultivated and 'polite' world. Above all, profoundly knit by the ties of the family, parent and child – oh, the mothers of Naples! Oh, *Filumena Marturano*! – warmth and bonds that the Anglo-Saxon can scarcely understand.

> (b) one must love Naples – anthill of vitality – cynical yet religious – religious yet superstitious – shadowed by the volcano and the thought of death – always a-boil with one passion or another, yet abounding in courtesy and charm.[58]

To transfer this world which De Filippo's characters inhabit to Anglo-Saxon shores entails a measure of acculturation, a process, in its most fully-fledged form illustrated by the English relocation of *Ducking Out* and *Napoli Milionaria*. However, just over a decade following Peter Tinniswood's Liverpool version, Europe no longer seemed as alien as it used to be, nor did Europeans on the English stage have to be presented as 'foreigners' through an over-emphasis on their ethnicity. On 13 July 1995, *La Grande Magia* (1948) premiered at the Lyttelton Theatre under its original Italian title, directed by Richard Eyre in a translation by Carlo Ardito. In this metaphysical comedy, Calogero di Spelta's wife disappears in the course of a magic show: the illusionist presents him with a lacquered box, with, he explains, his wife inside. If Calogero is a husband who has faith in his wife, when he opens it she will reappear. If he does not trust her, she will not.

When *La Grande Magia* first opened in 1948, critics did not fail to associate it with Pirandello whom De Filippo had first met in the 1930s and with whom he had collaborated. But De Filippo always rejected the suggestion that *La Grande Magia* was particularly Pirandellian, pointing out that no Italian playwright could entirely escape the influence of the master. The play, he stressed, was not a speculation about what was and what was not real but about faith in one's wife.[59] On the whole, the positive critical response to this 'uncharacteristic' De Filippo play showed a welcome, high degree of readiness to accept 'foreign imports' on the English stage. In *The Sunday Times* of 23 July 1995, Robert Hewison even went as far as to poke fun at traditional reservations about the appearance of European drama on the English Stage:

> People tempted to ask what the National Theatre is doing reviving an obscure comedy by a dead foreigner would have their chauvinist prejudices confirmed by the opening scenes of Richard Eyre's production of Eduardo de Filippo's *La Grande Magia*. The National's duty to conserve our cultural identity has been underlined by the addition of the word Royal to its title. Surely it should not be wasting a cast of 20 and talents of the calibre of Eyre, Alan Howard and Bernard Cribbins on this posey piece of nonsense set in some grand hotel that is clearly *abroad*?

Drawing attention to Eyre's decision to emphasise the illusionism of theatre, Hewison concluded:

> While the issue of faith may have more resonance in a culturally Catholic country such as Italy, the metaphor of theatrical illusion makes perfect sense in a hypocritically Protestant one. By presenting plays such as these the National reminds us of our European identity.

That an equal measure of comedy and tragedy are the correct components making up a De Filippo play has been confirmed by two more recent revivals of the Neopolitan playwright's work. In his review in the *Daily Mail* of 28 May 1998, covering Jude Kelly's production of *Saturday, Sunday…and Monday* as part of the Chichester Festival Theatre, in a translation by Jeremy Sams, Michael Coveney referred to its mixture of 'tears and laughter', which he equated with 'the very best theatre':

> Dearbhla Molloy [as Peppino's wife Rosa] and David Suchet [as Peppino] do themselves and this wonderful play much more than proud. By the time you watch them renewing their love affair as a new week dawns, you are lost in that precious vale of tears and laughter conjured only by the very best theatre, and the very best acting.

All aspects of the production were, however, not to everybody's liking. In what appears to have been an attempt to capture the use of the Neapolitan dialect in the original, the cast relied on cockney, intermixed with strands of Jewish and Irish idioms, an intercultural mixture which, according to Nicholas de Jongh in the *Evening Standard* of 28 May, succeeded in turning 'Eduardo de Filippo's comedy of Neapolitan family fall-out and fury into something like a bowdlerised episode of *EastEnders*'. The production was, he concluded in a review entitled 'When the Family Ragu Turns into a Spag Bowl', as 'Italian as Brighton rock and harder to swallow'.

Food also figured in the title of the *Independent on Sunday*'s review of the 1998 production of *Filumena* at the Piccadilly Theatre in the West End with Judy Dench and Michael Pennington, although this time with a reference picked from the dessert menu: 'For Real Neapolitan Colour, Try the Ice-cream'. For this production a more neutral approach to the translation had been chosen, with no attempt made to evoke the use of the regional dialect of the original. Wisely, Peter Hall, as the director, also rejected the option of caricaturing Italian accents, nor did he overly emphasise the exoticism of what Nicholas de Jongh, in his review in the *Evening Standard* on 9 October 1998, referred to as 'all that hand-waving volatility'; instead the production succeeded in 'persuasively discovering connections between reticent Anglo-Saxons and extrovert Italians'. In line with what had now become the more general trend for Pirandello translations into English, the translator, playwright Timberlake Wertenbaker, reduced the length of sentences, making the English text more concise – as in the speech in Act 1 by Domenico Soriano following Filumena's successful attempt to extract a marriage proposal. Below is a close to word-for-word translation of the Italian original, followed by Wertenbaker's version:

> DOMENICO: You are a devil... Who is near to you very much needs open eyes... And one's words have to be kept in mind, they have to be weighed. I know you. You are like a woodworm. A poisonous woodworm which, wherever it rests, it destroys. A little while ago you said something and I was thinking about it. You said 'There's another thing that I want from you...and you will give it to me.' [60]

> DOMENICO: You're a real devil. Whoever gets near you has to keep their eyes open. And you have to remember every word you say and weigh it carefully. You're like a poisonous insect who destroys anything it touches. A little earlier you said to me, there's something I want from you and you're going to give it to me. [61]

Wertenbaker's translation, which, in addition to contraction, shows further shared features with other more recently translated texts such as a switch from specific to generic, as in turning 'woodworm' into 'insect', was described by Maeve Walsh in the *Independent on Sunday* of 11 October 1998, as having 'sensibly eschew[ed] Italianese or a British regional idiom'. While the hot-blooded passions of the original remain in English translation they are now pitched at a lower, identifiably Anglo-Saxon emotional temperature. When Judy Dench's Filumena delivers her fiery speeches on the subject of love, law and responsibility she does so with dignity and a mediated bitterness. And while Michael Pennington's Domenico executes his rage with rapid gesticulating, frantic pacing and forehead-slapping – what Maeve Walsh refers to as Parma-hamming – she fixes him with a steely stare until finally she asks: 'Have you finished?' Awarded top marks for her performance by Nicholas de Jongh in the *Evening Standard* of 9 October, Judy Dench was lauded for her 'superb performance' as Filumena, 'a fusion of England and Italy: a rich, ripe, hip-swaying sensuality runs in train with a grim English introversion'. In shifting the emphasis and showing convincingly how Filumena, a put-upon outsider, in her later years manages to achieve her heart's desire, this revival of the play succeeded in being sufficiently rather than overtly specific in order to become convincingly universal.

As the heir to De Filippo, Dario Fo (*b*. 1926), together with Franca Rame (*b*. 1929), has kept alive the spirit of the *commedia dell'arte*, further developing its comic traditions into a special brand of theatre in order to deal with the social problems of today. In his work, Fo sees himself as the inheritor of the 'realistic' acting style of the Italian popular theatre, which also encompasses an epic dimension. Although derived from realism it is a style nevertheless characterised by the self-aware detachment of the actor who is himself critical of what he acts. According to Dario Fo:

> We Italians 'enjoyed' the industrial revolution after a long time lag. So we are not yet a sufficiently modern nation to have forgotten the ancient feeling for satire. That is why we can still laugh, with a degree of cynicism, at the macabre dance which power and the civilisation that goes with it performs daily, without waiting for carnival.[62]

Satire is not, however, to be equated simply with farce. Like De Filippo, fearful that farce might take over in the English staging of his plays, with the concomitant loss of the truth of the situation,[63] Dario Fo has also expressed concern about the balance between farce and social commentary in English stagings of his work. Interviewed by Jane Edwardes for *Time Out*, 8–15 April 1992, Fo voiced his fears about the stereotyping of his countrymen for comic effect and his disappointment at the characterisation of Italians on the English stage: 'Everywhere I go I see Italians with moustaches and sideburns, rings on their fingers and white shoes. It's as though all English plays were performed by men in bowler hats.' His wife, Franca Rame, has expressed similar sentiments:

> I think the image of Italy as seen from abroad is often ridiculous – in the London production of *Anarchist* the characters looked like nineteenth-century Mafioso types, with long sideburns. It was a very glossy production, with stock characters who were like dummies – they reduced the play to a simple farce.[64]

Before Dario Fo arrived on the English stage in the late 1970s, his work had already been staged for more than a decade in translation into other European languages. In 1964, Fo was the most frequently performed Italian playwright in Europe and by 1965 his plays had been produced in translation on stages in Stockholm, Oslo, Vienna, Prague, Copenhagen, Warsaw, Zurich, Hamburg, Reykjavik, Budapest, Bucharest, Amsterdam and Zagreb. When, in May 1978, *Non si paga! Non si paga! (We Can't Pay? We Won't Pay!*, 1974) opened at the Half Moon Theatre in the East End of London, Dario Fo was already one of the world's most widely performed playwrights: the Belgian collective NewsScene devoted a period of four years entirely to his work, producing most of Fo's plays that lent themselves to adaptation in translation, and in Vienna the Dario Fo Theatre performed his plays exclusively for a period starting in 1979. Further contributory factors to Fo's well-established popularity were the tours that he and Rame had undertaken to different parts of Europe, and, as is often the case, the support of committed individuals. In 1980, Fo's plays appear to have been better known in Denmark than anywhere else in the world except Italy.[65] This is likely to have been the result of the work of Italian theatre practitioner Euginio Barba who, since 1966, had been based in Denmark and in 1968 issued an invitation to Fo and Rame to visit and give seminars. Fo's work also found early recognition in Sweden, where the Italian director Carlo Barsotti had been based since the 1970s. Not only did Barsotti stage a number of Fo's plays, but, together with Birgitta Bergmark, he also produced a documentary television programme with extracts from Fo's and Rame's work, as well as interviews providing artistic and political information on the couple up to 1977.

In many respects, it is not surprising that Fo's plays found their way to other European theatres before they arrived on the English stage. In some cases there was the facilitating factor of easy geographical access across national borders; in others, European news coverage, in particular among the smaller nations of Europe, which ensures an overall sense of familiarity with the political systems of other countries. In spite of their often universal application, Fo's reference points are far from easy to transfer into English, especially when his plays have been written as a direct response to a particular Italian political development.

The problems inherent in 'English Fo' have been solved through the use of different strategies. While early productions often focussed on the 'Italianness' of the original, later stagings such as *Il papa e la strega* (*The Pope and the Witch*, 1989) favoured an in-between approach or even, as in the case of *Abducting Diana*, fully-fledged nationalisation. Presented at the Edinburgh Fringe in 1994, Stephen Stenning's adaptation of Fo's 1986 play *Il ratto della Francesca* (*Kidnapping Francesca*) turned the Italian protagonist into Diana Forbes-McKay, a media magnate. The masks worn by her Italian kidnappers became the masks of John Major, Saddam Hussein, Margaret Thatcher and Prince Charles, with the dialogue turned into colloquial London English.

In the 1978 Half Moon production of *We Can't Pay? We Won't Pay!*, a middle-of-the-road approach was used. The subject of this play is civil disobedience, with the main upholder of law and order, a Communist shop steward, struggling to come to terms with his wife taking action against rising costs of living in the form of a raid on a supermarket. Translated by Lino Pertile and adapted by playwright Bill Colvill and Rob Walker, at the time artistic director of the Half Moon Theatre and pioneer of Fo's work in the UK, *We Can't Pay? We Won't Pay!* opened at the Half Moon Theatre in May 1978. Three years later, following the commercial success of *Morte accidentale di un anarchico* (*Accidental Death of an Anarchist*, 1970) in London in 1980, the West End producer Ian Albery invited Rob Walker to remount the Half Moon production at the Criterion Theatre where, under the pruned title *Can't Pay? Won't Pay!*, it ran for almost two years. Fixing the play firmly in an English context, the Colvill/Walker team provided the English text with topical references and a London parlance, while maintaining Italian names and the Milan setting essential to the plot. For example, as the Maoist police sergeant encourages Luigi and Giovanni to take the contraband goods which they are helping him to load up, he informs them in a cynical parody of 'official' police language:

> SERGEANT: Do you want to know what'll happen from here? I shall
>   write a full report, a model of brevity and procedure, the result of
>   which charges will be laid. A brief item on News at Ten will allude to

a brilliant police operation where contraband has been seized and men are sought.[66]

The Colvill/Walker adaptation, subsequently further revised prior to its transfer to the West End, drew few kind words from purists, concerned that the text now bore little resemblance to Fo's original.[67] It was felt that the style of the production, something akin to music hall or vaudeville, betrayed a lack of understanding of the *commedia dell'arte* tradition. The attempt by the Colvill/Walker team to recreate an English working-class language also came in for its share of criticism. According to David Hirst it was 'a sign not so much of a working-class idiom as of bourgeois theatrical language posing as – and patronising – working class speech'.[68] The target of Hirst's criticism was the type of language used, for instance, in Giovanni's outburst:

> GIOVANNI: And goodnight! Well, fuck a brick! Lord love us. Whatever next. The die-in-the-wool, raving, steeped-on Marxisim, out-and-out red copper! Right in there with the lunatic fascists, psycho bullies and subnormal everyday street coppers. Well that's where the bleeding extremists fetch up, obviously. In the police! And he's got the neck to stand there in front of me, twenty years a member, and criticise the CP! From the left too! [69]

Recommending a glance at the plays of David Storey and D H Lawrence, or the opening scenes of Edward Bond's *Saved*, for the use of authentic working class language, the Colvill/Walker version was, Hirst felt, 'as near a genuine working-class idiom as is the language of Wilde or Coward'.

Against this charge it may be argued that while it is true that Giovanni's use of syntax and vocabulary is hardly characteristic of working-class language, the absence of realism in speech would not seem unjustified given that Fo's theatre does not claim to be naturalistic. Entitled *We Won't Pay! We Won't Pay!*, the play was also performed in the United States in a North American version by R G Davis. Again, Giovanni uses unashamedly 'bourgeois theatrical language'. In R G Davis' version, he expostulates:

> GIOVANNI: Altre tanto! Boy, the number of weirdos you run into! A cop who's a wild red subversive! I've met fascists, thugs, and bullies, and now. So here's where the political extremists wind up...in the police force...and he stands there criticising the Communist Party as not revolutionary enough! If only they knew it. Some 'sons of the people'.[70]

With its pastel pink and blue set, not unexpectedly reminiscent of Neapolitan ice cream, the remounted West End production of *Can't Pay? Won't Pay!* appears to have succeeded in evoking a distinctly Italian spirit, not least due to the presence of Alfred Molina, the London-born actor of Italian extraction in the role of the Fiat worker Giovanni. In the case of *Accidental Death of an Anarchist*, however, stereotyping left a far clearer mark on the production. The play was first staged in Italy in 1970, in response to audience demand following the 1969 Piazza Fontana bombs in Milan, the 'suicide' of the anarchist Giuseppe Pinelli and the ensuing court trials. Linguistically, the play gave rise to interesting neologisms such as *lo hanno suicidato*, 'they suicided him', in order to describe the fate of Pinelli, who, having been taken to police headquarters, 'fell' out of a fourth-floor window. In 1979, an English-speaking production opened at the Dartington College, then moved to the Half Moon Theatre in October. From there, the production transferred to the Wyndham's Theatre, where it opened on 5 March 1980, to remain a hit in the West End for nearly two years. Translated into English by Gillian Hanna, the play remained set in Italy but was adapted for the English stage by Gavin Richards, also the director, for the Belt and Braces Roadshow Company, whose stated primary aim was to 'entertain, but with material and forms which are articulate, progressive and created from the viewpoint of working and oppressed people'.[71] This English company would thus seem well matched to reflect the intentions of Collettivo Teatrale, 'La Comune'. Founded in 1970 by Dario Fo and Franca Rame, *Accidental Death of an Anarchist*, described by Fo as 'a grotesque farce about a tragic farce', was the company's second production.[72]

Belt and Braces' *Accidental Death of an Anarchist*, which was to become the most successful English production among all of Fo's plays, took the process of acculturation a step further than did Colvill/ Walker in *Can't Pay? Won't Pay!* Gavin Richards' adaptation was riddled with slapstick and 'easy jokes': Richards, an actor himself, who was only too familiar with the propensity of the English acting profession to judge a play by the number of laughs it elicits, often reduced the characters to caricatures, in particular simplifying the police into buffoons. In order to ensure that the English audience possessed sufficient knowledge of specifically Italian events, Belt and Braces ensured that some thorough research was undertaken. Where Fo was in a position to rely on his Italian audience's familiarity with events, English-speaking audiences were provided with a newspaper, explaining the background to the play, relating it to events in Northern Ireland and to the recent death of the teacher Blair Peach in clashes with the police in an anti-fascist demonstration in London. The fact remains however, as pointed out by Franca Rame, that Italian and British Fo productions will always differ in one important respect; the lack of real motivation for putting on the plays outside the country in which they were written. In Italy, both plays responded to real situations, whereas performed in translation in the UK they were just plays, without any real point of departure.[73] Without the audience being able to identify with the original inspiration behind the play, farcical elements can easily take over, however strenuous the efforts to link events to more closely-related happenings on the home front.

In November 1984, *Accidental Death of an Anarchist* opened on Broadway, only to close again on 5 December. The American version was adapted from a translation by Suzanne Cowan by American playwright Richard Nelson, well-known adapter of Ibsen, Chekhov and Strindberg. Nelson decided to transpose the action of the play from Milan to Rome, generously adding a number of topical American references including a fiasco at a Beach Boys concert, government cheese give-aways and Jimmy Carter's debate briefing book.[74] In addition to Nelson's adaptation, script doctors were called in to work in co-operation with Fo and Rame, effecting changes which included new political references. Writing in the *New York Times* of 15 February 1984, Mel Gussow found the American version of *Accidental Death of an Anarchist* less funny than Richards' British one, pointing to the need for a 'true adaptation of the play in the USA'. According to Mitchell the American failure was clearly the fault of the adaptation, describing the US political references to Reagan as 'clumsy and self-conscious', and the dialogue frequently 'turgid and limp'.[75]

In June 1981, a month before *Can't Pay? Won't Pay!* opened in the West End, *Tutta casa, letto e chiesa* (*All House, Bed and Church*, 1978), by Franca Rame and Dario Fo, premiered at the National Theatre in translation by Margaret Kunzle, adapted by Olwen Wymark. With no colloquial equivalent in English such as the German *Kinder, Küche und Kirche* ('children, kitchen and church'), the title of the play was changed to *Female Parts*, then retitled yet again, this time as *One Woman Plays*. In the English translation of this series of monologues on the theme of female oppression, one of the main problems proved to be the lack of a suitable linguistic idiom for each of the four characters. This was particularly evident in the language given to the working-class protagonist of *Waking Up*, a woman unable to leave for work and taking her child to the crèche, as she cannot find her house key. In English translation, the working-class vernacular of the source language became a tame, middle-class approximation of the original idiom, with the concomitant loss of the distinctive voice of the character. This was also the case in *A Woman Alone*, where a suspicious husband has locked his attractive wife in the house. Here the use of language was neutralised to the point of blandness, the hallmark of insufficiently adapted dialogue in translation. Given the universal nature of the subject, these translation problems suggest that in the case of the Fo/Rame women plays, naturalisation in the form of total Anglicisation may be the solution, as indeed Franca Rame herself has indicated.[76] Such an approach would also ensure that critics and audiences would be less likely to delegate the problems to other remote countries and instead be forced to face up to their universality.[77]

The Franca Rame and Dario Fo monologues also reached the United States when, in 1982, the American actress Estelle Parsons performed two monologues in the Kunzle-Wymark English translation at the summer arts festival in Purchase, New York. Not altogether happy with the translation, Parsons, after consulting with Fo and Rame, embarked upon a learning course of Italian in order to be able to do her own versions. The first major production of Estelle Parsons' adaptations of nine of the pieces took place at the Public Theatre in New York in July 1983. Convinced that in the United States the only successful way to present the monologues was to emphasise their 'Italianness', Parsons approached the plays, now entitled *Orgasmo Adulto Escapes from the Zoo*, as if 'Italian women were playing them and speaking a fluent second language',[78] interspersing the text with occasional Italian words as she went along. The success of Parsons' versions has indeed been ascribed to their 'Milanese flavour'.[79] As in productions of De Filippo, New York seems willing to embrace Italian plays in English translation as long as they conform to local notions of 'Italianness'. And not only in New York: in September 1998, three of Parsons' adaptations were revived successfully at the San Francisco Fringe Festival, from where they were transferred in November of that year to the Exit Theatre, retaining the title *Orgasmo Adulto Escapes from the Zoo*.

Prior to his founding of 'La Comune', Fo had made a previous attempt to dispense with traditional stage company roles *vis-à-vis* decision-making, through the Nuova Scena collective. Before its split in 1970, the most important production undertaken was Fo's one-man show *Mistero Buffo* (*The Comic Mysteries*). First performed on 1 October 1969, this one-man show was to become one of Fo's most enduring successes in Italy and abroad. For this performance, Fo used the counter-culture of the Middle Ages, drawing on the gospels as well as legends and tales for episodes where he himself played all the characters, using a language in part invented, in part originating in the dialects of Northern Italy, described as 'an imaginary Esperanto of the poor and disinherited'.[80] In May 1983, 14 years after Fo first performed *Mistero Buffo*, he was invited to present the play at the Riverside Studios, London. The following year, the play was given an English language production by the

1982 Theatre Company at the Half Moon Theatre in London, translated by Ed Emery. The text, which poses a formidable challenge to the translator on the semantic level alone, presents such problems that at times individual words require lengthy discussion for full understanding. One such word is *'giullare'*: originating from the Latin *iocus*, it has the same roots as the French *jongleur*, but the English word of the same origin, 'juggler', now has a much more specific sense. In the heyday of *commedia dell'arte*, the word had become one of abuse. In the terms of Dario Fo, who may be described as a modern *giullare*:

> The *giullare* was born from the people, and from the people he took their anger in order to be able to give it back to them, mediated via the grotesque, through 'reason', in order that the people should gain greater awareness of their own condition. And it is for this reason that in the Middle Ages, *giullare* were killed with such abandon; they flayed them alive, they cut out their tongues, not to mention other niceties of the time.[81]

Not surprisingly, in his 'Translator's Note' to *Mistero Buffo*, Ed Emery devotes a paragraph to explaining his method of translating the two words *'giullare'* and *'villano'*, informing the reader that to represent these Italian words in English, he has used two words, introduced into English by the Normans and current in the time of Chaucer: 'jongleur' and 'villeyn'. In addition, we are told, he has rendered *il populo*, innocuous as it would seem to us, as 'the people'. This is not, however, as straightforward as it may seem, as the Italian term has a political connotation.[82] As has been discussed (see Pirandello above), the translation of the title of a play can pose formidable problems; in the case of *Mistero Buffo* the degree of difficulty appears to have been such that the decision was taken to leave the title in the original language. According to Fo himself:

> *Mistero* is the term used since the second and third centuries AD to describe a sacred spectacle or performance. Even today in the Mass we hear the priest announce, 'On the first glorious mystery... In the second mystery...' and so on.[83]

Mistero means a sacred performance, and *Mistero Buffo* means a grotesque spectacle, as Fo informs readers and audiences, but, if not Italian, we are unlikely to smile in immediate recognition of the incongruous combination of the two words *'mistero'* and *'buffo'*. In fact, English speakers could hardly be blamed for asking the question who Mr Buffo might be, especially after seeing a picture of Robbie Coltrane on the cover of the published text which, through the BBC four-part dramatisation in 1990, helped *Mistero Buffo* to reach an even greater audience.

In 1984 *Clacson, trombette e pernacchi* (*Hooters, Trumpets and Raspberries*, 1981), Dario Fo's third play to arrive in the West End, played at the Phoenix Theatre under the shortened title *Trumpets and Raspberries*. Translated and adapted by Roger McAvoy and Anna-Maria Giugni, this play about Fiat boss Gianni Agnelli retained its Italian setting while, in a programme note written by Stuart Hood, the audience was provided with the most important facts about Agnelli. Still, given obvious political differences between Italy and the UK, the task of finding appropriate political equivalents proved to be far from easy, as indicated by Michael Billington's *Guardian* review of the opening night, including a reference to Agnelli as 'a cross between John de Lorean and the Duke of Kent'.[84] Like previous West End stagings of Dario Fo's work, in this production, a vehicle for Griff Rhys Jones to display his ability as a comic actor, the political aspect of Fo once again gave way to humour, pushing the play in its English translation further in the direction of pure farce.

The latter half of the 1980s saw some out-of-London and Fringe stagings of Fo and Fo/Rame plays. In the late autumn of 1986, *Gli archangeli non giocano a flipper* (*Archangels Don't Play Pinball*, 1959), Fo's satire on state bureaucracy, institutions and social status opened at the Bristol Old Vic, closely followed in November at the Half Moon Theatre by Fo's 1984 play *Quasi per caso una donna: Elisabetta* (*Elizabeth*), written after he had been living in London and researching Elizabethan theatre.

In addition to the problem in translation presented by the concept of *giullare*, the tradition of the great clowns of the *commedia dell'arte* to resort to the use of dialect and *grummelot* is yet another linguistic obstacle confronting the Fo translator. An extraordinary onomatopoeic rendering of a language, containing accurate sounds and intonations but few real words, still adding up to intelligible discourse, *grummelot* was developed through necessity by Italian players at the end of the seventeenth century as the result of being banished from Parisian theatres to fairground booths. This in turn forced them to make use of placards, scrolls and *grummelots*, since spoken dialogue was only allowed on the legitimate stage.[85] According to Fo himself, the technique, which he calls not grummelot but grammelot, is 'onomatopoeic patter used to imitate foreign languages and exotic dialects'.[86] In the Half Moon production of *Elizabeth*, Gillian Hanna, translator as well as lead role actress, transformed the seventeenth-century hybrid *grammelot* into an 'amalgam of Italian, Shakespeare, Cockney rhyming slang, spoonerisms [and] obscenities[…]'.[87] Through the addition of English jokes and frequent departures from Fo's text (the published version included an appendix of close translations of the passages that had been changed), the English version succeeded in capturing the complex word play of Fo's original. To give an example:

> Tis terril-ay! I comprehensive his stratagemical acts and monuments! Questo Shakespeare dicket to the rabblement: 'What do you fadge! Shift your ways! Go to! You perfect to be put upon like slaveys, like dumbo bruttoes – pimply on account of your terrorizzato of tripping off to hell? Arseholes! Dandiprats! hell be here, here sopra terra...not underbeyant. Divven be frit. Be a bravery! Arise! Shuffle off this governo of turd. Batter it to a tripes!' [88]

The problem with this attempt to reproduce in English the effect that Fo created from sound, intonation and gesture is that the resulting somewhat belaboured form of wordplay is far from easy to follow, particularly when spoken. The translation of *grammelot* appears to be a Hobson's choice: if transferred simply into standard English, something is lost, rendering the translation bland and lacking in bite, while on the other hand attempting to reproduce the special quality of the original language may be unjustly rewarded with an unnatural, over-wrought version of the unique linguistic variety of the source text.

An interesting perspective on two contrasting approaches to Fo on the English stage is offered by a comparison of *An Accidental Death of an Anarchist* in the Belt and Braces production of the 1980s and the revival of the play a decade later. In their 1990 and 1991 adaptation for the National Theatre, Alan Cumming and Tim Supple 'resolved to retain the open, uncharacterised language and to preserve the alien, rambling form'.[89] In this version, care was taken to avoid caricaturing the characters and to keep the subtlety of Fo's satire. The play's political references, however, were updated to include mention of the Guildford Four and the Birmingham Six, and Inspector Pisani's office was provided with a picture of British Police Chief Sir James Anderton: these were all changes made in the spirit of Fo's own approach adapting political and cultural references in order to contexualise a production.

Interestingly, on this occasion the critical response to the play was less favourable than the reaction to the earlier Belt and Braces production. One reason for the less enthusiastic response to the new updated production might have been the time factor: after more than a decade of Thatcherism the climate of artistic rebellion initially sparked by the Conservative government coming to power in 1979 had worn off and lost its muscle. But in addition, the success of the play in 1980 seems to have left an indelible imprint and created a set of expectations of an 'English Fo': inevitably comparisons were made. Some critics noted positively that the Cumming/Supple production was closer to Fo's original intentions, while others thought it was not close enough, focussing on marginal alterations in the new production, which were viewed as major departures from the 'original' by Gavin Richards. On 8 January 1991, the theatre critic for the *Evening Standard* felt that '[m]onstrous liberties have been taken with the original text to make the production an indictment of present abuses of authority'. The attempt to bring English audiences closer to the text seems, paradoxically, only to have drawn their attention to the problems inherent in the task: the play was now seen to have lost its power both as the farce of the 1980 production and as the more cutting satire of the original. On 9 January, *The Times* described the production as 'not as relentlessly burlesque as Richards's...[and] not as funny...marooned in some no-man's land between knockabout and realism'. And according to *The Sunday Times* of 13 January, the production was 'simply a batty farce', and 'essentially a harmless, jolly English production'. True to form, the American view voiced by *The Tribune* of 11 January 1991 followed the consistent American approach to Italian plays in English translation, complaining that the play's 'British filter' was not 'Italian enough'.

In contrast to the Cumming/Supple attempt to emphasise the authenticity of the original text, *The Pope and the Witch*, Dario Fo's farce about drugs, birth control and Pope John Paul II, was used as a vehicle to return to the stereotyping approach of times past. The fourth Fo play to reach the West End, it opened at the Comedy Theatre in April 1992, in an adaptation by Andy de la Tour, based on a translation by Ed Emery. Particularly interested in the theme of Vatican City corruption, de la Tour explained in his Adapter's Note that he had invented a character of his own, Cardinal Schilacci, 'to embody the corrupt and violent side of Vatican city politics in the hope of making this side of the play more accessible'.[90] Other changes in the adaptation of the play involved renaming all the characters after the players in the 1990 Italian World Cup football squad, a decision that did not meet with Fo's approval. The adaptation, which expanded on Richards' use of Italian stereotyping in *Accidental Death of an Anarchist*, did not go down well with the critics: Mitchell goes as far as to see a link between the unfavourable reception of this production and the absence of Dario Fo in the West End in subsequent years.[91]

Another perhaps more obvious reason for Fo's relative absence from the London stage during the 1990s was the change in political climate. Due to the government withdrawal of financial support, the number of alternative theatre groups, many with a political agenda, plummeted. Political theatre now began to find new means of expression, less overt than the social and political protest of Dario Fo and Brecht (see interview with David Hare, Chapter 6). But in addition to these factors, other reasons may have accounted for the decline in interest in Dario Fo's work. While the portrayal of 'the other' in the form of stereotyping and slapstick humour often associated with 'English Fo' had earlier been readily accepted, in the more recent climate of political correctness this approach had now begun to seem embarrassingly unsubtle. Instead, 'Italianness' gradually became more accessible to English audiences through a toning down of what might be too foreign. This is an approach that has been gaining ground in more recent productions of the plays by Pirandello and De Filippo, in which the adoption of English modes of expression has allowed universal aspects to emerge more clearly.

This approach, however, is less easily applied to the work of Dario Fo, where the role of the *giullare* and topical Italian political commentary figure as important ingredients. It is, for instance, difficult to envisage 'the Two-headed Anomaly' – Fo's latest political offering on the subject of Silvio Berlusconi, the Prime Minister of Italy, which has attracted heavy criticism in its country of origin – ever becoming fully accessible to West End theatre audiences.

In 1997, Dario Fo was awarded the Nobel Prize for Literature. In the press release issued by the Swedish Academy stating the reasons for its decision, a number of aspects of his work were singled out. Implicit in the statement were also many of the obstacles standing in the way of 'English Fo':

> For many years Fo has been performed all over the world, perhaps more than any other contemporary dramatist, and his influence has been considerable... With a blend of laughter he opens our eyes to abuses and injustices in society and also the wider historical perspective in which they can be placed... His independence and clear-sightedness have led him to take great risks, whose consequences he has been made to feel while at the same time experiencing enormous response from widely different quarters... As in *commedia dell'arte*, [Fo's texts] are always open for creative additions and dislocations, continually encouraging the actors to improvise...[92]

While this northern European communiqué pays little attention to the humorous aspect of Fo's work, referring only briefly to his role as an entertainer, it was instead the humorous element that tended to be singled out by the English press in its reaction to the choice of the 1997 recipient of the Nobel Prize for Literature. Having described 'Signor Fo' as 'one of the funniest playwrights and performers alive', *The Times* commentator expressed surprise at the decision, and, on the basis of a similar set of facts, provided a somewhat different commentary:

> What's interesting is that [Dario Fo] is basically a performer. His roots go back to the *commedia dell'arte* tradition. He writes for himself and performs himself, sometimes with his wife. He's a brilliantly talented clown. This choice is a wayward one. It's rather lightweight.[93]

While on its way to the English stage, the laughter of northern Europe often turns into 'doom and gloom', the humour of the South appears to suffer the opposite fate. Rather than being lost in translation, it seems instead to acquire added joviality and in the process lose some of its bite.

Notes

1 F Martini, 'Letter to Salvatore Barzilai, 6 December 1888', in *Lettere 1860–1926* (Milan, 1934). Discussed and trans. in L Richards, 'Italy, 1868–1919', in C Schumacher (ed.), *Naturalism and Symbolism in European Theatre, 1850–1918*, (Cambridge, Cambridge University Press, 1996), p. 443

2 Discussed in S Bassnett-McGuire, *Luigi Pirandello* (London, Macmillan, 1983)

3 S Taviano, *Italians on the Twentieth Century Stage: Theatrical Representations of Italianness in the English-Speaking World*, Unpublished PhD dissertation, University of Warwick, 2001

4 S Bassnett and J Lorch (eds.), *Luigi Pirandello in the Theatre. A Documentary Record* (Philadelphia, Pa, Harwood Academic Publishers, 1993), p. 72

5 *Scribner's*. Reprinted in *Immortal Shadows*, (New York, 1948)

6 S Taviano, *The Reception of Luigi Pirandello's Theatre in Great Britain: From the 1920s to the Present Day*, Unpublished MA Dissertation, University of Warwick, 1996

7 *Ibid.* p. 51

8 See list of performances in F Firth, 'Performances of Pirandello's plays in Britain and Ireland, 1922–1999', *Journal of the Society for Pirandello Studies* 20, 2000, pp. 75–100

9 D A Powell, 'Pirandellian humour and modern French drama', in J L DiGaetani (ed.), *A Companion to Pirandello Studies* (New York, Greenwood Press, 1991), p. 271

10 N de Jongh, 'The century's top twenty plays', *Evening Standard*, 1998, pp. 28–9

11 S Bassnett-McGuire, *op. cit.* p. 29

12 S Bassnett-McGuire, 'Pirandello's British première', *Yearbook of the British Pirandello Society*, (2), 1982, pp. 28–31

13 F May, 'Alfred Wareing and the production of Pirandello in the West Riding', *The University of Leeds Review*, 8 (3), 1963, p. 244

14 C Barker, 'La drammaturgia britannica fra le due guerre', in Enzo Scrivano (a cura di), *Pirandello e la drammaturgia fra le due guerre* (Agrigento, Edizione Centro Nazionale di Studi Pirandelliani, 1985). Discussed in S Taviano (1996), *op. cit.* pp. 20–1

15 S Bassnett-McGuire, (1983), *op. cit.* p. 10

16 *Ibid.* p. 11

17 S Bassnett and J Lorch, *op. cit.* pp. 98–100

18 S Bassnett-McGuire, (1983), *op. cit.* p. 135

19 S Bassnett and J Lorch, *op. cit.* p. 182

20 S Bassnett-McGuire, (1982), *op. cit.* pp. 28–31

21 S Bassnett, 'Pirandello and translation', *Journal of the Society for Pirandello Studies* 20, 2000, p. 9

22 Luigi Pirandello, *Three Plays (Sei personaggi in cerca d'autore, Enrico IV, La giara)*, ed. F Firth (Manchester , Manchester University Press, 1969), p. 21 (emphasis added)

23 Luigi Pirandello, *Six Characters in Search of an Author*, trans. E Bentley (London, Penguin, 1998), p. 20 (emphasis added)

24 *Sei personaggi in cerca d'autore*, *op. cit.* p. 46 (emphasis added)

25 *Six Characters in Search of an Author*, trans. E Bentley, *op. cit.* p. 44 (emphasis added)

26 *Sei personaggi in cerca d'autore*, *op. cit.* p. 55 (emphasis added)

27 *Six Characters in Search of an Author*, trans. E Bentley, *op. cit.* p. 53 (emphasis added)

28 J Lorch, 'Liolà', *Yearbook of the British Pirandello Society*, 3, 1983, pp. 100–1

29 S Bassnett-McGuire, (1983), *op. cit.* p. 6–7

30 *Ibid.* p. 2

31 Luigi Pirandello, *To Clothe the Naked and Two Other Plays*, trans. W Murray (New York, E P Dutton & Co. Inc., 1962), p. xiii

32 *Ibid.* p. xiv

33 *Ibid.* p. xiv

34 *Ibid.* p. 161

35 *Ibid.* p. 80

36 Luigi Pirandello, *The Rules of the Game*, adapt. D Hare (London, Absolute Classics, 1993), p. 6 (emphasis added)

37 *To Clothe the Naked and Two Other Plays*, trans. W Murray, *op. cit.* p. 87

38 *The Rules of the Game*, adapt. D Hare, *op. cit.* p. 13

39 G A Arsan, 'Six Characters at the National Theatre', *Yearbook of the British Pirandello Society*, 7, 1987, p. 35

40 K Worth, 'Six Characters at the National Theatre (2)', *Yearbook of the British Pirandello Society*, 7, 1987, p. 36

41 S Bassnett, in *Man, Beast & Virtue* performance programme (National Theatre, 1989)

42 *The Mountain Giants* performance programme (National Theatre, 1993)

43 *To Clothe the Naked and Two Other Plays*, trans. W Murray, *op. cit.* p. 4 (emphasis added)

44 Luigi Pirandello, *Naked*, adapt. N Wright (London, Nick Hern Books, 1998), p. 8 (emphasis added)

45 H Conway, *Daily Sketch*, January 1955, discussed in Robert Rietty's Introduction to Luigi Pirandello, *Collected Plays*, Vol. 3 (Paris, London, New York, Calder Publications, 1992)

46 Quoted in *Six Characters in Search of an Author* performance programme (National Theatre, 1987)

47 J L DiGaetani (ed.), Foreword to *A Companion to Pirandello Studies*, (New York, Greenwood Press, 1991), pp. xv–xvii

48 S Taviano and J Lorch, 'Producing Pirandello in England', *Journal of the Society for Pirandello Studies*, 20, 2000, p. 30

49 S Taviano (2001), *op. cit.*

50 C Barker (1981) 'Right you are (if you could only think so)', *Yearbook of the British Pirandello Society*, 1, 1981, pp. 26–34.

51 E Bentley, *In Search of Theater* (New York, Mentor Books, 1953), p. 274

52 J Fisher, 'An author in search of characters: Pirandello and commedia dell'arte', in F J Marker and C Innes (eds.) *Modernism in European Drama: Ibsen, Strindberg, Pirandello, Beckett* (Toronto, University of Toronto Press, 1998), pp. 151–69

53 S Taviano (2001), *op. cit.* p. 19

54 M Esslin, 'Filumena', *Plays and Players*, January 1978, pp. 28–9

55 S Taviano (2001), *op. cit.* p. 178

56 *Ibid.* pp. 182–3

57 S Bassnett-McGuire, 'Ways through the labyrinth: Strategies and methods for translating theatre texts', in T Hermans (ed.) *The Manipulation of Literature. Studies in Literary Translation* (London, Croom Helm, 1985), pp. 87–102

58 *Inner Voices* performance programme (National Theatre, 1983)

59 N Wright, in *La Grande Magia* performance programme (National Theatre, 1995)

60 Eduardo de Filippo, *Cantata dei giorni dispari* (Vol.1) (Torino, Einaudi, 1957), p. 223, trans. Sylvia Leone

61 Eduardo de Filippo, *Filumena*, trans. T Wertenbaker (London, Methuen, 1998), p. 21

62 Dario Fo, *Accidental Death of An Anarchist*, adapt. G Richards, from a trans. by G Hanna with an introduction by S Hood (London, Pluto Press, 1987), p. xviii

63 Interview by Michael Billington, *Guardian*, 7 Nov 1983

64 T Mitchell, *Dario Fo. People's Court Jester* (London, Methuen, 1999), p. 258

65 *Ibid.* pp. 241–3

66 Dario Fo, *Can't Pay? Won't Pay!*, adapt. R Walker and B Colvill, from a trans. by Lino Pertile (London, Pluto Press, 1978), p. 29

67 T Mitchell, *op. cit.* p. 251

68 D Hirst, *Dario Fo and Franca Rame* (London, Macmillan, 1989), p. 83

69 Dario Fo, *Can't Pay? Won't Pay!*, adapt. R Walker and B Colvill (London, Pluto Press, revised edition 1982), p. 12

70 Dario Fo, *We Won't Pay! We Won't Pay!*, trans. R G Davis (London, Samuel French, 1980), pp. 38–9

71 *Accidental Death of an Anarchist* performance programme (London: Pluto Press Ltd, 1980)

72 T Mitchell, *File on Dario Fo* (London, Methuen, 1989)

73 *Daily Telegraph*, 1981

74 T Mitchell (1999), *op. cit.* p. 298

75 *Ibid.* p. 30

76 *Ibid.* p. 27

77 *Ibid.* p. 271

78 Dario Fo/Franca Rame, *Orgasmo Adulto Escapes from the Zoo*, trans. and adapt. E Parsons (New York, Broadway Play Publishing, 1984), p. xi

79 S Taviano, (2001), *op. cit.* p. 254

80 Dario Fo, *Mistero Buffo*, trans. E. Emery, ed. and intro. S Hood (London, Methuen, 1988), p. xi

81 J Rudlin, *Commedia dell'arte. An Actor's Handbook* (London, Routledge, 1994), p. 227

82 *Mistero Buffo*, trans. E Emery, *op. cit.* p. xviii

83 *Ibid.*

84 *Guardian Weekly*, 25 November 1984, p. 20

85 J Rudlin, *op. cit.* p. 60

86 T Mitchell (1999), *op. cit.* p. 350

87 *Ibid.* p. 286

88 *Ibid.*

89 Dario Fo, *Accidental Death of an Anarchist*, adapt. A Cumming and T Supple (London, Methuen, 1991), p. xxiii

90 Dario Fo, *The Pope and the Witch*, adapt. A de la Tour (London, Methuen, 1992), p. xv

91 T Mitchell (1999), *op. cit.* p. 292

92 The Swedish Academy Press Release, 'The Nobel Prize for Literature' (The Permanent Secretary, 9 October 1997)

93 Dalya Alberge, *The Times*, 12 October 1997

Chapter 8

FEDERICO GARCÍA LORCA AND RAMÓN DEL VALLE-INCLÁN

WHILE IN THE 1890s European theatres felt the impact of the work of Ibsen, Chekhov and Strindberg, in Spain the stage continued to reflect the moral values of the Restoration and a heroic view of Spain's history. Spain's commercial theatre was dominated by the neo-romantic plays of José Echegaray (1832–1916). Audiences did not favour naturalism in the theatre and Spanish dramatists provided the theatrical escapism that they required, steering clear of serious or thought-provoking themes. Conscious of the cultural stagnation in Spain, Jacinto Benavente (1866–1954), the 1922 recipient of the Nobel Prize for Literature, mounted an early challenge to the status quo of Spanish theatre. However, in 1894, after his first play, *El nido ajeno* (*The Alien Nest*, 1894), was booed from the stage for its theme of adultery and family dishonour, Benavente grew more cautious. His social criticism was tempered, and his plays started to move in the direction of traditional theatrical fare with its emphasis upon nicely constructed plots and witty dialogue.

Commercially successful, bourgeois drawing-room theatre was also the penchant of other Spanish dramatists such as Manuel Linares Rivas (1867–1938) and Gregorio Martínez Sierra (1881–1947). Equally alien to progressive work in the theatre was the watered-down realism of the plays by Serafín Álvarez Quintero (1871–1938) and Joaquín Álvarez Quintero (1873–1944). The Quintero brothers wrote about 200 plays in the tradition of the so-called *género chico*: their vision of Spain, in particular Andalusia, invited grateful audiences into a world of nostalgia, firmly closing the door to the troubled Spanish world outside the theatre.

An alternative to the bourgeois world of Benavente was provided by the plays of Francisco Villaespesa (1877–1936) and Eduardo Marquina (1879–1946) which were often set in the medieval world or Spain's glorious past. This kind of historical verse drama was, however, equally resistant to any real change in the theatre.

Yet there were signs of changes to come. Although in the tradition of the *género chico* of the Quintero brothers, in his *Grotesque Tragedies*, Carlos Arníches (1866–1943) put on stage the lower depths of Madrid, a world inhabited by characters inviting not only the mirth but also the compassion of the audience. Pointing to the parochialism and prejudice of provincial life, Arníches anticipated not only the work of Beckett, Ionesco, Genet and Arrabal in European theatre but also the style of Ramón del Valle-Inclán, who more recently has joined Federico García Lorca as a twentieth-century Spanish dramatist whose work intermittently appears in translation on the English stage.

As a dramatist, Ramón del Valle-Inclán (1866–1936) reacted so strongly to the prevailing complacent Spanish theatre tradition of his time that, on the occasion of the national tribute to José Echegaray, the 1904 recipient of the Nobel Prize for Literature, he was moved to organise a formal protest. On another occasion when his wife, the actress Josefina Blanco, was due to appear in a play by Echegaray, Valle-Inclán went to the length of locking her up in an attempt to prevent her from leaving for the theatre.[1] *Aguila de blasón* (*Eagle of Honour*) and *Romance de lobos* (*Ballard of Wolves*), the two major plays of Valle-Inclán's *modernista*/symbolist period, were both published in 1907.[2] Together with *Cara de plata* (*Silver Face*), published in 1922, they form *Comedias bárbaras* (*Savage Plays* or *Barbaric Comedies*) with *Silver Face* constituting the opening part of the trilogy. This feudal family saga, which was never staged during Vallé-Inclán's lifetime, depicts the fall of the Galician House of Don Juan Miguel de Montenegro. In 1967, *Silver Face* was staged at Madrid's Teatro Infanta Beatriz and in 1991, it opened successfully as part of the whole trilogy at the Centro Dramático Nacional in Madrid.

The US annexation of Cuba in 1898 brought Spain's loss of empire sharply into focus: her decline as a world power now became a serious concern of Spanish intellectuals, who felt it their task to document in writing the declining state of Spain. A member of 'Generation of 98' – the name given to a group of writers who saw Spain's defeat in the Cuban American war of 1898 as the start of the national decline – Valle-Inclán's involvement in the social and political fate of his country intensified. In his 'tragi-comedia' *Divinas palabras* (*Divine Words*), published in 1920, the year which saw the publication of four of his major plays, Valle-Inclán drew on the Celtic traditions of his native rural Galicia, and what he saw as the repressive Catholicism of Spain. The first thread of action in the play concerns Laureano, a dwarf, who as a fairground freak constitutes a potential source of income, which results in a dispute over ownership between two interested parties. A second thread is the adulterous affair between Mari-Gaila and the tinker Séptimo Miau, and the ensuing reaction of the village to this liaison. Left to deal with the outraged morality of the villagers, Mari-Gaila's brother, the drunken, weak-willed sexton, Pedro Gailo, attempts to instil calm and order by reading from the Bible: 'Let he who be without sin among you cast the first stone.' These words, however, fail to calm the crowd and it is only when repeated in Latin, in the *divinas palabras* of the play's title, a language the villagers do not understand, that their tempers start to cool and peace can be restored.

In *Divine Words* Valle-Inclán abandoned the backward-looking, heroic view of the *Comedias bárbaras* for a more objective and less romanticised approach. In *Luces de bohemia* (*Bohemian Lights*), first published in 1920, with Scenes 2, 6 and 11 later added in 1924, he further altered his focus, arriving at his theory of *esperpento* (meaning scarecrow). Traditionally a term employed to denote someone of abnormal appearance or something absurd or foolish, Valle-Inclán turned it into a concept where distinctions were blurred between the tragic and the comic, the bizarre and the conventional, the real and the unreal, between fiction and history. In Valle-Inclán's characters, physical and psychological deformities are highlighted systematically to the point where they become grotesque caricatures, like the deformed images created by fairground mirrors.

Valle-Inclán's plays were written without the author giving a thought as to whether they would ever be performed, and for almost 40 years after his death in 1936 they remained largely unstaged. Before Valle-Inclán's death and the seizure of power by the Franco regime, *Divine Words* was performed by the Margarita Xirgu and Enrique Borras Theatre Company at Madrid's Teatro Español, in a production that opened on 16 November 1933. Early European stagings in translation included a production at Gothenburg City Theatre which opened on 3 February 1950, directed by Ingmar Bergman and, in the 1960s, a production at the Odéon Théâtre de France in Paris on 21 March 1963, directed by Roger Blin. The 1970s saw some German language productions: in 1971 the play opened at the Stuttgart Theatre and in 1974 at the Kammerspiele in Munich.

On 15 March 1998, *Divine Words* was broadcast on BBC Radio 3 in translation into English by David Johnston. For his translation, Johnston decided to draw upon his own Irish 'voice'. Underlying his decision were the parallels between Ireland and Galicia, the Celtic corner of north-west Spain in which Valle-Inclán's play is set. As has been pointed out by John Lyon in his study of the theatre of Valle-Inclán, symbolism in drama seems to have taken root in particular in European countries with a strong popular literary tradition such

as Belgium, Italy, Spain and Ireland: there is a clear parallel between Valle-Inclán's 'semi-feudal Galicia' and J M Synge's 'pagan and imaginative peasant culture of the West of Ireland'.[3] In addition, other points of contact between the world of Synge and that of Valle-Inclán may be found. Conscious of the position of Galicia within Spain, of its peripheral status in relation to the powerful forces of the centre, Valle-Inclán adopted the language of that overriding power only because he was able to turn it into a stage language of his own, which was markedly different. So too Synge, who succeeded in helping towards the formation of a definition of Irish 'otherness', through eliciting those language elements at odds with the prevailing discourse.[4] As the oral tradition from which much of Valle-Inclán's work derives can find its counterpart in a similar Irish custom of storytelling, for Johnston's radio transmission of *Divine Words*, one of the characters in the play was turned into a narrator. Opting for a strategy of verbal visibility crucial for the medium for which the play was intended, in Scene 2 of Act 1 Johnston transformed the stage directions into a monologue. First the stage directions as in the original, translated by Maria Delgado:

> *A clump of trees at the side of the road. There, half-hidden among the shadows, with her flowered handkerchief open, JUANA LA REINA can be seen begging. Her idiot son LAUREANO, smothered in the cart's straw mattress and patched blankets, groans and grimaces in his accustomed manner.*[5]

In Johnston's radio version, these stage directions are given to a narrator, the direction 'close' referring to the quality of voice required in order to distinguish the narrator from the other characters:

> BASTIAN: (*Close.*) That's when I saw Juana. There she was, sort of slumped under a big tree at the side of the road just outside the town, with her flowery handkerchief lyin' open in front of the idjit boy, him with his big jelly head poking out from the cart pullin' faces. And her the colour o' death.[6]

Thus Johnston drew on Irish voices and speech patterns in order to establish associations with another Catholic world, better known to English-speaking theatre audiences than that of Valle-Inclán's Galicia. In this way, connotations conjured up by Ireland provide a cultural bridge, helping to promote a better understanding of the functions and dysfunctions of sexuality in Valle-Inclán's male-dominated Spanish rural community. The setting was not, however, transported to Ireland but remained, in Johnston's version, firmly anchored in Spain. In contrast, the problems of translation into English of *Bohemian Lights* were of such a nature that Johnston opted for another solution. This time, Valle-Inclán's play, originally set in Madrid, was relocated to Ireland.

Bohemian Lights was the first of four dramatic works published during the last decade of Valle-Inclán's career, labelled *esperpentos*. The other three were: *Los cuernos de don Friolera* (*The Horns of Don Friolera*, 1921); *Las galas del difunto* (*The Dead Man's Suit*, 1926); and *La hija del capitán* (*The Captain's Daughter*, 1927). In 1930, the trilogy was published as *Martes de carnaval* (*Carnival Tuesday*). In Scene 12 of *Bohemian Lights*, just before he dies, Max Estrella comments on his role as an artist in Spain. It is at this point that the concept of *esperpento* is discussed. Half in jest, half seriously, Max Estrella suggests to the parasitical hanger-on Don Latino that reality should be dramatised as if seen in a distorting concave mirror. According to Anthony Zahareas, co-translator with Gerald Gillespie of Valle-Inclán's play into English, the style of writing and manner of portraying the world is 'a principle of art, not necessarily a fact of experience'.[7]

The Zahareas and Gillespie translation containing the oft-quoted passage where the concept of *'esperpento'* is first introduced, here translated as 'the Grotesque', is provided with numerous references to explanatory endnotes:

> MAX: The avant-garde are humbugs. (303) It was Goya who invented the Grotesque. (304) The classical heroes have gone to take a stroll in Cat Alley. (305)
> LATINO: You're completely balmy.
> MAX: Classical heroes reflected in concave mirrors yield the Grotesque. The tragic sense of Spanish life (306) can be rendered only through an aesthetic that is systematically deformed.
> LATINO: Cat shit! You're about to catch that disease yourself!
> MAX: Spain is a grotesque deformation of European civilisation.
> LATINO: Perhaps! I'm staying out of all this!
> MAX: In a concave mirror, even the most beautiful images are absurd.
> LATINO: Agreed. But I enjoy looking at myself in the mirrors in Cat Alley.
> MAX: Me too. Deformation stops being deformation when subjected to a perfect mathematic. (307) My present aesthetic approach is to transform all classical norms with the mathematics of the concave mirror.
> LATINO: And where is the mirror to be found?
> MAX: At the bottom of the drinking glass. (308)
> LATINO: You are ingenious! I take my head off to you.[8]

The concept of *'esperpento'* is explained in endnote (307). But before the reader reaches this point, information is provided about other aspects of Spanish life and culture that might confound the uninitiated: through endnote (303) we learn that '*los ultraístas*' has been rendered in English as the 'avant-garde' and that '*ultraísmo*' was the most advanced literary movement around 1918, related to the imagism, cubism and dadaism of other countries.[9] The next endnote (304) tells us that the Spanish painter Goya (1746–1828) was well known for 'his grotesque *Caprichos* and *Disparates* in which he systematically deformed reality. Valle-Inclán was particularly influenced by such *Caprichos* as the one in which a mirror distorts a man's face and converts it into that of a monkey or a serpent.' Further information in endnote (305) reveals the source of the concave mirrors which reportedly appears to have influenced the concept of '*esperpento*':

> (305) Álvarez Gato is the name of a real alley off the Plaza de Santa Ana, next to the Puerta del Sol. In front of a hardware store there were, in the 1920s, some distorting mirrors, like those found in fairs and carnivals, and the passers-by would stop and amuse themselves by being reflected: a concave mirror elongates the figure while a convex one shortens and broadens it. The heroes of tragedy are deformed in an *esperpento* in the same way as the onlookers who stopped before the mirrors in the alley of Álvarez Gato.

In (306), the next endnote, we learn that Max's reference to 'the tragic sense of Spanish life' is not as straightforward a comment as it may first appear: it turns out to be an 'allusion to Unamuno's famous work, *Del sentimiento trágico de la vida en los hombres y en los pueblos* (1913)'. Finally, footnote (307) deals with the concept of '*esperpento*'. It states:

> (307) The *esperpento* does not catch reality according to classical norms, but as in a concave mirror that distorts and ridicules appearances. In the imaginative reflection of the artist's mind, human deformations, like disparate numbers arranged systematically in a mathematical formula, acquire their own order and become, aesthetically speaking, 'beautiful'.

And in case we have not realised it, Max's reply to Don Latino's question 'where is the mirror to be found?' is clearly explained in endnote (308), where we learn that '*en el fondo del vaso*' (at the bottom of the drinking glass) is a euphemism for 'being drunk'.[10]

Undoubtedly, the endnotes provided by Zahareas and Gillespie are invaluable to readers lacking information about Valle-Inclán's Spain, not to say necessary in order for the non-Valle-Inclán specialists to comprehend and enjoy the play. They are, however, of little help to an English-speaking theatre audience. For instance, in the original Spanish, the word '*esperpento*' occurs twice, once in the derived form '*el esperpentismo*', when linked with Goya , and once with a capital 'E', '*el Esperpento*', when Max announces that 'concave mirrors yield the Grotesque'. It is here rendered in English as 'the Grotesque' but the use of the capital letter 'G', an attempt to signal a new aesthetic concept, is again only helpful to readers, not spectators. The problem of conveying the concept of *'esperpento'* in English is evident: in his translation of *Bohemian Lights*, John Lyon chose to render *'esperpento'* as a 'travesty'. Maria Delgado's version left it in the Spanish original, while David Johnston opted for a 'groteskery', none of which fully match the startling force achieved by Valle-Inclán in Spanish in his elegant shift to a novel use of an already existing term.[11] The translation of *esperpento* into English remains an obstacle to the translator, as do the cultural allusions peppering Valle-Inclán's text, amply illustrated by the numerous endnotes provided in the Zahareas and Gillespie translation.

The degree of difficulty inherent in Valle-Inclán translation has been widely acknowledged by translators trying their hand at transferring his work into English. In her introduction to *Valle-Inclán: Plays One*, translator Maria Delgado draws attention to the problem of the tendency of Valle-Inclán's characters suddenly to burst out in a language completely out of character: prostitutes and low-life figures may for instance start quoting from literary sources or declaiming in elevated Spanish when least expected. A further problem is presented by the multitudinous references to people and places of the time, the parodies of Biblical and literary language, the use of neologisms, slang and colloquialisms as well as expressions with Galician, Portuguese and Latin American roots. Valle-Inclán's plays have been described as 'a montage of languages which clash and collide – drawing constant attention to their own artificiality and self-reflexivity', all forming part of what critics are fond of referring to as the 'spirit' of Valle-Inclán.[12]

The abundance of couched quotations, echoes, pastiche and parodies of past literature appearing in almost all of his work has also earned Valle-Inclán the epithet of 'a writer's writer, often an intellectual in spite of his intention to write for everybody'.[13] Selected for praise are his precise and tactile sense of the power of words in Spanish and his mastery of tone and impression. Valle-Inclán possesses a 'linguistic virtuosity [...] especially evident in his capacity to coin and compound new words'.[14] Considered by some a liberator of Spanish prose, he has been described as having 'freed the Spanish language from dross and clichés, investing it with a new intensity and colour'.[15]

From these observations Valle-Inclán emerges as a writer who has created a language of his own: for translators this means that they are confronted with the problem of having to transfer into another language the work of an innovator of the Spanish tongue, a challenge comparable to that facing the translator of Strindberg's novel use of language in Swedish. Viewed in this light, it comes as no surprise that *Bohemian Lights* had to wait 48 years for its British premiere, although the play was not helped on its way to the English stage by the censorship that prevented it from being performed in Spain until 1972. Had Valle-Inclán's esperpentos been performed in Spain at the time that they were written, his position among European dramatists might have been different. Instead, his plays were staged after Brecht, Beckett, Ionesco and Genet, too late for him to be acknowledged as one of the foremost innovators of the language of the theatre. In the circumstances, *Bohemian Lights* was first performed in France by the theatrical company of Jean Vilar in 1963.

For Valle-Inclán's play to be performed in the UK took another five years, until 1968 when *Bohemian Lights* was chosen by the Oxford Theatre Group as their opening Fringe production at the Edinburgh Festival, the first time a major work by Valle-Inclán was performed to an English-speaking audience. Directed by Nic Renton, it was staged in a surrealist avant-garde manner, utilising masks, lights, colour and sound. Little prepared for Valle-Inclán's treatment of the Madrid Bohemian underworld in the early part of the twentieth century, according to most critics the production was 'shooting at difficult game', with reviews ranging from 'controversial', 'stunning', 'truly haunting' and full of 'Valle-Inclán's exquisite poetry', to 'theatre of the minority', 'harsh' and a 'tragedy-travesty'.[16] Two years after the showing of *Bohemian Lights* to English-speaking audiences in Edinburgh, a Valle-Inclán follow-up took place in New York. In 1970, two short plays written after *Bohemian Lights*, *La cabeza del Bautista* (*The Head of John the Baptist*, 1924) and *Rosa de papel* (*Paper Rose*, 1924) were performed Off-Broadway, at the La Mama Experimental Theater Club. The plays were selected as offering innovative theatre of potential interest to Americans unfamiliar with Spanish culture, yet 'relevant enough to the theatrical problems of the New York community'.[17] In the event, however, American theatre audiences proved to be no more open than the British in embracing the remote world of Valle-Inclán.

If early productions that attempted to introduce Valle-Inclan's Spain in unadulterated form to English-speaking audiences met with little success, it could be that a more promising alternative would be to bring the Spanish text closer to the audience by relocating it to a more familiar milieu. This was the approach taken by David Johnston's in his version of *Bohemian Lights*, which relaunched the refurbished London Gate Theatre in 1993. Seeing in the twosome of Valle-Inclán's play, Max Estrella and his disreputable crony Don Latino de Hispalis, a similarity with the male double-act in O'Casey's *Juno and the Paycock,* Johnston decided to set *Bohemian Lights* not in Madrid but in Dublin. Thus in Scene 4 of Johnston's version, the drunken Max Starr, Johnston's Irish counterpart to Valle-Inclán's Max Estrella and his companion Captain Sweeney, the Spanish Don Latino de Hispalis, stagger around Dublin trying to find a bar still open to serve them. The year is 1915, just one year before the Easter Rising:

> *Night. Maximus Cornelius Starr and Captain Sweeney stagger arm in arm along a lonely street. The smell of violence lingers on the air, signs of it are all around: smashed bottles, windows and doors closed and boarded up. A weak greenish light shivers from those few lamps still lit, while the moon shines on the tenement roofs, plunging one side of the street into darkness. Every now and then the road rumbles, as though with the approach of a train, as yet another patrol or armoured convoy passes nearby. Shadows of soldiers or of police. Archetypal. The sense of centuries' violence. As the swing doors of the Palace Bar open and close, a triangle of yellow light spills onto the pavement. Max and Sweeney, drunk under the moon, scholars staggering along a line of streetlights, are drawn irresistibly towards it.*[18]

Setting *Bohemian Lights* in a trouble-torn Dublin not only brought Valle-Inclán's play onto more familiar grounds for an English-speaking audience than the Madrid of 1918/19, but the use of a specifically Dublin vernacular also helped Johnston to overcome the problem in English translation of the slang, cultural references and poetry in the heated bar-room discussions of the Spanish original. In his review of the play for *The Times Literary Supplement*, Barry Ife found the comparison between Ireland and Spain particularly apt, because:

> Valle-Inclán worked hard at his text, publishing it first in 1920, and revising it twice before the definitive version of 1924. What becomes stronger in the successive versions was the overt political commentary. The move away from the generalised post-Bolshevik disturbances of Madrid to Dublin before the Easter Rising gives extra force to Valle's final vision of the play.[19]

Other reviewers on the other hand, such as Michael Billington in the *Guardian*, expressed a preference for having the play staged as rooted in its original soil. Against this view, Johnston has pointed to the impossibility of conveying the mass of linguistic as well as social and cultural information contained in endnotes accompanying the 1976 translation by Zahareas and Gillespie, as evidence of the play's unperformability in an unadapted form.[20]

However, relocating Valle-Inclán's work to Ireland does not seem to constitute a fool-proof recipe for theatrical success. In August 2000 the Abbey

Theatre staged an English-language version of the *Barbaric Comedies* at the Edinburgh festival. Having first played at the Dublin Theatre Festival, this English version by Frank McGuiness drew on another Spanish-Irish parallel, this time between Galicia and Galway. In spite of praise for the acting, production, lighting and direction – by the Catalan director Calixto Bieito – there appears to have been limited appreciation of this pageant of carnivalesque scenes charting the slow descent of the Monte Negro clan into madness and murder. On 10 June 2000, the *Irish News* expressed the opinion that '[f]or the most part and in Frank McGuiness' laborious translation and director Calixto Bieito's overwrought production, the *Barbaric Comedies* are overblown and histrionic dramatisations of Valle-Inclán's religious and psychosexual angst'. And from the Edinburgh Festival Michael Billington commented that '[d]rama is always translatable, but it is not always transposable', and that 'the play is like some wild beast and I suspect works best in Spanish'. Unlike the Gate production of *Bohemian Lights*, in this Anglicised version of *Barbaric Comedies*, the assumed parallels between the Irish and the Spanish situation seem to have failed to emerge sufficiently distinctly: an oppressive church, a dispossessed underclass and a preoccupation with land. The un-English acting style also appears to have added to the feel of 'foreignness' of the production, making it difficult for the audience to identify with what was happening on stage: Bieito's direction seems to have encouraged actors' lines to be bellowed and overcoats to be flung to the ground. All in all, this cross-cultural attempt at making Valle-Inclán's intentions more easily understandable to English-speaking audiences only seems to have resulted in inviting the conclusion from Michael Billington that '[t]here is simply nothing in Anglo-Irish drama that matches Valle-Inclán's delight in violent grotesquerie'.

Aspects of Valle-Inclán's theatrical use of the grotesque and his generally visually-orientated approach to theatre as a means of breaking through the barriers of middle-class morality are also found in the work of Federico García Lorca (1898–1936), the only twentieth-century Spanish writer to be represented in a number of different English translations. With Valle-Inclán, Lorca shared the tendency to favour a rural setting. Permeating Lorca's writing is the Spanish countryside: Lorca was born in Fuente Vaqueros, a village in the Vega of Granada, and his childhood years remained with him as a constant present. In an interview published in 1934, the year following the premiere in Madrid of *Bodas de sangre* (*Blood Wedding*, 1932), the play that marked his break-through as a playwright, Lorca acknowledged his debt to the land:

> I love the countryside. I feel myself linked to it in all my emotions. My oldest childhood memories have the flavour of the earth. The meadows, the fields have done wonders for me. The wild animals of the countryside, the livestock, the people living on the land, all these have a fascination that very few people grasp. I recall them now exactly as I knew them in my childhood. Were this not so I could not have written *Blood Wedding*.[21]

Lorca's work sprang from an early and total immersion in the folk poetry, music and rural speech of his native Andalusia. On 18 February 1935, an article appeared in the Madrid evening newspaper *La Voz* written by Angel Lázaro, following an interview with Lorca in his home. Insisting that he most of all loved simplicity, Lorca talked about his early days in Fuente Vaqueros and, when mentioning the life, speech and rhythms of the countryside, his face lit up with enthusiasm. 'It was the look of the Lorca who, in Buenos Aires, had said that he suffered from what psychoanalysts would call "an agrarian complex".'[22] In this respect, although hailing from a different part of Europe, the work of Lorca presents the English translator with a problem similar to that of Strindberg. At a time when the wit and sophistication of Oscar Wilde was keeping London theatre audiences amused in a country that had seen early industrialisation, playwrights in southern and northern Europe, deeply rooted in agrarian societies, still viewed simplicity as a virtue and communion with nature as one of life's primary sources of enjoyment. The problems resulting from this asymmetry in historical and cultural background and its effect on the translation of their work have not as yet been fully grasped, as can be gleaned from the reception of the plays by both playwrights when first performed on the English stage.

Always present in Lorca's work, Andalusia provides the physical setting for books of his poems such as *Romancero gitano* (*Gypsy Ballads*, 1928), as well as for his trilogy of rural tragedies which, starting with *Blood Wedding*, was followed by *Yerma* (1934) and *La casa de Bernarda Alba* (*The House of Bernarda Alba*, 1936). Another theme running through Lorca's writing is that of lost love, of a love that could and should have been but which was thwarted. Not surprising then that an incident that took place on 22 July 1928 involving a young Andalusian bride who left her bridegroom to run off with her childhood sweetheart attracted Lorca's attention. Reported in the national as well as the local press in the province of Almería, the 'crime of Níjar' provided Lorca, the poet, with a powerful metaphor for a drama of his own which, in turn, established him as a playwright.[23]

In Lorca's hands, the incident became *Bodas de sangre*, literally 'marriage of blood', the first, in the poet's own words, of a 'dramatic trilogy of the

Spanish earth'.[24] Written in 1932, *Blood Wedding* describes the elopement of the Bride with Leonardo Felix to whom she was once engaged. Through the guidance of the figure of Death, disguised as an Old Beggar Woman, the elopers are entrapped, and a knife fight ensues. Her lover now dead, the Bride returns to the family of the Bridegroom and, still a virgin, his honour can be declared to be intact. On 8 March 1933, the play premiered at the Theatre Beatriz in Madrid, directed by Lorca himself. The same year it was also an immediate success in Buenos Aires. For a Spanish play to be successfully launched in South America, this was crucial for its success at the box office. At last Lorca had hit on a money-spinning dramatic formula: on 4 August he was told that *Blood Wedding* had already earned him the equivalent of some 3,500 pesetas, a sum corresponding to the annual salary of the highest paid miner or metal worker in Spain at the time.[25]

The first English-speaking performance of *Blood Wedding* took place in New York in 1935. Under the title *Bitter Oleander*, it was staged at the Lyceum Theatre just east of Broadway on 44th Street by the Neighbourhood Playhouse, in order to mark the company's twentieth anniversary. The interest of the founders of the Playhouse, the philanthropist sisters Irene and Alice Lewisohn, was almost ethnographic: they were concerned with 'song and dance and ritual as direct expressions of the beauty of life' [26] and, in order to provide authentic material for the production, emissaries were sent off to Spain. Given the Neighbourhood Playhouse's reputation for worthy exoticism, *Bitter Oleander* was likely to arouse certain kinds of expectations even before it opened; this was confirmed by the mixed, critical reception of the play. In the *New York Times* of 12 February 1935, headed '*Bitter Oleander* to celebrate the founding of the Neighbourhood Playhouse', Brooks Atkinson lamented the staging of 'a peasant play from the Spanish' which, he felt, had 'been removed from the soil and clapped in the straightjacket of style'. Other critical voices, such as that of the *New York World Telegram* of the same date, focused on the translator, José Weissberger, with the anti-Semitic jibe 'he's not so spick and Spanish either', and suggested that 'these adaptations from the Spanish [should not] be exposed to the biting winds on Broadway'. In the *New York Evening Post* of 12 February a dispute in the audience was reported as to whether an oleander is a flower, a tree, or a Spanish onion – on the whole, what were referred to as 'horticultural references' in the dialogue attracted unfavourable comment. Lorca's characters, it was pointed out, were 'great ones for talking as if they had eaten whole libraries full of seed catalogues'.[27] On 16 February, in 'Flowers of Spain', the review in the *New York Sun* started by summing up floral motifs in the dialogue:

A deceased gentleman is lovingly remembered by his widow not only as 'my carnation', but also as one of her 'two geraniums'. Her dead son was the other geranium. A mother looks affectionately on her sleeping baby and breathes: 'My little rose-bush'.

In its close linguistic faithfulness to the original, *Bitter Oleander* clearly shows the hallmark of early translation approaches. For example, while in Spanish, pronominal subjects may be left out, this is not the case in English. Nevertheless, translators of the past were often scrupulous in reproducing the original. When, for instance, the Mother expresses her reservations about the Bride:

Amasa su pan y cose sus faldas, y siento, sin embargo...[28]

the Spanish construction is dutifully replicated in English:

Kneeds her bread, sews her skirts and yet...

Judging from the reaction of the New York critics, the 1935 translation of *Bitter Oleander* appears to have stayed dangerously close to the original. 'What *Bitter Oleander* was like in its original tongue', the *New York Times* reviewer wrote at the time, 'this reporter has no way of knowing...[here]...it is overwrought...filled with clipped phrases...nothing comes out of it.'[29]

New York critics also reacted to the foreign feel of the play: one review entitled 'Andalusians of Grandeur' referred to the play as a 'torrid melodrama...[which] seems fated to do little more to American audiences than reminding them of the size of the Atlantic'.[30] The audience response was however not altogether adverse and although most of the critical reviews were not favourable, some were encouraging.

Culturally and socially the Anglo-American and the Spanish worlds appear to be too far removed and the languages spoken, English and Spanish, not sufficiently similar in structure for a simple transfer of Lorca's text to be possible without some degree of acculturation. The fidelity of José Weissberger's translation was in fact praised by García Lorca himself, who collaborated with the translator, helping with untranslatable words and phrases which were replaced by others suggested by the author himself. This is corroborated by the resulting, unpublished text which shows the evolution of what the Neighbourhood Playhouse considered to be an 'actable' version, the prompt book indicating the actors' lines as actually spoken on stage.[31] It would not, however, have been the first time that the original author's inclination to view the text from the point of view of the source language speaker did little to help the translator arrive at a version likely to match the theatrical expectations of the target audience. In sum, the 1935 New York reception of

Blood Wedding, targeting aspects such as Lorca's floral imagery and the inherent element of melodrama, foreshadowed the reaction to 'English Lorca' in years to come.

In the UK, *Blood Wedding* had an early showing by The Under Thirty Theatre Group, in a translation by the South African poet Roy Campbell. The initiative was praised by the critics who were willing to ascribe weaknesses in the performance to the lack of experience of the young company. In the *Daily Telegraph* of 1 December 1947, W A Darlington gave Lorca the benefit of the doubt, stating that 'good verse badly spoken sounds like bad verse, and only one or two of last night's cast had much idea how to tackle Roy Campbell's translation'. Seven years later, the play opened at the Arts Theatre in a production by Peter Hall, which was on the whole respectfully received. In his review of 4 March headed 'Fierce, Stark, Spanish Drama', W A Darlington found Peter Hall's handling of the play both imaginative and effective while raising questions about what had gone missing in translation. In the then Manchester *Guardian* of the same date, Philip Hope-Wallace also found that 'some quality has failed to "travel"', his review headed 'Lorca's Inner Music Lost in Transit?'

In an interview in 1933 with José S Serna, a young Spanish journalist, Lorca revealed that he was busy at work on the second play in his 'dramatic trilogy of the Spanish earth'.[32] At the time the work did not have a title but the subject with which it was concerned was female sterility. A few weeks later it was common knowledge that the title of the play on which Lorca was working was *Yerma*. As in *Blood Wedding*, in his new play Lorca drew on his familiarity with Spanish country life, reaching back to his childhood, when he first became conscious of the annual 'cuckold's pilgrimage' to the village of Mochlín.[33] The first wife of Lorca's father, Matilde Palacios, had died childless, and might well have provided the model for the female protagonist of the play. On a personal level Lorca was also acutely aware, as a homosexual male, of his own fate to remain childless: the Mochlín pilgrimage provided him with a ready-made framework for the subject of infecundity.

Yerma, whose name is derived from the Spanish adjective *yermo*, meaning 'barren', is desperate for children, but the man to whom she is married values his role as a farmer more highly than that as her husband. Prevented by her sense of honour from following her instincts and yielding to Victor who could give her the love that she needs, Yerma sees no other way out of her dilemma but to kill her husband, thus destroying all hope of conceiving the child that she craves. The play opened on 29 December 1934 at the Teatro Español in Madrid, with the Catalan actress Margarita Xirgu in the part of Yerma. When, at the end of the performance, the curtain went down, the applause was deafening. But there was also vociferous opposition from right-wing newspapers, which were unanimous in condemning the play, seeing in it an implicit rejection of Catholic values; it was considered to be 'immoral, anti-Spanish, irreligious and odious'.[34] The author of Yerma had now become an enemy of the Church and the intense and widespread dislike of Lorca that was felt by many Catholics dated back to Yerma and the arrival of the play on the Spanish stage.

The first English performance of Yerma opened at the Arts Theatre Club in London on the 31 July 1957, produced by Clifford Williams. On the whole, the encounter between Spanish peasant culture with its passionate emotions and English restrained gentility does not appear to have been an altogether happy one. On 1 August, under the heading 'The Lorca legend may suffer', F B of the Evening News chose to 'state its entire theme in one sentence', which was followed by a further sentence dismissing the play out of hand: 'It is about a woman who cannot have a baby. But all the anguished sighs, long pauses, guitar music and semi-poetic dialogue do not really help it to achieve the status of tragedy.'

For the part of Yerma, the choice of Madalena Nicol, an actress born in Brazil, appears to have been determined by her 'vibrant intensity'. According to some critics, it was her 'dignified performance' through three acts of 'conspicuous suffering' that greatly helped to save the production, and, thanks to her efforts, the 'nobility' of the play was rescued. For Richard Findlater, however, the radiance of the lead actress' performance failed to offset the 'monotony of her broken-Englished Yerma. Meaningful pauses, whose timing is so important in Lorca's work, are sometimes prolonged to yawning-point, and dignity congeals into dullness.'[35] Acknowledging the problems inherent in transferring Hispanic peasant drama onto the London stage, Findlater's review for the Observer, entitled 'Poet and Peasant' started:

> For most English actors, peasants are – like Americans – unactably beyond the pale, among the less picturesque accessories of holidays abroad. Even English villagery on stage usually seems, at best, a subtopian *fête champêtre*, and putting on the Home Counties style in cross-Channel folk drama leads to certain disaster.

Under the heading 'Spanish passion is stifled', the problem was also identified by Milton Schulman in the Evening Standard of 1 August:

> Something disturbing happens when Spanish poetic drama is translated

into English and produced over here. The hot passion is frozen into prim Kensingtonian vowel sounds; the lyric verse is heightened into lush rhetoric; the symbolism acquires an unbelievable artificiality.

Milton Schulman's review proceeds to pay tribute to direction and design, acknowledging the 'conscientious' attempt to 'evoke Lorca's brooding poetic mood', while pointing to the shortcomings of the acting and the translation which 'prove too onerous an Anglo-Saxon obstacle'. In *The Sunday Times* of 4 August, the translation similarly came under attack:

> True, the company is handicapped by a translation which, whenever it has created any sense of dark and ominous illusion, destroys it by some unfeeling colloquialism. The poetry of Shakespeare himself could hardly survive the constant interruption of such phrases as 'That's up to you' or 'Let's go eat'.

The English text used for the 1957 Arts Theatre production of *Yerma* was the result of the co-operation between Richard L O'Connell and James Graham-Luján, two Americans, who were also responsible for the translation of *Blood Wedding* used in Peter Hall's 1954 production. The O'Connell & Graham-Luján translations were the first English-language translations of Lorca's plays published in the United States in the 1940s; at a later date, their Lorca translations were also published in two volumes in the UK by Penguin Books.[36] Sanctioned by the Lorca Estate and further authorised by the preface written by Lorca's brother, Francisco, they were the only published translations available until 1986, fifty years after the playwright's death, when copyright restrictions lapsed. Described as 'reverential to the point that the source language is wholly audible beneath the English', it has been suggested that the 'officially sanctioned translations by Luján and O'Connell […] performed a great disservice to Lorca in terms of his potential for influencing the English-speaking stage'.[37] In their concern to protect Lorca's work from the maraudings of unscrupulous translators, the Lorca Estate decreed that all translations should be as close to the original as possible, an approach often resulting in O'Connell and Graham-Luján failing to capture the Spanish spoken by Lorca's country people. It does, for instance, not seem very likely that a rough-speaking English country equivalent to Lorca's peasant would dismiss his mother's reservations about his girlfriend in Scene 1 of *Blood Wedding* as 'Foolishness'. It is equally difficult to imagine that the gossipy Neighbour in the latter part of the same scene would reply, 'that was not discussed',[38] in answer to the Mother's attempt to elicit information about the mother of the bride. Not only does this approach to translation deprive Lorca's country people of a voice, making his characters sound uniformly middle class, it also gives them a language never used in conversation between English-speakers. Differently put, in the officially sanctioned translations, Lorca's plays do not read as if they have been translated but as if they have 'simply been photocopied into English'.[39]

Copyright restrictions do not appear to have prevented permission to be granted by the Lorca Estate for specific English-language performances, and on 21 March 1973, *The House of Bernarda Alba*, the last of Lorca's rural tragedies, premiered at the Greenwich Theatre, in an English version by Tom Stoppard. The reason for the long lapse between the time when the play was written and its arrival on the London stage was closely linked to the play's content and the political context in which it was written.

As testified by the date at the end of the manuscript, *The House of Bernarda Alba* was completed on 19 June 1936. As a source of inspiration for Bernada Alba, Lorca drew on Frasquita Alba Sierra, a woman of domineering temperament, born in 1858, who lived next door to Lorca's Aunt Mathilde and her family in Asquerosa, although the tyranny imposed on her daughters by the widow in the play was the work of Lorca the dramatist. With her hypocrisy, her inquisitorial Catholicism and her determination to suppress her daughters' freedom of expression, Bernarda represented a mentality only too familiar to Lorca. Both La Barraca – Lorca's travelling theatre company, taking Spanish dramatic classics to the people as part of a widespread campaign to eradicate illiteracy in the early 1930s – and *Yerma* had been viciously attacked by *El Debate*, Spain's leading Catholic newspaper. Calling his play not just *Bernarda Alba* but *The House of Bernarda Alba*, Lorca ensured that the emphasis was placed on the locale in which the tyrant reigned, making his play an indictment on Spain and Spanish intolerance. Within the four walls of her house, everyone falling under Bernarda's rule is crushed, her daughters as well as her servants, a category of the poor denounced by Bernarda as 'animals'. When, in 1933, the Right came to power in Spain, the agrarian reform promised by the Republic and initiated during the first two years of democratic rule was paralysed, and in June 1936, as Lorca finished the play, it still remained unimplemented. Two months later, after the completion of *The House of Bernarda Alba*, Lorca was assassinated by custodians of the mentality closely akin to that of the protagonist of the play, and for the next 40 years, the manner of his death was effectively concealed by the Franco regime. Although not performed in Spain until 10 January 1964, *The House of Bernarda Alba* did, however, appear on other Spanish-speaking stages –

almost twenty years earlier, on 8 March 1945, it had opened in Buenos Aires. Its first London performance took place on 17 June the following year when the Studio des Champs Elysées from Paris presented the play in French at the Mercury Theatre, while its first English-language staging had to wait until the 1973 Greenwich Theatre production.

In his *Guardian* review of 23 March 1973 of Stoppard's English version of *The House of Bernarda Alba*, Michael Billington pointed to two crucial requirements for Lorca's play to work: the notion of honour and its preservation at all costs; and the almost tangible atmosphere of suppressed sexuality among the women of the Bernarda household, as doors and windows are blocked up and a mourning period of eight years is announced following the death of the man, father, husband and master of the house. While the Spanish concept of honour appears to have been successfully captured in the Greenwich production, any feeling of pent-up sexual longing among Bernarda Alba's five daughters seems to have been absent, according to *The Times* theatre critic, the possible result of the director Robin Phillips' practice 'of exposing classics in an environment of antiseptically modern materials. We might be in a convent furnished by Habitat.'[40] Similar sentiments were echoed in the *Daily Telegraph* of 23 March 1973, where John Barber's opening paragraph refers to the production as 'cool and beautiful…a rare classic of the modern theatre', bemoaning the fact that 'the Greenwich's open stage cannot suggest claustrophobia'. Other responses went further. On 25 March 1973 the opening line of the *Observer* review asked, 'What's wrong with [the Greenwich] production of Lorca's *The House of Bernarda Alba*?', then proceeded to give a one-word answer: 'plenty'. A list of flaws were listed, starting with the set, which was described as 'more appropriate to Scandinavia than to Spain'. Also varied were the responses to the English actresses and their attempt to convey the emotional turmoil of the women in Bernarda Alba's household. While *The Times* saw virtue in their efforts to Anglicise Lorca's play, bestowing praise on the actress in the part of the soured eldest sister, 'who sensibly opts for the arrogant cadences of a Home Counties wallflower in preference to any Spanish impersonation', the *Observer* faulted the English Bernarda Alba for coming on 'with the stern indignation of a suburban English matron, or a Trust House Lady who has been interrupted at tea by tourists who mistakenly entered the private quarters'. It is plain that the *Observer* critic would have favoured a reduced degree of English acculturation, and the review ended by denouncing the use of middle-class gentility in Lorca's peasant dramas, calling for 'a lot less breeding and reserve' and more of an 'injection of working-class blood'. Similar reservations were voiced about Mia Farrow in the part of Adela,

Bernarda's youngest daughter, described as 'too ethereal and Bohemian to capture the irrepressible eroticism of Adela, scurrying around as she does in bare feet, and curling her legs beneath her like a cuddly debutante', while the *Daily Telegraph* reviewer suggested she would have made 'a good Peter Pan'.

In the absence of other English language productions of *The House of Bernarda Alba*, the part played by Stoppard's adaptation received limited critical attention. In the *Observer* the Stoppard version was described as 'crisp, colloquial but overly jocular', and *The Daily Telegraph* concurred, finding it 'surprisingly humourless and there are some unwanted laughs'. With no published version following the production, Stoppard's adaptation appears to have enjoyed a short life-span, leaving it to later translator/adapters to create new English versions of Lorca's plays once the 50-year copyright restrictions were lifted.

When, in 1986, the rights of the Lorca Estate lapsed, two new American translators were approached. In 1987, *The Rural Trilogy* appeared in the United States published by Bantam Books in translation by Michael Dewell and Carmen Zapata, authorised by Isabel García Lorca, the playwright's sister, and his nephew, Manuel Fernández-Montesinos. In 1992, the Dewell/Zapata translations appeared in the UK,[41] but, with the rights no longer tied exclusively to one set of translators, other Lorca translators started to emerge. On 8 September 1986, *The House of Bernarda Alba* was presented at the Lyric Theatre Hammersmith, London, in a translation by Robert David MacDonald, directed by the celebrated, classical actress, Nuria Espert. On 1 January 1987 the production was transferred to the Globe Theatre. Other productions followed: in 1991, Helena Bonham-Carter took the part of Adela at the Nottingham Playhouse and, in 1996, the play was staged at the Theatre Clwyd, both productions making use of the translation by Robert David Macdonald.

With the Lyric production, which starred Glenda Jackson as Bernarda and Joan Plowright as the shrewd housekeeper Poncia, the last vestiges of middle-class gentility that had plagued previous productions were removed, allowing 'an Andalusian point of view that to date has proved virtually impossible for British directors and actors to interpret with any sense of verisimilitude'.[42] In his review in the *Observer* of 14 September 1986, Michael Ratcliff now hailed Lorca as a playwright who 'has been rescued from the people who take themselves too solemnly, which he did not; we no longer need to accept his reputation on trust or nod in agreement when told that he does not survive in translation'. For the translation, the English used by Robert David MacDonald was described as 'sardonic, robust and austere'. Referring to the English text as 'the highly speakable translation by Robert David MacDonald' and 'quite the best text of the play we have come across', in the *Spectator* of 20 October 1986, Christopher Edwards welcomed the 'staging of a little-known European classic'. And in *Time Out* of 17 October 1986, Steve Grant concurred, paying tribute to the translation as 'splendidly [A]nglicised', while still painted in Lorca's 'vivid colours: the red of blood and sexuality (inseparable in his work); the blackness of Catholic piety, in the veils of its woundedly faded and unloved women; white for purity and grace and for the towering, windowed walls of Bernarda Alba's fortress home....'

Less than a year after the successful staging of *The House of Bernarda Alba* at the Lyric, the National Theatre followed with another Lorca play. On 26 March 1987 *Yerma* opened at the Cottesloe Theatre with Juliet Stevenson in the title role. Judging from its critical reception, this production seems to have succeeded in moving yet another Lorca play closer to audience understanding and enjoyment. In an apparent attempt to create an appropriately 'Southern European atmosphere', the walls of the Cottesloe were draped with washing which, although to some members of the audience more reminiscent of the neo-realism of Italian films of the 1950s than Spain at the time of Lorca, provided non-stereotypical but unmistakable pointers in the general direction of Mediterranean countries.[43] Lingering doubts about the country of origin of the play were also emphatically dispelled by the flamenco dancing marking the fertility festival in Act 3, moving Michael Billington to comment in the *Guardian* of 28 March 1987 that 'the Bacchanalian ritual in the hills, embodied by some tasteful gypsy dancing accompanied by a decorous trio on guitar and violin, is about as far from pagan sexuality as a night in an ethnic Spanish eatery in West London'. Also alluded to in Billington's review was the Anglicisation of the direction: *Yerma* is as much a poem as it is a play, not sufficiently clearly remembered in Di Trevis' production, 'played for the most part with quiet, naturalistic intensity'. Although the use of music and set helped to locate the play in its country of origin, to some, the actors still remained irretrievably English. Writing on 29 March 1987, the theatre critic of the *Sunday Telegraph* found 'Juliet Stevenson's Yerma [...] more like the daughter of a Home Counties vicar than an Andalusian shepherd'. The English Victor, the man whom Yerma loves, played by Neil Dudgeon, in flat cap and corduroy trousers, also came in for his share of criticism as not likely to be the 'strong' and 'vigorous' man of the Spanish original. Lorca's characters in the rural plays are, according to Edwards, 'uninhibited, passionate, rough',[44] the very opposite of any association with good breeding, sophistication and polish.

The 1987 National Theatre production of *Yerma* suggests that if some aspects of 'otherness' are accentuated, with which an English audience is familiar and able to identify, an understanding of Lorca may more easily be achieved. A similar strategy seems to have influenced the choice of language and translator used for the translation. According to the National Theatre performance programme note:

> Peter Luke's ten years as a farmer in Andalusia resulted in a book, *The Mad Pomegranate and the Praying Mantis*, in which he examines the mores of the country people and the villagers among whom he lived. What he learned then intensified his interest in Lorca and gave him a deeper insight into the background of the poet's work, resulting in the present new translation of *Yerma*.

In Luke's version, English Yerma, socially equivalent to Lorca's childless and frustrated protagonist, uses four-letter words to indicate strong emotions and a firm stand. When her husband reproaches her, having been stirred by a man singing: 'people will start talking if they see you out and about like this', dismissing his warning Yerma answers, 'Fuck people', arguably somewhat out of character, given that Yerma's tragedy is that of the ultra-conservative woman.[45] Nevertheless, although it may not have provided a truly authentic English voice for Lorca, the 1987 National Theatre production, closely following in the *glasnost* created by the lapse of the copyright restrictions in 1986, marked another step in the Anglicisation of the Spanish playwright, slowly pushing open the door to greater popular audience acceptance. A recurring problem, however, appears to be the bridging of the gap between Lorca's Spanish villagers of the source text and the middle class world which they seem to inhabit in English translation. One of the stumbling blocks having proved to be the middle-class associations created by the use of standard English, Gwynne Edwards, Hispanist scholar and Lorca translator, has suggested as an alternative that Lorca's work be translated into another variety of English. According to Edwards, 'Lorca is best served in English by the much more blunt, strong, no nonsense character of northern English, as well as by the lyrical and poetic nature of southern Irish'.[46] (See Chapters 2, 4 and 6 for the use of this strategy in the translation from French, Russian and German.)

The production of *Yerma* at the Cottesloe was soon followed by other Lorca performances in new translations, and the once uncomfortable critical response to the playwright on the English stage now seemed to be changing. On 17 August 1988, Joseph Farrel reported in the *Scotsman* that the translation by David Johnston for the Communicado production of *Blood Wedding* at the Edinburgh festival 'has in turns, the lilt of song and the flint of peasant speech, and the production opens vistas and touches the heart, which indicates how poetic drama can be done with powerful effect on the modern stage'.

Towards the end of the twentieth century, other Lorca plays also started to appear on English stages, in addition to the rural tragedies. In the autumn of 1989, the Theatre Royal in Bristol staged *Doña Rosita la soltera* (*Doña Rosita, the Spinster*, 1935), directed by Phyllida Lloyd and translated by Gwynne Edwards. Born, like Lorca's mother, in 1870, Doña Rosita is only 20 years old when the first act of this social tragedy begins. The second act is set in 1900 and the last act in 1910. An orphan living with her uncle, aunt and nurse in Granada, Doña Rosita falls in love with her cousin who is called away to Argentina. Fifteen years pass and Doña Rosita receives a letter asking for her hand in marriage. But her cousin never returns: instead he marries in Argentina, leaving Doña Rosita to end her days as a spinster.

In his review of the play for the *Guardian* of 16 October 1989, entitled 'Sex, Lies and Lorca', the reaction of Nicholas de Jongh to *Doña Rosita, the Spinster* indicated that 'English Lorca', if he had not fully arrived, was standing at the threshold. Two extraneous factors appear to have been instrumental in this process: Chekhov and the development of interest in Gender Studies. Rosita's hopes for another life which never come to fruition are not unlike those of Chekhov's three sisters and their vain longing for the start of a new life in Moscow. The popularity already achieved by English Chekhov as an Anglicised foreign playwright on the subject of unfulfilled dreams, now seems to be encouraging a closer English understanding of Lorca. 'Rosita's great arias of regret,' according to de Jongh, 'her sense of being stranded barrenly in anachronistic youthfulness, and the final Chekhovian scene in which she, her aunt and servant totter out of their deserted home, combine to achieve a quiet but fierce pathos.' In addition, a more profound understanding of the themes that informed Lorca's writing was now available. The year that saw the Bristol production of *Doña Rosita, the Spinster* also saw the publication of Ian Gibson's full-scale biography of Lorca.[47] While it is clear that the play castigates Spanish hypocrisy, that women forcibly have to repress their desire for sensual pleasure, more recently accessible knowledge of Lorca and his life now allows the play to speak with greater clarity of the hypocrisy shrouding Lorca's own sexual orientation. The question 'How much longer will all the Doña Rositas of Spain have to carry on like this?' that Lorca asks can now be viewed as having a broader concern.[48] In de Jongh's words, Rosita represents 'Lorca's own shadow, speaks covertly of his struggle to come to terms with his homosexuality and failure to find the enduring gay love he craved'. From the appearance of Gibson's biography, information has been culled helping to reveal that 'if ever Lorca came close to identify with one of his protagonists, it was with Rosita'.[49]

The *Guardian* review of *Doña Rosita* also covered a report on the staging of another Lorca play in English translation. In the production by the Asian Co-operative Theatre of *Blood Wedding* at the Half Moon Theatre in London, Lorca's peasant culture was found a suitable correlative by transporting the play to a non-European location. In translation by the director Jonathan Martin and the Peruvian actress Mary Ann Vargas, with the emphasis on simplicity and earthy epithets, the Bride is described as 'soft as wool', whom the Bridegroom leaves to hunt down 'like a raging star'. In summing up, the two productions would suggest, according to de Jongh, that 'we are on the way to discovering conventions by which to render Lorca in English'.

Three years later, in October 1992, these conventions were explored even further as well as put to highly successful theatrical effect. For her production of *Bernarda Alba* at the Gate Theatre, Katie Mitchell managed to establish links between Lorca's intentions and present-day issues, adding:

> Camp touches of religious iconography and a chilling awareness of the fascism without that reflects the tyranny within. As the lynch mob pass by Bernarda's back door, the entire family gathers to salute 'il duce' [*sic*]; as the lights go down after the interval, they are frozen in a tableau based on Leonardo's Last Supper, with Adela, the youngest daughter, encased in a crown of thorns.[50]

In a translation by Matthew Banks described as 'sinewy', 'the unspoken issue' of the play, according to Andrew St George in the *Financial Times* of 12 October 1992, 'is the oppression of women by men and of women by each other. This speaks to the 1990s: for as gender becomes sect, great oppression is now gathering in the name of equality'. In Katie Mitchell's direction, the play has now been allowed to express itself metaphorically: it speaks of 1930s Spain, beset by violence and tyranny, with Bernarda's daughters' dilemma suggesting the deeper, underlying malaise in Spanish society.

Giving voice to the overall theme of a Lorca play by allowing it to speak metaphorically may arguably be a simpler task than attempting to transfer discreet aspects of his symbolism in translation. Not only are Lorca's metaphors and images difficult to capture, there is also the problem of 'fixing' the meaning of a word or phrase in the original. As a result, translators are likely to find themselves in the unenviable position of having to transfer into English what Lorca wrote in Spanish, the meaning of which he was unable to explain himself.[51] For example, as might be expected, key terminology used by Lorca throughout *Blood Wedding* revolves around expressions containing the word 'blood'. One such phrase is 'man of blood', used by Leonardo in reference to himself. But while to a Spanish audience *hombre de sangre* is a phrase encoded with a range of different associations including masculinity, virility, pride and honour, in English there is no single word encapsulating all the resonances of the Spanish phrase. As a result, in translations into English, translators are likely to capture one or more but not all of the associations linked to the Spanish phrase. Examples below show some of the options chosen:

Federico García Lorca:

LEONARDO: *No quiero hablar, porque soy **hombre de sangre**, y no quiero que todos estos cerros oigan mis voces.*[52]

Langston Hughes:

LEONARDO: I'd better shut up. I'm **a man with blood running through my veins**, and I don't want those hills to know what I have to say.[53]

Dewell and Zapata (p.25):

LEONARDO: I don't want to talk about it, because I'm **hot-blooded**, and I don't want all these hills to hear my shouts.

Graham-Luján and O'Connell (p. 59):

LEONARDO: I don't walk to talk. I'm **hot-blooded** and I don't want to shout so all these hills will hear me.

Edmunds:

LEONARDO: I'd best say nothing; I **have blood in my veins**, and I don't want my voice ringing all round the hills.[54]

Edwards:

LEONARDO: I don't want to speak out. I'm **a man of honour** and I don't want all these hills to have to listen to my complaints.[55]

Johnston:

LEONARDO: Look, I'm not going to talk about this any more because I **can feel my blood boil**, and I don't want the whole countryside to hear what I've got to say.[56]

Ted Hughes:

LEONARDO: I don't want to raise my voice. I **am a man of honour**. I
   don't want all these hills hearing my complaints.[57]

The Graham-Luján/O'Connell and Dewell/Zapata translations both focus
on Leonardo's 'hot blood' and fiery temperament as does Johnston's, but in
the latter case the translation, 'a man of blood' is provided in an endnote. In
contrast, Edwards and Ted Hughes both opt for a different choice, preferring
to associate the meaning of *hombre de sangre* with the notion of honour.

More recently, the 'fixing' of the meaning of words and phrases referring
more directly to imagery linked to Lorca's homosexuality has attracted scholarly
attention. Paul Julian Smith has argued that a comparison with *Fate at the
Wedding*, an early translation by Langston Hughes, and the prompt book of
Bitter Oleander, the 1935 New York text used for the production of *Bodas de
sangre*, reveals successive revisions and emendations, indicative of a nervous-
ness with the use of Lorca's language and its application to the male body.[58]
The version by Langston Hughes (1902–67), a poet and leader of the Harlem
Renaissance, was drafted in Paris in 1938 but remained in manuscript form
until 1984. Found by Melia Bensussen, it was developed and finalised in March
and April 1992 during rehearsals of the play for production at the New York
Shakespeare Festival. Together with *Yerma*, as translated by the poet and
translator S Merwin (*b.* 1927), the translations of these two parts of Lorca's
rural trilogy were published in 1994 by The Theatre Communications Group
with an introduction by Melia Bensussen. As discussed in the introduction,
bodas, the first noun of the original title of the play, is in fact in the plural,
'suggesting that perhaps more than one wedding takes place during the course
of the play'. The use of the plural in the original Spanish title in turn forces
audiences to look at other relationships in the play, specifically the 'marriage'
of Leonardo and the Boy in their midnight bloodshed'.[59] Of particular interest
here are the opening and closing parts. After a cursory exchange, the Mother
of The Bridegroom soon introduces the play's 'grammar of imagery', the images
of 'cutting, pinning, slicing and piercing'.[60] Below is the opening scene in the
Spanish original (emphasis added):

Lorca (p. 93):

NOVIO: (*Entrando.*) *Madre.*
MADRE: *¿Qué?*
NOVIO: *Me voy.*
MADRE: *¿Adónde?*
NOVIO: *A la viña.* (*Va a salir.*)
MADRE: *Espera.*

NOVIO: *¿Quiere algo?*
MADRE: *Hijo, el almuerzo.*
NOVIO: *Déjelo. Comeré uvas. Déme **la navaja**.*
MADRE: *¿Para qué?*
NOVIO: (Riendo.) *Para **cortarlas**.*
MADRE: (Entre dientes y buscándola.) ***La navaja**, **la navaja**… Maldita*
    sean todas y el bribón que las inventó.
NOVIO: *Vamos a otro asunto.*
MADRE: *Y las escopetas y las pistolas y el **cuchillo** más pequeño, y **hasta***
    ***las azadas y los bieldos** de la era.*
NOVIO: *Bueno.*
MADRE: *Todo lo que puede **cortar** el cuerpo de un hombre. Un hombre*
    hermoso, con su flor en la boca, que sale a las viñas o va a sus olivos
    propios, porque son de él, heredados…
NOVIO: (Bajando la cabeza.) *Calle usted.*

Graham-Luján and O'Connell (p. 34) translate the scene thus:

BRIDEGROOM: (*Entering.*) Mother.
MOTHER: What?
BRIDEGROOM: I'm going.
MOTHER: Where?
BRIDEGROOM: To the vineyard.
    (*He starts to go.*)
MOTHER: Wait.
BRIDEGROOM: You want something?
MOTHER: Your breakfast son.
BRIDEGROOM: Forget it. I'll eat grapes. Give me the **knife**.
MOTHER: What for?
BRIDEGROOM: (*Laughing.*) To **cut** the grapes with.
MOTHER: (*Muttering as she looks for the knife.*) **Knives**, **knives**. Cursed
    be all knives, and the scoundrel who invented them.
BRIDEGROOM: Let's talk about something else.
MOTHER: And guns and pistols and the smallest little **knife** – and
    even hoes and pitchforks.
BRIDEGROOM: All right.
MOTHER: Everything that can **slice** a man's body. A handsome man,
    full of young life, who goes out to the vineyards or to his own olive
    groves – his own because he has inherited them…
BRIDEGROOM: (*Lowering his head.*) Be quiet.

Words referring to knives and sharp-edged instruments in different shapes seem to constitute key lines in 'a play whose emotional action begins and ends with the image of the knife, an image of violence overhanging the play like a Damoclean sword dangling precariously over the head of a humankind on the horns of a cruel and impossible dilemma'. Thus 'the first mention of the *navaja*, the knife, creates a shiver of expectation; the audience confronts the tragedy of a relentless chain of cause and effect which it recognises as being its own trauma'.[61]

Invested with the important function of foreshadowing the violence to come, how then would the force of the word '*navaja*' best be conveyed in English? For his own translation of the opening lines of the play, David Johnston first considered the possibility of drawing on what was familiar to him, that is his own Irish situation where 'gun' would have an immediately recognisable association to the violence linked to social and political feuds with which Lorca is concerned. The word 'gun' does not, however, have the obvious phallic implications of the word 'knife', which in turn might obscure the sexual overtones of the death of the two men in Act 3. Hence in his translation Johnston opted to retain 'knife'.

The next obstacle to be overcome is the translation of the remaining cutting instruments which could inflict mortal injury to man, listed by the Bridegroom's Mother as the threat of escalating violence mounts. In the case of '*las azadas y los bieldos*', the original Spanish has, as Johnston points out, an English dictionary equivalence that translates as 'draghoes and winnowing-forks'. The translator now faces three choices: to heighten the impact of the instruments to reinforce the aura surrounding the '*navaja*'; to convey the specificity of the agricultural instruments in order to stress the play's rural setting; or to attempt to capture the particularly Spanish form of assonance resulting from Lorca's choice of words in '*hasta las azadas*'. Through the introduction of the recurring s-feature in 'the sickle and the scythe', in compensation for the loss of the Spanish assonance, Johnston opts for a combination of the first and the last, making the exact nature of Lorca's agricultural tools the unavoidable victim of this choice.[62] This leaves the translation of the relevant exchange between Bridegroom and Mother as follows:

> MOTHER: (*Muttering as she looks for it.*) Damn the knife, damn them
>   all and the devil who brought them into the world...
> BRIDEGROOM: Just forget it.
> MOTHER: Knives...guns...pistols, even the **sickle** and the **scythe**...[63]

While Johnston's preference is to neutralise specificity at the cost of reduced accuracy in his choice of agricultural instruments, this is not the solution favoured by Edwards:

> MOTHER: (*Muttering and looking for it.*) The knife, the knife... Damn
>   all of them and the scoundrel who invented them.
> BRIDEGROOM: Let's change the subject.

MOTHER: And shotguns...and pistols...even the tiniest knife...and
mattocks and **pitchforks**...[64]

Closer specificity of Lorca's agricultural instruments was similarly the
preference of Edmunds, also choosing mattocks and pitchforks,[65] as did Ted
Hughes. However in Hughes' sparse but rhythmically sonorous version, the
sequence of the order of the two instruments is changed in order to allow
'pitchforks' to further strengthen the presence of the 'i' feature:

MOTHER: The knife, the knife! Damn the knife, damn all knives,
   damn the devil who created knives.
BRIDEGROOM: Enough of that, mother.
MOTHER: And guns and pistols, even the tiniest little knife, even
   pitchforks and mattocks.[66]

A similar rhythmic flow is achieved in the translation by Langston Hughes,
reproduced below showing the building up of tension starting with the bare
one word exchange of the opening lines, then mounting:

BOY: Mama!
MOTHER: What?
BOY: I'm going.
MOTHER: Where?
BOY: To the vineyards.
MOTHER: Wait.
BOY: There's something you want?
MOTHER: Your lunch, son.
BOY: Never mind. I'll eat grapes. Give me my knife.
MOTHER: For what?
BOY: Why, to cut them!
MOTHER: A knife! Always a knife! Knives are no good, like the
   scoundrels who invented them.
BOY: Let's talk about something else, then.
MOTHER: Guns and pistols and pocket-knives, and even **spades** and
   garden forks, are no good.
BOY: You're right.
MOTHER: Anything that can split the body of a man apart – a fine-
   looking man, with a flower in his mouth, starting out to vineyards or
   his olive trees. His, handed down to him...
BOY: But stop talking about it, Mama! [67]

While in Langston Hughes' American version, Lorca's agricultural implements have been turned into 'spades and garden forks', the translation by
Dewell and Zapata, also for American audiences, has opted for 'the pitch fork
and the hoe':

MOTHER: (*Muttering as she looks for it.*) The knife! The knife! Damn
    all of them! And the monster who invented them!
BRIDEGROOM: Let's change the subject.
MOTHER: And the shotguns and the pistols and the smallest knife –
    and even **the pitchfork** and **the hoe**! [68]

The problems in translation created by the Spanish references to sharp
implements in the opening scenes of *Blood Wedding* is matched by those
presented by the closing scene of the play. As the Mother and the Bride lament
the mutual penetration of the two men, references to the knife recur, this
time in the form of repeated use of *'con un cuchillo'* (with a knife) and *'con un
cuchillito'* (with a small knife):

MADRE: *Vecinas, con un cuchillo,*
    Con un cuchillito
    En un día señalado, entre las dos y las tres,
    se mataron los dos hombres del amor.
    Con un cuchillo,
    con un cuchillito
    que apenas cabe en la mano,
    pero que penetra fino
    por las carnes asombradas,
    y que se para en el sitio
    donde tiembla enmarañada
    la oscura raíz del grito.[69]

The variation *cuchillo/cuchillito* pivots on the addition of the diminutive
ending '-ito' to the Spanish noun for 'knife', rendered in translation either as
'little', 'small' or, in some cases simply omitted. However, Spanish diminutive
suffixes may have a number of different functions: in addition to expressing
size, they are often used in order to convey an emotional tone to a word or a
phrase ranging across 'affection, endearment, contempt, irony, repugnance…'.[70]
Like Russian suffixes, which often suffer loss of emotional nuances in
translation into English (see Chapter 4), capturing the exact meaning of Spanish
diminutives often presents a challenge to the translator. A further problem in
the translation of the closing scene of Lorca's play is the interpretation of the
fourth line *'se mataron los dos hombres del amor'*. What Lorca has written
here does not lend itself to a single, unambiguous interpretation. It can either
be translated as favouring one interpretation (the translations by Graham-
Luján and O'Connell, 1955, Dewell and Zapata, 1987, Gwynne Edwards, 1987
and John Edmunds, 1997) or translated into English in a way that makes the
possibility of another interpretation more obvious (Langston Hughes, 1989,

David Johnston, 1989 and Ted Hughes, 1996). First, the passage in full in the translation by Graham-Luján and O'Connell (p. 98):

> MOTHER: Neighbours: with a knife,
> with a little knife
> On their appointed day, between two and three,
> these two men killed each other for love.
> With a knife,
> with a tiny knife
> that barely fits the hand,
> but that slides in clean
> through the astonished flesh
> and stops at the place
> where trembles, enmeshed,
> the dark root of a scream.[71]

The relevant line is dealt with very similarly by Dewell and Zapata (p. 64), Edwards (p. 92) and Edmunds (p. 64). Langston Hughes's translation, however, is less clear-cut (p. 70):

> MOTHER: Friends! With a knife, one day with a knife, between two
> and three, **two men in love killed each other**. With a knife. With a
> little knife almost too small to hold in your hand, but sharp to find its
> way through startled flesh to stop entangled in the trembling roots of
> a cry!

Johnston's translation is similarly ambiguous (p. 104):

> MOTHER: Neighbours, it was with a knife,
> just a little knife,
> that on the appointed day between two and three,
> **two men in love killed each other**.

So is the version by Ted Hughes (p. 71):

> MOTHER: Neighbours. With a knife,
> With a small knife,
> On an appointed day
> Between two and three in the morning,
> Two men who were in love
> Killed each other.
> With a knife
> With a small knife
> that hardly fits the hand
> But slides in cleanly
> Through surprised flesh
> Till it stops
> there,

In the quivering
Dark
Roots.

The opening scene of *Blood Wedding* also contains the recurring imagery that, in the critical response to the 1935 New York production of *Bitter Oleander*, earned Lorca's play the epithet 'verbal gardening'. Beautiful flowers tend to stand for the good and positive aspects of life: these are flowers that are associated with water, with fertile land in contrast to the dry, barren areas of southern Spain, and flower and water imagery are found in abundance in Lorca's plays. When the Bridegroom's mother talks of *un hombre hermoso, con su flor en la boca* (a beautiful man with a flower in his mouth), the flower here represents life and vitality, acting as a further reinforcement to *un hombre hermoso*. Although in English translation the immediate impression created may be that of emphasising male physical beauty, the expression also means 'a good example of a man, a fine man'. While not 'the language of a man, it could be the language of a woman, the mother in this case', expressing general approval not only of appearance but also of character and personality. [72] Linking men metaphorically to flowers is however not a commonly-found Anglo-American literary practice, leaving the English translator with the problem of determining the extent to which a faithful rendering of Lorca's floral symbols might result in 'nudging the audience towards the comic stereotype of Spaniards strutting around Andalusia with carnations gripped grimly between their teeth'.[73] In *Blood Wedding*, translations of the phrase veer between 'a fine-looking man with a flower in his mouth' (Langston Hughes) to 'a glorious man, an angel, his mouth like a flower' (Ted Hughes) and 'an angel of a man, in the flower of his life' (David Johnston).

Lorca, however, makes use not only of generic floral references but also of specific ones, drawing on the flowers typical of southern Spain, such as jasmine, carnations, geraniums, dahlias, poppies and roses. In *Yerma* the concluding line of the washerwomen's chorus in Scene 1, Act 2, *como un jazmin caliente tienes la risa*,[74] translates into English as 'You have laughter like hot jasmine'. The flower theme reappears again in the play when *Yerma* talks of her yearning for a child and her plea is answered by the breeze offering her *dalia de luna dormida* (dahlias of the sleeping moon).[75] The obstacle to overcome here is a culture-specific one in that a particular type of flower, in this case dahlias, has a certain set of associations in one language not matched in another. The problem presented by Lorca's expression in English translation has been discussed by David Johnston:

In terms of Spanish cultural resonance, dahlias are flowers with funereal overtones; in Britain they are faintly funny, with overtones of an Eastenders' type allotment. My solution was to turn the menace of Lorca's dahlias into 'frozen flowers of the sleeping moon', additionally helped by the assonance.[76]

By turning the specific into the generic, Johnston's translation leads English audiences to a closer understanding of an unfamiliar aspect of Hispanic culture. Other instances, however, of Lorca's use of specific floral imagery might present greater problems in English translation. Lamenting the death of her husband and her son in *Blood Wedding*, the Bridegroom's mother first compares the smell of the husband she has lost to that of carnations, then likens him and her son, also killed, to two geraniums – not likely to be the imagery chosen by an English mother wishing to describe her family as sturdy, erect and healthy. Less difficult to convey into English are the plants characteristic of the dry and barren parts of Spain. Here nothing but thistles will grow, standing for life's failures and disappointments, rather like Yerma's infertility, which moves her to liken herself to 'a dry field'.[77]

As in the work of Valle-Inclán, where opposites such as darkness versus light continually assert themselves,[78] in Lorca's plays powerful forces are pitched against each other: water stands against heat and dryness as the backdrop against which Yerma's barrenness and lack of sexuality is set; the pulsing of blood and the threat to life by the knife in *Blood Wedding*; the fascism inside the 'house' of Bernarda Alba, and the freedom from tyranny outside. As in Ibsen, these are stark contrasts, which in a less than subtle English translation may easily be perceived as bordering on melodrama by audiences more accustomed to indirectness and understatement. Directing *The House of Bernarda Alba* for the Abbey Theatre in Dublin in 1950, in addition to the use of the polarity axis, Eric Bentley astutely registered other points of contact between Ibsen and Lorca. 'Lorca's use of the Ibsenite device of a single, central metaphor that spreads itself, horizontally as it were, onto different levels of meaning. Like Ibsen, Lorca puts his central image in the title. The house is the main character of the play.'[79]

The Spanish original of *The House of Bernarda Alba*, the last play that Lorca was to write, starts and finishes with the word 'Silence!' Lorca did not, however, observe the requested silence: in the summer of 1933, when La Barraca presented *Fuente Ovejuna* (*The Sheep Well*), Lope de Vega's play on the exploitation of the peasants in Spain, Lorca removed references to Ferdinand and Isabella and dressed up his stage peasants in contemporary clothing, in order to highlight the immediate applicability of the issues of the play. His social commitment did not weaken, and three years later, while putting the finishing touches to *The House of Bernarda Alba*, in an interview on 10 June 1936, Lorca stressed the importance of the social mission of the theatre, as he had been known to do with increasing frequency. The words he chose to express his political involvement echo the language of his plays, his use of binary oppositions with their resulting, strong emotional impact, his stark imagery, and his floral symbolism:

> At this dramatic moment in time, the artist should laugh and cry with his people. We must put down the bouquet of lilies and bury ourselves up to the waist in mud to help those who are looking for lilies.[80]

Nine days after the interview, *The House of Bernarda Alba* was completed. Less than a month later General Franco and the Falangists set about cleansing Spain of the curse of liberalism, with Lorca falling early victim to the regime.

Notes

1   Valle-Inclán, *Plays: One (Divine Words, Bohemian Lights, Silver Face)*, trans. and intro. M Delgado (London, Methuen, 1993) p. xix

2   *Ibid.* p. viii

3   J Lyon, *The Theatre of Valle-Inclán* (Cambridge, Cambridge University Press, 1983), p. 17

4   D Johnston, 'Valle-Inclán: The mirroring of esperpento', *Modern Drama*, XL1 (1), 1998, pp. 30–1

5   *Divine Words*, trans. M Delgado, *op. cit.* p. 10

6   D Johnston, 'Valle-Inclán: the meaning of form', in C-A Upton (ed.) *Moving Target. Theatre, Translation and Cultural Relocation* (Manchester, St Jerome, 2000), p. 92

7   Valle-Inclán, *Luces de Bohemia*, trans. A N Zahareas and G Gillespie, with an Introduction and commentary by A N Zahareas (Edinburgh, Edinburgh University Press, 1976), p. 38

8   *Ibid.* pp. 183–5

9   *Ibid.* p. 255

10 *Ibid.*

11 D Johnston, 'Theatre pragmatics', in D Johnston (ed.), *Stages of Translation* (Bath, Absolute Classics, 1996), p. 63

12 Valle-Inclán, *Plays: One*, *op. cit.* pp. xxxviii–ix

13 *Luces de Bohemia*, trans. A N Zahareas and G Gillespie, *op. cit.* p. 16

14 *Ibid.* p. 17

15 *Ibid.* p. 17

16 *Ibid.* p. 1

17 *Ibid.* p. 6

18 D Johnston, (2000), *op. cit.* p. 91

19 Discussed in D Johnston, (1996), *op. cit.* p. 65

20 D Johnston (1996), *op. cit.* p. 66

21 Discussed in I Gibson, *Federico García Lorca: A Life* (London, Faber and Faber, 1989), p. 21

22 *Ibid.* p. 401

23 *Ibid.* p. 336

24 *Ibid.* p. 355

25 *Ibid.* p. 357

26 P J Smith, 'Black Wedding: García Lorca, Langston Hughes and the translation of introjection', *Donaire*, 10, 1998, p. 49

27 Discussed in *ibid.* p. 50

28 García Lorca, *Bodas de sangre* (Edición de A Josephs and J Caballero, Madrid, Catedra, 1998), p. 96

29 Discussed in Handley, 'The increasing visibility of the translator: approaches to the translation of *Bodas de sangre*', *Donaire*, 11, 1998, p. 33

30 Discussed in P J Smith, *op. cit.* p. 50

31 P J Smith, *op. cit.* pp. 50–1

32 I Gibson, *op. cit.* p. 355

33 *Ibid.* p. 356

34 *Ibid.* p. 398

35 Richard Findlater, *Observer*, 4 August 1957

36 García Lorca, *Three Tragedies (Blood Wedding, Yerma, Bernarda Alba)*, trans. J Graham-Luján and R L O'Connell (New Directions, New York, 1955)

37 D Johnston, 'Translating García Lorca: the importance of voice', *Donaire*, 11, 1998, p. 55

38 G Edwards, 'Translating Lorca for the theatre: *Blood Wedding, Yerma* and *The House of Bernarda Alba*', *Donaire* 11, 1998, p. 16

39 D Johnston, (1998), *op. cit.* p. 56

40 Irving Wardle, *The Times*, 23 March 1973

41 García Lorca, *Three Plays (Blood Wedding, Yerma, The House of Bernada Alba)*, trans. M Dewell and C Zapata, with an Introduction by C Maurer (London, Penguin, 1992), p. xxviii

42 Trader Faulkner, *Guardian* 24 March 1993

43 Discussed in G Edwards, 'Lorca in the United Kingdom', *Donaire*, 10, 1998, p. 29

44 *Ibid.*

45 R Bolt, 'Interview. Translating verse plays', in D Johnston (ed.), (1996), *op. cit.* p. 255

46 G Edwards, *Donaire*, 10, *op. cit.* p. 28

47 I Gibson, *op. cit.*

48 *Ibid.* p. 404

49 *Ibid.* p. 407

50 Claire Armitstead, *Guardian*, 13 October 1992

51 S Handley, *op. cit.* p. 31

52 García Lorca, *Bodas de sangre*, *op. cit.* p. 119 (emphasis added)

53 García Lorca, *Blood Wedding and Yerma*, trans. L Hughes and W S Merwin, with an Introduction by Melia Bensussen (New York, Theatre Communications Group, 1994), pp. 31–2 (emphasis added)

54 García Lorca, *Four Major Plays* (*Blood Wedding, Yerma, The House of Bernarda Alba, Doña Rosita the Spinster*), trans. J Edmunds (Oxford, Oxford University Press, 1997), p. 26 (emphasis added)

55 García Lorca, *Plays: One* (*Blood Wedding, Doña Rosita the Spinster*), trans. and intro. G Edwards, *Yerma*, trans. P Luke (London, Methuen, 1987), p. 56 (emphasis added)

56 García Lorca, *Blood Wedding*, trans. D Johnston (Kent, Hodder and Stoughton, 1989), p. 59 (emphasis added)

57 García Lorca, *Blood Wedding*, trans. T Hughes (London, Faber and Faber, 1996), p. 27 (emphasis added)

58 P J Smith *op. cit.* pp. 48–54

59 *Blood Wedding*, trans. L Hughes, in L Hughes and W S Merwin, *op. cit.* p. xi

60 D Johnston (1998), *op. cit.* p. 57

61 *Ibid.* p. 57

62 *Ibid.* pp. 57–8

63 *Blood Wedding*, trans. D Johnston, *op. cit.* p. 30 (author's emphasis throughout notes 63–8)

64 *Blood Wedding*, trans. G Edwards, *op. cit.* p. 33

65 *Blood Wedding*, trans. J Edmunds, *op. cit.* p. 30

66 *Blood Wedding*, trans. T Hughes (1996) p. 7

67 *Blood Wedding*, trans. L Hughes, in L Hughes and W S Merwin, *op. cit.* p. 5

68 *Blood Wedding*, trans. Dewell and Zapata, *op. cit.* p. 25

69 García Lorca, *Bodas de sangre*, *op. cit.* p. 165 (emphasis added)

70 J Butt and C Benjamin *A New Grammar of Modern Spanish* (London, Edward Arnold, 1998), p. 401

71 Emphasis added to all translations of the passage discussed

72 M Paul, *Federico García Lorca: His Theatre, Use of Metaphors and Their Translation into English*, Unpublished MA Dissertation, University of Surrey, 2001, p. 36

73 D Johnston, (1998), *op. cit.* p. 58

74 García Lorca, *Yerma*, Edición de Ildefonso-Manuel Gil (Madrid, Catedra, 1998), p. 74

75 *Ibid.* p. 80

76 D Johnston, 'Theatre pragmatics', (1996), *op. cit.* p. 65

77 García Lorca, *Yerma*, *op. cit.* pp. 94–5

78 G Edwards, 'The Comedias Barbaras: Valle-Inclán and the Symbolist Theatre', *Bulletin of Hispanic Studies*, (LX), 1983, pp. 293–303

79 E Bentley, *In Search of Theater* (London, Dennis Dobson, 1954), p. 220

80 I Gibson, *op. cit.* p. 439

Chapter 9
LOST AND GAINED IN TRANSLATION

ALTHOUGH THE SUBJECT MATTER of Ibsen's plays may have reflected the concerns of the 'real' world, in early English translations the language used to express his ideas did not. At the time, translation for the stage seems to have adhered to the 'ledger principle': information left unaccounted for in the original due to the lack of equivalents in the target language was conveyed by explanations contained in footnotes, leaving problems of 'untranslatability' to be solved in performance. Also, at the time, little was known about the differences between spoken and written language; when, in 1914, the vernacular appeared on the stage in the form of Eliza Dolittle's 'kerbstone' English, it sent London audiences and critics reeling. Not infrequently, theatre practitioners were also confronted with another hurdle: it was not unknown for a translation to be of a quality that made it difficult for readers to fully understand its content (see Chapter 1).

The first known translation of *A Doll's House* was undertaken by a Danish schoolteacher by the name of T Weber. Published in Copenhagen in 1880, it was dedicated to his countrywoman, Her Royal Highness Alexandra, Princess of Wales. In Mr Weber's version, the opening dialogue between Helmer and Nora reads:

> HELMER: Has my thoughtless bird again dissipated money?
> NORA: But, Thorwald, we must enjoy ourselves a little. It is the first Christmas we need not to spare.
> HELMER: Know that we cannot dissipate.
> NORA: Yes, Thorwald; we may now dissipate a little, may we not?
> HELMER: Nora! (*Goes up to her and catches her in jest by her ear.*) Is thoughtlessness again there? Suppose that I borrowed £50 to-day, and you dissipated this sum during the Christmas week, and a tile fell down on my head New Year's eve, and I were killed –
> NORA: O fy! don't speak so badly.
> HELMER: Yes, suppose that such happened, what then?
> NORA: If such bad were to happen, it might be indifferent to me either I had debt or no...[1]

In contrast, in Michael Meyer's translation the exchange takes the following form:

> HELMER: Has my little squander bird been overspending again?

NORA: Oh, Torvald, surely we can let ourselves go a little this year! It's
    the first Christmas we don't have to scrape.
HELMER: Well, you know, we can't afford to be extravagant.
NORA: Oh yes, Torvald, we can be a little extravagant now. Can't we?
    Just a tiny bit? You've got a big salary now, and you're going to make
    lots and lots of money.
HELMER: Next year, yes. But my new salary doesn't start till April.
NORA: Pooh; we can borrow till then.
HELMER: Nora! (*Goes over to her and takes her playfully by the ear.*)
    What a little spendthrift you are! Suppose I were to borrow fifty
    pounds today, and you spent it all over Christmas, and then on New
    Year's Eve a tile fell off a roof on to my head –
NORA: (*Puts her hand over his mouth.*) Oh, Torvald! Don't say such
    dreadful things!
HELMER: Yes, but suppose something like that did happen? What then?
NORA: If anything as frightful as that happened, it wouldn't make
    much difference whether I was in debt or not.[2]

According to William Archer, 'Mr Weber' emerges as 'some gentleman who seems to have conceived that in order to write our language he had but to procure a Danish-English dictionary, look up all the words and take the first meaning that came to hand'.[3]

In one respect, Weber's translation of *A Doll's House* appears to have served a useful purpose, although somewhat different from that intended. When, in the finale, Nora informs her husband that the only way to save their marriage is if they both change, in its stiltedness, Weber's translation so impressed Harley Granville-Barker that he proposed using it as an entrance test for female applicants to drama school. If candidates succeeded in delivering Weber's line 'cohabitation between you and me would then become a matrimony' with feeling, they would have provided irrefutable proof of their talent.[4]

Granville-Barker does not appear to be the only English director finding a use for 'dreadful translations'. For Laurence Boswell, one time Artistic Director at The Gate, the London theatre dedicated to the staging of foreign drama, a translation that cannot be used by actors may nevertheless be useful in helping the director arrive at the hidden depths of a foreign play. According to Laurence Boswell:

> In terms of the process of coming to terms with the play and its meanings, what I find incredibly useful is the most dreadful translation, which I consciously seek out, the most archaic, academic, unactable, gobbledegook translation, which you can't even imagine presenting to a group of actors. Even a translation like that can lead you to a quantum leap of perception that would, otherwise, be very difficult to make.[5]

More frequently, however, poor translations do not serve such a useful purpose. Instead they may easily obscure the playwright's intentions and, as a result, invite 'adaptations', often reflecting the thinking of the adapter more closely than the ideas of the playwright. Thus, in 1884, a less than subtle German translation of Ibsen's *A Doll's House* gave rise to a play called *Breaking a Butterfly*, the result of a collaboration between Henry Arthur Jones, a young British playwright, and an Alsatian colleague, Henry Herman. In this version, Ibsen's Nora becomes Flora, the pretty wife of one Humphrey Goddard. A new character, a kindly old book-keeper named Martin Grittle, who has always loved Flora, manages to get possession of the incriminating note that Flora has written. This does not happen, however, until Flora has learnt that independent action without the wise guidance of her Humphrey can lead to disaster, and when the curtain comes down, Flora knows not to be a foolhardy wife.

In 1914, after the Censor's ban had been lifted, *Ghosts* also spawned a different English version, this time in the form of a sequel. A new play appeared called *Realities*, purportedly written by Ibsen. After a six-month stay in an asylum, Oswald's health is much improved, and the drama now gains a new momentum when after a visit to Paris, he becomes engaged to a French actress who follows him to Norway. In spite of William Heinemann, Ibsen's publisher, exposing the hoax through a letter to *The Times* presenting conclusive evidence from both George Brandes and Ibsen's son Sigurd that Ibsen never wrote such a play, on 18 February 1918 *Realities* reached the stage of the Royal Court Theatre. The play, however, met with a less than fulsome response from the London critics, all agreeing that it lacked the characteristics of Ibsen's customary writing.[6]

A more recent example of a more personal interpretation of an Ibsen play is provided by John Osborne's 1989 version of *Hedda Gabler*. Here, the adapter, working from a 'literal' translation, has succeeded in extracting an interpretation from the text that seems to accord more closely with his own thinking than that of Ibsen's. Hedda's problem, according to Osborne, is basically nothing more than the customary boredom of an upper-class female, echoing views not infrequently associated with the British playwright's own work (see Chapter 3).

Paradoxically, an adapter at one remove with no axe to grind is often able, through sheer lack of knowledge of the language in which a play has been written and the culture in which it originates, to assess objectively the aspects of 'otherness' in the work of a foreign playwright and the extent to which this needs adjusting for English audiences. Sometimes this is a more difficult task for the linguist, who is more inclined to consider it a matter of conscience to ensure that the specific cultural details of the original are all acknowledged in translation. Without a doubt, to safeguard the authenticity of the original is as crucial as the need to make the play in translation more accessible to the audience in the theatre. If the translation moves too far away from the culture of its origin, it might reduce the impact of the playwright's voice and as a result lessen the overall theatrical effect. Yet there is a fine line to be drawn between the loss of the authenticity of the original and respect for its uniqueness to the point of risking audience bewilderment.

Amongst linguists, a strategy of 'marking' has been suggested for the translation of plays such as Lorca's *Bernarda Alba, Yerma* and *Blood Wedding*. Pointing to the combination of the Spanish playwright's use of stylised language and unfamiliar cultural components, Hispanist Leo Hickey advocates an approach whereby the alien aspects of the original should be accentuated to ensure that the 'otherness' of these works is clearly acknowledged.[7] And in the words of another Lorca translator and scholar, Gwynne Edwards:

> I have always been interested in the theatre, but not as an actor – rather as an observer, an analyst of the lives and emotions which are expressed on stage, and of the language in which those emotions are expressed. This also means for me a preference for those dramatists who lay bare the emotions of the characters in a direct, no-nonsense way, devoid of the reserve and the distancing irony which is associated with so many English writers.[8]

However, Edwards goes on to qualify his statement by acknowledging that this 'affinity may be that of a Celt for an Andalusian'. Another vote in support of allowing the distinctive voice of the foreign writer to speak for him/herself comes from Joseph Farrell, translator from Italian. According to Farrell:

> First-rate writers from abroad are now more frequently heard than they were in the past but are all too often asked to keep their voices down. My own preference is for those companies – Glasgow Citizens, The Gate, Cheek by Jowl, to choose a few at random – who allow foreign writers to remain foreign and slightly strange...[9]

This voice raised in defence of bringing the audience 'abroad' to the original text is that of yet another linguist with a knowledge of the culture of the language in which the play was written.

The debate over whether the original is to be made more easily accessible to the audience or whether it should be left as foreign, at the risk of appealing only to a well-informed elite, has been raging since time immemorial (see Chapter 1). More recently, the discussion has been rekindled by the work of

Laurence Venuti, who has invoked Schleiermacher's two approaches to translation, drawing a distinction between a 'domesticating' method that brings the author back home, and a 'foreignising' method, sending the reader abroad.[10]

The domesticating method, which ensures greater public appeal, and, as a consequence, longer queues at the box-office, entails adapting the imported, foreign theatrical product. However, the extent to which it is deemed necessary for a foreign play to be acculturated has varied greatly and, at times, has been known to give the original playwright something of a surprise. In an oft-quoted incident, Christopher Hampton found himself forced to withdraw his play *The Philanthropist* from production in France after discovering that the French translator had provided it with a different ending. 'Permit me, Monsieur, to know the French audiences better than you', the translator declared in answer to Christopher Hampton's protestations. To which the British playwright replied, 'Permit me, Monsieur, to withdraw my play.'[11] A similar, outraged reaction from Dario Fo in 1979, following the West End production of *Accidental Death of an Anarchist* by Belt and Braces, is also well-documented.

From the discussion in previous chapters of the work of European playwrights on the English stage the conclusion is not difficult to draw: for a foreign playwright to find his or her own voice in translation into English is not an overnight occurrence and often entails, in the initial stages, a phase of over-domestication. This, for instance, happened to Swedish playwright Lars Norén (b. 1944), when in the early 1980s his sparse dialogue in *Courage to Kill* emerged in English translation as middle-class chit-chat.[12] Two decades later and in the 2003 Royal Court production of *Blood* (1995) where Norén applies the laws of Greek tragedy to contemporary life, the dialogue of the original was allowed to remain virtually intact in English translation. Still, although hailed by Michael Billington in his *Guardian* review of 26 September, the foreign feel of the play was not altogether to the liking of other reviewers. A similar critical fate befell Jon Fosse (b. 1959), the Norwegian playwright who makes use of a near-poetic stage language. While *Nightsongs* (1997) escaped Anglicisation in the 2003 production at the Royal Court, in English translation Fosse's language, in its simplicity, struck some as banal rather than attractively minimalist.

For writers from southern Europe, the wait to obtain an authentic voice in English translation seems to be as long. Contemporary Spanish playwrights such as Fermín Cabal (b. 1948) whose *Shoot* (1990) played at the Jermyn

Street Theatre in June 1999 and José Sanchis Sinisterra (*b.* 1940), whose *Ay, Carmela* (1989) was staged during the same period at the Riverside Studios, seem to have joined the queue of contemporary European playwrights waiting for their turn to become more familiar to English theatre audiences. The same goes for living, Italian playwrights. Giuseppe Manfridi (*b.* 1956), whose work has been produced in Canada, South America and Europe – including Finland, where the Manfridi Theatre in Helsinki is named after him – only briefly touched down in London with *Cuckoos* (1990), staged in April 2000 at The Gate in direction by Peter Hall.

The European playwrights whose plays are now considered to belong to the European canon have all had to serve their apprenticeship, and few have achieved the status of 'honorary British playwrights'. In the case of Ibsen and Chekhov, initial resistance to their introduction on the English stage was lessened by external factors working in their favour. Ibsen's *A Doll's House* arrived on the English stage at a time when the subject of feminism was an eagerly debated issue, and when the theatre had not as yet become a forum for debate about social issues. In addition there was William Archer, highly proficient in Norwegian and, as a libertarian, willing to take on the fight to get Ibsen on the English stage (see Chapter 3). In the case of Chekhov, there was also some initial help at hand: the émigré director, Theodore Komisarjevsky, saw to it that the work of the Russian dramatist was subjected to some 'Anglicising', helping to make Chekhov accessible to more than just a cultured elite (see Chapter 4).

Strindberg, in contrast, had no early spokesman advocating his cause, and, in spite of some recent successes, is still waiting to be given a fully authentic voice and to be embraced in English translation in the manner of Ibsen and Chekhov. In some cases the slow progression of breaking down the resistance to what is foreign and unfamiliar has been further impeded by the restrictions imposed by copyright law. Pirandello did not help his own cause when he entrusted the Italian actress Marta Abba with sole copyright to the English translation of some of his work, delaying the start of the gradual process of English adaptation of his plays until 1986, 50 years after his death. When, in 1995, EU legislation lengthened the period of 50 to 70 years, easy access to some of Pirandello's plays continued to be denied. A similar fate befell Lorca. In its concern to protect the Spanish dramatist's work, the insistence of Lorca's Estate on faithful, commissioned translations added years to the period it appears to take for the work of a foreign playwright to be eased into the consciousness of English theatre audiences, accustomed to plays modelled on their own literary and cultural traditions. For a long time Brecht's Estate also made it difficult for any adjustments to be made to the German playwright's work. More recently, perhaps as a result of the fall of the Berlin Wall, an indirect but serious attack on Brecht's thinking, the Estate appears to have realised that the end of Communism might also have the effect of diminishing interest in Brecht's work. This is the view put forward by David Hare, after experiencing no problems with the Brecht Estate when adapting *The Life of Galileo* for the Almeida Theatre in 1994.[13] Nor did the National Theatre find it difficult three years earlier when it commissioned an English version of *The Resistible Rise of Arturo Ui* from Ranjit Bolt. Representatives of the Estate asked to come and see Bolt's other translations, but once they had seen them they were happy for work to carry on, even without submission of the final text for approval.[14] In the early days, however, the obstacles placed in the way of adaptation of Brecht's plays added further delay to the slow-moving process of breaking down the resistance to the 'foreign' feel of the German playwright's work in English translation.

Part of the problem of staging European work in translation is the frequent treatment of the plays as if they have been written for the prevailing English acting and directorial style, something that may, in fact, present a greater problem than aspects of content. Accustomed to the naturalism of Ibsen's plays, the symbolist-influenced approach of the dramatist's later plays was bound to disappoint William Archer, the crusader for social issues to be aired in the theatre. While *Miss Julie,* Strindberg's best known play in the English-speaking world, represents naturalistic theatre at its peak – perhaps the reason for its popularity on English stages – the case of *The Father* is not as clear-cut. In his letter to Zola offering him the play, Strindberg referred to it as naturalistic, but then, writing to the father of naturalistic drama, it was in his interest to present it in this way: it was written at a time of straitened circumstances when owing to Swedish censorship, Strindberg was experiencing problems getting his plays staged in his own country. If, however, *The Father* is viewed as more expressionistic, the ranting and raving, the contempt and loathing that the Father pours over his female household may be viewed not merely as simplistic misogyny, but as forming part of an internal monologue, as Swedish expressionistic revivals of the play have shown. A similar preference for naturalistic acting has, at times, also failed to do justice to Brecht, and to Pirandello, whose lightness of touch has often been weighed down in English-speaking, more naturalistic productions. Reviews of English productions of

Lorca have also frequently pointed to the danger of stifling Lorca's dramatic poetry by overly naturalistic interpretations.

The failure to 'translate' direction and acting style may in fact have more serious implications for the reception of a foreign play than verbal mistakes in the translation of a play text. As a result of rushed planning and rehearsal schedules, mistakes often occur, and yet do not necessarily prevent a play from acquiring its place in the canon. For example, in 1949, the German director Berthold Viertel translated Tennessee Williams' *A Streetcar Named Desire* into German as *Endstation Sehnsucht* in three to four weeks, dictating to his wife from the American manuscript as she typed. The play was translated for performance purposes only, but in spite of later revisions to the production script, Viertel's subsequent corrections were never incorporated into the published version, an omission that may account for *Endstation Sehnsucht* meaning something different to a German audience than *A Streetcar Named Desire* means to American theatregoers. In one instance, Viertel's hasty translation even seems to have resulted in an interpretation of the original text as meaning the opposite of that intended. Engraved on Mitch's cigarette case are two lines from a sonnet by Elizabeth Browning:

| I shall but love thee better | *Werd ich Dich nach dem Tod* |
| after death | *Nur um so besser lieben* |

In German, however, *besser lieben*, 'to make love in a better way', has clear physical and sexual connotations, while *mehr lieben* as later amended by Viertel, more clearly conveys the sense of the deeper, genuine feeling intended in the original, hinting at a relationship based on mutual love and understanding of the kind that Blanche is looking for. Through mistranslations of this nature, a picture of German Blanche appears to have been formed which is somewhat different from that of her American counterpart. Far less vulnerable, she has not infrequently been referred to, by German critics with little sympathy for her tragic fall, as arrogant and malicious, a hypocrite and a liar.[15]

That *A Streetcar Named Desire* has retained its appeal to German audiences attests to the fact that great drama may survive in spite of mistakes in translation: the voice of Blanche, telling us of the tragic fate of an American Southern belle, is too distinct to be lost in translation. If, however, the source text offers fewer clues with only scant information about the social class or the locale which the characters inhabit, the chances are that in translation they may all come out sounding the same, little more than cardboard figures with whom English audiences would find it difficult to identify.

A speaker's voice is the outcome of the interaction of several different variables. Dialect, one such variable, reflects the particular region from which a speaker comes. Another variable is social: the way a person's speech is influenced by their background, such as social class. Finally, every speaker has an individual and personal way of using their language, their so-called idiolect. These provide everyone, including characters on stage, with an individual voice. For instance, while attending a performance of *Doña Rosita the Spinster*, Lorca's cousin Mercedes Delgado García immediately recognised that the protagonist's manner of expressing herself derived from the speech of Asquerosa.[16] In the case of Brecht's *Mother Courage*, the protagonist speaks in a language strongly coloured by her Bavarian dialect. And in his comments to his translation of *The Cherry Orchard*, Michael Frayn tells us that each of Chekhov's characters has their own distinctive voice, the result of their education, place of birth, social class or their own set of idiosyncratic speech characteristics. A governess of German extraction, Charlotta's idiolect is strongly influenced by her non-Russian linguistic background, which results in some predictable grammatical errors. This situation is cleverly used by Chekhov to his advantage by making Charlotta experience problems in remembering the use of the feminine endings in Russian, poignantly reflecting her own sexual ambivalence, one among many features easily lost in English translation.

In the case of dramatists writing in Italian, the conflict between national language and dialects in Italy has long tended to make translation into other language more difficult. In 1861, according to one estimate, the number of speakers able to use Italian could not have amounted to many more than 600,000, that is 2.5 per cent of the total population. Major Italian writers such as Pirandello had to work in a language which they did not regularly use, and the individual manner in which they grappled with language often constitutes an essential element of their achievement as writers. At one point the fight against dialects was considered central to the educational process, and schoolchildren and illiterate adults learning Italian had to suppress the use of the dialect which was their native tongue. In 1923, *Riforma Gentile* acknowledged the importance of dialects as a spontaneous form of expression, but under the centralising approach of the Fascist regime, dialects tended to be swept under the carpet as if they were a national disgrace.

In more recent years the gulf between standard and dialect Italian has been exploited deliberately in order to achieve stylistic effects on stage or in film. In his *The Gospel According to Saint Matthew*, the Italian film director Pasolini made poignant use of dialects, letting the disciples speak with a southern dialect, Caiphus in the prestige-laden Tuscan, and Christ (dubbed) with a non-identifiable stage accent. In 1964 Pasolini acknowledged that Italy had a national language, although he described it as 'a thin, bloodless language, well suited to the squalid neo-capitalist society that uses it'.[17]

In Norway, there are also different language varieties for playwrights to draw upon. In contrast to Dano-Norwegian, the use of 'New Norwegian', the language that started to develop after Norway gained independence from Denmark in 1814, is frequently associated with a particular set of values such as radical versus conservative, rural versus urban, west versus east. As a result, writers have at their disposal the linguistic means of providing information about their characters simply through choosing a New Norwegian word over a Dano-Norwegian one: although pointed in the original, it is, however, a dramatic device doomed to lose its effect in translation.

If a particular dialect or language variety is viewed as having peripheral rather than majority status, the choice of an English dialect of matching status may prove successful in translation. In Bill Findlay's Scots translation, *The Weavers*, Hauptmann's Silesian play, was given an authentic voice through the use of the contrasting linguistic features of varying degrees of genuine Scots and standard English. Matching dialect with dialect is also the approach chosen by Bill Findlay and Martin Bowman, Findlay's co-translator of a number of Quebec plays including seven plays by contemporary Montreal playwright Michel Tremblay (*b.* 1942). In his first successful play, *Les Belles-Soeurs* (*The Guid Sisters*, 1968), Tremblay turned *joual*, the stigmatised 'horse-language' of Montreal, into art, packing into the play 'virtually every expression he had ever heard his mother say'.[18] Seen as a language of the underclass, polluted in particular by Anglicisms, Tremblay's variety of French finds a fitting match in Scots, which, to many, stands in relation to standard English as does *joual* to French. The introduction of *joual* as a language variety for the stage has also succeeded in broadening the translatability of the non-standard language variety of some Anglo-American plays into French. Whereas the elevated, literary language of the French stage has been known to create problems for the translation of the vernacular language used by Tennessee Williams, Eugene O'Neill and Edward Albee, the use of *joual* has successfully helped to provide the American playwrights with a convincing French voice. In addition, it has also resulted in more earthy and down-to-earth translations of the European canon such as Brecht's *Mother Courage*, Strindberg's *Miss Julie* and Chekhov's *Uncle Vanya*.[19]

The use of imagery, of crucial importance to language on stage, constitutes another important source of difficulty for translators. If there is a relatively high degree of social and cultural overlap between speakers of different languages,[20] concepts and images may often be transferred directly in translation. For example, British and German Euro-debates both employ metaphors related to *family, love* and *marriage,* although the particular point of view that such metaphors are used to support may be different. While the British media might comment somewhat triumphantly on any *marriage problems* of the Franco-German *couple* that might lead to a *break-up of the partnership,* giving Britain the chance to *flirt* or establish a *ménage à trois,* the German press would be more inclined to see such a development as dangerous.[21] An image may also be transferred successfully in translation if the physical environments of the speakers of different language communities are not too dissimilar. When an action is described as being only of limited significance, it may be described in English as 'only a drop in the ocean'. Since this expression is not culture specific to a particular language area but uses an image drawn from one of the four elements, it corresponds closely to metaphors already existing in a number of different languages: German *ein Tröpfchen im Meer,* French *une goutte d'eau dans la mer* and Swedish en *droppe i havet.*

Other images, however, may be more culture and language specific. While Shakespeare's 'gilding the lily' may also be described as 'carrying coals to Newcastle' or 'selling fridges to Eskimos', all referring to a redundant action in English, in German the metaphor is that of 'carrying owls to Athens' (*Eulen nach Athen tragen*). Bringing wisdom to the city ruled by the goddess of wisdom is also the essence of the Greek saying, while in French, the image used is that of carrying water to the river (*porter de l'eau à la rivière*), which recurs in Norwegian as 'to cross the river to get water' (*gå over bekken etter vann*).

A type of imagery that may also create difficulties when transferred between languages is animal metaphors: a particular animal providing an image in one language may not be the same in another. For example, if in English someone is felt to have more important things to do, they may be described as having 'other fish to fry', while the French would draw on a different image and refer to 'other cats to whip' (*autres chats à frapper*). Again, in English someone may be described as behaving like 'a bull in a china shop', while a clumsy person in French is likened to a dog in a game of skittles (*un chien dans un jeu de quilles*), and in Spanish their awkward counterpart is referred to as an elephant in a china shop (*un elephante en una cacharrería*). The use of a different image but with the same sense may often be preferable to direct transfer of an alien image from a foreign culture. However, in replacing one image with another, translators may run the risk that some elements in the source text, perhaps chosen by the original author for their part in a symbolic continuity, will be lost in the translation from one language to another.

Perhaps most frequent among the images used for dramatic purposes are flowers, which in many languages serve as potent symbols. Again, what they stand for often tends to be culture specific. 'By themselves flowers have no power other than the power of men and women who protect them and take care of them,' the German-born Marxist philosopher Herbert Marcuse told American college students, garlanding him at the height of the Vietnam War, at a time when the flower-power movement represented opposition to the war effort. At the end of Act 2 of Ibsen's *Little Eyolf* it is through flowers that Asta says a last farewell to her brother Alfred. The flowers are water lilies, their beauty suggesting purity: through this symbolism, Alfred's obsession is shown as something more than just a weakness, something beautiful in its own way, but a beauty that, like the water lily, has reached the surface from the deep bottom. And it is precisely because lilies are seen as sombre religious symbols of purity, that Robert Mapplethorpe's famous photograph of a lily as a symbol becomes erotic and disturbing because the flower is traditionally seen in religious iconography rather than in homosexual art.[22] Lilies may however also say something else. On the subject of the language of floral imagery, the *Independent* of 26 March 2000 reported the dampened enthusiasm of the recipient of a beautiful bouquet of lilies, when she was informed, 'Don't you realise that they are for funerals! If you want to say to someone: "You are history", you send them a bunch of those.' In addition, the language of the lily may also be political. In April 2001, to the fury of loyalists, there were moves afoot to display lilies at Stormont Castle, plans resulting in the hasty recall of the Northern Ireland Assembly from its Easter recess. 'The lilies would have to go,' Dr Paisley's supporters thundered, the flower being a republican symbol, to be used at Easter to commemorate dead IRA terrorists. In short, the battle was between the lilies and the colour green representing the Republicans, and the red poppies and the orange of the Loyalists. But again, the political symbolism of the poppy is not confined to the Irish context: it also seems to function in a similar capacity in other more distant parts of the world. Refusing to remain silent on the eve of her appearance in the Delhi Supreme Court, Arundhati Roy, the Booker prize-winner for *The God of Small Things*, concluded: 'It's dangerous to be a tall poppy in India today'.[23]

Hyacinths too seem to offer varying images in different languages. In Sweden, at the time of Strindberg, they were associated with death and funerals, as illustrated by the Young Lady in *The Ghost Sonata*, languishing in the Hyacinth Room. In more recent times, in Italy hyacinths seem to be viewed as representing prosperity.[24] Lilacs on the other hand, which in Italy may represent envy, in Sweden stand for light and early summer as in *Miss Julie*, where they preside prominently on the kitchen table when Julie and Jean meet. In England, the field lilac reportedly stands for humility, purple lilac for the first emotions of love and white lilac for youthful innocence. And in some English villages, a lilac branch also signifies a broken engagement,[25] potentially applicable to the situation of the protagonist of *Miss Julie*.

When in 1935 *Blood Wedding* opened in New York as *Bitter Oleander*, Lorca's play was likened to a seed catalogue. Although Lorca's work has its roots in Andalucia and Strindberg's plays originated in northern Europe, both playwrights derived their inspiration from mainly non-industrialised settings. As a result, flower imagery figures prominently in the work of the Spanish as well as the Swedish playwright, but the choice of flower is rarely random: the selection of the flower image is often sensitive to the fabric of the individual play. In Strindberg's *Easter*, the daffodil represents the coming of light after a winter of physical and spiritual darkness. If replaced by a lily, as has often been the case in English-speaking productions of the play, the change in flower also means a change in the language it speaks. A white lily speaks of sombre occasions, a language different from that of a sun-soaked daffodil, resulting in yet further fuel added to the well established notion of the introspective and angst-ridden Swedish playwright. This firmly entrenched association with Scandinavian 'doom and gloom' continues to be passed down and to be applied to new generations of writers: on 5 July 2001, the *Evening Standard*'s reception of the acclaimed new comedy *Together* by Swedish director Lukas Moodysson was headed 'Not gloomy but moody'. 'Young Swedish director Lukas Moodysson,' it was reported, had 'been praised by the master of Scandinavian angst, Ingmar Bergman.' And in a travel feature in the *Observer* of 21 January 2001, Arthur Smith confirmed the consensus on the subject of the lack of mirth in a cold climate, now extended to include Norway: '[A]sking myself what I knew about our host nation [Norway], I realised that the answer was confined to the melancholy playwright Ibsen, the depressive novelist Knut Hamsun and Munch's *The Scream*.'

What a theatre audience in one country is in a position to know about the people and culture of another often amounts to little more than broad generalisations and, as a result, a certain amount of cultural stereotyping is difficult to avoid. For translation for the stage, a distinction may usefully be drawn between two types of stereotyping. If a translator or director attempts to impose stereotypical features on a translated text in order to highlight the 'foreignness' of a play, and does so with insufficient subtlety, the play's characters may often be exposed to an easy laugh, as in early stagings of Italian playwrights. In addition to this type of *intercultural* stereotyping, there is a further kind used by playwrights for the purpose of social satire, as a means of highlighting aspects of their own culture or society. This *intra-cultural* form of stereotyping is often used for comic effect, as immortalised by John Cleese's bowler-hatted businessman in *Monty Python*, or the archetypical British civil servants in *Yes, Minister*. Due to global awareness of Anglo-American culture, these stereotypical English characters are all familiar to other nations and enjoy great popularity in translation into other languages.

When travelling in the opposite direction, however, the comic elements of stereotypical characters seem to fare less well in translation. For instance, in Ekdahl junior of *The Wild Duck*, Ibsen gives us a stereotypically comic daydreamer who believes himself to be a genius waiting to be discovered. Ekdahl senior, his father, is an equally comic figure, who continues to live in the past and engages in wild bear hunts among the bedraggled Christmas trees in the attic. In its use of such stereotypes, which are easily recognisable to Norwegians, *The Wild Duck* mixes comedy with tragedy to a considerably greater extent than is immediately obvious in many English translations of Ibsen's play.

However, the laughter arising from stereotyping in its inflated, parodied form constitutes only one type of humour. In addition there are many others, as generated and determined by the culture in which they are found. Nevertheless, critical reviews of European plays in English translation often seem to suggest that the humour of a foreign play should be of the kind favoured by the receiving culture. In his review of 19 February 2002, the *Guardian* theatre critic decried the lack of 'wit' in the Lyric production of *Feast of Snails* starring David Warner:

> Now [David] Warner returns to the London stage, after 30 years, as another money-loving tycoon in this seriously weird Icelandic import from Olaf Olafsson; but I spent much of the endless 100-minute evening hungering not for a feast of snails but for one iota of Shaw's subversive wit.

The expectations here on the part of one member of the audience, no doubt shared by many others, appear to have been for verbal 'wit', closely linked to the use of puns and word games, both notoriously difficult to transfer from one language to another.

While the success of jokes in translation for the stage is usually most at risk if the humour is exclusively verbal, other categories of humour may travel with greater ease. One category, that of 'aggressive humour', appears to be found in most Western societies; it is represented by the 'ethnic joke'. Just as in the UK the Irish are often the butt of 'underdog' jokes, in Australia it is the New Zealanders, in the United States the Poles and the Italians, in Canada the Newfoundlanders, in Sweden the Norwegians and Finns, in Greece the Pontians (the Greeks living by the Black Sea), in the Netherlands it is the Belgians and in France it is the Belgians as well as the Swiss.[26] With migration, new ethnic, minority groups are constantly being formed, followed by new ethnic jokes which seem to fulfil the function of making a larger group of people feel superior to another, smaller one. As the feeling giving rise to this type of humour is universal, it can be transferred and, if need be, replaced in translation into another language with similar less locally-based references.

Less easy to transfer, however, is the humour found in different types of wordplay such as malapropisms and spoonerisms. These involve the confusion of words to comical effect as in Sheridan's *The Rivals*, where Mrs Malaprop refers not to an 'alligator' but an 'allegory' on the banks of the River Nile. A more recent example was provided by a speaker at the 2002 Conservative Party conference paying respect not to the 'revered' or 'venerable' Iron Lady but the 'veneered' Margaret Thatcher. Spoonerisms on the other hand derive their name from the Reverend Spooner, the Dean and Warden of New College, Oxford, around the turn of the century, who, when proposing a toast, raised his glass, not to 'the dear old queen' but to 'the queer old Dean'. While malapropisms involve the incorrect use of similar sounding words, spoonerisms involve the inadvertent transposition of sounds, in the case of the Dean's toast, the consonants 'd' and 'q'. Although semantically both sentences will probably need to be replaced by different examples in translation, malapropisms and spoonerisms are both known to exist among speakers of other languages and do not defy ingenious translation solutions. One example of the use of such humour is found in *The Wild Duck* where, in Norwegian, Gina shows her lack of education through her use of malapropisms, which are not always captured successfully in English translation.

Other forms of wordplay, however, are more difficult to transfer from one language to another. Instances of homophony where two identical-sounding words have different meanings often cause considerable problems in translation. A study of one English television sitcom series subtitled into Danish showed a loss of approximately 50 per cent of the humour achieved through this form of wordplay.[27] Another example, from the subtitling of a full-length feature film, clearly illustrates the problems confronting the translator. In *The Big Chill*, a group of friends reunite for a weekend following the funeral of one of their college friends. During the course of the evening, one of the female characters, now a successful career woman, approaches one of the men with the request that he fathers her child. In response to his question, 'Why me?', she answers, 'You've got good genes,' to which Kevin Kline, as the chosen candidate for the role, responds by looking down, puzzled, at his 'jeans'. For this joke to work in translation is clearly against the odds: it can only happen if the language into which the line is translated happens to have identical sounding words for 'genes' and 'jeans'. Another form of wordplay, equally difficult to transfer in translation, takes the form of replacing well-known allusions with almost identical sounding words and expressions. This type of joke turns expressions such as 'the days of wine and roses' into 'the days of whine and noses', the description of the drug-taking past of Tara Palmer-Tomkinson in an interview with the It girl in the *Observer* of 20 October 2002.[28]

As this is the type of humour with which English audiences are familiar and which they are inclined to expect, puns and wordplay are not infrequently injected when foreign plays are adapted for performance in English. In some cases, this approach has been raised to the status of a virtual art form. In providing the plays by European playwrights with English verbal wit to compensate for loss in translation, Tom Stoppard emerges as the foremost exponent of the technique, as vividly demonstrated by his English reworking of *Einen Jux will er sich machen*. In 1981, Stoppard successfully transformed this comedy by Johann Nestroy (1801–62), written in Viennese dialect with satirical and comic songs interwoven between the scenes, into *On the Razzle*. Below, in a scene from Act 1, Zangler, the prosperous proprietor of a provision emporium, and his assistant, Sonders, in love with Zangler's niece Marie, have the following exchange:

ZANGLER: Sonders!
SONDERS: Herr Zangler!
ZANGLER: Unhand my foot, sir!
SONDERS: I love your niece!
ZANGLER: (*Outraged.*) My *knees*, sir?
(*Mollified.*) Oh, my *niece*.
(*Outraged.*) Well, my niece and I are not to be prised apart so easily, and nor are hers, I hope I make my meaning clear?[29]

The ambiguity derived from the wordplay (knees/niece) amply demonstrates how the local humour of the original Viennese text has been replaced by the verbal wit more customarily found on the English stage. What has been lost in translation has been compensated for through gains in adaptation.

Another area where loss is inevitably incurred in translation into English is the European pronominal system of address, where the practice still prevails of making use of a formal/informal form of address such as *tu/vous* in French, the so-called T/V distinction (see for instance Chapters 3, 5 and 8). In Early Modern English, the distinction could be established through the use of the two pronominal forms thou/you. In, for instance, *As You Like It*, the complex relationship that exists between Celia and Rosalind, friends and cousins, is portrayed by Shakespeare through the varying choice of personal pronouns with which they address each other.[30] More recently, attention has been drawn to the fact that the pronouns of address in Early Modern English are likely to have fulfilled other functions in addition to those of conveying 'expressive' or 'attitudinal' overtones. They might also have served to mark in-group or out-group relations in the negotiations of social identities.[31]

According to Brown and Gilman, whose linguistic study of the pronouns of address in European languages first attracted attention to the subject, the use of the plural pronoun in Latin might have started as a form of address to the emperor. At the time the ruler of the Eastern Empire was based in Constantinople, while the ruler of the West was presiding in Rome; the use of the plural *vos* might be interpreted as meaning that everything proposed to one would by implication also be put to the other.[32] The practice of addressing someone in a superior position with the plural form of a pronoun and receiving an answer back in the plural may also be viewed simply as a well-established manifestation of power, aptly illustrated by Mrs Thatcher's announcement following the birth of her grandchild that 'we have become a grandmother'.

The extent to which European playwrights during the latter part of the nineteenth century drew their inspiration from translations of Shakespeare, and his effective use of the switch in pronominal address on stage, would be an interesting avenue to explore. In Strindberg's *Miss Julie*, the device is used throughout the play to mark the shift of power between the two contestants, Julie and Jean, and, to an extent, Kristin. (There are other signs of Shakespearean influence on Strindberg, such as quotes and use of flower imagery.) The pronominal switch is also found in Ibsen, in a number of plays including *A Doll's House* and *Hedda Gabler*. Among the Russian literary giants of the epoch, not predominantly dramatists, instances of the practice of pronominal switching between *ty* and *vy* as a means of expressing a no-longer-existent nineteenth-century social structure, illuminate discriminations involving age, generation, sex, kinship status, group membership, judicial and political authority as well as emotional solidarity. During a conversation, sudden changes in the use of pronouns may serve to illustrate speakers adjusting to each other emotionally, socially and culturally. In, for instance, *Anna Karenina*, generations of English readers will never know that Tolstoy had Kitty vacillating between using T and V to Levin until their wedding day, or that Dolly addressed Oblonsky with V while she felt estranged from him because of his infidelity. On a particular occasion when she breaks the practice and addresses him with T, the reader's attention is drawn to the effect that this has on Oblonsky, although Dolly immediately resumes the use of V for the remainder of the period of their estrangement.[33] In Italian, the pronominal switch is used to dramatic effect by Pirandello in his best-known play *Six Characters in Search of an Author* to reflect the stepdaughter's changing attitude in her relationship with her father.

Observance of the T/V distinction in social intercourse appears to have been preserved to a greater extent in French than in, for instance, the Scandinavian languages, leaving it as a device still available for use by French writers. Its loss in translation into English has been commented upon with reference to twentieth-century French playwrights such as Marguerite Duras, as well as in other everyday situations. In the run-up to the French presidential election in the spring of 2002, the husband-wife teams of Bernadette and Jacques Chirac, and Sylviane Agacinski and Lionel Jospin, came under public scrutiny. In addition to comments related to Madame Chirac's staunch loyalty to her husband in the face of multiple sleaze allegations and rumours of extramarital affairs, the *Guardian* of 2 March 2002 also saw it as important to report on the now presidential couple's practice of referring to each other as *vous*. In Germany, language textbooks printed thirty years ago provide the information that the use of the informal *Du* is confined to children and the intimacy of family life. Although this is no longer absolutely true, in 1998, Hollywood films were reportedly dubbed into German with lovers addressing each other with *Sie*, the formal pronoun of address, with the cut-off point and a switch to the informal *Du* only triggered by the consummation of their passion.[34]

Also indicative of interpersonal attitudes between speakers and equally problematic for the translator are the monosyllabic words used in many European languages to invest a declarative statement with a set of wide-ranging, subtle nuances. Often the same word can be used to express a range of different, emotional attitudes. In German for instance, the word *denn* may convey astonishment, as in: *Bist du **denn** schon in London gewesen?* (Have you already been to London?). Although in English surprise expressed may be conveyed through the use of intonation, this option is obviously ruled out in a translated play text. On other occasions, however, *denn* may be used to slightly alter the basic meaning of a question to inject doubt, as in: *Kommst du **denn**?* (Are you coming?). In English, this may be conveyed through turning the question into a negative: 'Aren't you coming?' But it is also possible to add yet a further shade of meaning through the use of *wohl*: *Kommst du **denn** **wohl**?* The question now not only expresses doubt, but the presence of *wohl* has further added a note of personal concern and involvement on the part of the speaker.[35]

Modal particles of this kind as exemplified here in German are also used in other Germanic languages. In the case of Swedish, a corpus-based study of five English translations of Strindberg's *Miss Julie* showed *ju* to be the most frequently occurring particle, with *nog* in second position, closely followed by *väl*, as used by Jean to Kristin:

> JEAN: *Du är **väl** inte svartsjuk på henne.*
> You are **väl** not jealous of her.[36]

In translation by Elizabeth Sprigge Jen's line reads:

> JEAN: You're not jealous of her, surely?[37]

Consultation of a bilingual dictionary listing one-word equivalents would have yielded 'surely', a word that might have belonged to the linguistic register of Miss Julie but is less likely to have been used by someone in Jean's social position. Instead, in Kenneth McLeish's translation the negated statement has been turned into the affirmative, providing a forceful and actable line:

> JEAN: You're jealous.[38]

In other cases, a modal particle left untranslated may also leave nuances of the original untransferred from the source language. In the case of *ju*, this often results in the sentiments of anxiety and insecurity expressed in the original turning into assertive statements in English translation. For instance, in the Swedish original of Ingmar Bergman's *Scener ut ett äktenskap* (*Scenes from a Marriage*, 1974),[39] Marianne, the female protagonist, is considerably more hesitant and lacking in self-confidence in her relationship with her husband Johan, about to leave her for another woman, than she appears in English:

> MARIANNE: *Du skulle **ju** inte komma förrän i morgon.*

You weren't coming until tomorrow. [40]

Transferring the meaning of *ju* in translation, the original lends itself more closely to an interpretation such as:

MARIANNE: But I thought you weren't coming until tomorrow.

In a study of Ibsen's *An Enemy of the People* in the original Norwegian, *da* was shown to be a frequently occurring particle in the play.[41] In a comparison of different English traditions, the favoured solution proved to be the introduction of an exclamation mark to indicate the need for some form of emphasis. In James McFarlane's 1960 translation, Stockmann's daughter says to her mother:

PETRA: *Nej men mor **da**, – hvor kan du snakke slig?*
No, mother ***da***, how can you talk like that?
Oh, Mother! How can you say such a thing? [42]

Occurring even more frequently than *da* is *jo*, which similarly invites different translations into English. *Han gjør det* jo can express surprise, as in 'He's doing it after all', or correction, as in 'He's doing it, so you're wrong'. While *Han er her* simply provides the information that 'He is here', *Han er* jo *her*, may suggest an additional, 'I'm pleased to see' or 'as you ought to know' or a number of other renderings, depending on context. The word *jo* in Norwegian has in fact proved to be such a difficult word to translate that in the great majority of cases, English translations of *A Doll's House* have simply left it untranslated. In William Archer's translation, only twelve instances of Nora's *jo* were given explicit equivalents, in James McFarlane's fifteen and in Michael Meyers' six.[43] Still, it is nevertheless a word of crucial importance in the original. Overtaken by anxiety because of her money problems and her secret debt, Nora's repeated use of *jo* reflects her worried state of mind and is indicative of her need to persuade herself that in the end everything will work out.[44]

More recently, the study of the translation of a different type of particle has started to attract attention. Discourse particles such as 'oh', 'well', 'now' may express attitudes or emotions and need to be interpreted by the translator in accordance with their context. In Norwegian, *å*, corresponding to English 'oh', occurs with striking frequency in Nora's language. According to one calculation, Nora says it 82 times while Hedda Gabler only uses it 30 times. But then Nora is close to euphoria about her husband's sudden prosperity while Hedda's unwanted pregnancy makes her view the world through gloomy eyes. There is in fact evidence that Ibsen was concerned to ensure that the emotional signifier *å* was closely associated with Nora's language: a study of the printed version of Nora's penultimate speech shows the exclamatory *akk* of an earlier version carefully replaced by *å*.[45]

The loss of dialectal features, metaphors and humour, as well as language-specific characteristics such as the T/V distinction or the use of different particles to turn a straightforward statement into a more emotionally nuanced exchange, all interact to render work in translation much blander than plays originally written in English. In an attempt to compensate for the loss incurred, earlier English versions of European plays often added colour through stereotyping. In Italian plays, the accent convention ruled, in Lorca productions flamenco music was considered a necessary ingredient, while Russian plays gained additional Slavonic flavour through Cossack dancing. In the staging of French plays, on the other hand, English familiarity with French language and culture has tended to minimise the degree of acculturation required. However, during the last few decades, plays in translation from other European languages have similarly been allowed to remain relatively unadapted, showing fewer signs of Anglicisation. Not infrequently, the English version has been prepared by an English playwright, but increasingly without the culture-specific characteristics previously thought to be necessary ingredients.

A playwright who has produced a number of successful, moderately acculturated English versions of plays written by European playwrights, is Nick Dear. An adapter of *Le Bourgeois Gentilhomme* after Molière in 1992 for the National, *A Family Affair* by Ostrovsky in 1988 for Cheek by Jowl and, in 1999, Maxim Gorky's *Summer Folk*, again for the National, Nick Dear has described the number of translations which sprang up in the late 1960s and early 1970s partly as an answer to the dearth of new writing. 'If the English theatre was in crisis, engaging in dialogues with the dead at that time, as Stafford-Clark said, was a way of broadening a repertoire when there was very little theatre about.' Dear has also drawn attention to two other factors: first, the adaptation for the stage of the nineteenth-century European novel, starting with the Royal Shakespeare Company staging of *Nicholas Nickelby* and a large audience desire for a good story; second, the link between the rise of the translator/adapter and the version, which came to prominence in the mid- to late-1980s, directly linked to the years of the Thatcher government. Finding themselves without subsidy, theatres were forced out into the market place, and in order to sell tickets the quick response was often, 'Let's do a new adaptation of something', rather than finding an original work with the more uncertain prospect of selling tickets.[46] Although this shift in approach might need to be viewed within the framework of the social changes of the 1980s, the last few decades have continued to show evidence of a growing interest in European plays as confirmed by the National Theatre Platform Papers of 1992, in which the topic chosen for discussion was translation. In his interview with the translator Ranjit Bolt, Giles Croft, National Theatre literary manager at the time, opened the session by referring to the increasing number of productions of European drama in English translation since the middle of the 1980s. At the end of the interview, among Bolt's concluding remarks was his observation that 'England is beginning to discover foreign drama'.

In 1972, the United Kingdom joined what is now known as the European Union. In May 2004, the membership of the EU was enlarged to include 25 member states. Together with the sophistication of communications and the growth of globalisation in business and culture, this is now beginning to open up Europe as never before. Although the national languages of the different European member states may remain well known only to a few, the emergence of English as the global language and the *lingua franca* of Europe will increasingly provide access to the life and culture of individual nations. For contemporary European playwrights the chances seem better than ever before that their work will arrive on the English stage during the course of their own lifetime.

Notes

1   M Egan (ed.), *Ibsen: The Critical Heritage*, (London, Routledge, 1972), pp. 134–5

2   Henrik Ibsen, *A Doll's House*, trans. M Meyer, with Commentary and Notes by Non Worrall (London, Methuen, 1982), p. 24

3   Archer, quoted in M Egan (ed.), *op. cit.* p. 67

4   Discussed in G Ackerman, *Ibsen and the English Stage 1889–1903* (New York and London, Garland Publishing, 1987), p. 28

5   L Boswell 'Interview. The director as translator', in D Johnston (ed.), *Stages of Translation* (Bath, Absolute Classics, 1996), p. 147

6   G Ackerman, *op. cit.* p. 171

7   L Hickey, 'Pragmatic comments on translating Lorca', *Donaire*, 11, 1998, pp. 47–60

8   G Edwards, 'Translating Lorca for the theatre: *Blood Wedding*, *Yerma* and *The House of Bernarda Alba*', *Donaire*, 11, 1998, p. 15

9   J Farrell, 'Servant of many masters', in D. Johnston (ed.), *op. cit.* p. 55

10 L Venuti, *The Translator's Invisibility* (London, Routledge, 1995), pp. 19–20

11 *Platform Papers I: Translation* (London, National Theatre, 1992), p. 117

12 G Anderman, 'A funny thing happened on the way to the production. Some thoughts on translating drama', *Swedish Book Review*, (1), 1984, pp. 33–9

13 'David Hare: Interview: Pirandello and Brecht', in D. Johnston (ed.), *op. cit.* p. 139

14 *Platform Papers I: Translation, op. cit.* pp. 36–7

15 O Zuber, 'Problems of propriety and authenticity in translating modern drama', in O. Zuber (ed.), *The Languages of Theatre. Problems in the Translation and Transposition of Drama* (Oxford, Pergamon Press, 1980), pp. 96–102

16 I Gibson, *Federico García Lorca: A Life* (London, Faber and Faber, 1989), p. 406

17 A L Lepschy and G Lepschy, *The Italian Language Today* (London, Routledge, 1988), p. 32

18 M Bowman, 'Scottish horses and Montreal trains. The translation of vernacular to vernacular', in C-A Upton (ed.), *Moving Target. Theatre Translation and Cultural Relocation* (Manchester, St Jerome, 2000), p. 27

19 A Brisset, 'The search for a native language: translation and cultural identity', in L Venuti (ed.) *The Translation Studies Reader* (London, Routledge, 2000), pp. 342–75

20 G Lakoff, 'The contemporary theory of metaphor', in A Ortony (ed.), *Metaphor and Thought*, (Cambridge, Cambridge University Press, 1993), pp. 202–51

21 A Musolff, 'Cross-language metaphors: parents and children, love, marriage and divorce in the European family', in J Cotterill and A Ife (eds.), *Language Across Boundaries* (London, BAAL in association with Continuum, 2001), pp. 119–34

22 A C Grayling, *Independent on Sunday*, 15 April 2001

23 *Independent*, 6 March 2002

24 P Newmark, 'Notes on floriography or the language of flowers', *The Linguist*, 40(5), 2001, pp. 144–5

25 *Ibid.* p. 145

26 C Davies, *Jokes and their Relation to Society* (Mouton de Gruyter, Berlin, 1998), pp. 11–25

27 H Gottlieb, 'You got the picture? On the polysemiotics of subtitling wordplay', in D Delebaslita (ed.), *Essays on Punning and Translation* (Manchester, St Jerome, 1997), p. 216

28 E Ferguson, 'The Powder and the Glory', *Observer Review*, 20 October 2002

29 J Nestroy, *On the Razzle*, version T Stoppard (London, Faber and Faber, 1981), p. 10 (emphasis added)

30 A McIntosh, '*As you like it*: a grammatical clue to character', *Review of English Literature*, 4(2), 1963, pp. 68–81

31 C Calvo, 'Pronouns of address and social negotiation in *As You Like It*', *Language and Literature*, 1(1), 1992, pp. 5–27

32 R Brown and A Gilman, 'The pronouns of power and solidarity', in J Laver and S Hutcheson (eds.) *Communication in Face to Face Interaction* (Harmondsworth, Middlesex, Penguin, 1960), pp. 104–5

33 J Lyons, 'The pronouns of address in *Anna Karenina*; the stylistics of bilingualism and the impossibility of translation', in S Greenbaum, G Leech and J Svartvik (eds.) *Studies in English Linguistics for Randolph Quirk* (London, Longman, 1980), pp. 235–49

34 Imre Karacs, *Independent*, 7 August 1998

35 For further discussion of particles in German, see D Nehls, 'German modal particles rendered by English auxiliary verbs', in H Weydt (ed.), *Sprechen mit Partikeln* (Berlin, De Gruyter, 1989), pp. 282–92

36 G Gustafsson, *'Ju', 'nog' and 'väl' – Swedish Attitudinal Adverbs in English Translation. A Corpus Study of Five Translations of* Miss Julie *by August Strindberg*, Unpublished MA dissertation, University of Surrey, 1997

37 *Six Plays of Strindberg*, trans. E Sprigge (Garden City, NY, Doubleday & Company, 1955), p. 103

38 August Strindberg, *Miss Julie*, trans. and intro. K McLeish (London, Nick Hern Books, 1995), p. 38

39 Ingmar Bergman, *Scener ur ett äktenskap* (Stockholm, P A Norstedt & Söners Förlag, 1973), p. 77

40 Ingmar Bergman, *The Marriage Scenarios*, trans. Alan Blair (New York, Random House, 1973), p. 82

41 A Howden, *Norwegian Particles in English Translation: A Contrastive Analysis*, Unpublished MA dissertation, University of Surrey, 1999, p. 24

42 Discussed in *ibid.* pp. 27–8

43 K Smidt, 'Idiolectic characterisation in *A Doll's House'*, *Scandinavica*, 41(2), 2002, pp. 191–206

44 *Ibid.*

45 *Ibid.*

46 'Nick Dear: Interview. Translation as conservative writing' in D Johnston (ed.), *op. cit.* p. 279

BIBLIOGRAPHY

Aaltonen, S *Acculturation of the Other. Irish Milieux in Finnish Drama Translation* (Joensuu , Joensuu University Press Oy, 1996)

Ackerman, G *Ibsen and the English Stage 1889–1903* (New York and London, Garland Publishing, 1987)

Aitchison, J *The Articulate Mammal. An Introduction to Psycholinguistics*, 3rd edition (London, Unwin Hyman, 1989)

Akerholt, M B 'Henrik Ibsen in English translation', in O Zuber (ed.) *The Languages of Theatre. Problems in the Translation and Transposition of Drama* (Oxford, Pergamon Press, 1980), pp. 104–20

Amundsen Le Maire, R 'Ibsen's use of the pronouns of address in some of his prose plays', *Scandinavica*, 20 (1), 1980, pp. 43–61

Anderman, G 'A funny thing happened on the way to the production. Some thoughts on translating drama', *Swedish Book Review*, 1, 1984, pp. 33–9

Anderman, G 'Finding the Right Word', in K Malmkjaer (ed.) *Translation and Language Teaching. Language Teaching and Translation* (Manchester, St Jerome, 1998), pp. 39–48

Archer, C *William Archer: Life, Work and Friendships* (New Haven, Yale University Press, 1931)

Arsan, G A 'Six Characters at the National Theatre', *Yearbook of the British Pirandello Society*, 7, 1987, pp. 32–5

Barker, C 'Right you are (if you could only think so)', *Yearbook of the British Pirandello Society*, 1, 1981, pp. 26–34

Barker, C 'La drammaturgia britannica fra le due guerre', in Enzo Scrivano (a cura di) *Pirandello e la drammaturgia fra le due guerre* (Agrigento, Edizione Centro Nazionale di Studi Pirandelliani, 1985)

Barthes, R 'Seven photo models of *Mother Courage*', *Tulane Drama Review*, 12 (1), 1967, pp. 44–53

Bassnett, S and Lefevere, A (eds.) *Constructing Cultures* (Clevedon, Multilingual Matters, 1998)

Bassnett, S and Lorch, J (eds.) *Luigi Pirandello in the Theatre. A Documentary Record* (Philadelphia, Pa, Harwood Academic Publishers, 1993)

Bassnett, S 'Still trapped in the labyrinth: further reflections on translation and theatre', in S Bassnett and A Lefevere (eds.) *Constructing Cultures* (Clevedon, Multilingual Matters, 1998) pp. 90–108

Bassnett, S 'Pirandello and translation', *Journal of the Society for Pirandello Studies*, 20, 2000, pp. 9–17

Bassnett-McGuire, S 'Pirandello's British première: *Lazzarro*', *Yearbook of the British Pirandello Society*, 2, 1982, pp 28–31

Bassnett-McGuire, S *Luigi Pirandello* (London, Macmillan, 1983)

Bassnett-McGuire, S 'Ways through the labyrinth: Strategies and methods for translating theatre texts', in T Hermans (ed.) *The Manipulation of Literature. Studies in Literary Translation* (London, Croom Helm, 1985), pp. 87–103

Becker, G *Documents of Modern Realism.* (Princetown University Press, 1963)

Bentley, E *In Search of Theater* (London, Dennis Dobson, 1954)

Bergfeldt, P *Insiderisms in Pinter. Problems in the Translation of Pinter's Formulaic Expressions into Swedish*, unpublished PhD dissertation, University of Surrey, 2003

Bergman, I *Scener ur ett äktenskap* (Stockholm, P A Norstedt & Söners Förlag, 1973)

Bergman, I 'Scenes from a Marriage', trans. A Blair, in *Ingmar Berman: The Marriage Scenarios* (New York, Random House, 1973), pp. 7–202

Billington, M *Peggy Ashcroft.* (London, John Murray, 1988)

Bolt, R *Platform Papers I Translation.* (Royal National Theatre, 1992)

Bolt, R 'Interview. Translating verse plays', in D Johnston (ed.) *Stages of Translation* (Bath, Absolute Classics, 1996), pp. 249–61

Boswell, L 'Interview. The director as translator', in D Johnston (ed.) *Stages of Translation* (Bath, Absolute Classics, 1996), pp. 145–52

Bowman, M 'Scottish horses and Montreal trains. The translation of vernacular to vernacular', in C-A Upton (ed.) *Moving Target. Theatre Translation and Cultural Relocation* (Manchester, St Jerome Press, 2000), pp. 25–33

Brandell, G *Drama i tre avsnitt* (Stockholm, Wahlström & Widstrand, 1971)

Bratus, B V *The Formation and Expressive Use of Diminutives. Studies in Modern Russian Language*, 6 (Cambridge, Cambridge University Press, 1969)

Brecht, B *Seven Plays* (*In the Swamp*, *A Man's a Man*, *Saint Joan of the Stockyards*, *Mother Courage*, *Galileo*, *The Good Woman of Setzuan*, *The Caucasian Chalk Circle*), ed. and trans. E Bentley (New York, Grove Books Inc, 1961)

Brecht, B *Brecht on Theatre*, ed. and trans. John Willett (London, Methuen, 1964)

Brecht, B *Mutter Courage und Ihre Kinder* Berlin, Suhrkamp Verlag, 1963)

Brecht, B *Mother Courage*, trans. H R Hays (New York, New Directions, 1941)

Brecht, B *Mother Courage and Her Children*, trans. J Willett, with commentary and notes by Hugh Rorrison (London, Methuen, 1983)

Bredsdorff, E *Sir Edmund Gosse's Correspondence with Scandinavian Writers* (Copenhagen, 1960). Discussed in O Lausund, 'Edmund Gosse: Ibsen's first prophet to English readers', in I-S Ewbank, O Lausund and B Tysdahl (eds.) *Anglo-Scandinavian Cross-Currents* (Norwich, Norvik Press, 1999), pp. 139–58

Brisset, A 'The search for a native language: translation and cultural identity', in L.Venuti (ed.) *The Translation Studies Reader* (London, Routledge, 2000), pp. 343–75

Bristow, E K 'On translating Chekhov', *Quarterly Journal of Speech*, 52, 1966, pp 290-4

Brooker, P 'Keywords in Brecht's theory and practice of theatre', in P Thomson and G Sacks (eds.) *The Cambridge Companion to Brecht* (Cambridge, Cambridge University Press, 1994), pp. 185–200

Brown, R and Gilman, A 'The pronouns of power and solidarity', in J Laver and S Hutcheson (eds.) *Communication in Face to Face Interaction* (Harmondsworth, Middlesex, Penguin, 1960), pp. 103–27

Brusewitz, G *Guldörnen och duvorna. Fågelmotiv hos Strindberg* (Stockholm, Wahlström & Widstrand, 1989)

Brustein, R 'Foreword', *Chekhov: The Major Plays (Ivanov, The Seagull, Uncle Vanya, Three Sisters, The Cherry Orchard)*, trans. Ann Dunnigan (New York, Signet Classics, 1964)

Buchanan, R 'The modern drama and its critics', *The Contemporary Review*, 56, Dec 1889, pp. 908–25

Butt, J and Benjamin, C *A New Grammar of Modern Spanish* (London, Edward Arnold, 1998)

Calvo, C 'Pronouns of address and social negotiation in *As You Like It*', *Language and Literature*, 1 (1), 1992, pp. 5–27

Chambers, C *The Story of Unity Theatre* (London, Lawrence & Wishart, 1998)

Charteris, E *The Life and Letters of Sir Edmund Gosse* (London, Collins, 1931)

Chekhov, A *The Cherry Orchard*, adapt. R Brustein, from a translation by George Calderon (Chicago, Ivan R Dee, 1995)

Chekhov, A *The Cherry Orchard, Three Sisters, Ivanov*, trans. E, Fen (Harmondsworth, Middlesex, Penguin, 1951)

Chekhov, A *Three Sisters*, trans. E Fen (Lyme, NH, Smith and Kraus, 1951)

Chekhov, A *Plays (Ivanov, The Seagull, Uncle Vanya, Three Sisters, The Cherry Orchard, The Bear, The Proposal, A Jubilee)*, trans. and intro. E Fen (Harmondsworth, Middlesex, Penguin, 1959)

Chekhov, A *Plays (The Seagull, Uncle Vanya, Three Sisters, The Cherry Orchard)*, trans. M Frayn (London, Methuen, 1988)

Chekhov, A *The Cherry Orchard*, trans. M Frayn (London, Methuen, 1995)

Chekhov, A *Uncle Vanya*, National Theatre, version Pam Gems (London, Nick Hern Books, 1992)

Chekhov, *Three Sisters*, trans. B Friel (Loughcrew, Ireland, The Gallery Press, 1981)

Chekhov, A *The Seagull*, National Theatre, version Pam Gems (London, Nick Hern Books, 1994)

Chekhov, A *The Cherry Orchard*, version P Gill, from a literal translation by T Braun (London, Oberon Books, 1995)

Chekhov, A *The Seagull*, version P Gill, from a literal translation by H Molchanoff (London, Oberon Books, 1999)

Chekhov, A *The Cherry Orchard*, adapt. T Griffiths, from a trans. by H Rappaport (London, Faber and Faber, 1989)

Chekhov, A *The Cherry Orchard*, adapt. D Mamet from a literal trans. by Peter Nelles (London, Samuel French, 1985)

Chekhov, A *The Three Sisters*, adapt. D Mamet from a literal trans. by V Chernomordik (New York, Grove Press, 1990)

Chekhov, A *The Seagull*, trans. and intro. S Mulrine (London, Nick Hern Books, 1997)

Chekhov, A *Three Sisters*, adapt. R Nelson, from a trans. by Olgo Lifson (New York, Broadway Play Publishing, 1991)

Chekhov, A *The Seagull*, version T Stoppard (London, Faber & Faber, 1997)

Chekhov, A *Three Sisters*, trans. L Wilson (Lyme, NH, Smith and Kraus, 1984)

Clyman, T (ed.) *A Chekhov Companion* (Westport, Conn., Greenwood Press, 1985)

Cocteau, J *Les parents terribles* (Paris, Gallimard, 1938)

Cocteau, J *Les Parents Terribles (Indiscretions)*, trans. J Sams, intro. S Callow. Royal National Theatre (London, Nick Hern Books, 1994)

Davies, C *Jokes and their Relation to Society* (Mouton de Gruyter, Berlin, 1998)

De Filippo, E *Cantata dei giorni dispari*, Vol. I (Torino, Einaudi, 1957)

De Filippo, E *Filumena*, trans. T Wertenbaker (London, Methuen, 1998)

Dear, N 'Interview. Translation as conservative writing', in D Johnston (ed.) *Stages of Translation* (Bath, Absolute Classics, 1996), pp. 271–80

Decker, C *The Victorian Conscience* (New York, Twayne Publishers, 1952)

Dehn, P 'Oklahomov!', in B Lowrey (ed.) *Twentieth Century Parody American and British* (New York, Harcourt Brace, 1958)

DiGaetani, J L (ed.) *A Companion to Pirandello Studies* (New York, Greenwood Press, 1991)

Dort, B 'Crossing the desert: Brecht in France in the eighties', in P Kleber and C Visser (eds.) *Re-interpreting Brecht: His Influence on Contemporary Drama and Film* (Toronto, Cambridge University Press, 1990), pp. 90–103

Duras, M *Four Plays (La Musica (La Musica Deuxième), Eden Cinema, Savannah Bay, India Song)*, trans. B Bray (London, Oberon Books, 1992)

Durbach, E 'A century of Ibsen criticism', in J McFarlane (ed.) *The Cambridge Companion to Ibsen* (Cambridge, Cambridge University Press, 1994), pp. 233–51

Eddershaw, M *Performing Brecht. Forty Years of British Performances* (London, Routledge, 1996)

Edwards, G 'The Comedias Barbaras: Valle-Inclán and the Symbolist Theatre', *Bulletin of Hispanic Studies*, LX, 1983, pp. 293–303.

Edwards, G 'Translating Lorca for the theatre: *Blood Wedding*, *Yerma* and *The House of Bernarda Alba*', *Donaire*, 11, 1998, pp. 15–30

Edwards, G 'Lorca in the United Kingdom', *Donaire*, 10, 1998, pp. 23–30

Egan, M (ed.) *Ibsen: The Critical Heritage* (London, Routledge, 1972)

Elwin, M *Charles Reade* (London, Jonathan Cape, 1931)

Emeljanov, V *Chekhov. The Critical Heritage* (London, Routledge and Kegan Paul, 1981)

Engwall, G '"Det knastrar i hjärnan". Strindberg som sin egen franske översättare', in B Meidal and N Å Nilsson (eds.) *August Strindberg och hans översättare*. Konferenser 33. Kungl. Vitterhets Historie och Antikvitets Akadamien (Stockholm, Almqvist & Wicksell International, 1995), pp. 35–51

Esslin, M 'Brecht and the English theatre', *Tulane Drama Review*, 11(2), 1966, pp. 63–70

Esslin, M 'Pinter translated. On international non-communication', *Encounter*, 1968, pp. 45–7

Esslin, M 'Filumena', *Plays and Players*. January 28–9, 1978

Esslin, M 'Chekhov and the modern drama' in T Clayman (ed.) *A Chekhov Companion* (Westport, Conn., Greenwood Press, 1985), pp. 135–45

Even-Zohar, I 'The position of translated literature within the literary polysystem', in L Venuti (ed.) *The Translation Studies Reader* (London, Routledge, 2000), pp. 192–7

Ewbank, I-S 'Ibsen's language: literary text and theatrical context', in G K Hunter and C J Rawson (eds.) *The Yearbook of English Studies*, IX (London, Modern Humanities Research Association, 1979), pp. 102–15

Ewbank, I-S 'Ibsen on the English Stage: the proof of the pudding is in the eating', in E Durbach (ed.) *Ibsen in the Theatre* (London, Macmillan, 1980), pp. 27–48

Ewbank, I-S, Lausund, O and Tysdahl, B (eds.) *Anglo-Scandinavian Cross- Currents* (Norwich, Norvik Press, 1999)

Farrell, J 'Servant of many masters', in D Johnston (ed.) *Stages of Translation* (Bath, Absolute Classics, 1996), pp. 45–55

Ferguson, R *Henrik Ibsen. A New Biography* (London, Richard Cohen Books, 1996)

Feydeau, G *A Flea in Her Ear*, trans. and intro. K McLeish (London, Nick Hern Books, 2000)

Findlater, R *At the Royal Court* (London, Amber Lane Press, 1981)

Findlay, B 'Silesian into Scots: Gerhart Hauptmann's *The Weavers*', *Modern Drama*, XLI(1), 1998, pp. 90–104

Firth, F 'Performances of Pirandello's plays in Britain and Ireland, 1922–1999', *Journal of the Society of Pirandello Studies*, 20, 2000, pp. 75–100

Fisher, J 'An author in search of characters', in F J Marker and C Innes (eds.) *Modernism in European Drama: Ibsen, Strindberg, Pirandello, Beckett* (Toronto and London, Toronto Press, 1999), pp. 151–69

Fo, D *Accidental Death of an Anarchist*, adapt A Cumming and T Supple (London, Methuen, 1991)

Fo, D *We Can't Pay. We Won't Pay*, trans. R G Davis (London and New York, Samuel French, 1980)

Fo, D *The Pope and the Witch*, adapt. A De la Tour (London, Methuen, 1992)

Fo, D *Mistero Buffo*, trans. E Emery, ed. and intro. S Hood (London, Methuen, 1988)

Fo, D/Rame, F *Orgasmo Adulto Escapes from the Zoo*, trans. and adapt. E Parsons (New York, Broadway Play Publishing, 1984)

Fo, D *Accidental Death of An Anarchist*, adapt. G Richards from a trans. by G Hanna, with an introduction by S Hood (London, Pluto Press, 1987)

Fo, D *Can't Pay? Won't Pay!*, adapt. R Walker and B Colvill, from a trans. by L Pertile (London, Pluto Press, 1978, 1982 revised ed.)

Freeborn, R *A Month in the Country* (Albery Theatre performance programme, 1994)

Friel, B trans. *Three Sisters* (Loughcrew. Old Castle. County Meath. Ireland, The Gallery Press, 1981)

Genet, J *Splendid's*, trans. N Bartlett (London, Faber and Faber, 1995)

Genet, J *Les Bonnes, Le Balcon*, Collection Balises (Paris, Nathan, 1998)

Gibson, I *Federico García Lorca: A Life* (London, Faber and Faber, 1989)

Gilula, D 'Greek drama in Rome: Some aspects of cultural transposition', in H Scolnicov and P Holland (eds.) *The Play Out Of Context: Transferring Plays from Culture to Culture* (Cambridge: Cambridge University Press, 1989), pp. 99–109

Gottlieb, H 'You got the picture? On the polysemiotics of subtitling wordplay', in D Delebastita (ed.) *Essays on Punning and Translation* (Manchester, St Jerome, 1997), pp. 207–32

Gottlieb, V *Chekhov and The Vaudeville. A Study of Chekhov's One-Act Plays* (Cambridge University Press, 1982)

Gottlieb, V 'Chekhov in limbo: British productions of the plays of Chekhov', in H Scolnikov and P Holland (eds.) *The Play out of Context. Transferring Plays from Culture to Culture* (Cambridge, Cambridge University Press, 1989), pp. 163–85

Guest, H 'Samuel Beckett', in O Classe (ed.) *Encyclopedia of Literary Translation into English*, I (London, Fitzroy Dearborn, 2001), pp. 122–6

Gustafsson, G *'Ju', 'nog' and 'väl' – Swedish Attitudinal Adverbs in English Translation. A Corpus Study of Five Translations of* Miss Julie *by August Strindberg*, unpublished MA dissertation, University of Surrey, 1997

Hale, T 'The imaginary quay from Waterloo Bridge to London Bridge: Translation, adaptation and genre', in M Salama-Carr (ed.) *On Translating French Literature and Film*, II (Amsterdam, Rodopi, 2000), pp. 220–38.

Hall, P 'Directing Pinter', *Theatre Quarterly*, 4(16), 1974/75, pp. 4–17

Handley, S 'The increasing visibility of the translator: approaches to the translation of *Bodas de Sangre*', *Donaire*, 11, 1998, pp. 31–7

Hare, D 'Interview. Pirandello and Brecht', in D Johnston (ed.) *Stages of Translation* (Bath, Absolute Classics, 1996), pp. 137–43

Hauptmann, G *Plays*, ed. and intro. R Grimm (New York, Continuum, 1994)

Heiberg, J L/Holberg, L, *Three Danish Comedies. Heiberg: No, Holberg: Jeppe of the Hill, The Scatterbrain*, trans. M Meyer (London, Oberon Books, 1999)

Hemmer, B 'Ibsen and the realistic problem drama', in J McFarlane (ed.) *The Cambridge Companion to Ibsen* (Cambridge University Press, 1994), pp. 68–88

Heylen, R *Translation, Poetics and the Stage. Six French Hamlets* (London, Routledge, 1993)

Hickey, L 'Pragmatic comments on translating Lorca', *Donaire*, 11, 1998, pp. 47–60

Hiley, J *Theatre at Work* (London, Routledge, 1981)

Hirst, D *Dario Fo and Franca Rame* (London, Macmillan, 1989)

Hobson, H *French Theatre Since 1830* (London, John Calder, 1978)

Holderness, G (ed.) *The Politics of Drama and Theatre* (London, Macmillan, 1992)

Howden, A *Norwegian Particles in English Translation: A Contrastive Analysis*, Unpublished MA dissertation, University of Surrey, 1999

Ibsen, H *Samlade værker* (Kristiania og Kobenhavn: Gyldendalske Boghandel. Nordisk Forlag, 1907)

Ibsen, H *Hedda Gabler*, adapt. J R Baitz, from a translation by A-C Hanes Harvey, with a foreword by Susan Faludi (New York, Grove Press, 2000)

Ibsen, H *The Wild Duck*, adapt. R Brustein (Chicago, Ivan R Dee, 1997)

Ibsen, H *Hedda Gabler*, adapt. M Faber (London, Heinemann, 1966)

Ibsen, H *Hedda Gabler* (Dover Thrift Editions: New York, Dover Publications, 1990)

Ibsen, H *Four Major Plays (A Doll's House, Ghosts, Hedda Gabler, The Master Builder)*, trans. R Fjelde (New York, Signet Classics, 1965)

Ibsen, H *The Collected Works* (Vol X) *(Hedda Gabler, The Master Builder)*, trans. E Gosse and W Archer (New York, Charles Scribner's Sons, 1907)

Ibsen, H *An Enemy of the People*, trans. C Hampton (London, Faber and Faber, 1997)

Ibsen, H *Eight Plays*, trans. E Le Gallienne (New York, Mc Graw-Hill, 1992)

Ibsen, H *The Oxford IBSEN* (Vol. VI): *An Enemy of the People, The Wild Duck, Rosmersholm*, ed. and trans. J McFarlane (London, New York, Toronto, Oxford University Press, 1960)

Ibsen, H *The Oxford IBSEN* (Vol. VII): *The Lady from the Sea, Hedder Gabler, The Master Builder*, trans. J McFarlane and J Arup, intro. J McFarlane (London, New York, Toronto, Oxford University Press, 1966)

Ibsen, H *A Doll's House*, adapt. F McGuiness (New York, Dramatists Play Service, 1998)

Ibsen, H *Plays: One (Ghosts, The Wild Duck, The Master Builder)*, trans. M Meyer (London, Methuen Drama, 1980)

Ibsen, H *Plays: Three (Rosmersholm, The Lady from the Sea, Little Eyolf)*, trans. M Meyer (London, Eyre Methuen, 1980)

Ibsen, H *A Doll's House*, trans. M Meyer, with Commentary and Notes by Nan Worrall (London, Methuen, 1982)

Inverne, J *Jack Tinker. A Life in Review* (London, Oberon Books, 1997)

Jarry, A *The Ubu Plays* trans. and intro. K McLeish (London, Nick Hern Books, 1997)

Johnston, D 'Theatre pragmatics', in D Johnston (ed.) *Stages of Translation* (Bath, Absolute Classics, 1996), pp. 57–66

Johnston, D 'Translating García Lorca: the importance of voice', *Donaire*, 11, 1998, pp. 54–60

Johnston, D 'Valle-Inclán: The mirroring of esperpento', *Modern Drama*, XL1 (1), 1998, pp. 30–48

Johnston, D 'Valle-Inclán: the meaning of form', in C-A Upton (ed.) *Moving Target. Theatre Translation and Cultural Relocation* (Manchester, St Jerome, 2000), pp. 85–99

Josephson, L *Strindbergs drama Fröken Julie* (Stockholm, Almqvist & Wiksell, 1965)

Kärnell, K-A *Strindbergs bildspråk. En studie i prosastil* (Stockholm, Almqvist & Wiksell, 1962)

Kelly, L G *The True Interpreter: A History of Translation. Theory and Practice in the West* (Oxford, Blackwell, 1979)

Klimenko, S 'Who killed Hedda Gabler? Playing the evidence of discourse against the alibi of the mise en scène', *Assaph. Studies in the Theatre*, 16, 2000, pp. 27–42

Klimenko, S 'Anton Chekhov and English nostalgia', *ORBIS Litterarum. International Review of Literary Studies*, 56(2), 2001, pp. 121–37

Koon, H and Switzer, R *Eugène Scribe* (Boston, Twayne Publishers, 1980)

Labiche, E and Marc-Michel. *An Italian Straw Hat*, trans. and intro. K McLeish (London, Nick Hern Books, 1996

Lakoff, G, 'The contemporary theory of metaphor', in A Ortony (ed.) *Metaphor and Thought* (Cambridge, Cambridge University Press, 1993), pp. 205–51

Lamm, M *Strindbergs dramer*, II (Stockholm, Albert Bonniers Förlag, 1926)

Lamm, M *Det moderna dramat* (Stockholm, Albert Bonniers Förlag, 1948)

Lefevere, A (ed. and trans.) *Translating Literature: The German Tradition from Luther to Rosenzweig* (Amsterdam and Assen, van Gorcum, 1977)

Lefevere, A 'Acculturating Bertolt Brecht', in S Bassnett and A Lefevere (eds.) *Constructing Cultures. Essays on Literary Translation* (Clevedon, Multilingual Matters, 1998), pp. 109–22

Leppihalme, R *Culture Bumps. An Empirical Approach to the Translation of Allusions.* (Cleveland, Multilingual Matters, 1997)

Lepschy, A L and Lepschy, G *The Italian Language Today* (London, Routledge, 1988)

Long, J 'An Irish Seagull: Chekhov and the new Irish theatre', *Revue de Litterature Comparée*, 4, 1995, pp. 409–16

Lorca, F G *Yerma* (Edición de Ildefonso-Manuel Gil. Madrid, Catedra, 1998)

Lorca, F G *Bodas de sangre* (Edición de A Josephs y J Caballero. Madrid, Catedra, 1998)

Lorca, F G *Three Plays (Blood Wedding, Yerma, The House of Bernarda Alba)* trans. M Dewell and C Zapata, with an Introduction by C Maurer (London, Penguin, 1992)

Lorca, F G *Four Major Plays (Blood Wedding, Yerma, The House of Bernarda Alba, Doña Rosita The Spinster)*, trans. J Edmunds (Oxford, Oxford University Press, 1997)

Lorca, F G *Plays: One (Blood Wedding, Dona Rosita the Spinster, Yerma)* trans. and intro. G Edwards, *Yerma*, trans. P Luke (London, Methuen, 1987)

Lorca, F G *Three Tragedies (Blood Wedding, Yerma, Bernarda Alba)*, trans. J Graham-Luján and R O'Connell (New York, New Directions, 1955)

Lorca, F G *Blood Wedding and Yerma*, trans. L Hughes and W S Merwin, with an Introduction by M Bensussen (New York, Theatre Communications Group, 1994)

Lorca, F G *Blood Wedding*, trans. T Hughes (London, Faber and Faber, 1996)

Lorca, F G *Blood Wedding*, trans. D Johnston (Kent, Hodder and Stoughton, 1989)

Lorch, J & Taviano, S 'Producing Pirandello in England', *Pirandello Studies.Journal of the Society for Pirandello Studies*, 20, 2000, pp. 18–30

Lorch, J 'Liolà', *Yearbook of the British Pirandello Society*, 3, 1983, pp. 100–1

Lyon, J *The Theatre of Valle-Inclán* (Cambridge, Cambridge University Press, 1983)

Lyons, J, 'The pronouns of address in Anna Karenina; the stylistics of bilingualism and the impossibility of translation', in S Greenbaum, G Leech and J Svartvik (eds.) *Studies in English Linguistics for Randolph Quirk* (London, Longman, 1980), pp. 109–22

Malcolm, J *Reading Chekhov. A Critical Journey* (London, Granta, 2003)

Malmkjær, K (ed.) 'Introduction: Translation and language teaching' in *Translation and Language Teaching. Language Teaching and Translation* (Manchester, St Jerome, 1998), pp. 1–11

Marshall, G 'Duse and Ibsen in the 1890s', in I-S Ewbank, O Lausund and B Tysdahl (eds) *Anglo-Scandinavian Cross-Currents* (Norwich, Norvik Press, 1999), pp. 203–14

Maurer, W *Gerhart Hauptmann* (Boston, Twayne Publishers, 1982)

May, F 'Alfred Wareing and the production of Pirandello in the West Riding', *The University of Leeds Review*, 8(3), 1963, pp. 242–51

McFarlane, J (ed.) *The Cambridge Companion to Ibsen* (Cambridge, Cambridge University Press, 1994)

McIntosh, A '*As you like it*: a grammatical clue to character', *Review of English Literature*, 4 (2), 1963, pp. 68–81

Meidal, B '"En klok råtta måste ha många hål!" Strindberg och översättarna', in B Meidal and N Å Nilsson (eds.) *August Strindberg och hans översättare*, Konferenser 33, Kungl. Vitterhets Historie och Antikvitets Akademien. (Stockholm, Almqvist & Wiksell International, 1995), pp. 11–24

Meyer, M 'Strindberg in England', in C.R Smedmark (ed.) *Essays on Strindberg* (Stockholm, Beckman, 1966), pp. 65–73

Meyer, M 'On translating plays', *20th Century Studies*, 11, 1971, pp. 44–51

Meyer, M *Strindberg. A Biography* (New York, Random House, 1985)

Miller, A 'Ibsen and the drama of today', in J McFarlane (ed.) *The Cambridge Companion to Ibsen* (Cambridge, Cambridge University Press, 1994), pp. 227–32

Mitchell, T *File on Dario Fo* (London, Methuen, 1989)

Mitchell, T *Dario Fo. People's Court Jester* (London, Methuen, 1999)

Musolff, A 'Cross-language metaphors: parents and children, love, marriage and divorce in the European family', in J Cotterill and A Ife (eds.) *Language across Boundaries* (London, BAAL in association with Continuum, 2001), pp. 119–34

Müssener, H '"Det är synd om...": Strindberg och de tyska översättarna', in B Meidal and N Å Nilsson (eds.) *Strindberg och hans översättare*, Konferenser 33, Kungl. Vitterhets Historie och Antikvitets Akademien (Stockholm, Almqvist & Wiksell International, 1995), pp. 25–34

Nathan, G J *Since Ibsen: A Statistical Historical Outline of the Popular Theatre since 1900* (New York, Alfred A Knopf, 1939)

Nehls, D 'German modal particles rendered by English auxiliary verbs', in H Weydt (ed.) *Sprechen mit Partikeln* (Berlin, de Gruyter, 1989), pp. 282–92

Nestroy, J *On the Razzle*, version T Stoppard (London, Faber and Faber, 1981)

Newmark, P 'Notes on floriography or the language of flowers', *The Linguist*, 40(5), 2001, pp. 144–5

Nilsson, N Å *Ibsen in Russland* (Stockholm, Almqvist & Wiksell, 1958)

Northam, J *Ibsen. A Critical Study* (Cambridge, Cambridge University Press, 1973)

Ollén, G *Strindbergs dramatik* (Stockholm, Sveriges Radio, 1961)

Paul, M *Federico García Lorca: His Theatre, Use of Metaphors and Their Translation into English*, Unpublished MA Dissertation, University of Surrey, 2001

Pavis, P *Theatre at the Crossroads of Culture*, trans. Loren Kruger (London, Routledge, 1992)

Philips, J 'Marguerite Duras', in O Classe (ed.) *Encyclopedia of Literary Translation into English*, I (London, Fitzroy Dearborn, 2000), pp. 385–8

Pinter, H *Plays I* (London, Faber and Faber, 1991)

Pirandello, L *Three Plays (Sei personaggi in cerca d'autore, Enrico IV, La giara)*, ed. F Firth (Manchester, Manchester University Press, 1969)

Pirandello, L *Six Characters in Search of an Author*, trans. E Bentley (London, Penguin, 1998)

Pirandello, L *The Rules of the Game*, adapt. D Hare (London, Absolute Classics, 1993)

Pirandello, L *To Clothe the Naked and Two Other Plays*, trans. W Murray (New York, E P Dutton & Co. Inc., 1962)

Pirandello, L *Collected Plays 3 (The Rules of the Game, Each in His Own Way, Grafted, The Other Son)*, ed. and intro. R Rietty (Paris, London and New York, Calder Publications, 1992)

Pirandello, L *Naked*, adapt. N Wright, from a literal trans. G McFarlane (London, Nick Hern Books, 1998)

Platform Papers I: Translation (London, National Theatre, 1992)

Postlewait, T (ed.) *William Archer on Ibsen: the Major Essays, 1889–1919* (Westport, Conn., Greenwood Press, 1984)

Postlewait, T *Prophet of the New Drama. William Archer and the Ibsen Compaign* (Westport, Conn., Greenwood Press, 1986)

Powell, D A 'Pirandellian humour and modern French drama', in J L DiGaetani (ed.) *A Companion to Pirandello Studies* (New York, Greenwood Press, 1991), pp. 271–82

Rapp, E H 'Strindberg bibliography. Strindberg's reception in England and America: Part A: Strindberg in England', *Scandinavian Studies* 23(1), Feb. 1951, pp. 1–22

Rayfield, D 'Chekhov', in P France (ed.) *The Oxford Guide to Literature in English Translation* (Oxford, Oxford University Press, 2000), pp. 598–601

Redfearn, W D (ed.), Jean-Paul Sartre *Les Mains Sales*, Twentieth Century Texts (London, Routledge, 1985)

Reed, P 'Jean Anouilh', in O Classe (ed.) *Encyclopedia of Literary Translation into English*, I (London, Fitzroy Dearborn, 2000), pp. 56–8

Rees, R *Fringe First: Pioneers of Fringe Theatre on Record* (London, Oberon Books, 1992)

Reid, I 'Hazards of adaptation: Anouilh's Antigone in English', in O Zuber (ed.) *Languages in the Theatre. Problems in the Translation and Transposition of Drama* (Oxford, Pergamon Press, 1980), pp. 82–91

Rem, T 'Cheerfully dark: Punchian parodies of Ibsen in the early 1890s', in I-S Ewbank, O Lausund and B Tysdahl (eds.) *Anglo-Scandinavian Cross-Currents* (Norwich, Norvik Press, 1999), pp. 215–30

Richards, L 'Italy 1868–1919', in C Schumacher (ed.) *Naturalism and Symbolism in European Theatre 1850–1918* (Cambridge, Cambridge University Press, 1996), pp. 417–75

Robb, G *Victor Hugo* (London, Picador, 1997)

Robins, E *Ibsen and the Actress*, 2nd Series, XV (London, Hogarth Essays, 1928)

Robinson, M 'Aldrig längre än till Gravesend: Strindberg och England', in B Meidal and N Å Nilsson (eds.) *August Strindberg och hans översättare*, Konferenser 33. Kungl. Vitterhets Historie och Antikvitets Akademien (Stockholm, Almqvist & Wiksell International, 1995), pp. 109–21

Robinson, M 'England's Ibsen, or performing Ibsen's dramas of contemporary life today', *Scandinavica*, 39(2), 2000, pp. 171–90

Rosslyn, F *Tragic Plots. A New Reading from Aeschylus to Lorca* (Aldershot, Ashgate, 2000)

Rudlin, J *Commedia dell'arte. An Actor's Handbook* (London, Routledge, 1994)

Salama-Carr, M (ed.) *On Translating French Literature and Film*, II (Amsterdam, Rodopi, 2000)

Sandbach, M 'Translating Strindberg', *Swedish Book Review*, 1, 1985, pp. 30–3

Sartre, J.P *Crime Passionnel*, trans. K Black (London, Methuen, 1949)

Sartre, J.P *Les Mains sales*, ed. W D Redfearn. Twentieth Century Texts (London, Routledge, 1985)

Sartre, J.P *Loser Wins (Les Séquestrés d'Altona)*, trans. S and G Leeson (London, Hamish Hamilton, 1960)

Schnitzler, A *La Ronde (Reigen)*, adapt. J Barton, from a translation by Sue Davies (Harmondsworth, Penguin, 1982)

Schnitzler, A *The Blue Room*, adapt. D Hare (New York, Grove Press, 1998)

Schnitzler, A *The Round Dance and Other Plays*, trans. C Osborne (Manchester, Carcanet New Press, 1982)

Schnitzler, A *Plays and Stories 1862–1931 (Flirtations, La Ronde, Countess Mitzi or the Family Reunion)*, trans. E Schwartz (New York, Continuum Publications, 1982)

Schnitzler, A *Dalliance and Undiscovered Country*, adapt. T Stoppard (London, Faber and Faber, 1986)

Schumacher, C (ed.) *Naturalism and Symbolism in European Theatre, 1850–1918* (Cambridge University Press, 1996)

Scott, J S *Children of the Age* (New York, Alfred A Knopp, 1924)

Senelick, L (1987) 'Stuffed seagulls. Parodies and the reception of Chekhov's plays', *Poetics Today*, 8(2), 1987, pp. 285–98

Shaw, G B *The Quintessence of Ibsenism* (New York, Dover Publications, 1904)

Shaw, G B *Our Theatres in the Nineties*, III. (London, Constable, 1948)

Schück, H and Warburg, K *Illustrerad svensk litteraturhistoria* IV (Stockholm, Hugo Gebers Förlag, 1916)

Skrine, P *Hauptmann, Wedekind and Schnitzler* (London, Palgrave, Macmillan, 1989)

Slonim, M *Russian Theater. From the Empire to the Soviets* (London, Methuen, 1963)

Smedmark, C R *Essays on Strindberg*, Published by the Strindberg Society (Stockholm, Beckman, 1966)

Smidt, K 'Idiolectic characterisation in *A Doll's House*', *Scandinavica*, 41(2), 2002, pp. 191–206

Smith, P J 'Black Wedding: García Lorca, Langston Hughes and the translation of introjection', *Donaire*, 10, 1998, pp. 48–54

Spencer, C *The Translation of Theatre Texts – An Analysis of Translations of Arthur Schnitzler's* Liebelei *into English*, Unpublished MA in Translation, Dublin City University, 1996

Sprinchorn, E 'The unspoken text in Hedda Gabler', in F J Marker and C Innes (eds.) *Modernism in European Drama: Ibsen, Strindberg, Pirandello, Beckett* (Toronto and London, Toronto Press, 1998), pp. 40–56

Steene, B 'Alf Sjöberg's Film *Fröken Julie*: Too much Cinema, too much Theater?', in O Bandle (ed.) *Strindbergs Dramen im Lichte neuerer Methodendiskussionen: Beiträge zum IV. Internationalen Strindberg – Symposion in Zürich 1979* (Basel, Helbing & Lichtenhahn, 1981), pp. 179–95

Stockenström, G 'Strindberg i Amerika 1988', in H-G Ekman, A Persson and B Ståhle Sjönell (eds.) *Strindbergiana*, 4, (Stockholm, Atlantis, 1989), pp. 73–99

Strindberg, A *Samlade verk.* Nationalupplaga (27): *Fadren. Fröken Julie, Fordringsägare* (Stockholm, Almqvist & Wiksell, 1984)

Strindberg, A *Samlade verk.* Nationalupplaga (46): *Ett drömspel.* (Stockholm, Norstedts, 1988)

Strindberg, A *Samlade verk.* Nationalupplaga (58): *Kammarspel, Oväder, Brända tomten, Spöksonaten, Pelikanen, Svarta handsken* (Stockholm, Almqvist & Wiksell, 1991)

Strindberg, A *Five Plays (The Father, Miss Julie, The Dance of Death, A Dream Play, The Ghost Sonata)*, trans. and intro. H G Carlson (Berkeley, Los Angeles and London, University of California Press, 1981)

Strindberg, A *Miss Julie*, trans. H Cooper, from a literal translation by Peter Hogg with an Introduction by Helen Cooper (London, Methuen Drama, 1992)

Strindberg, A *Miss Julie and The Stronger*, version F McGuiness, from a literal trans. by Charlotte Barslund (London, Faber and Faber, 2000)

Strindberg, A *Miss Julie*, trans. and intro. K McLeish (London, Nick Hern Books, 1995)

Strindberg, A *A Dream Play: An Interpretation by Ingmar Bergman*, trans. and intro. M Meyer (London, Secker and Warburg, 1973)

Strindberg, A *The Plays: Volume One (The Father, Miss Julie, The Comrades, Creditors)*, trans. G Motton (London, Oberon Books, 2000)

Strindberg, A *A Dream Play and the Ghost Sonata*, trans. C R Mueller, with selected Notes to the members of The Intimate Theatre (San Francisco, Chandler Publishing Company, 1966)

Strindberg, A *The Father*, adapt. R Nelson (London, Oberon Books, 1998)

Strindberg, A/Ibsen, H *The Father and Hedda Gabler*, adapt. J Osborne (London, Faber and Faber, 1989)

Strindberg, A *Six Plays of Strindberg (The Father, Miss Julie, The Stronger, Easter, A Dream Play, The Ghost Sonata)*, trans. E Sprigge (Garden City, NY, Doubleday & Company Inc., 1955)

Strindberg, A *Selected Plays (Master Olof, The Father, Miss Julie, Creditors, The Stronger, Playing with Fire, To Damascus I, Crimes and Crimes, The Dance of Death, A Dream Play, The Ghost Sonata, The Pelican)*, trans. E Sprinchorn (Minneapolis, University of Minnesota Press, 1986)

Strindberg, A *Three Plays (The Father, Miss Julie, Easter)*, trans. P Watts (London, Penguin Books, 1958)

Strongin, C 'Irony and theatricality in Chekhov's *The Seagull*', *Comparative Drama*, 15(4), 1981, pp. 366–80

Sutherland Edwards, H *Personal Recollections* (London, Cassell & Co., 1900)

Taviano, S *Italians on the Twentieth Century Stage: Theatrical Representations of Italianness in the English-Speaking World*, Unpublished PhD dissertation, University of Warwick, 2001

Taviano, S *The Reception of Luigi Pirandello's Theatre in Great Britain: from the 1920s to the Present Day*, Unpublished MA Dissertation, University of Warwick, 1996

Taviano, S and Lorch, J 'Producing Pirandello in England', *Journal of the Society of Pirandello Studies*, 20, 2000, pp. 18–30

Thody, P *Anouilh* (Edinburgh, Oliver and Boyd, 1968)

Thwaite, A *Edmund Gosse: A Literatury Landscape* (Oxford, Granite Impex, 1984)

Tolles, W *Tom Taylor and the Victorian Drama* (New York, AMS, 1966, first published 1940)

Törnqvist, E 'Att översätta Strindberg. Spöksonaten på engelska', *Svensk litteraturtidskrift*, 39(2)1976/77, pp. 4–31

Törnqvist, E 'Unreliable narration in Strindbergian drama', *Scandinavica*, 38(1), 1999, pp. 61–79

Tynan, K *Tynan on Theatre* (London, Methuen, 1964)

Tynan, K (ed.) *Kenneth Tynan's Letters* (London, Minerva, 1994)

Ustinov, P *The Love of Four Colonels* (New York, Dramatists Plays Service, 1953)

Ustinov, P *Dear Me* (Harmondsworth, Middlesex, Penguin, 1979)

Valle-Inclán R del. *Plays: One (Divine Words, Bohemian Lights, Silver Face)*, trans. and intro. M Delgado (London, Methuen, 1993)

Valle-Inclán, R del. *Luces de Bohemia*, trans. A N Zahareas and G Gillespie, with an introduction and commentary by A N Zahareas (Edinburgh, Edinburgh University Press, 1976)

Van Dijk, M 'Blocking Brecht', in P Kleber and C Visser (eds.) *Re-interpreting Brecht: His Influence on Contemporary Drama and Film* (Toronto, Cambridge University Press, 1990), pp. 117–34

Venuti, L *The Translator's Invisibility* (London, Routledge, 1995)

Venuti, L 'Neoclassicism and Enlightenment', in P France (ed.) *The Oxford Guide to Literature in English Translation* (Oxford, Oxford University Press, 2000), pp. 55–64

Venuti, L *The Translation Studies Reader* (London, Routledge, 2000)

Willett, J 'Ups and downs of British Brecht', in P Kleber and C Visser (eds.) *Reinterpreting Brecht: His Influence on Contemporary Drama and Film* (Toronto, Cambridge University Press, 1990), pp. 76–89

Wilson, A E *Theatre Guide. The Baedeker of Thespia* (London, Methuen, 1935)

Worth, K 'Six Characters at the National Theatre 2', *Yearbook of the Pirandello Society* 7, 1987, pp. 36–43

Zuber, O 'Problems of propriety and authenticity in translating modern drama', in O Zuber (ed.) *The Languages of Theatre. Problems in the Translation and Transposition of Drama* (Oxford, Pergamon Press, 1980), pp. 92–103

INDEX

A

Abba, Marta, 245–6, 249, 253, 322
  The Mountain Giants and Other Plays, 245, 249
Abbey Theatre, Dublin, 312
  Is Life Worth Living, 151
  Pleasure of Honesty, The, 242
  Six Characters in Search of an Author, 240
Accidental Death of an Anarchist, 267–70, 274–5, 321
Acculturation of plays, 26–9, 239, 256–7, 261–2, 299, 321, 337
  Brecht, 221
  Plays for English audiences, 86
  Russian names, 147
  Strindberg into French, 165
Actability of translations, 133
Adamov, Arthur, 65
Adaptation of original translations, 41, 131–3
After Miss Julie, 25, 197
Albery Theatre, London
  Month in the Country, A, 123
  See You Next Tuesday, 68
  Vassa Zheleznova, 122
Aldwych Theatre, London
  Becket, 59
  Threepenny Opera, The, 218
  Uncle Vanya, 126
Alexandrinsky Theatre, St Petersburg
  Revizor, 120
  Seagull, The, 122
Alfred Jarry Theatre, Paris, 172
Alienation effect, 228–30, 232
All House, Bed and Church, 270–1
Allusions, difficulty of translating, 20
Almeida Theatre London, 225–6
  Conversations after a Burial, 67
  Life of Galileo, 323
  Mains sales, Les, 62
  Naked, 30, 254
  Rules of the Game, The, 27, 250
  Storm, The, 122
  Uncle Vanya, 152–3
Allouette, L' (*Lark, The*), 53
Álvarez Quintero, Joaquín, 281

Álvarez Quintero, Serafín, 281
Amateur Dramatic Club Theatre, Cambridge
  Henry IV, 240
  Pleasure of Honesty, The, 242
Amour et Piano (*Love and a Piano*), 48
Amphitryon 38, 53
Anatol, 7
Anderman, Gunilla
  Haven't We Met Before?, 9
  Munich-Athens, 9
  Night of the Tribades, The, 9
  Seven Girls, 9
Anglicisation, 129, 137, 146, 321–2
Anouilh, Jean, 60
  Alouette, L', 53
    Lark, The, 54, 58
  Antigone, 53–5, 57–9
  Bal des voleurs, Le, 53
  Becket, 53–4, 58–9
  Cher Antoine, 54
  Collected Plays, 54
  Colombe, 59
  Eurydice, 53
  Hermine, L', 53
  Invitation au château, L', 53, 55
  Nombril, 54
  Pauvre Bitos, 54
  Répétition, La, 54
    Rehearsal, The, 55
  Valse des toréadors, La, 54
    Waltz of the Toreadors, 58
  Voyageur sans bagage, Le, 54
Antigone (Anouilh), 53–5, 57–9
Antigone (Sophocles), 55
Anti-realism, 65
Antoine, André, 45
Apollo Theatre, London
  Dance of Death, The, 174
Aguila de blason (*Eagle of Honour*), 282
Archangeli giocano a flipper, Gli (*Archangels Don't Play Pinball*), 273
Archer William, 7, 16, 19, 22–3, 76–8, 81, 84, 86, 89–90, 100, 114, 130–1, 160, 163, 167, 174, 318, 322–3
  Doll's House, A, 336

Hedda, 107, 109, 112
  John Gabriel Borkman, 98
  Pillars of Society, 92
  Quicksands, 92
  When We Dead Awaken, 90
Ardito, Carlo
  Grande Magia, La, 262
Arniches, Carlos
  Grotesque Tragedies, 281–2
Arnold, Matthew, as translator, 18
Arrabal, Fernando, 282
Art, 67–8
Art of the Theatre, The, 163
Arts and Theatre Club, London
  Easter, 170
Arts Theatre Club, London
  Balcon, Le, 65
Arts Theatre, London, 242, 244
  Blood Wedding, 294
  Yerma, 295–6
Arup, Jens, 103, 114
As You Desire Me, 243, 248
As You Like It, 333
Asian Co-operative Theatre Company
  Blood Wedding, 303
Assommoir, L' (*Drink*), 44, 201
Aufhaltsame Aufstieg des Arturo Ui, Der
  (*Resistible Rise of Arturo Ui, The*), 220, 222,
  225, 233, 323
Aufstieg und Fall der Stadt Mahagonny (*Rise and
  Fall of the City of Mahagonny, The*), 220
Augier, Émile, 40, 43, 158
  Contagion, La, 37–8
  Fourchambault, Les, 38
  Gendre de M. Poirier, Le, 37
Aveling Edward, 77, 83
  Playgoers Club, 85
Avenue Theatre
  Little Eyolf, 88
Aveugles, Les (*Blind, The*), 46
Ayckbourn Alan
  Forest, The, 122

B

Bachelor, The, 120
Bal des voleurs, Le (*Thieves' Carnival, The*),
  53–4
Balcon, Le (*Balcony, The*), 65
Bald Prima Donna, The, 65
Ballard of Wolves, 282

Bandet (*Bond, The*), 161
Bankrupt, The, 121
Banks, Matthew
  House of Bernarda Alba, The, 303
Barba Eugenio, 266
Barbican Theatre
  Solemn Mass for a Full Moon in Summer, 70
Barker, Howard
  Uncle Vanya, 129–32
Barnes, Peter
  Purging, The, 48
Barnett, Ben and Johnstone, J B
  The Pride of Poverty, 40
Barsacq, André, director, 53
Barthes, Roland, 229
Bartlett, Neil
  Splendid's, 66
Barton, John, 213
BBC *Divine Words* (radio play), 283
Bear, The, 125
Beatriz Theatre, Madrid, 292
Beaumarchais, 35
Becket, 53–4, 58–9, 65
Beckett, Samuel, 244, 282, 288
  En attendant Godot, 63–4
  Fin de Partie, 64
  translation of own works, 63–4
Before Sunrise, 201–2
Behrman, S N and Gellert, Roger
  Amphitryon 38, 53
Belt and Braces Theatre Company, 321
  Accidental Death of an Anarchist, 269–279,
  274
  Mother, The, 221
Benavente, Jacinto, 281
  Nido ajeno, El (*Alien Nest, The*), 281
Benjamin, Walter, 18
Bentley, Eric, 257, 312
  Brecht, 24
  Caucasian Chalk Circle, The, 217, 219
  Mother Courage and her Children, 233
  Naked Masks, Five Plays by Luigi Pirandello,
  245
  Pirandello, 24
  Playwright as thinker, 92
  Six Characters in Search of an Author, 246–
  7
Bergman, Ingmar 173, 283
  Scener ut ett äktenskap, 335–6

INDEX

Berliner Ensemble Theatre Company, 215–16, 217, 218, 221

Berne Convention, 42

Bieito, Calixto, 291

Big Chill, The (film), 332

Birthday Party, The, 20, 134

Bitter Oleander, 292–3, 305, 311

Björkman, Edwin
  Easter, 170
  Strindberg plays, 162

Bjørnsen, Bjørnstjerne, 37–8, 75, 90, 158
  Hanske, En, 95
  Magnhild, 95

Black, Kitty
  Crime Passionel, 60–2
  Diable et le bon Dieu, Le, 60–1

Blacks, The, 65

Blin, Roger, 283

Blind, The, 46

Blood Wedding, 291–2, 294, 296–7, 302–12, 320, 329

Bloomsbury Group, 213

Blue Room, The, 25, 213–5

Bodas de sangre (*Blood Wedding* / *Bitter Oleander*), 291, 305

Bohemian Lights, 25, 283–9

Bolt, Ranjit, 225, 233, 323, 338
  Resistible Rise of Arturo Ui, The, 225, 323
  Ubu Roi, 47

Bon Soir, Monsieur Pantalon!, 41

Bond, Edward
  Saved, 268

Bond, The, 161

Bonnes, Les (*Maids, The*), 65

Börjesson, Johan
  Eric XIV, 158

Boswell, Laurence, 318

Boucicault, Dion
  Streets of London, The, 40–1

Bowman, Martin and Findlay, Bill
  Solemn Mass for a Full Moon in Summer, 70

Brahm, Otto, 201

Brand, 101, 158

Brandes, Georg, 75, 158

Bray Barbara, 55, 66
  Antigone, 55
  Marguerite Duras: Four plays, 66

Brecht, Bertolt, 10, 24, 213, 215–34, 244, 276, 288, 322
  Aufhaltsame Aufstieg des Arturo Ui, Der, 220
    Resistible Rise of Arturo Ui, 220, 222, 225, 233, 323
  Aufstieg und Fall der Stadt Mahagonny, 220
  Brecht Estate, 322–3
  Coriolan, 220, 223
  Dreigroschenoper, Die, 218
    Threepenny Opera, The, 218, 220
  Edward II, 223
  Ensemble style, 220
  Epic Theatre, 228
  Gewehre der Frau Carrar, Die, 217
    Riders to the Sea, based on, 217
  Gute Mensch von Sezuan, Der, 217, 220
    Good Person of Setzuan, The, 217–221, 224
    Santa Monica text, 224–5
  Kaukasische Kreidekreis, Der, 215
    Caucasian Chalk Circle, The, 215, 217, 219–21, 224
  Leben des Galilei, 223
    Life of Galilei, 223–7, 233, 323
  Mann ist Mann, 221
    Man is a Man, A, 221–2
  Marxist philosophy of, 216
  Mutter Courage und Ihre Kinder, 215
    Mother Courage and Her Children, 217, 219–23, 226–8, 230–3, 325–6
  Pauken und Trompeten (adaptation of *The Recruiting Officer*), 215
  Rundköpfe und die Spitzköpfe, Die, 217
  Schweyk im Zweiten Weltkrieg, 222
    Schweyk in the Second World War, 222, 224
  Tage der Commune, Die, 220
    Days of the Commune, The, 220, 222
  Trommeln in der Nacht, 215
    Drums in the Night, 215, 221
  Use of opposites, 231–2
  Weigel, Helene, 229

Brechtian style, 218, 229–30

Brenton, Howard
  Life of Galilei, 223

Brisebarre, Edouard and Nus, Eugène
  Pauvres de Paris, Les, 40

Bristol Old Vic Theatre, Bristol
  Archangels Don't Play Pinball, 273

Brook, Peter, 54, 56, 65

Brustein, Robert
  Cherry Orchard, The, 145
Buchanan, Robert, 78
Burnett, Constance
  And Chekhov, 19
Burgtheater, Vienna, 206
  Liebelei, 206
Bygmester Solness (Master Builder, The), 84

C

Cabal, Fermin, Shoot, 321–2
Calderon, George
  Cherry Orchard, The, 131, 145
  Seagull, The, 125
Calomnie, La (Calumny), 35
Campbell, Roy
  Blood Wedding, 294
Can't Pay! Won't Pay!, 266–70
Captain's Daughter, The, 285
Carnival Tuesday, 285
Casa de Bernarda Alba, La, 291
Cat Among the Pigeons, A, 48
Caucasian Chalk Circle, The, 215, 217, 219, 220, 221, 224
Chaika (Seagull, The), 122
Chaîne, Une (Chain, A), 35
Chaises, Les (Chairs, The), 64
Chapeau de paille d'Italie, Le (Italian Straw Hat, The), 39
Château de Grantier, Le, 41
Cheek by Jowl Theatre Company, 320
  Family Affair, A, 122, 337
Chekhov, Anton, 8, 10–11, 46, 101, 186, 189–91, 202, 213, 228, 232, 270, 281, 302, 322
  Chaika, 122
    Seagull, The, 22, 123–7, 131–5, 140–1, 147, 152–3, 189
  Dyadya Vanya, 126
    Uncle Vanya, 144, 147, 150, 152–3
  Hiberno-English Voice, 133–4
  Humour in, 150, 154
  Ivanov, 128, 130
  Leshy, 128
  Medved, 125
  Tri sestry, 127
    Three Sisters, 14, 130, 138–9, 141 145–6, 148–50, 153–4, 165
  Vishnyovyi Sad, 126

Cherry Orchard, The, 25, 123, 127–9, 131, 135–9, 144–5, 147, 150, 32
Chekhovian style, 123, 128, 136–8, 151–2, 302
  Geyer, pastiche by, 151
Cher Antoine (Dear Antoine), 54
Cherry Orchard, The, 123, 126–9, 131, 135–9, 144–5, 147, 153
  Relocation of, 25
Chevaliers de la Table Ronde (Knights of the Round Table), 49
Chichester Festival Theatre, Chichester
  Saturday, Sunday...and Monday, 263–4
Christmas at the Cupiello's, 261
Churchill, Caryl
  Serious Money, 122
Ciascuno a suo modo (Each in His Own Way), 239
Cicero
  De optimo genere oratorum, 16–17
  Greek into Latin, 16
Circle Dance, The, 207
Citizens' Theatre, Glasgow, 221–2
City Theatre, Gothenburg
  Divine Words, 283
Clacson, trombette e parnacchi (Hooters, Trumpets and Raspberries), 273
Cleese, John, 39, 138, 330
Cocteau, Jean
  Chevaliers de la Table Ronde, 49
  Machine infernale, La, 49
  Orphée, 49
  Parents terribles, Les, 49–52
Collettivo Teatrale La Comune Theatre Company, 269, 271
Colombe, 59
Colvill, Bill and Walker, Rob
  Can't Pay! Won't Pay!, 267–269
Come tu mi vuoi (As You Desire Me), 243, 248
Comédie Française
  Hamlet, 13
Comedy Theatre, London
  Ghosts, 80
  Pope and the Witch, The, 275
Comic Mysteries, The, 271–2
Commedia dell'Arte, 253, 257–8, 265, 268, 272–3, 276–7
Communicado Theatre Company
  Blood Wedding, 302

INDEX

Compounds, translation of in other languages, 96–100

Condemned of Altona, 60

Contagion, La, 37

Conversations après un enterrement (Conversations after a Burial), 67

Cooper, Helen
  Miss Julie, 175–8, 181

Copyright, 42, 249, 299, 322

Coriolan (Coriolanus), 220, 223

Corrigan, Robert
  Cherry Orchard, The, 131

Cort Theatre, New York
  Antigone, 58

Cosí è (se vi pare) (Right You Are (If You Think So)), 240–2, 248

Cottesloe Theatre, London
  Cyrano, 47
  Man, Beast & Virtue 253
  Yerma, 300–02

Council for Proletarian Art (see also Workers' Theatre Movement), 216

Court Theatre, London
  Wild Duck, The, 88

Cowan, Susan and Nelson, Richard
  Accidental Death of an Anarchist, 270

Coward, Noël, 268

Coyne, J Stirling
  Fraud and its Victims, 40

Craig, Edward Gordon
  Art of the Theatre, The, 163

Créanciers, 168

Creditors, 160, 162, 165–6

Crimp, Martin
  Chairs, The, 64

Criterion Theatre, London
  Can't Pay! Won't Pay!, 267
  Lady from Maxim's, The, 48

Cuernos de don Friolera, Los (Horns of Don Friolera, The), 285

Culture
  of receiving country, 81–2
  French
    domination of, 13
    familiarity with in other cultures, 13

Cumming, Alan and Supple, Tim
  Accidental Death of an Anarchist, 274–5

Cyrano de Bergerac, 47

D

Dachniki (Summer Folk), 123

Dalliance, 207–12

Dame aux camélias, La, as play, 36

Dame de chez Maxim, La (Lady from Maxim's, The), 48

Dance of Death, The, 159, 169–71, 174, 196–7
  Death Dance, The, 171

Danish Student Association, Staging of Miss Julie, 168

Dano-Norwegian, 91

Dario Fo Theatre, Vienna, 266

Weite Land, Das (The Vast Country / Undiscovered Country), 207

Davies, Sue, 213

Davies, Howard, 222–3

Davis, R G
  We Don't Pay! We Won't Pay!, 268
  Ronde, La, 213

Days of the Commune, The, 220, 222

De Filippo, Eduardo, 11, 257–65, 276
  Filumena Marturano, 30, 258–60, 264–5
  Grande Magia, La, 262–3
  Napoli milionaria!, 261–2
  Natale in casa Cupiello, 262
    Ducking Out, 261–2
  Sabato, domenica, e lundi, 258
    Saturday, Sunday, Monday, 258–60, 263
  Voci di dentro, Le, 261

de la Tour, Andy
  Pope and the Witch, The, 275

Dead Man's Suit, The, 285

Dear, Nick, 123
  Bourgeois Gentilhomme, Le, 337
  Family Affair, A, 337
  Summer Folk, 123, 337

Delgado, Maria
  Ballard of Wolves, 282
  Bohemian Lights, 287
  Divine Words, 284
  Eagle of Honour, 282
  Valle-Inclán: Plays One, 287

Demi-Monde, Le (Half-World, The), 36

Dennery, Adolphe Phillipe, 40

Deutsches Theater
  Weber, Die, 202

Devil and the Good Lord, The, 60

Dewell, Michael and Zapata, Carmen
  Rural Trilogy, The, 299, 304–5, 309–10

Diable et le bon Dieu, Le (*Devil and the Good Lord, The / Lucifer and the Lord*), 60

Diaghilev, Sergei
  Parade, 49

Dialect, 7–8, 10, 325–6
  Hauptmann's use of Silesian, 203
  In translations, 180
  Difficulties in translation, 70

Dickens, Charles
  Nicholas Nickleby (as play), 337

Diminutives in Russian, 143–6

Dindon, Le (*The Turkey*), 48

Dîner de cons, Le (*See You Next Tuesday*), 68

Dödsdansen (*Dance of Death, The*), 159

Doll's House, A, 76–9, 82, 84, 86–7, 100–1, 109–11, 126, 317–8, 322, 333, 336
  German to Russian, 82

Doll's House, A (short story by Strindberg), 163–4

Doña Rosita la soltera (*Doña Rosita, the Spinster*), 302–3, 325

Donmar Warehouse Theatre, London
  After Miss Julie, 25
  Henry IV, 241
  Ronde, La, 213

Dossor, Alan and Mitchell, Adrian
  Good Woman of Setzuan, The, 221

Double Marriage, The, 41

Drama at Inish (*Is Life Worth Living*), 151

Dream Play, A, 165, 171–3, 193–4

Dreigroschenoper, Die (*Threepenny Opera, The*), 218, 220

Drink, 44, 201

Drömspelet (*Dream Play, A*), 165

Drums and Trumpets, 215

Drums in the Night, 215, 221

Dryden, John, 17–18

Ducis, Jean-François
  Hamlet, 13

Ducking Out, 261–2
  as relocation of *Natale in casa Cupiello*, 25

Duke of York's Theatre, London
  Ducking Out, 261–2
  Ivanov, 128
  Uncle Vanya, 128

Dukkehjem, Et (*Doll's House, A*), 76

Dumas, Alexandre *père*, 69

Dumas, Alexandre *fils*, 35–6, 39–40, 43, 121, 158, 238
  Dame aux camélias, La, 36

Demi-monde, Le, 36

Fils naturel, Le, 37

Dunnigan, 131
  Cherry Orchard, The, 131

Duras, Marguerite, 66, 334
  Duras: Four Plays, 66
  Hiroshima mon amour (film), 66

Dyadya Vanya (*Uncle Vanya*), 126

E

Each in His Own Way, 239

Eagle of Honour, 282

Earth, 45

Easter, 162, 169–70, 192

Echegaray José, 281–2

Edmunds
  Blood Wedding, 304, 308, 310

Educating Rita, 33

Edward II, 223

Edwards, Gwynne, 302, 304–5, 308, 310
  Blood Wedding, 304–5, 308, 310
  Doña Rosita, the Spinster, 302
  Works of Lorca, 301, 302

Elisabetta (*Elizabeth*), 273

Emery, Ed, 275
  Mistero Buffo, 272

Emperor and Galilean, 92

En attendant Godot (*Waiting for Godot*), 63–4

Endgame, 64

Endstation Sehnsucht, 324

Enemy of the People, An, 38, 86–8, 98, 103–4, 336
  Stanislavsky, 87

English Stage Company
  Threepenny Opera, The, 217–18

'English' voice of
  Borkman, 10, 102
  Brecht, 224, 226–7, 302
  Chekhov, 8, 129, 138, 302
  Eduardo (de Filippo), 261, 267
  Fo, 274, 276
  Ibsen, 8, 94, 96
  Lorca, 8, 302, 294
  Pirandello, 239, 248–9, 257
  Sartre, 63
  Strindberg, 8, 159, 197

Enquist, Per Olov
  Night of the Tribades, The, 9

Enrico IV (*Henry IV*), 240–1, 244
  Living Mask, The, 240

Epic theatre, 215, 229
Eric XIV, 158
Erichsen, Nellie
  Father, The, 167
Ericsson, Stig-Ossian
  Haven't We Met Before?, 9
Eurydice, 53
Everyman Theatre, London, 174
  Henry IV, 241–2
Evolution of the Theatre, 151
Existentialism, 49, 244–5
Expressionism, 323
  start of, 169
Eyre, Richard, 62

F

Faber
  Hedda Gabler, 114
Fadren (Father, The), 159
Fagan, J B, 173–4
Famille Benoîton, La, 38, 158
Family Affair, A, 122
Farquhar, George
  Recruiting Officer, The, 215
Farrell Joseph, 29, 320
Father, The, 45, 159, 164–7, 169, 174, 182–4, 186, 192, 201, 323
Fathers and Sons, 120
Fawlty Towers, 39
Fen, Elisaveta, 129, 136, 144–6, 148–50
  Cherry Orchard, The, 129, 135–6
  Three Sisters, 146, 148–50
  Uncle Vanya, 144–5
Feydeau, Georges, 39, 47, 49, 69, 70, 121
  Amour et piano, 48
  Dame de chez Maxim, La, 48
  Dindon, Le, 48
  Hôtel du Libre-Échange, L', 48
  Occupe-toi d'Amélie, 48
  On Purge Bébé, 48
  Par la fenêtre, 48
  Puce à l'oreille, La, 48
Fil à la patte, Un, 48
Fils naturel, Le (Illegitimate Son, The), 37
Filumena Marturano, 30, 258–60, 264–5
Fin de partie (Endgame), 64
Findlay, Bill, 70, 204–06
  Weavers, The, 204–06
Flea in the Ear, The, 48

Flies, The, 60
Flirtation, 207–12
Fo, Dario, 11, 29, 222, 265–77
  Archangeli giocano a flipper, Gli, 273
  Clacson, trombette e pernacchi, 273
  Elisabetta, 273
  Grummelot dialect, 273–4
  Mistero Buffo, 271–2
  Morte accidentali di un anarchico, 267
    Accidental Death of an Anarchist, 267–70, 274–5, 321
  Non si paga! Non si paga!, 266
    Can't Pay! Won't Pay!, 266–70
  Papa e la strega, Il, 267
  Ratto della Francesca, Il, 267
  Translated as farce, 273
  Tutta casa, letto e chieso, 270–1
Foco Novo Theatre Company
  Drums in the Night, 221
Folkefiende, En (Enemy of the People, An), 85–6
Fordringsägare (Creditors), 160
Forest, The, 122
Fosse, Jon
  Night Songs, 321
Fourchambault, Les, 38
Fraud and its Victims, 40
Frayn, Michael, 54, 132–3, 136, 145
  Noises Off, 256
  Cherry Orchard, The, 136
  Seagull, The, 132
  Number One, 54
Frechtman, Bernard, 65
Freeborn, Richard
  Month in the Country, A, 12
Freie Bühne Theatre, Berlin
  Weber, Die, 201–2
  Father, The, 166
  Fräulein Julie, 168
French
  Drama, 33–71
  Light comedies, 16
  Novelists, 45
  Novels, translation of, 43–4
Friel, Brian
  Month in the Country, A, 123
  Three Sisters, 146, 149–50
  Uncle Vanya, 152–3
Fröken Julie (Miss Julie), 159
Fruen fra havet (Lady from the Sea, The), 83
Fruits of Enlightenment, The, 121

Fry, Christopher, 55–7
  Invitation to the Castle, 56–57
  Tiger at the Gate, 53
Fuegi, John, The Life and Lies of Bertolt Brecht, 233
Funny Peculiar, 261

G

Galantière, Lewis, 55, 57–59
  Antigone, 55, 57–8
Galas del difunto, Las, 285
Garland, Patrick, 47
Garnett, Constance
  12 Plays by Chekhov, 125–6
  Chekhov's Plays, 130
  Uncle Vanya, 128
Gaskill, William, 253
Gate Theatre, Dublin
  Uncle Vanya, 152–3
Gate Theatre, London, 318
  Bohemian Lights, 289
  Cuckoos, 322
  House of Bernarda Alba, The, 303
Gate Theatre Company, London, 320
Gebler, Carlo
  10 Rounds, 25
Gems, Pam
  Seagull, The, 131–3, 140, 142
  Uncle Vanya, 144, 147
Gendre de M. Poirier, Le (Monsieur Poirier's Son-in-law), 37
Genet, Jean, 65, 69, 282, 288
  Balcon, Le, 65
  Bonnes, Les, 65
  Nègres, Les, 65
  Paravents, Les, 65
  Splendid's, 65
Gengangere, 79
  Ghosts, 79
  Gespenster, 79
  Revenants, Les, 82
German drama, 201–34
German Strindberg, 161
Getting Married, 163–4, 179
Gewehre der Frau Carrar, Die
  based on Riders to the Sea, 217
Geyer, Boris Petrov
  Evolution of the Theatre, 151
Ghost Sonata, The, 26, 172–3, 187–9, 191, 196, 328–9

Ghosts, 14, 45, 76, 79–82, 84–5, 98, 125, 167, 201
  Negative response to, 81
Giftas (Getting Married), 163–4
Giganti della montagna, I (Mountain Giants, The), 242–5, 249, 253
Gilbert, Stuart
  Huis Clos, 60
  Mouches, Les, 60
Gill, Peter
  Cherry Orchard, The, 136
  Seagull, The, 140, 142
Gillespie, Gerald, 285–7, 290
Giraudoux, Jean
  Amphitryon 38, 53
  Guerre de Troie n'aura pas lieu, La, 53
Giuoco delle parti, Il (Rules of the Game, The), 27, 242, 245, 250–3, 257
Globe Theatre (Strand), London, 242
  House of Bernardo Alba, The, 299
  Spook Sonata, The, 173–4
Goethe, 78
  and Weltliteratur, 17
Gogol, Nikolai, 120–1
  Revizor, 120
Gooch, Steve
  Man is a Man, A, 222
Good Person of Setzuan, The, 217–21, 224
Gorky, Maxim
  Dachniki, 123
    Summer Folk, 337
  Vassa Zheleznova, 122
Gosse, Edmund, 76, 87, 93, 102, 167
  Editor of Bjørnstjerne Bjørnson, 90
  Hedda Gabler, 91, 109, 112
  Life of Ibsen, 91
  Master Builder, The, 91
Government Inspector, The, 120
Graham-Luján, James, 296–7, 304–06, 310
Grande Magia, La, 262–3
Granville-Barker Harley, 88, 318
Gray, Simon, 28
Green Cockatoo, The, 207
Greenberg, Richard
  Dance of Death, A, 196–7
Greenwich Theatre, London
  Ducking Out, 261–2
  House of Bernarda Alba, The, 297
Grein, J T, 80
Griboedov, Alexander, 120–1

Griffiths, Trevor
  Cherry Orchard, The, 129, 145
Grisar
  Bon Soir, Monsieur Pantalon!, 41
Grosses Schauspiel-Haus Berlin
  Dance of Death, The, 171
Groza (The Storm), 121
Grüne Kakadu, Der (Green Cockatoo, The), 207
Guerre de Troie n'aura pas lieu, La
  Tiger at the Gate, The, 53
  The Trojan War Will Not Take Place, 53
Gute Mensch von Sezuan, Der (Good Person of
  Setzuan, The), 217, 220
Guthrie, Tyrone
  Cherry Orchard, The, 128, 131
Gypsy Ballads, 291

H

Hagberg, Karl August
  Shakespeare into Swedish, 158
Halévy, Ludovic, 40
Half Moon Theatre, London, 269
  Arturo Ui, 222
  Blood Wedding, 303
  Elizabeth, 273
  Mistero Buffo, 272
  We Can't Pay! We Won't Pay!, 266–7
Hall, Lee
  Mother Courage, 226–7
Hall, Peter, 111, 132, 134–5, 137, 223, 229,
  244, 258, 264, 294
  Waiting for Godot, 63
Hamlet, 13
Hampstead Theatre, London
  Enemy of the People, An, 85–6
  Miss Julie, 180
  Musica, La, 66
  Tribades, The, 9
Hampton, Christopher, 26–9
  Art, 68
  Enemy of the People, An, 98, 103–04
  Hedda Gabler, 114
  Ibsen, 67–8
  Liaisons Dangereuses, Les, 70
  Life x 3, 68
  Ödön von Horváth, 26
  Philanthropist, The, 321
  Yasmina Reza, 26, 67
Hamsun, Knut, 22, 329
Hands, Terry, 65

Hanna, Gillian
  Acccidental Death of an Anarchist, 269–70
  Elizabeth, 273
Hanske, En (Gauntlet, A), 95
Hardy, Thomas, 83, 167
Hare, David, 233, 276, 323
  Blue Room, The, 25, 213–15
  Ivanov, 130
  Life of Galileo, The, 225–6
  Rules of the Game, The, 27, 250–2
Harrison, John, 27
Harrison, Tony
  Prince's Play, The, 25
Harwood, Ronald
  Dîner de cons, Le, 68
Hauptmann, Gerhard
  Nobel Prize for Literature, 202–03
  Ratten, Die, 20
  Vor Sonnenaufgang, 201–202
  Weber, Die, 201
    dialect of Silesia in, 203
  Weavers, The, 7, 201–06, 326
Haymarket Theatre, London, 85–6, 180
Hays, H R
  Mother Courage and Her Children, 232–3
Head of John the Baptist, The, 288
Hedda Gabler, 79, 82–3, 91, 94, 97, 102, 104–
  11, 112, 114, 153, 319, 333
  and Elvira Madigan / Marie Vestera, 106–7
Henry IV (Pirandello), 240–1, 244
Hermine, L' (Ermine, The), 53
Hiberno-English voice in Chekhov, 133–4
Hickey, Leo, 320
Hija del capitán, La (Captain's Daughter, The),
  285
Hill, Lucienne
  Collected Plays, 54
Hingley, Ronald
  Cherry Orchard, The, 131, 136
Hiroshima mon amour (film), 66
His Majesty's Theatre, London
  Pygmalion, 23
Hofmann, Michael
  Good Person of Sichzuan, The, 224–5
Holberg, Ludvig, 94–5
  Vægelsindede, Den, 95
  Jeppe paa Bjerget, 95
Home-abroad dichotomy, 161, 197, 253,
  260–1, 288–90, 320–1

Homme du hasard, L' (Unexpected Man, The), 67

Hooters, Trumpets and Raspberries, 273

Horace
  Translation of Greek into Latin, 16

Horns of Don Friolera, The, 285

Horváth, Ödön von, 26

Hôtel du Libre-Échange, L' (Hotel Free-Exchange / Hotel Paradiso / A Little Hotel on the Side), 48

House of Bernarda Alba, The, 291–2, 297–300, 303, 312–3, 320

Hughes, Langston
  Blood Wedding, 304–05, 308–09, 310–11

Hughes, Ted
  Blood Wedding, 305, 308, 310–11

Hugo, Victor, 13, 121
  Roi s'amuse, Le, 25

Huis Clos (In Camera / No Exit), 60

Humour, 7, 9–10
  Importance of Being Earnest, The and, 19–20
  In Chekhov, 150–4
  Lack of, in translations, 330–332
  Loss of in translation, 19, 99, 131
  Undue emphasis on, 259

Hunter's Club, Moscow
  Plody prosveshcheniya, 121

I

Ibsen, Henrik, 7–8, 10–11, 16, 19, 23–4, 37, 57, 75–115, 123–4, 127, 152, 158–9, 163–4, 174, 179, 206, 246, 270, 281, 312
  Anglicisation of, 87
  Brand, 158, 101
  Bygmester Solness, 84
    Master Builder, The, 7, 89, 91, 100, 102
  Dover Thrift Edition, 97, 104–5, 109, 112
  Dukkehjem, Et, 76
    Doll's House, A, 82, 84, 86–7, 100–101, 109–11, 126, 317–18, 322, 333, 336
    Breaking a Butterfly, 319
  English Ibsen, 94, 96
  Folkefiende, En, 85–6
    Enemy of the People, An, 38, 86–8, 98, 103, 336
  Fruen fra havet, 83
    Lady from the Sea, The, 46, 79, 84, 109
  Gengangere, 79
    Ghosts, 14, 45, 76, 79, 81–2, 84–5, 98, 125, 167, 201, 319

Hedda Gabler, 79, 82–3, 91, 94, 97, 102, 104–08, 112, 153, 319, 333
    Hostility to, 84
  John Gabriel Borkman, 79, 89, 98–100, 111
  Kejser og Galilæer, 92
  Kjærlighedens komedie, 92
  Lille Eyolf, 88–9
    Little Eyolf, 93, 95, 326
  Naar vi dode vaagner, 89
  Peer Gynt, 75–6
  Poems, 90
  Realities (hoax play), 319
  Rosmersholm, 46, 79, 109
  Samfundets støtter, 76
    Pillars of Society, 92, 103
    Quicksands, 92
  Use of polarity effect, 181
  Vildanden, 88
    Wild Duck, The, 24, 45, 99, 102–03, 109, 165, 189, 330–1
    Iceman Cometh, The, 24, 99
  When We Dead Awaken, 90

Ibsenites, 77, 162, 167, 241

Iceman Cometh, The
  as rewrite of Ibsen's *Wild Duck, The*, 24, 99

Il Teatro di Eduardo Theatre Company, 258

Imagery, 7, 10, 327–9
  Chekhov, 124, 145
  Flora and fauna, 26, 147–50, 189–96, 311–12, 327–9
  Ibsen, 93
  Lorca, 292–3, 306–07
  Natural environment, 147–9
  Strindberg, 189–96

Imperial Theatre, London, 121
  When We Dead Awaken, 90

Importance of Being Earnest, The, 19

In Camera, 60

Incorporated Stage Society Theatre Company, 126

Independent Theatre Company
  Ghosts, 80

Independent Theatre Society, 167

Indiscretions, 49–52

Infernal Machine, The, 49

Inferno, 169

Inner Voices, 261

Inspector General, The, 120

Institute for Contemporary Arts, 217

Intimate Theatre, New York
  Creditors, 162

Intimate Theatre, Stockholm, 163
  Starkare, Den, 1 62
  Påsk, 162
  Strindberg's Chamber Plays, 172–3
Intruse, L' (Intruder, The), 46
Invitation au château, L', 54
  Invitation to the Castle, 53, 55–6
  Ring Round the Moon, 54–5
Ionesco, Eugene, 64, 227, 282, 288
  Cantatrice chauve, La, 64
    Bald Prima Donna, The, 64–5
  Leçon, La, 64
  Chaises, Les, 64
Irving Place Theatre New York
  Staging Strindberg plays, 162
Is Life Worth Living (Drama at Inish), 151
Italian drama, 138–77
  And grummelot, 273–4
Italian Straw Hat, The, 39
It's A Family Affair – We'll Settle it Ourselves,
  121
Ivanov, 128, 130

J

James Henry, 81, 83–4, 89, 94, 167
James Theatre, New York
  Filumena, 259
Jarry, Alfred
  Ubu cycle, 46
Jeppe paa Bjerget (Jeppe of the Hill), 95
John Gabriel Borkman, 79, 89, 98–102, 111
Johnson, Samuel, Life of Pope, 17
Johnston, David, 25–6, 283–5, 287, 289–90,
  302, 305, 307, 310–12
  Blood Wedding, 302, 305, 307, 310–12
  Bohemian Lights, 25, 285, 297, 289–290
  Divine Words, 283–4
  Imagery in Lorca, 26
Jones, Henry Arthur and Herman Henry
  Breaking a Butterfly, 319
Joyce, James, 90
Junge Medardus, Der (Young Medardus, The),
  207
Jux will er sich machen, Einen (On the Razzle),
  332–3

K

Kammerspiele, Munich
  Divine Words, 283

Kaukasische Kreidekreis, Der (Caucasian Chalk
  Circle, The), 215, 217, 219–21, 224
Kejser og Galilæer (Emperor and Galilean), 92
Kent, Jonathan, 226
Key Theatre, New York
  Last Dance, The, 171
Kholastyak (The Bachelor), 120
Kidnapping Francesca, 267
Kilroy, Thomas, 133
Kingsway Theatre, London
  Six Characters in Search of an Author, 252
  Bear, The, 125
Kjærlighedens komedie (Love's Comedy), 92
Knights of the Round Table, 49
Komisarjevsky, Theodore, 240, 242, 322
  Cherry Orchard, The, 127–8
Kunzle, Margaret and Wymark, Olwen
  All House Bed and Church, 270–1
Kureishi, Hanif, 223
  Mother Courage and Her Children, 222

L

La Barraca Theatre Company, 297
  Cabeza del Bautista, La (Head of John the
  Baptist, The), 288
  Fuente Ovejuna, 313
La Mama Experimental Theatre Club
  Head of John the Baptist, The, 288
Labiche, Eugène-Marin, 40, 47, 48
  Chapeau de paille d'Italie, Le, 39
Laclos
  Liaisons dangereuses, Les (novel), 70
Lady from the Sea, The, 46, 83–4, 109
Lady from Maxim's, The, 48
Leka med elden (Playing With Fire), 161
Language
  Distinctive voice of characters, 179–80
  Domination of English, 14
  Strindberg's use of, 159
Lark, The, 54, 58
Last Dance, The, 171
Lawrence, D H, 268
Lazzarro (Lazarus), 242–3
Leben des Galilei (Life of Galileo), 223–7, 233
Leçon, La (Lesson, The), 64
Ledger principle of translation, 130, 144, 317
Leeson, Sylvia and George
  Loser Wins, 60–61
Lermontov Mikhail

Lyudi i strasti, 120
  Strannyi chelovek, 120
Les (Forest, The), 122
Leshy (Wood Demon, The), 128
Lesson, The, 64
Liaisons Dangereuses, Les, 70
Liebelei (Flirtation), 207–12
Life and Lies of Bertolt Brecht, The, 233
Life of Galileo, 223–7, 233, 323
Life x 3, 67–8
Life That I Gave You, The, 243, 249
Lille Eyolf (Little Eyolf), 88–9, 93, 95
Linares Rivas, Manuel, 281
Little Theatre, London
  Miss Julie, 168
Living Mask, The, 240
Livingston, Arthur
  Naked, 242
Lloyd, Phyllida, 302
Locock, C D
  Dance of Death, The, 174
Look After Amelia, 48
Look Back in Anger, 138, 202, 218
Lorca, Federico García 24, 26, 282, 290–313
  Assassination of, 298
  Bodas de sangre, 291, 305
    Bitter Oleander, 292–3, 305, 329
    Blood Wedding, 291–2, 294, 296–7,
      302–12, 320, 311
    Fate at the Wedding, 305
  Casa de Bernarda Alba, La, 291
    House of Bernarda Alba, The, 291–2,
      297–300, 303, 312–3, 320
  Doña Rosita la soltera, 302
    Doña Rosita, The Spinster, 302–3, 325
  Lorca Estate, 296–297, 322
  Romancero gitano (Gypsy Ballads) (poems),
    291
  Yerma, 291, 294–7, 300–02, 305, 311, 320
Lorch, Jennifer, 257
Lord, Henriette Francis
  Doll's House, A, 77
Loser Wins, 60
Love and a Piano, 48
Love Games, 208–09
Love of Four Colonels, The, 151–2
Love's Comedy, 92
Luces des Bohemias (Bohemian Lights), 25,
  283–9
Lugné-Poe, Aurélien, director, 46

Luke, Peter
  Yerma, 301
Lyceum Theatre, New York
  Bitter Oleander, 292
Lyric Theatre, London, 299–300
  Dance of Death, A, 197
  Splendid's, 65
  Cherry Orchard, The, 127
Lyttelton Theatre, London
  Forest, The, 122
  John Gabriel Borkman, 111
  Parents Terribles, Les, 49
  Grande Magia, La, 262–3
  Napoli milionaria!, 261
  Trojan War Will Not Take Place, The, 53
Lyudi i strasti (Men and Passions), 120

M

McAvoy, Roger and Giugni, Anna-Maria
  Trumpets and Raspberries, 273
MacDonald, Robert David
  German plays, translator of, 221
  House of Bernard Alba, The, 299–300
MacFarlane James
  Doll's House, A, 336
MacFarlane, James and Arup, Jens
  Enemy of the People, An, 103
  Hedda Gabler, 114
McGuiness Frank, 291
  Barbaric Comedies, 290
  Doll's House, A, 101
  Miss Julie, 175–8, 190, 193
McLeish, Kenneth
  Feydeau, 69
  Italian Straw Hat, The, 39
  Miss Julie, 335
  Ubu Roi, 46–7
Machine infernale, La (Infernal Machine, The),
  49
Madman's Defence, A, 165
Maeterlinck, Maurice
  Aveugles, Les, 46
  Intruse, L' 46
  Pelléas et Mélisande, 7, 46
Magarshack, David
  Cherry Orchard, The, 131
Magnhild, 95
Maids, The, 65
Mains sales, Les (Novice, The), 62
  Assassin, The, 60

Crime Passionel, 60–1
    Dirty Hands, The, 60
    Red Gloves, 60
Maly Theatre, 121
Mamet, David
    Three Sisters, 141, 146, 149–50
    Cherry Orchard, The, 136–7, 145
Man Beast & Virtue, 253
Man is a Man, A, 221–2
Man With the Flower in His Mouth, The, 241–2
Manfridi, Giuseppe
    Cuckoos, 322
Mann ist Mann (Man is a Man, A), 221–2
Mann, Thomas, 202
Maquet, Auguste
    Château de Grantier, Le, 41
Marber, Patrick
    After Miss Julie, 197
Margarita Xirgu and Enrique Borras Theatre
    Company
    Divine Words, 283
Marivaux, 35, 228
Marowitz, Charles, 174
Marquina, Eduardo, 281
Martes de Carnival (Carnival Tuesday), 285
Martin, Jonathan and Vargas, Mary Ann
    Blood Wedding, 303
Martínez Sierra, Gregorio, 281
Marx, Eleanor, 76, 77, 90
Marx, Eleanor and Aveling, Edward
    Lady from the Sea, The, 83
Master Builder, The, 7, 84–5, 89, 91, 100, 102
Mäster Olof (Master Olaf), 159, 258–9
Mathias Sean, 196
May, Frederick
    Pirandello, 24, 245–6
Medved (Bear, The), 125
Meilhac, Henri, 40
Men and Passions, 120
Merchant of Venice, The, 182
Mercury Theatre, London
    House of Bernarda Alba, The, 298
Meredith, George, 83
Merwin, S
    Yerma, 305
*Messe solennelle pour une pleine lune d'été
    (Solemn Mass for a Full Moon in Summer)*, 70
Mesyats v derevne (Month in the Country, A),
    120

Meyer, Michael, 99, 114, 136–7, 181, 187–8,
    233
    Doll's House, A, 317–8, 336
    Dream Play, A, 194–5
    Ibsen, 24
    Jeppe of the Hill, 95
    John Gabriel Borkman, 111
    Scatterbrain, 95
    Strindberg, 24
    Wild Duck, The, 99
Mill at Sonning Theatre, Sonning
    Haven't We Met Before?, 9
Miller, Arthur, 88, 96
    Enemy of the People, An, 88
Miss Julie, 14, 45, 163, 165–6, 167–9, 174–5,
    182, 184–5, 193, 323, 326, 329, 333, 335
    censorship of, 168
    relocation of in *After Miss Julie*, 25
Mistero Buffo (Comic Mysteries, The), 271–2
    dramatisation on BBC Television, 272
Mitchell, Katie, 303
Molière, 121, 228
    Bourgeois Gentilhomme, Le, 337
Monsieur Poirier's Son-in-Law, 37
Month in the Country, A, 120, 123
Moodysson, Lukas, *Together* (film), 329
Moore, George, 84
Morris, May, 77
Morris, William, as translator, 18
Morte accidentale di un anarchico, 267
Mortimer, John
    Feydeau, 69
    Flea in her Ear, A, 48
    Lady from Maxim's, The, 48
Moscow Arts Centre
    Enemy of the People, An, 87
    Hare's Ivanov, 130
Moscow Art Theatre, 122, 153, 202, 123–4,
    129
Mother Courage and Her Children, 215, 217,
    219, 220–3, 226–8, 230–3
Motton, Gregory, 194
    Father, The, 184
    Miss Julie, 175–7, 179, 188, 190
Mouches, Les (Flies, The), 60
Mountain Giants, The, 242–5, 249, 253
Mueller, C R
    Dream Play, A, 195
Mulrine, Stephen
    Seagull, The, 140, 146–7

Munch, Edvard, 329
Murray, William
  Naked, 30
  Works of Pirandello, 249–52, 254
Mutter Courage und Ihre Kinder (Mother Courage and Her Children), 215, 217, 219–23, 226–8, 230–3

N

Na vsyakogo mudretsa dovol'no prostoty (Too Clever by Half), 122
Naar vi døde vaagner (When We Dead Awaken), 89
Naked, 29–30, 254
Nakhlebnik (Parasite, The), 120
Napoli milionaria! (Naples Millionaire), 261–2
Natale in casa Cupiello (Christmas at the Cupiello's), 25, 262
  Relocation of, 25
National Theatre, Bergen, 94
National Theatre, Christiania
  and Scribe, 33
National Theatre, London, 11, 27, 50–52, 224–5, 252–3, 263, 300–01, 338 (See also Cottesloe / Lyttelton / Olivier)
  Accidental Death of an Anarchist, 274
  All House, Bed and Church, 270–1
  Amphitryon 38, 53
  Bourgeois Gentilhomme, Le, 337
  Brand, 101
  Cyrano, 47
  Dance of Death, The, 174
  Enemy of the People, An, 98
  Father, The, 174
  Filumena, 258
  Flea in Her Ear, A, 48
  Liebelei (Dalliance), 207, 212
  Man Beast & Virtue, 253
  Mother Courage and Her Children, 220, 223
  Prince's Play, The 25
  Rules of the Game, The, 250
  Saturday, Sunday, Monday, 258
  Six Characters in Search of an Author, 252
  Summer Folk, 337
  Undiscovered Country, 26
National Vigilance Association, 45
Naturalism, 7, 10–11, 23, 38, 44, 46–7, 76, 201, 238, 248, 271, 281, 323–4
  Rejection of, 216
  Verismo, 238

Naturalistic drama, 36, 43, 52, 54, 75, 122, 124, 165–7, 170, 203, 206, 215, 225, 230, 256, 268
Naturalistic novels, 45
Nègres, Les (Blacks, The), 65
Neighbourhood Playhouse Theatre Company
  Bitter Oleander, 292
Nelson, Richard, 270
  Father, The, 182–3, 192
  Three Sisters, 146, 149
Nemirovich-Danchenco, 122
Nesostoyatelnyi dolzhnik (Bankrupt, The), 121
Nestroy, Johann
  Jux will er sich machen, Einen, 332–3
  On the Razzle, 20
New Ambassadors Theatre, London
  Mother Courage, 226–7
New Century Theatre Company
  John Gabriel Borkman, 79, 89
New Colony, The, 242–3
New International Theatre, London
  Liola, 248
New Oxford Theatre, London, 240
New Scene, Belgium, 266
New Theatre, Cambridge
  Henry IV (Pirandello), 240
New Theatre, London
  Rules of the Game, The, 250
Nietzsche, Friedrich
  The Twilight of the Gods, 108
Night of the Tribades, The, 9
Nobel Prize for Literature, 11, 15
  Benavente, Jacinto 281
  Bjørnsen, Bjørnstjerne, 95
  Fo, Dario, 276
  Hamsun, Knut, 22
  Hauptmann, Gerhardt, 202–3
  Pirandello, Luigi, 239, 244
Nombril (Navel / Number One), 54
Non si paga! Non si paga! (We Can't Pay! We Won't Pay!), 266
Norén, Lars
  Blood, 321
  Courage to Kill, 321
  Munich-Athens, 9
Norske Theater, Bergen, 75
Norske Theater, Christiania
  Ibsen as director, 75
  Refuses Ibsen play, 86
Norwegian drama, 75–115

And Denmark, 75
As new technique and content, 79
In tune with the Zeitgeist, 79
Norwegian, idiomatic, 93
Nottingham Playhouse Theatre
House of Bernarda Alba, The, 299–300
Novelty Theatre, London, 78
Doll's House, A, 77
Novice, The, 60
Nuit de la Garde Nationale, Une (Night of the National Guard, A), 34
Nuova colonia, La (New Colony, The), 242–3
Nuova Scena Collective Theatre Company, 271–2

O

O'Casey, Sean, 162
Juno and the Paycock, 290
Occupe-toi d'Amélie (Look After Amelia), 48
Ockrent, Mike, 261
O'Connell, Richard L and Graham-Luján, James
Blood Wedding, 296–7, 304–06, 310
Yerma, 296–7
Odéon Théâtre de France, Paris
Divine Words, 283
Oedipus Rex, 49
Olafsson, Olaf
Feast of Snails, 330
Old Vic Theatre, London
Antigone, 57
Cherry Orchard, The, 128
John Gabriel Borkman, 111
Purging, The, 48
Seagull, The, 125, 132
Too Clever by Half, 122
Olivier Theatre, London
Fruits of Enlightenment, The, 122
Summer Folk, 123
Olivier, Laurence, as director, 54
On Purge Bébé
On the Razzle, 20, 332–3
O'Neill, Eugene, 162, 171–2
Iceman Cometh, The, 24, 99
Open Space Theatre, London
Seven Girls, 9
Ophüls, Max, 213
Orange Tree Theatre, London
Cherry Orchard, The, 25
Orgasmo Adulto Escapes from the Zoo, 270–1

Orphée, 49
Osborne, Charles
Love Games, 208–09
Osborne, John
Hedda Gabler, 97, 107–08, 114, 319
Father, The, 183–4, 192
Look Back in Anger, 138, 202, 218
Ostrovsky, Alexander, 120
Groza, 121
Storm, The, 121–2
Les, 122
Na vsyakogo mudretsa dovol'no prostoty, 122
Nesostoyatelnyi dolzhnik, 121
Svoi lyudi-sochtemsyai, 121
Family Affair, A, 122, 337
Othello, 182
Ottsy i deti (Fathers and Sons), 120
Ours
misidentified as L'Ours, 40
Oxenford, John
Twice Killed, 41
Oxford Players Theatre Company
Cherry Orchard, The, 127
Oxford Playhouse Theatre, London
Easter, 170
Oxford Theatre Group
Bohemian Lights, 288

P

Pandolfi, Gwenda and Wood, Charles
Man Beast & Virtue, 253
Papa e la strega, Il (Pope and the Witch, The), 267, 275
Paper Rose (Rosa de papel), 288
Par la fenêtre (Through the Window), 48
Parade, 49
Libretto by Jean Cocteau, 49
Designs by Picasso, 49
Parasite, The, 120
Paravents, Les (Screens, The), 65
Parents terribles, Les (Indiscretions), 49–52
Paria (Pariah), 162
Parsons, Estelle
Orgasmo Adulto Escapes from the Zoo, 270–1
Particles, use of, 110–15
Påsk (Easter), 162
Pasolini

Gospel According to Saint Matthew, The (film), 325
Patrie, 39
Patronymics in Russian, 146
Pauken und Trompeten (Drums and Trumpets), 215
Paulson, Arvid
    John Gabriel Borkman, 111
Pauvre Bitos (Poor Bitos), 54
Pauvres de Paris, Les (Poverty and Pride), 40
Pax Robertson Salon, London
    Easter, 170
Peer Gynt, 76
Pelikanen (The Pelican), 162
Pelléas et Mélisande, 46
Père, 166, 168
Pertile, Lino, 267–8
    Can't Pay? Won't Pay!, 267
Phillips, Robin, 298
Phoenix Theatre, London
    Trumpets and Raspberries, 273
Piacere dell'onestà, Il (Pleasure of Honesty, The), 242, 250, 254–6
Picasso, 49
Piccadilly Theatre, London
    Filumena, 30, 264
Pillars of Society, 92, 103
Pinter, Harold, 136–7, 227
    Birthday Party, The, 20, 134–5
Pirandellian style, 242, 263
Pirandello, Luigi, 11, 24, 213, 238–57, 258, 260, 263–4, 272, 276, 322–3
    Ciascuno a suo modo, 239
    Come tu mi vuoi, 243, 248
    Copyright, 249, 253, 322
    Cosí è (se vi pare), 240–2, 248
        Absolutely (Perhaps), 248
    Enrico IV, 240–1, 244
    Fascist Party, joins, 243–4
    Giganti delle montagna, I, 242–5, 249, 253
    Giuoco della parti, Il, 27, 242, 245, 250–3, 257
    Illustratori, attori e traduttori (Illustrators, Actors and Translators), 246
    Impressions of London, 256
    Nuova colonia, La, 242–3
    Vita che ti diedi, La, 243, 249
    Lazzarro, 242–243
    Liolà, 248
    Mussolini, support for, 243–244
    Piacere dell'onestà, Il, 242, 250, 254–6

Questa sera si recita a soggetto, 239
Sei personaggi in cerca d'autore, 238
    Six Characters in Search of an Author, 238–42, 245–7, 252–3, 256334
    Unauthorised translation of, 240
Uomo, la bestia e la virtù, L', 253
Uomo dal fiore in bocca, L', 241–242
Vestire gli ignudi, 240
    Naked, 29–30, 254
    To Clothe the Naked, 240, 250, 254
Plaidoyer d'un fou, Le (Madman's Defence, A), 165
Playhouse Theatre, Salisbury
    Colombe, 59
Playing with Fire, 161
Pleasure of Honesty, The, 242, 250, 254–6
Plody prosveshcheniya (Fruits of Enlightenment, The), 121
Plowright, Joan, 258–60, 299
Poem of the Cid, 24
Polar opposites, 231–2
Polarity effect, 181
Pomerance, Bernard
    Man is a Man, A, 221
Pope and the Witch, The, 267, 275
Pope, Alexander
    Translations of Iliad and Odyssey, 17–18
Post-modernism, 49
Power of Darkness, The, 45, 201
Pride of Poverty, The, 40
Priestley, J B, 141
Prince's Play, The, 25
Professor Bernhardi, 207
Progress Theatre, Reading
    Good Woman of Setzuan, The, 217
Promenade Theatre, New York
    Unexpected Man, The, 67
Pronominals, 109, 180–1, 293
Provincetown Players, New York
    Dream Play, A, 173
Puce à l'oreille, La (Flea in the Ear, The), 48
Punctuation
    Problems in translation, 66
Puns
    Genet's use of, 69
    Problems in translation, 66
Purging, The, 48
Pygmalion, 23

INDEX

Q

Queen's Theatre, London
Double Marriage, The, 41
Saturday, Sunday, Monday, 259
Questa sera si recita a soggetto (Tonight We Improvise), 239
Quicksands, 92
Quintessence of Ibsenism, 79, 84

R

Racine, Shakespeare as contemporary of, 13
Rame, Franca, 7, 265–77
Ratten, Die (Rats, The), 202
Ratto della Francesca, Il (Kidnapping Francesca), 267
Kidnapping Diana, 267
Ravenhill, Mark
Shopping and Fucking, 130
Reade, Charles, 45
Double Marriage, The, 41
Drink, 44
Château de Grantier, Le, 41
Poverty and Pride, 40
White Lies (novel), 41
Realism, 121–4, 215, 265, 281
Move from, 257
Realistic drama, 35–6
Recruiting Officer, The, 215
Rees, Roland, 221
Rehearsal, The, 55
Rehearsal Theatre, London
Father, The, 167
Reigen, 212–15
Circle Dance, The, 207
Ronde, La, 25, 213
Reinhardt, Max, 172–3, 239–40
Relocation, 197
As translation tool, 24
Bohemian Lights, 25
Cherry Orchard, The, 25
Mains sales, Les, 62
Miss Julie, 25
Natale in casa Cupiello, 25
Renton, Nic, 288
Répétition, La (Rehearsal, The), 54
Resistible Rise of Arturo Ui, The, 220, 222, 225, 233, 323
Resnais, Alain, 66

Revizor (Inspector General, The / Government Inspector, The), 120
Reza, Yasmina, 10, 26
Art, 67–8
Conversations après un enterrement, 67
Trois Versions de la vie, 67
Life x 3, 67–8
Richards, Gavin
Accidental Death of an Anarchist, 269–70
Riders to the Sea, 217
Rietty, Robert, 250
Right You Are (If You Think So), 240–2, 248
Ring Round the Moon, 56–7
Rise and Fall of the City of Mahagonny, The, 220
Riverside Studio Theatre, London, 322
Mistero Buffo, 271–6
Cherry Orchard, The, 136
Robertson, T W
Ours, 40
Robespierre, 39
Robins, Elizabeth and Lea, Marion, 83
Robins, Elizabeth, 83, 88–9, 94
Hedda Gabler, 93
Robinson, Lennox
Is Life Worth Living (Drama at Inish), 151
Röda Rummet (The Red Room) (novel), 176
Roi s'amuse, Le (Prince's Play, The), 25
Roman experimental, Le (Experimental Novel, The), 43
Romance de Lobos (Ballard of Wolves), 282
Romancero gitano (Gypsy Ballads), 291
Romeo and Juliet, 159
Ronde, La, 25, 207
Film, 213
Rosa de papel, La (Paper Rose), 288
Rosmersholm, 46, 79, 109
Poor reception of in London, 79
Acceptance in Russia, 79
Rostand, Edmond
Cyrano de Bergerac, 47
Roundheads and Peakheads, 217
Roy, Arundhati
God of Small Things, The (novel), 328
Royal Court Theatre, London, 319, 321
Chairs, The 64
Seagull, The, 133
Three Sisters, 127
Threepenny Opera, The, 218
Royal Haymarket Theatre, London

Blue Room, The, 215
Royal National Theatre, Copenhagen
  Gengangere, 79
Royal National Theatre, Stockholm
  Dream Play, A, 172
  Gengangere, 79
Royal Shakespeare Company, 220, 222–3, 337
  Balcon, Le, 65
  Cherry Orchard, The, 136
  Liaisons Dangereuses, Les, 70
  Month in the Country, A, 123
  Nicholas Nickleby, 337
  Ronde, La, 213
  Unexpected Man, The, 67
Royal Theatre, Bristol, 30
Royalty Theatre, Glasgow
  Seagull, The, 125, 127
Royal Theatre, Huddersfield, 242–3, 245
Royalty Theatre, London, 242
  Ghosts, 80
  Naked, 242
  Wild Duck, The, 88
Rudman, Michael, director, 9
Rules of the Game, The, 27, 242, 245, 250–3, 257
  Role-playing in, 252
Rundköpfe und die Spizköpfe, Die (Roundheads and Peakheads), 217
Russell, Willy, *Educating Rita*, 33
Russian Drama, 120–4

S

Sabato, domenica e lunedi (Saturday, Sunday, Monday), 258–60, 263
Salomé (Salome), 7
Samfundets støtter (Pillars of Society), 76
Sams, Jeremy, 50–1, 59, 263–4
  Becket, 59
  Colombe, 59
  Parents terribles, Les, 49–50
Sanchis Sinisterra, José
  Ay, Carmela, 322
Sand, George, 69
Sandbach, Mary
  Strindberg's novels, 179
Sardou, Victorien, 33, 40, 43, 238
  Famille Benoîton, La, 38, 158
  Patrie, 39
  Robespierre, 39
  Thermidor, 39

Sartre Jean-Paul, 60–3, 65
  Diable et le bon Dieu, Le, 60
  Huis Clos, 60
  Letters of, 62–3
  Main sales, Les, 60
  Mouches, Les, 60
  Séquestrés d'Altona, Les, 60
  Witness to my Life, 62
Saturday, Sunday, Monday, 258–9, 263
Saved, 268
Savoy Theatre, London, 174
Scandinavian late-romanticism, 75
Scandinavian Socialist Club, 162
Scatterbrain, 95
Scener ut ett äktenskap (Scenes from a Marriage), 335–6
Schering, Emil, 160–3, 170, 232
  German Strindberg, 161
  Mistranslations of Strindberg, 19
  Strindberg's *Collected Works*, 16
  Word for word translations, 160
Schiller, 121
Schleiermacher, Friedrich, 18, 30, 321
  Home-abroad dichotomy, 161
Schnitzler, Arthur, 11, 206–215
  Anatol, 7
  Grüne Kakadu, Der, 207
  Junge Medardus, Der, 207
  Liebelei, 207–12
    Dalliance, 207–12
    Flirtations, 208
    Love Games, 208–09
  Professor Bernhardi, 207
  Reigen, 25, 207, 212–15
    10 Rounds, 25
    Blue Room, The, 25, 213–15
  Weite Land, Das, 207
    Undiscovered Country, 26–7, 207
Schwarz, Egon
  Flirtations, 208
Schweyk im Zweiten Weltkrieg (Schweyk in the Second World War), 222, 224
Scott, T S
  Work of Knut Hamsun, 22
Scott Moncrieff, C K
  Rules of the Game, The, 242–3
Screens, The, 65
Scribe, Eugène, 33–4, 36, 38–9, 68, 120–1
  Calomnie, La, 34–5
  Chaîne, Une, 35
  Verre d'eau, Le, 35

INDEX

Scribe, Eugène and Délestre-Poirson, *Nuit de la Garde Nationale, Une*, 34

Scribean, 158
  Genre, 40
  Plot, 42

Seagull, The, 22, 123–7, 131–6, 140–1, 147, 152, 189
  Dehn, Paul, satire by, 152
  Irish *Seagull*, 134

See You Next Tuesday, 68

Sei personaggi in cerca d'autore (Six Characters in Search of an Author), 238

Señora Carrar's Rifles, 217

Séquestrés d'Altona, Les (Condemned of Altona, The / Loser Wins), 60

Serious Money, 122

Seth, Carl-Johan
  Seven Girls, 9

Shakespeare, William, 121, 129, 195, 228
  As You Like It, 333
  Hamlet, 13
  Merchant of Venice, 182
  Othello, 182
  Romeo and Juliet, 159
  Tempest, The, 159, 194

Shared Experience Theatre Company
  Mother Courage, 226

Shaw, (George) Bernard, 76–8, 81, 83–4, 89–90, 125–6, 167, 163
  Pygmalion, 23
  Quintessence of Ibsenism, 79, 84
  Widowers' Houses, 7

Shelley, Percy Bysshe, *Defence of Poetry, A*, 257

Sheridan, Richard Brinsley, *The Rivals*, 331

Sherman, Martin
  Absolutely (Perhaps), 248

Shopping and Fucking, 130

Simpson, N F
  Inner Voices, 261–2

Six Characters in Search of an Author, 238–42, 245–7, 252–3, 256, 334
  Hamlet in, 252–3

Social and cultural references, 8, 102–8

Social realism, 82

Société des Auteurs et Compositeurs Dramatiques, 34

Soho Poly Theatre, London
  Munich-Athens, 9

Song of Roland, 24

Songe, Le, 172

Sophocles, *Antigone*, 55

Spanish drama, 281–313

Speirs, Ronald, 233

Splendid's, 65–6

Spöksonaten (Ghost Sonata, The), 172–3

Sprigge, Elizabeth
  Miss Julie, 335

Sprinchorn, Evert
  Dream Play, A, 195

Stage directions in Archer's translations, 93

Stage Society Theatre Company
  Six Characters in search of an Author, 240
  Uncle Vanya, 128

Stanislavsky, Konstantin, 87–8, 122, 124, 153, 202

Starkare, Den (Stronger, The), 162

Stereotyping, 7, 264–6, 275
  Inter / intracultural, 329–30
  In Pirandello, 247

Stoppard, Tom, 22, 130
  Dalliance, 207–12
  House of Bernarda Alba, The, 297–9
  Ledger principle, 22, 144
  On the Razzle, 20, 332–3
  Seagull, The, 125, 132–3, 140–2
  Undiscovered Country, 26–7, 207

Storer, Edward
  Living Mask, The, 240–1

Storey, David, 268

Storm, The, 122

Stott, Mike
  Ducking Out, 25, 261
  Funny Peculiar, 261

Strange Man, A, 120

Stronger, The, 162, 167

Strannyi chelovek (Strange Man, A), 120

Strasfogel Ian, 233

Streetcar Named Desire, A (Endstation Sehnsucht), 324

Streets of London, The, 40

Strehler, Giorgio, 253

Stretford Civic Theatre, Manchester
  Caucasian Chalk Circle, The, 217

Strindberg August, 8–11, 19, 24, 39, 46, 77, 104, 136, 152, 158–197, 232, 246, 270, 281, 288, 291, 322, 328
  Acculturation of plays in French, 165
  Bandet, 161
  Chamber plays, 172
  Collected Works, 160

Doll's House, A (short story), 163–164
Dödsdansen, 159
   Dance of Death, The, 169–71, 174,
    196–7
   Last Dance, The, 171
Drömspelet, 165
   Dream Play, A, 171–3, 193–4
   Songe, Le, 172
Fadren, 159
   Father, The, 45, 165–7, 169, 174, 182–
    4, 186, 192, 201, 323
   Père, 166, 168
Fordringsägare, 160
   Créanciers, 168
   Creditors, 160, 162, 165–6
Fröken Julie, 159
   Miss Julie, 14, 25, 45, 163, 165–166–9,
    174–5, 182, 184–5, 193, 323, 326,
    329, 333, 335
Giftas, 163–4
   Getting Married, 179
   Alleged blasphemy in, 164
Imagery in, 189–96
Inferno, 169
Laka med Elden, 161
Plaidoyer d'un fou, Le, 165
Mäster Olof, 258–9
Move to Europe, 164
Paria, 162
Påsk, 162
   Easter, 169–70, 192, 329
Pelikanen, 162
Polarity effect, 181
Röda Rummet (novel), 176
Spöksonaten, 172–3
   Gespenstersonate, 173
   Ghost Sonata, The, 26, 187–9, 191,
    196, 328–9
   Sonate des spectres, La, 173
Starkare, Den, 162
   Stronger, The, 162, 167
Till Damascus, 169
Translates plays into French, 165
Translation into other languages, 161–2
Use of language and linguistic structures,
   159, 179
Use of pauses in, 186–8
Strindbergians, 162
Studio des Champs-Elysées, Paris, 298
Stuttgart Theatre, Stuttgart
   Divine Words, 283
Sue, Eugène, 69

Summer Folk, 123
Sunday Players Theatre Company, London
   Death Dance, The, 171
Supple, Tim, 274–5
Surrealist Drama, 172
Suzman, Janet, 25
Svoi lyudi-sochtemsyai (It's a Family Affair –
   We'll Settle it Ourselves), 121
Swan Theatre, Stratford upon Avon
   Cherry Orchard, The, 136
   Month in the Country, A, 123
Swedish drama, 158–97
   French comedies and plays, 158
Sweet, Henry and Pygmalion, 23
Swinging the Gate, 128
Symbolism, 46–7, 283, 304, 323
Symons, Arthur, 84
Synge, J M, 284
   Riders to the Sea, 217

T

Tage der Commune, Die (Days of the
   Commune, The), 220, 222
Tara Theatre Company
   Cyrano, 47
Taviano, Stefano, 257
Taylor, C P
   Drums in the Night, 221
Taylor, Tom, 41
Teatro d'Arte Theatre Company, 240–1
Teatro Español, Madrid
   Divine Words, 283
   Yerma, 295
Teatro Valle, Rome
   Six Characters in Search of an Author, 239
Tempest, The, 159, 194
Terre, La (Earth), 45
Theater am Schiffbauerdamm, Berlin, 215
Théâtre Alfred Jarry, Paris
   Songe, Le, 172
Theatre and Text Congress, 129–30
Théâtre Babylone, Paris
   En attendant Godot, 63
Theatre Beatriz, Madrid
   Blood Wedding, 292
Théâtre Bouffes-du-Nord, Paris
   Pelléas et Mélisande, 46
Theatre Clwyd
   House of Bernard Alba, The, 299–300

Théâtre de Champs-Elysées, Paris
  Six Characters in Search of an Author, 239
Théâtre de Complicité Theatre Company
  Chaises, Les, 64
Théâtre de l'Avenue, Paris
  Sonate des spectres, La, 173
Théâtre de l'Œuvre
  Hermine, L', 53
  Père, 166
  Rosmersholm, 46
  Ubu Roi, 46
Théâtre des Ambassadeurs, Paris
  Parents terribles, Les, 49
Théâtre des Bouffes-Parisiens, Paris
  Enfants terribles, Les, 49
Théâtre du Gymnase, Paris
  Balcon, Le, 65
Théâtre du Palais-Royal, Paris
  Chapeau de paille d'Italie, Le, 39
Théâtre Libre, Paris, 121, 165– 6, 201
  Father, The, 45
  Ghosts, 45
    Revenants, Les, 82
  Miss Julie, 45
    Mademoiselle Julie, 168
  Power of Darkness, The, 45, 121
  Wild Duck, The, 45
Théâtre Nationale Populaire, Paris
  Mother Courage and her Children, 228
Theatre of Action Theatre Company, 217
Theatre of the absurd, 49, 65, 239, 244
Theatre Royal, Bristol
  Doña Rosita, The Spinster, 302
Theatre Royal, Huddersfield
  Right You Are (If You Think So), 242–3
Theatre Royal, London
  Becket, 59
Theatre Workshop Theatre Company, 217
Thérèse Raquin, 201, 238
Thermidor, 39
Thieves' Carnival, The, 54
Three Sisters, 14, 127, 130, 138–9, 142, 145–
  6, 148–50, 153–4, 165
Threepenny Opera, The, 218, 220
Tiger at the Gate, The, 53
Till Damascus (To Damascus), 169
Tinniswood, Peter, 262
  Napoli milionaria!, 261
To Clothe the Naked, 240, 250, 254
To Damascus, 169

Tolstoy, Leo, 120
  Anna Karenina, 334
  Vlast' t'my, 121
    Power of Darkness, The, 45, 201
  Plody prosveshcheniya, 121
    Fruits of Enlightenment, The, 122
Tonight We Improvise, 239
Too Clever by Half, 122
Trafalgar Square Theatre, London
  Master Builder, The, 85
Translation
  Actability of, 133
  Adaptations in, 77, 131–2
  Alterations to text, 56–8
  Attribution to translator, 27, 131
  Awful translations, usefulness of, 8, 317–18
  Bible, of, 16, 17
  Conversation, of, 24
  Dialect, 70, 180, 203, 261, 325–6
  English style, to, 29
  Education purposes, for, 69–70
  French names into English, 69
  French novels, 43, 69
  French, 10, 13, 68, 701
  German, 17, 20, 28
  Grummelot in Dario Fo's work, 273–4
  Home-abroad dichotomy, 7–8, 16, 30, 66,
    19, 260–1, 288–90, 320–1
  Humour, 330–1
    Loss of, 19, 98–9, 131
    Satire and farce 273, 283
    Undue emphasis on, 2 59
    Wordplay and puns, 66, 69, 174–5,
      332–3
  Italian, 11, 29
  Judgment in Burnett v Chetwood, 17
  Lack of, from English, 15, 41
  Language expertise, poets / playwrights and,
    18–19
  Ledger principle or word-for-word, 22, 63,
    93, 130, 317
    using sense instead of, 66
  Linguistic structure, 8, 21–2, 61, 66, 96–
    101, 110–15, 179, 187–8, 203, 229,
    334–7, 139–42
  Literal, 26–8, 319
  Locally understood allusions, 20
  Lost and gained in, 95–6, 317–38
  Norwegian, 23
  Obscuring author's intention, 319
  Over-domestication as route to English
    voice, 321

Pindar, on, 16, 17
Plays known only from, 94
Pronominals in, 66–7, 109, 180–1, 143–6, 333–4
Relocation and, 24–5
Social and cultural custom, 61, 81–2, 188–9
Spanish, 11
Stage directions in, 93
Stereotyping, 264–6
Surrealism in Pinter and, 21
Swedish, 9
Titles, of, 141–2
Valle-Inclán, 287
Via other languages, 19
Travelling Theatre Company
Last Dance, The, 171
Traverse Theatre Company
Solemn Mass for a Full Moon in Summer, 70
Tree, Herbert Beerbohm
Enemy of the People, An, 86
Tremblay, Michel
Belles-Soeurs, Les (Guid Sisters, The), 326
Messe solennelle pour une pleine lune d'été, 70
Trevis, Di, 225, 300–01
Tri sestry (Three Sisters), 127
Tricycle Theatre, London
10 Rounds, 25
Trois Versions de la vie (Life x 3), 67
Trommeln in der Nacht (Drums in the Night), 215, 221
Trumpets and Raspberries, 273
Turgenev, Ivan
Kholastyak, 120
Mesyats v derevne, 120
Month in the Country, A, 120, 123
Nakhlebnik, 120
Ottsy i deti, 120
Turkey, The, 48
Tutta casa, letto e chiesa
All House, Bed and Church, 270–1
Female Parts, 270–1
One Woman Plays, 270–1
Orgasmo Adulto Escapes from the Zoo, 270–1
Waking Up, 270–1
Woman Alone, A, 270–1
Twice Killed, 41
Twilight of the Gods, 108
Tyndale, William, 17–18

U

Ubu Roi, 46–7
Unamuno
Del sentimiento trágico de la vida en los hombres y en los pueblos, 286
Uncle Vanya, 126, 128, 130, 144, 147, 150, 152–3
Under Thirty Group Theatre Company
Blood Wedding, 294
Undiscovered Country, 26–7, 207
Unexpected Man, The, 67
Unity Theatre Theatre Company, London
Señora Carrar's Rifles, 217
Unreliable narration, 182–5
Uomo dal fiore in bocca, L' (Man With the Flower in His Mouth, The), 241–2
Uomo, la bestia, e la virtù, L' (Man Beast & Virtue), 253
Ustinov, Peter
Chekhov's intertwined monologues, 128–9
Leshy, 128
Love of Four Colonels, The, 151–2
Swinging the Gate, 128

V

Vægelsindede, Den (Scatterbrain), 95
Valle-Inclán, Ramón del, 282–90, 312
Aguila de blason, 282
Cabeza del Bautista, La, 288
Cara de plata, 282
Comedias Barbaras, 282, 290
Cuernos de don Friolera, Los, 285
Divinas palabras, 282–284
Esperpento and, 283, 285–7
Galas del difunto, Las, 285
'Generation of 98' and, 282
Hija del capitán, La, 285
Luces de Bohemia, 25, 283–9
Martes de Carnival, 285
Romance de lobos, 282
Use of language in, 288
Valse des toréadors, La (Waltz of the Toreadors, The), 54
Vargas, Mary Ann, 303
Vassa Zheleznova, 122
Vast Country, The, 207
Vaudeville Theatre, London
Master Builder, The, 85
Rosmersholm, 79

INDEX

Vaudeville Theatre, Paris
  Nuit de la Garde Nationale, Une, 34
Veber, Francis
  Dîner de cons, Le, 68
Verfremdungseffekt or V-effect (alienation effect), 228–30, 232
Venuti, Laurence, 321
Verma, Jatinda
  Ubu Roi, 47
Verre d'eau, Le (Glass of Water, The), 35
Vestire gli ignude (To Clothe the Naked), 240, 250, 254
Victoria Theatre, London
  Easter, 170
Viertel, Berthold
  Streetcar Named Desire, A, 324
    And changed meanings, 324
Vildanden (Wild Duck, The), 88
Villaespesa, Francisco, 281
Vishnyovyi Sad (Cherry Orchard, The), 126
Vita che ti diedi, La (The Life that I gave you), 43, 249
Vizetelly, Henry, 44–5
Vlast t'my (Power of Darkness, The), 121
Voci di dentro, Le (Inner Voices), 261
Vor Sonnenaufgang (Before Sunrise), 201–2
Voyager sans bagage, Le (Traveller Without Luggage), 54

W

Waiting for Godot, 63
Walker, Rob, 267–9
Waltz of the Toreadors, 58
Waterhouse, Keith and Hall, Willis
  Saturday, Sunday, Monday, 258–9
Watts, Peter
  Easter, 192
  Father, The, 183–4
  Miss Julie, 177–8, 189–90
Weber, Die (Weavers, The), 201–6
Weber, T
  Doll's House, A, 77, 317
Weigel, Helene, 229
Weissberger, José
  Bitter Oleander, 292–4
    And Lorca, 293
Well-made play, 34, 40, 42–3, 47–8, 84, 92, 123–4, 158
  Outdated, 36

Wertenbaker, Timberlake
  Filumena, 264–5
Whatmore, Arthur R, 243
When We Dead Awaken, 89–90
Whiting, John
  Collected Plays, 54
Widowers' Houses, 7
Wild Duck, The, 45, 88, 99, 102–04, 109, 165, 189
Wilde, Oscar, 44, 167, 268, 292
  Importance of Being Earnest, The, 19
  Salomé, 7
  Woman of No Importance, A, 85
Willett, John, 24, 233
  Brecht, 24, 219, 227, 230, 232
Williams, Tennessee
  Streetcar Named Desire, A, 324
Williams, Clifford, 295
Wilson, Lanford
  Three Sisters, 146, 149
Witness to My Life, 62
Wood, Charles, 253–4
Wood Demon, The, 128
Woolf, Virginia, 213
Workers' Theatre Movement, 216–17
Wright, Barbara, 65
  Naked, 30, 254–6
  Six Characters in Search of an Author, 252–3
Wright, Barbara and Hands, Terry
  Balcon, Le, 65
Wymark, Olwen, 270–1
Wyndham's Theatre London, 269

Y

Yarmolinsky, Avrahm
  Cherry Orchard, The, 131
Yeltsin, Boris, 137
Yerma, 291, 294–7, 300–2, 305, 311, 320
Yes, Minister, 330
YMCA Theatre, Sheffield
  Rules of the Game, The, 242
Young Medardus, The, 207
Young Vic Theatre, London
  Six Characters in Search of an Author, 256

Z

Zahareas, Anthony and Gillespie, Gerald
  Bohemian Lights, 285–7, 290

Zapata, Carmen, 299, 304–05, 309–10
Zeffirelli, Franco, 11, 258–9
Zola, Émile, 42–4, 76, 81–2, 165–6, 238, 323
    Assommoir, L', 44, 201
    Jacques Damour, 45
    Naturalisme au théâtre, Le, 43
    Negative response to, 81–2
    Terre, La, 45
    Thérèse Raquin, 43, 201, 238